INTRUSIVE
PARENTING

INTRUSIVE PARENTING

*How Psychological Control Affects
Children and Adolescents*

Edited by Brian K. Barber

AMERICAN PSYCHOLOGICAL ASSOCIATION
WASHINGTON, DC

Published by
American Psychological Association
750 First Street, NE
Washington, DC 20002
www.apa.org

To order
APA Order Department
P.O. Box 92984
Washington, DC 20090-2984
Tel: (800) 374-2721,
    Direct: (202) 336-5510
Fax: (202) 336-5502,
    TDD/TTY: (202) 336-6123
Online: www.apa.org/books/
E-mail: order@apa.org

In the U.K., Europe, Africa, and the
    Middle East, copies may be ordered
    from
American Psychological Association
3 Henrietta Street
Covent Garden, London
WC2E 8LU England

Typeset in Goudy by World Composition Services, Inc., Sterling, VA

Printer: Sheridan Books, Ann Arbor, MI
Cover Designer: NiDesign, Baltimore, MD
Production Editor: Catherine Hudson
Project Manager: Debbie Hardin, Carlsbad, CA

The opinions and statements published are the responsibility of the authors, and such opinions and statements do not necessarily represent the policies of the American Psychological Association.

Library of Congress Cataloging-in-Publication Data

Intrusive parenting : how psychological control affects children and adolescents / edited by Brian K. Barber.
    p. cm.
    Includes bibliographical references and index.
    ISBN 1-55798-828-5 (alk. paper)
    1. Parent and child. 2. Parent and teenager. 3. Parenting—Psychological aspects.
    4. Child psychology. 5. Adolescent psychology. 6. Control (Psychology).
    7. Manipulative behavior. I. Barber, Brian K., 1954–
HQ755.85 .I585 2001
306.874—dc21   2001041341

British Library Cataloguing-in-Publication Data
A CIP record is available from the British Library.

Printed in the United States of America
First Edition

*This book is dedicated to Earl Schaefer for his pioneering work
in identifying and studying psychological control,
to Larry Steinberg for his insight and work in reviving
the appreciation of the uniqueness of the construct,
and to all those who may further explore understanding it.*

CONTENTS

CONTRIBUTORS

Shelli Avenevoli, Yale University School of Medicine, New Haven, CT
Brian K. Barber, University of Tennessee, Knoxville
Roy L. Bean, Ohio State University, Columbus
Cheryl Buehler, University of Tennessee, Knoxville
Nicki R. Crick, Institute of Child Development, University of
     Minnesota, Twin Cities Campus, Minneapolis
Lance D. Erickson, University of North Carolina at Chapel Hill
Marilyn J. Essex, Wisconsin Psychiatric Institute and Clinics, Madison
Elizabeth Lovelady Harmon, Brigham Young University, Provo, UT
Craig H. Hart, Brigham Young University, Provo, UT
Grayson N. Holmbeck, Loyola University of Chicago
Jennifer S. Hommeyer, Loyola University of Chicago
Shenghua Jin, Beijing Normal University, China
Robert D. Laird, University of Rhode Island, Kingston
Amanda Sheffield Morris, University of New Orleans, LA
David A. Nelson, Brigham Young University, Provo, UT
Larry J. Nelson, Brigham Young University, Provo, UT
Susanne Frost Olsen, Brigham Young University, Provo, UT
Gregory S. Pettit, Auburn University, Auburn, AL
Clyde C. Robinson, Brigham Young University, Provo, UT
Frances M. Sessa, Pennsylvania State University—Abington
Wendy E. Shapera, Loyola University of Chicago
Jennifer S. Silk, Temple University, Philadelphia, PA
Laurence Steinberg, Temple University, Philadelphia, PA
Gaye Stone, Chattanooga, TN
Jianzhong Wo, Beijing Normal University, China
Peixia Wu, Brigham Young University, Provo, UT
Chongming Yang, Brigham Young University, Provo, UT

FOREWORD

JACQUELYNNE S. ECCLES

To be asked to write the foreword for such a fine book is truly an honor. But what does one write about in a foreword? Typically one provides an overview of the book, laying out major themes and putting these themes in the broader context. Brian, characteristic of his very thorough and thoughtful style, has already done this. In the opening chapters, he provides an excellent overview of the book and its goals and a thorough review of the previous literature on psychological control; his final chapter offers an impressive discussion of where the field should go. Chapters 3 through 8 fill in the meal with a fine sampling of the essential nutrients needed for continued growth. So what could be added? A little personal background for an appetizer and some added speculations of new directions for dessert.

When I first met Brian about 12 years ago, he had just received a FIRST award from the National Institute of Mental Health to begin his work on adolescent development. He had organized a meeting of many of the major researchers in the field of adolescent development—researchers from several different disciplines and perspectives—to discuss the best ways to conceptualize and then measure the multiple influences on adolescent development. Because I was in the middle of similar research, I was both honored to be invited and delighted to attend.

It was at that meeting that I first became familiar with Brian's approach to the distinction between psychological and behavioral control in parenting behaviors. I was also struggling with the best way to think about the changing role of parents in supporting autonomy while at the same time providing adequate structure and supervision as their children passed through adolescence. Based on my work on the debilitating impact of the junior high school transition on many of America's youth, my colleagues and I were exploring the notion of stage–environment fit. Issues related to adolescents' need for increasing autonomy and respect from adults were central to our conceptualization. We had demonstrated that early adolescents often experience a decline in the opportunities for taking responsibility for one's own learning in a respectful classroom environment as they moved from elementary schools to junior high schools. Furthermore, we documented that this contributed to a decline in early adolescents' interest in school and confidence in their own ability to master the academic content of school. My colleagues and I concluded that this increase in emphasis on adult control at the expense of student autonomy was an example of stage–environment misfit, because it was counter to what one might design if one wanted to create a developmentally appropriate and challenging educational context for early adolescents. Junior high schools, for a variety of reasons, were treating their young adolescent students in a manner that was not respectful of their increasing maturity—less respectfully, in fact, than many early adolescents had experienced during the last years of elementary school. Brian's distinction between psychological and behavioral control provided us with a very useful framework for extending our stage–environment fit perspective from the school environment to the family. Thus began my admiration for Brian and his work.

Both of us have matured intellectually since that meeting. Brian has gone on to do incredibly comprehensive cross-cultural work on parenting during adolescence. He has successfully demonstrated that (a) the distinction between psychological and behavioral control is relevant to, and can be validly measured in, a wide variety of cultures; and (b) psychological control has debilitating effects on adolescent development in every culture he studied. Although developmentalists regularly call for such work, it is still quite rare. I invited Brian to present his work at my MacArthur Research Network on Successful Pathways Through Middle Childhood. This group had had many discussions about the validity of parenting constructs derived from work on European-based Western cultures for other cultures, particularly those with quite different perspectives on life and relationships. Most of these discussions ended with speculation and rhetoric. Brian was able to cut through the rhetoric with solid empirical work. Everyone was rightly impressed and acknowledged that Brian had accomplished what we had only talked about. (Chapter 8 gives further evidence of the cross-cultural validity of the construct of parental psychological control.)

This book provides the stepping stones needed to take our understanding of psychological control to new levels. Chapters 3 and 4 ask us to consider parental psychological control during adolescence in the larger contexts of both marital relations and earlier histories of parent–child interaction. By focusing on both the contemporary correlates and historical precursors of parenting behaviors, these chapters make salient the importance of personal characteristics, relationships and relational styles, the dance of the changing nature of relationships over time, and the underlying meaning of behavioral interactions to all participants. Psychological control is a fundamental characteristic of the interaction between individuals. As a consequence, it is not surprising that individual characteristics of the actors in the relationship play a major role in the likelihood of either actor trying to use psychological control as part of the interaction. Its use by parents in parent–child interactions is made doubly complex by the fact that parents must parent as well as interact with their children. Parenting by its very nature involves major power differences between the actors— increasing the probability that the adult will get away with psychological control and that the child's psychological development will suffer as a result. Finally, given individual differences in temperament, it is also not surprising that some children will suffer more than others because they are more vulnerable to the undermining effects of psychological control. These two chapters, along with chapters 5 to 7, make the need to study these dynamics quite clear.

I would add one additional dimension to the study of the precursors of parental psychological control: attachment style. I was struck in reading several of the chapters with the similarity between the descriptions of parents who rely heavily on psychological controlling strategies in their interactions with their children and their spouse and the growing body of work on adult attachment styles. Once one places psychological control in the context of relationship patterns, the issue of relationship styles becomes quite salient. Theorists in the attachment tradition are increasingly focusing their attention on the connection between early parent–child interaction patterns and subsequent adult relationship styles. It would be quite productive to let this body of work inform our thinking about the origins of individual differences in the use of parental psychological control strategies. This frame of reference also makes salient the importance of following up with the children who have been studied as recipients of parental psychological control to study the connection between childhood exposure and subsequent adult parenting strategies.

Chapters 5 to 8 provide the theoretical and methodological tools to extend the work on parental psychological control to young children. As Brian points out, until quite recently most of the work on parental psychological strategies has focused on adolescents because the major researchers in this area have linked psychological control to the issues of autonomy and self. The work reported in chapters 5 to 8 makes it clear that psychological control is used by parents throughout their children's development and that its use has consequences for children's development from early on. The results reported throughout this book also make it clear that psychological control influences a much broader range of development than those aspects linked to internalizing symptoms and issues of adolescent autonomy.

These findings reminded me of the work by various scholars aimed at identifying fundamental human needs. Several of these authors have stressed that the need for autonomy is central to human development early in life. Recent cultural critiques of the salience of autonomy in Western psychology have led me to reconsider whether autonomy is the right conceptualization of this need. The work in chapters 4, 5, and 7 reinforced this concern. What exactly does psychological control undermine? Several of the authors in the volume include self-processes as part of what is being undermined. We often translate the notion of self-processes into notions of autonomy and individuality, particularly when we discuss adolescents. Perhaps this is a particularly easy translation within our Western frame of reference. Notions of autonomy and individuality are less salient in more communal cultures, even when considering adolescence as a developmental period.

But even in these cultures it is likely that self-processes are important. In these cultures it may be easier to think of self-processes in terms of respect and being included as an important member of one's social group. I lived in Africa for two years, and while there I was struck by the inclusion of even the very youngest children in the "work" of the family. Mothers would go to the river to fetch water followed by all of their children—each carrying an appropriately sized container of water on his or her head. Clearly, no one expected the youngest children to actually succeed in getting their water back to the family compound. Nonetheless, all children were considered critical to the family's survival and all were given responsibilities to help. In this culture, this form of "respect," I believe, provided the essence of support for self-processes by making it clear to each child that she or he mattered in a very fundamental way to the family. It would be interesting to study what the nature of parental psychological control is in such a culture and what are its consequences.

This example brings me back to one of the issues Brian raises as critical for the future: understanding the nature of the effects of psychological control on children's development. I have already mentioned one additional set of mechanisms of influence—the mechanisms linked to the socialization of attachment styles and fundamental psychological models of the nature of human relationships. The African example suggests that we focus more on the impact of psychological control strategies on both fundamental aspects of mental health and emerging confidence and trust in oneself. The stress in several of the chapters on maltreatment as a model of possible influence fits nicely with this perspective. Incorporating findings and theoretical perspectives from the clinical literature will further work in this direction in important ways.

I end my comments by reinforcing the authors' stress on the need to bring both a developmental and a phenomenological perspective to the study of parental psychological control. I began by mentioning stage–

environment fit and ended by talking about self-processes. It is clear across the chapters that parental psychological control can be, and is being, operationalized in many different ways. It is also clear that the exact behaviors that produce the effects characteristic of psychological control vary across children's ages and temperament. Finally, it is clear that parents walk a fine line between respecting and socializing their children—a line that changes as their children mature. Specific interactional sequences will have different meanings to both parents and children, depending on the history of interaction, the ages and maturity of the participants, and the specific needs and characteristics of the participants. We need to develop theories and methods that capture this complexity. The chapters in this book are an excellent beginning for this intellectual journey.

INTRUSIVE PARENTING

1

REINTRODUCING PARENTAL PSYCHOLOGICAL CONTROL

BRIAN K. BARBER

For three quarters of a century, social scientists from a variety of disciplines have been studying the interpersonal relationship between parents and their children and adolescents. This long-standing and actively continuing research effort has focused primarily on two tasks: (a) understanding, describing, and categorizing behaviors that parents engage in as they raise their children; and (b) discerning if and to what degree these parental behaviors are associated with types and patterns of child and adolescent cognitive, social, emotional, and behavioral development. Although scores of varying parental behaviors have been labeled, most reviewers of these literatures have posited a limited number of general categories of parenting behaviors. Two of these categories are common among organizational schemes: parental support and parental control (e.g., Darling & Steinberg, 1993; Peterson & Hann, 1999; Peterson & Rollins, 1987; Rollins & Thomas, 1979; Schaefer, 1965).

The broad-band construct of parental support is most often considered a unidimensional construct—with the more specific variables such as nurturance, warmth, responsiveness, acceptance, attachment, and so forth apparently tapping the same central supportive processes that are uniformly related to positive child development. The broad-band construct of parental control, however, is much more complex and varied. Not only have there been numerous dimensions of control that have been labeled (e.g., discipline, maturity demands, coercion, induction, guilt induction, supervision, monitoring, love withdrawal, hostile control, inconsistent control, restrictive, punishment, etc.), but the effects of control on child and adolescent development often vary from weak to strong, from positive to negative, and from linear to nonlinear. Hence, much of the focus in parent control studies is on the absolute level of control, critical thresholds of control, and when or if the effect of a certain form of control shifts from positive to negative or vice versa. Because of this complexity, the aggregate research literature on parental control of children and adolescents has not provided a very clear understanding of the effects of parental control on children and adolescents.

Another complication in studying parental control has been that various forms of control, along with other noncontrolling parenting behaviors, have been aggregated into typologies of parenting behavior (e.g., Baumrind, 1967, 1978, 1991; Steinberg, Lamborn, Dornbusch, & Darling, 1992; Steinberg, Mounts, Lamborn, & Dornbusch, 1991). Although this work has produced many important findings relative to parenting composites and their associations with child and adolescent development, it has precluded specific analyses of different types of parental control, because, by conceptual definition and measurement methodology, different types of control are merged together.

ISOLATING PSYCHOLOGICAL CONTROL
FROM BEHAVIORAL CONTROL

One way to advance the understanding of the processes of parental control is to make the distinction between behavioral control and psychological control. This distinction between control over a child or adolescent's behavior (e.g., home responsibilities, daily activities, manners, etc.) versus control over the child or adolescent's psychological world (e.g., feelings, verbal expressions, identity, attachment bonds, etc.) was made early in the scientific research on parenting (Schaefer, 1965), but, for reasons speculated on in chapter 2 of this volume, was not pursued regularly until it was revived around 1990 (Steinberg, 1990; Steinberg, Elmen, & Mounts, 1989). Essentially what was lost in the meantime was a concerted effort to develop understanding of the construct of psychological control, defined by Schaefer (1965, p. 555) as covert, psychological methods of control that "would not permit the child to develop as an individual apart from the parent." Perhaps because parental behavioral control can be more overt and more common, attention to its various forms continued systematically over the decades. But understanding of the more passive and insidious psychological control that Schaefer (and others before him who did not specifically use the label of *psychological control*) defined conceptually and empirically in the 1960s was not pursued explicitly.

Since 1990, however, there has been a dramatic increase in scientific attention to distinguishing between parental psychological control and parental behavioral control, as recommended and demonstrated by Steinberg (Steinberg, 1990; Steinberg et al., 1989). This distinction has shifted the focus from the level or amount of control a parent exercises (as in the study of behavioral control) to the locus in the child of the parental control (e.g., the psychological processes of the child versus the child's behavior; Barber, 1996). This recent effort to isolate parental psychological control from parental behavioral control has demonstrated that psychological control can be measured reliably and that it has a remarkably consistent, negative relationship to healthy child and adolescent development. These findings have been robust enough to warrant a thorough treatment of the construct of psychological control (see chapter 2 of this volume for a review of these findings).

REVIEWING RESEARCH ON PARENTAL PSYCHOLOGICAL CONTROL

One purpose of this volume is to thoroughly review the literatures related to parental psychological control. In an earlier effort to integrate Schaefer's original conceptualization of parental psychological control with subsequent research efforts that appear to measure the essential aspects of psychological control (although they did not conceive of them specifically as such) I wrote the following:

> Psychologically controlling processes involve socialization pressure that is nonresponsive to the child's emotional and psychological needs (Maccoby & Martin, 1983), that stifles independent expression and autonomy (Baumrind, 1965, 1978; Hauser, 1991; Hauser, et al., 1984). Such an environment makes it difficult for a child to develop a healthy awareness and perception of self for several reasons: the implied derogation of the child, the lack of healthy interaction with others that is required for adequate self-definition (Youniss & Smollar, 1985), limited opportunities to develop a sense of personal efficacy (Seligman & Peterson, 1986), and, particularly for adolescents, interference with the exploration needed to establish a stable identity (Erikson, 1968; Marcia, 1980). Psychological control has consistently been found to be correlated with patterns marked by feelings of guilt, self-responsibility, confession, and indirect or nonexpression of aggression (see Becker, 1964), dependency (Baumrind, 1978; Becker, 1964), alienation (Baumrind, 1968), social withdrawal (Baumrind, 1967; Baumrind & Black, 1967), low ego strength (Hauser, 1991; Hauser et al., 1984; Siegelman, 1965), inability to make conscious choice (Baumrind, 1966), low self-esteem (Coopersmith, 1967), passive, inhibited, and overcontrolled characteristics (Beavers, 1982), and depressed affect (Allen, Hauser, Eickholt, Bell, & O'Conner, 1994; Barber, Olsen, & Shagle, 1994; Burbach & Bourdin, 1986, Fauber, Forehand, Thomas, & Wierson, 1990). (Barber, 1996, p. 3299)

From the breadth of disciplines and methods represented by the references cited in this quotation, it is apparent that the essence of parent psychological control of children and adolescents has not been ignored in the research literatures. When this evidence is combined with the numerous studies that are now being conducted that explicitly measure the construct of parental psychological control, it is apparent that a thorough review of this literature is warranted. Barber and Harmon provide such a review in chapter 2 of this volume. In tracing the history of conceptualization, measurement, and findings in some 100 studies over a 50-year period, we had two central tasks: (a) to review and integrate the historical conceptualizations of parental psychological control and identify the aspects of child or adolescent development these conceptualizations appear to have targeted, and (b) to review and discuss the known child and adolescent correlates of parental psychological control.

Regarding the first task, we concluded that varied descriptions of parent behaviors, attitudes, and intents related to psychological control converge around a conceptualization that this form of parental control is psychologically intrusive in manipulating and constraining children and adolescents. Further, we advanced the assessment that parental psychological control appears not to be an objective strategy for training children for healthy psychological and emotional development; rather, it reflects a type of interpersonal interaction in which the parent's psychological status and relational position to the child is maintained and defended at the expense and violation of the child's development of self.

Regarding the second task, we concluded that the empirical evidence from studies linking parental psychological control (or variables similar to it) to aspects of child and adolescent development reveals consistent findings that link these parenting variables to disturbances in self-processes, increased internalized and externalized problems, and decreased academic achievement. We concluded that there is growing evidence that these empirical associations are discernible in a variety of cultures and subcultures throughout the world.

Another purpose of this volume is to extend the research on parental psychological control. In chapter 2 we note that the literatures that have specifically measured parental psychological control have used samples of adolescents predominantly over samples of younger children, and that the majority of studies have used self-report survey designs. Chapters 3 through 8 of this volume were solicited to expand the literature on psychological control in these two areas. The criteria for selection of these chapters were (a) that they report empirical data from major research projects that have a specific focus or subfocus on parental psychological control, and that they meaningfully advance the research on parental psychological control by (b) extending the extensive existing work on parental psychological control of adolescents, (c) testing the measurement and predictive aspects of parental psychological control of younger children, and (d) using new methodologies and designs to further test the generalizability of the findings reviewed in chapter 2.

EXTENDING WORK ON PARENTAL PSYCHOLOGICAL CONTROL OF ADOLESCENTS

As noted previously, much of the evidence of the consistent negative effects of parental psychological control comes from work with adolescents. Thus, more studies that simply replicate this association (at least with adolescent-reported data) would not necessarily extend the understanding of psychological control. Instead, chapters 3 and 4 of this volume extend the work on psychological control of adolescents by studying its relationship with other key variables in family and individual development.

In chapter 3, Stone and colleagues broaden the understanding of parental psychological control of adolescents by setting it in the larger family context. They make a compelling theoretical and empirical link between parental psychological control and interparental conflict (particularly covert interparental conflict), both "indirect and insidious family patterns that disrupt the development of social and emotional competence in children" (p. 53). They show empirically that psychological control is distinct from interparental conflict, and that their findings of both direct and indirect associations of conflict (through parental psychological control) with adolescent functioning are independent of demographic variation. Further, although their adolescent self-reported measurement is common to the established work on psychological control, their multisample replication design adds confidence to the validity of the findings. In sum, their chapter provides an instructive and systematic analysis of the various ways in which multiple family processes can be understood, and they provide interesting initial information on the role of parental psychological control amid other key family processes.

In chapter 4, Pettit and Laird extend the work on psychological control of adolescents by providing an interesting assessment of potential antecedents of parental psychological control. In looking at both characteristics of adolescents when they were children and previous parenting patterns when they were children, they extend not only the general work on the antecedents of parenting but they provide useful new information on psychological control, particularly how parental orientations to parenting over the course of the life of the child might inform and conditionalize the use and effects of psychological control. Like others before them, their strategy to understand parental psychological control is to compare it empirically with parental behavioral control (monitoring). In terms of antecedents of psychological control, their findings replicate the often noted differences in findings when comparing child reports and parents reports of family phenomena, in their case showing that, from parental reports of parenting, earlier proactive parenting predicts later psychological control and, from adolescent reports of parenting, earlier hostile parenting predicts later psychological control. In contrast, from both parent and child reports of parenting, earlier proactive parenting predicts later parental monitoring. These findings are refined more by the demonstration that the links between earlier proactive parenting and both psychological and behavioral control are conditioned on the degree of earlier child adjustment difficulty: earlier proactive parenting predicts later psychological control for children with low levels of adjustment difficulty, but it predicts later behavioral control for children high in adjustment difficulty.

The distinction between parental psychological and behavioral control is further refined in the Pettit and Laird chapter (chapter 4) when documenting that parents high on behavioral control remain so over time if they are otherwise high on parental involvement, but that parents high on psychological control remain so over time in conjunction with their otherwise low involvement in parenting. The authors suggest, therefore, that such findings may reveal that parental psychological control is a manifestation of general parental "insensitivity."

Other interesting findings clarifying the nature of parental psychological control are reported in the Pettit and Laird study, which also adds substantially to the sophistication of the research on parental psychological control by way of its large sample, long-term longitudinal, multiple-informant design and its search for key interactions among parenting and child characteristics.

EXTENDING WORK ON PARENTAL PSYCHOLOGICAL CONTROL OF YOUNGER CHILDREN

Chapters 5 through 8 of this volume present studies on parental psychological control of younger children in an effort to extend the general work on psychological control beyond the predominant focus on adolescents. In addition, all of these chapters use designs or methodologies heretofore not common to the work on psychological control. Both of these foci help substantially to increase confidence in the robustness of the construct of psychological control.

In chapter 5, Morris and colleagues extend the work on psychological control in several ways. A unique part of their multi-informant, multiracial design is the development and testing of a puppet interview method for assessing psychological control as perceived by young children. As far as we know, this is the first effort to creatively test the ability of young children to reliably report on the psychological control they perceive from their parents. Their findings provide initial evidence that young children have this capability. Although they find no direct link between their new measure of parental psychological control and child functioning (perhaps because of their small sample size), they do find an interesting interaction between parenting and child temperament: Psychological control was related to internalizing and externalizing problems for children high in temperamental negative reactivity. This search for how the effects of psychological control might be conditionalized by child temperament is important and it, along with inconsistencies discerned in their measurement efforts, leads Morris and colleagues to advance the conceptual beginnings of an effort to refine the understanding of parental psychological control by defining the areas of child functioning (cognitive, emotional, behavioral) over which the psychological control is exercised.

In chapter 6, Nelson and Crick also explore a small sample of young children. The conceptual portion of their chapter is a good example of how the work on psychological control can be merged with different but relevant literatures. Specifically, they make the theoretically compelling link between psychological control and relational aggression, as distinguished from physical aggression. This link is consistent with our contentions (see chapters 2 and 9, this volume) that parental psychological control is symptomatic of relational difficulties in the parent–child/adolescent relationship. Nelson and Crick use somewhat limited measures of parent-reported psychological control, but their findings add to the evidence for the distinction of psychological control and behavioral control, in their case coercive control (particularly, corporal punishment). With regard to psychological control, their solitary finding of the association between paternal psychological control and daughter's relational aggression provides, like Morris and colleagues in the preceding chapter, another example of the potential conditionalized aspect of the effects of psychological control, in this case conditionalized by gender of parent and child.

In chapter 7, Holmbeck and colleagues provide additional evidence of the salience of parental psychological control to the functioning of young children. Like Morris and colleagues in chapter 5, these authors also provide methodological validation for the importance of psychological control through their use of a multi-informant design, in their case through the use of child-, mother-, and father-reported psychological control, as well as a rare videotape observational measure of psychological control. In addition, they extend the work significantly by demonstrating that the effects of psychological control can be found in unique populations—in their case, children with spina bifida. According to expectations, parents of children with spina bifida were rated higher on psychological control than parents of children without physical limitations. Consistent with the areas of child/adolescent functioning that parental psychological control has been shown to predict (as reviewed in chapter 2, this volume), links between parental psychological control and child internalized problems, externalized problems, school grades, and adaptive behavior were discerned across source of informant and observation, and, almost uniformly, were salient for both children with and without disabilities.

In chapter 8, Olsen and colleagues look at the cross-cultural validity of the psychological control construct, using samples of young children from the United States, Russia, and China. In addition to demonstrating some variance in the levels of parent-reported psychological control (highest for mothers of Russian girls; lowest for mothers of U.S. girls), they found psychological control to be predictive of internalized and externalized child problems in all of the samples. The patterns of association varied by type of problem and by sex of child, which, together with the findings from chapter 6, suggest the importance of testing for child sex differences, at least when studying younger children. The Olsen et al. study provides a good foundation for comparative work on the relevance of parental psychological control to younger children's functioning, in demonstrating that psychological control of younger children can be reliably measured via parental reports and that the growing evidence of the salience of psychological control to adolescent functioning cross-culturally (as reported in chapter 2, this volume) can also be discerned among children in a variety of cultures.

Finally, in chapter 9, Barber and colleagues briefly summarize the volume and offer a two-fold extension. First, they recommend a number of areas in which the research on parental psychological control can be strengthened. The recommendations include paying more careful attention to subgroup differences in the use of psychological control, clarifying the effects of psychological control through more sophisticated modeling and analyses, more effort to understand the determinants of parental psychological control, and the value of alternative methodologies in understanding specific parameters of psychological control. Second, they lift the construct of psychological control out of the restricted realm of the study of normative parent–child relationships by demonstrating its theoretical, conceptual, and empirical similarity to other work. This includes other parenting research, such as the literatures on child maltreatment and abuse but also research that extends beyond the parent–child dyad to sibling relationships and to broader levels of family process and functioning. They discuss also the relevance of the psychological control to environments outside the family, including school, peer, community, and occupational contexts, concluding that there is substantial evidence from a variety of arenas that intrusion into the psychological autonomy of individuals is problematic.

INTENDED AUDIENCE OF THE VOLUME

This volume is intended to be a useful resource for scholars and others interested in parent–child relationships. It highlights an area that has to date received inconsistent and inadequate attention, and it provides a source that both thoroughly reviews the literatures on parental psychological control and presents new methodologies and findings that enhance the study of this intrusive type of parenting. It is hoped that the volume will stimulate interest and much more work on a construct that appears to be an important component of the socialization of children. It is also hoped that the volume will stimulate thought and research focused on the intrusion into the psychological autonomy of children, adolescents, and other age groups in the variety of contexts that make up human social life.

REFERENCES

Allen, J. P., Hauser, S. T., Eickholt, C., Bell, K. L., & O'Connor, T. G. (1994). Autonomy and relatedness in family interactions as predictors of expressions of negative adolescent affect. *Journal of Research on Adolescence, 4,* 535–552.

Barber B. K. (1996). Parental psychological control: Revisiting a neglected construct. *Child Development, 67,* 3296–3319.

Barber, B. K., Olsen, J. A., & Shagle, S. (1994). Associations between parental psychological control and behavioral control and youth internalized and externalized behaviors. *Child Development, 65,* 1120–1136.

Baumrind, D. (1965). Parental control and parental love. *Children, 12,* 230–234.

Baumrind, D. (1966). Effects of authoritative parental control on child behavior. *Child Development, 37,* 887–907.

Baumrind, D. (1967). Child care practices anteceding three patterns of preschool behavior. *Genetic Psychology Monographs, 75,* 43–88.

Baumrind, D. (1968). Authoritarian vs. authoritative parental control. *Adolescence, 3,* 255–272

Baumrind, D. (1978). Parental disciplinary patterns and social competence in children. *Youth and Society, 9,* 239–276.

Baumrind, D. (1991). The influence of parenting style on adolescent competence and substance use. *Journal of Early Adolescence, 11,* 56–95.

Baumrind, D., & Black, A. E. (1967). Socialization practices associated with dimensions of competence in preschool boys and girls. *Child Development, 38,* 291–327.

Beavers, W. R. (1982). Healthy, midrange, and severely dysfunctional families. In F. Walsh (Ed.), *Normal family processes* (pp. 45–66). New York: Garland.

Becker, W. C. (1964). Consequences of different kinds of parental discipline. In M. L. Hoffman & W. W. Hoffman (Eds.), *Review of child development research* (Vol. 1, pp. 169–208). New York: Russell Sage Foundation.

Burbach, D. J., & Bourdin, C. M. (1986). Parent-child relations and the etiology of depression. A review of methods and findings. *Clinical Psychology Review, 6,* 133–153.

Coopersmith, S. (1967). *The antecedents of self-esteem.* San Francisco: W. H. Freeman.

Darling, N., & Steinberg, L. (1993). Parenting style as context: An integrative model. *Psychological Bulletin, 113,* 487–496.

Erikson, E. E. (1968). *Identity: Youth and crisis.* New York: Norton.

Fauber, R., Forehand, R., Thomas, A. M., & Wierson, M. (1990). A mediational model of the impact of marital conflict on adolescent adjustment in intact and divorced families: The role of disrupted parenting. *Child Development, 61,* 1112–1123.

Hauser, S. T. (1991). *Families and their adolescents.* New York: Free Press.

Hauser, S. T., Powers, S. I., Noam, G., Jacobson, A., Weiss, B., & Follansbee, D. (1984). Familial contexts of adolescent ego development. *Child Development, 55,* 195–213.

Maccoby, E. E., & Martin, J. A. (1983). Socialization in the context of the family: Parent-child interaction. In P. H. Mussen (Series Ed.) and M. E. Hetherington (Ed.), *Handbook of child psychology: Vol. 4, Socialization, personality, and social development* (pp. 1–101). New York: Wiley.

Marcia, J. E. (1980). Identity in adolescence. In J. Adelson (Ed.), *Handbook of adolescent psychology* (pp. 159–187). New York: Wiley.

Peterson, G. W., & Hann, D. (1999). Socializing parents and children in families. In S. Steinmetz, M. Sussman, & G. W. Peterson (Eds.), *Handbook of marriage and the family* (Rev. ed.; pp. 327–370). New York: Plenum Press.

Peterson, G. W., & Rollins, B. C. (1987). Parent-child socialization. In M. Sussman & S. K. Steinmetz (Eds.), *Handbook of marriage and the family* (pp. 471–507). New York: Plenum Press.

Rollins, B. C., & Thomas, D. L. (1979). Parental support, power, and control techniques in the socialization of children. In W. R. Burr, R. Hill, F. I. Nye, & I. L. Reiss (Eds.), *Contemporary theories about the family: Vol. 1. Research-based theories* (pp. 317–364). New York: Free Press.

Schaefer, E. S. (1965). A configurational analysis of children's reports of parent behavior. *Journal of Consulting Psychology, 29,* 552–557.

Seligman, M. E., & Peterson, C. (1986). A learned helplessness perspective on childhood depression: Theory and research. In M. Rutter, C. E. Izard, & P. B. Read (Eds.), *Depression in young people* (pp. 223–249). New York: Guilford Press.

Siegelman, M. (1965). College student personality correlates of early parent-child relationships. *Journal of Consulting Psychology, 29,* 558–564.

Steinberg, L. (1990). Autonomy, conflict, and harmony in the family relationship. In S. S. Feldman & G. R. Elliott (Eds.), *At the threshold: The developing adolescent* (pp. 255–276). Cambridge, MA: Harvard University Press.

Steinberg, L., Elmen, J. D., & Mounts, N. S. (1989). Authoritative parenting, psychosocial maturity, and academic success among adolescents. *Child Development, 60,* 1424–1436.

Steinberg, L., Lamborn, S. D., Dornbusch, S. M., & Darling, N. (1992). Impact of parenting practices on adolescent achievement: Authoritative parenting, school involvement, and encouragement to succeed. *Child Development, 63,* 1266–1281.

Steinberg, L., Mounts, N. S., Lamborn, S. D., & Dornbusch, S. M. (1991). Authoritative parenting and adolescent adjustment across varied ecological niches. *Journal of Research on Adolescence, 1,* 19–36.

Youniss, J., & Smollar, J. (1985). *Adolescent relations with mothers, fathers, and friends.* Chicago: University of Chicago Press.

2

VIOLATING THE SELF: PARENTAL PSYCHOLOGICAL CONTROL OF CHILDREN AND ADOLESCENTS

BRIAN K. BARBER AND ELIZABETH LOVELADY HARMON

During the past decade, there has been a pronounced increase in scientific attention to the construct of parental psychological control of children and adolescents. The increase began when Laurence Steinberg (1990; Steinberg, Elmen, & Mounts, 1989) reminded the field of important distinctions between this form of control and other, more behaviorally focused, forms of parental control. Since that time there has been a steady focus on the construct, and the attention continues to increase. During this period, findings of numerous studies have consistently demonstrated that parental psychological control is a meaningful aspect of the parent–child relationship that is negatively associated with a variety of aspects of healthy child development. As this volume shows, the research literature on psychological control is expanding to incorporate a variety of methodologies for indexing psychological control, to define its developmental parameters, to understand its position among other family process variables, to investigate its antecedents, and to assess its relevance across cultures.

As discussed in chapter 1, *psychological control* refers to parental behaviors that are intrusive and manipulative of children's thoughts, feelings, and attachments to parents. These behaviors appear to be associated with disturbances in psychoemotional boundaries between the child and parent, and hence with the development of an independent sense of self and identity. It is also predictive of numerous forms of psychological and social maladaption. Psychological control differs from most other types of parental control. Most traditional measures of parental control define parental attempts to regulate the behavior of their children, either through various disciplinary strategies, control of rewards and punishments, or through supervisory functions. Psychological control, as traditionally and contemporaneously defined, is not concerned with behavioral regulation, but with control—and violation—of the child's psychological self.

From the very beginnings of formal scientific explorations of the parent–child relationship, researchers have been aware of and concerned about the tendency of parents to act in psychologically controlling ways toward their children. Our review concerns 108 studies we have found ranging in time from 1946 to 2001. The distribution of these studies across the decades reveals the dramatic increase in attention to psychological control in the most recent decade. Figure 2-1 shows the trend of relatively minor but consistent attention to the construct from the 1940s to the 1990s, and then the steep rise in attention during the 1990s when 71 of the 108 studies (66%) were published.

This chapter extends an earlier, less comprehensive, review of psychological control (Barber, 1996). The chapter is organized into two parts. The first part reviews and integrates the historical conceptualizations of parental psychological control, focusing particularly on how psychological control has been conceptualized and measured over the decades and toward which aspects of the child this type of control appears to be targeted. This section makes clear that this form of control uniquely implicates the self—both that of the child and the parent. The second part reviews and discusses the known child and adolescent correlates of parental psychological control. It discusses the consistent association between psychological control and disturbances in self as well as between psychological control and varieties of internalized and externalized forms of behavior.

Before proceeding, it is important to make one comment on the logic of the use of specific references as they relate to psychological control. Much

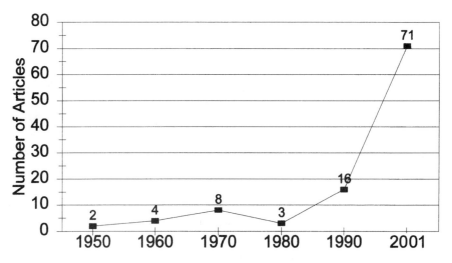

Figure 2-1. Chronological Trend in Studies on Psychological Control

of the work reviewed for this chapter has explicitly used the term *psychological control* in its conceptualization or measurement. However, we have also included numerous studies, which, although they do not use the specific term *psychological control*, do clearly in our opinion relate directly to the construct. The best example of this is the work by Diana Baumrind. Although she has not used the precise term *psychological control* in her work, her conceptual descriptions and measurement of parent–child relations refer to the same processes. Indeed, she has written more than any other researcher about parental attitudes and behaviors that violate the psychological integrity of children in the context of her description of authoritarian parenting. Another example is the work by Helm Stierlin and those who have expanded on his concepts of binding interactions between parents and adolescents.

CHARACTERIZATIONS OF PSYCHOLOGICAL CONTROL

As is the case with the socialization literature in general, the work on psychological control has included numerous labels or descriptors of this intrusive form of parental behavior. As a way of managing this abundance of characterizations, our strategy has been to conduct a content analysis of the construct definitions across the many studies and organize them according to the generality or specificity of the characterization. We created four types of characterizations: (a) higher order characterizations, which include general descriptors of psychological control; (b) lower order, more measurement-specific labels for psychological control; (c) characterizations that implicate the parental self in the interaction with the child; and (d) characterizations that focus on aspects of the child that are targeted or affected by psychological control.

Higher Order Characterizations of Psychological Control

Earl Schaefer was the first researcher to attend explicitly to the construct of psychological control. His work in the 1950s and 1960s set the standard for both the definition and the measurement of the construct (see also Droppleman & Schaefer, 1963; Renson, Schaefer, & Levy, 1968; Schaefer, 1965a, 1965b; Schaefer & Bell, 1958). In configurational analyses of parent- and child-reported parenting data, Schaefer (1965b) discerned three replicated factors, which he labeled *acceptance versus rejection, firm control versus lax control,* and *psychological autonomy versus psychological control.* This latter factor was defined primarily by the multiple-item scales of intrusiveness, parental direction, and control through guilt. Also related empirically to these were the scales of possessiveness, protectiveness, nagging, negative evaluation, strictness, and punishment. Schaefer characterized this complex of variables as, "covert, psychological methods of controlling the child's activities and behaviors that would not permit the child to develop as an individual apart from the parent" (Schaefer, 1965b, p. 555).

Psychological Methods

This founding definition of psychological control has been relied on through much of the ensuing work that has explicitly explored the construct, with many researchers quoting Schaefer's precise definition and others paraphrasing it. The most obvious and important element of the characterization is the term *psychological* in describing the methods parents use when relating with their children. Others' characterizations have been similar, such as psychological discipline (Becker, 1964), psychological pressure techniques (Schludermann & Schludermann, 1970), and psychological means of controlling (Dusek & Litovsky, 1988). Schaefer's definition also implicated the psychological development of the child in describing the effect of psychological control to be inhibiting the child from developing as an individual apart from the parent.

Most recent work on psychological control has focused on these consequences to the psychology of the child. Examples of this are when psychological control is equated with "the absence of psychological autonomy [of the child]" (Steinberg, 1990, p. 274) and in definitions such as the following:

> Psychological control is defined as patterns of family interaction that intrude upon or impede the child's individuation process, or the relative degree of psychological distance a child experiences from his or her parents and family. (Barber, Olsen, & Shagle, 1994, p. 1121)

Thus, definitions refer to either or both descriptions of psychologically oriented parental behavior as well as the psychological processes of children that are either targeted or effected by such behavior. As we will discuss later in the chapter, we believe this dual psychological involvement of parent and child is a unique element of this form of interpersonal interaction.

The psychological nature of this type of parental control is its most distinguishing characteristic. Most other forms of parental control describe "psychologically neutral" parental behaviors that have as their intent the control of children's behavior toward normative goals of internalization of or conformity to parental or societal standards. The distinction between psychological and behavioral control was made clear by Steinberg:

> A word or two is in order on the difference between psychological and behavioral control and their respective effects on the developing adolescent. Some readers may find it inconsistent, or perhaps confusing, that the two forms of control appear to have opposite effects on the adolescent. (Many researchers do not distinguish between these different

forms of control, which is clearly a mistake.) Adolescents appear to be adversely affected by psychological control—the absence of "psychological autonomy"—but positively influenced by behavioral control—the presence of "demandingness." Too little behavioral control may leave the youngster without adequate guidance and supervision and may, as a consequence, expose him or her, especially in contemporary society, to an array of developmentally risky temptations and dangers. Too much psychological control, in contrast, may facilitate dependency and impede the development of psychological competence and self-direction. The challenge for parents—and it may be a difficult one—is to grant sufficient psychological autonomy to their child without being behaviorally permissive. (1990, pp. 273–274; note 6)

This assertion of the important qualitative difference between psychological and behavioral control, and the differences in their effects on adolescent development, were based in part on Steinberg's study (Steinberg et al., 1989) of adolescent academic success and psychosocial maturity. The assertion was also the impetus for Barber's (e.g., 1992, 1996; Barber et al., 1994) subsequent investigations that were designed to test the distinctions outlined by Steinberg. These studies supported the distinctions by demonstrating that psychological control was negatively related to behavioral control, and, that whereas behavioral control was negatively related to antisocial behavior, psychological control was positively related to both depression and antisocial behavior.

The characterization that this form of control is psychological in nature has often been paired with other adjectives such as *covert* and *indirect*, descriptors that further qualify the psychological state or intent of parents who engage in this behavior (Armentrout & Burger, 1972; Droppleman & Schaefer, 1963; Garber, Robinson, & Valentiner, 1997; Litovsky & Dusek, 1985; Schaefer, 1965b; Schludermann & Schludermann, 1970; Teleki, Powell, & Claypool, 1984).

Intrusive

A second, common characterization of psychological control in the literature is that it is parenting that is intrusive. This helps clarify that psychological control is behavior that violates the child's psychological world. The label *intrusive* has commonly been used in general descriptions of psychological control (e.g., Barber, 1996; 1997; Crockenberg & Litman, 1990; Siegelman, 1965), and in some cases it has been used as a label for a measured scale (e.g., Baumrind, 1989, 1991; Weiss & Schwartz, 1996). Psychological control has been seen as behavior that intrudes on the "child's person" (Crockenberg & Litman, 1990), opportunity for self-discovery

(Constanzo & Woody, 1985), differentiation from parents (Barber, 1992), individuation (Constanzo & Woody, 1985), psychological competence and self-direction (Steinberg, 1990), and identity, efficacy, and worth (Barber, 1997a).

There are numerous other higher order terms that have been used to describe psychological control. Some are quite general, and could be (and are at times) used to describe nonpsychological control if they were not paired with other more psychologically related descriptors. Examples of these are *controlling* (Baumrind, 1966; Schaefer, 1965b), *demanding* (Marcus & Tisne, 1987), and *strict* (Siegelman, 1965). Others refer more directly to negative, psychologically based forms of control, such as *binding* and *constraining* (Barber, 1996; Hauser, 1991; Hauser et al., 1984; Stierlin, 1974), *manipulative* (Hart, Nelson, Robinson, Olsen, & McNeilly-Choque, 1998), *coercive* (Baumrind, 1987), *hostile* (Becker, 1964; Conger, Conger, & Scaramella, 1997; Schludermann & Schludermann, 1970), *invalidating* (Barber, 1996; Hart et al., 1998), *protective* (Becker, 1964; Droppleman & Schaefer, 1963; Schaefer, 1965a; Siegleman, 1965), *possessiveness* (Becker, 1964; Droppleman & Schaefer, 1963), and *overprotection* (Becker, 1964), a summary term for a constellation of psychological control, intrusion, excessive contact, infantilization, and prevention of independent behavior (Parker, Tupling, & Brown, 1979).

Lower Order Characterizations of Psychological Control

As was the case for the higher order characterizations of psychological control, the literature is filled with more specific descriptors, many of which are labels for measurement scales. We have grouped these into three main types, using our own general labels: (a) manipulative, (b) constraining, and (c) miscellaneous.

Manipulative

Several characterizations of psychological control appear to describe specific, tactical parental strategies to manipulate the child, or more specifically, the relationship between the parent and the child. Specifically, manipulating parents attempt to shape their children's behavior or adjust the emotional balance between parents and children by three main strategies: inducing guilt, instilling anxiety, and withdrawing love.

Parental *control through guilt* was one of the original defining scales in Schaefer's work (1965a, 1965b), and it has persisted both as a conceptual description of psychological control and as a measurement of it, as would be expected given that most investigators still use Schaefer's measurement instrument or one of the many revisions of it (Armentrout & Burger, 1972;

Barber, 1996; Barber et al., 1994; Dusek & Litovsky, 1988; Fauber, Forehand, Thomas, & Wierson, 1990; Forehand & Nousiainen, 1993; Hart et al., 1998; Litovsky & Dusek, 1985; Renson et al., 1968; Schludermann & Schludermann, 1970, personal communication, 1988; Schwarz, Barton-Henry, & Pruzinsky, 1985).

Control through the *withdrawal of love*, or making the parent's attention or affection contingent on the child being or behaving as the parent wishes, is a second common element of the manipulative aspects of parental psychological control. It was included among some of the earliest formulations of psychological control and continues today as a central element of the construct (Barber, 1996; Barber et al., 1994; Baumrind, 1966; Becker, 1964; Conger, Conger, & Scaramella, 1997; Hart et al., 1998; Hoffman, 1963; Litovsky & Dusek, 1985; Renson et al., 1968; Schludermann & Schludermann, 1970; Schwarz et al., 1985; Siegelman, 1965).

Instilling anxiety in the child as a means of control has also been historically a common element of psychological control conceptually and empirically (Armentrout & Burger, 1972; Dusek & Litovsky, 1988; Fauber, Forehand, Thomas, & Wierson, 1990; Forehand & Nousiainen, 1993; Litovsky & Dusek, 1985; Renson et al., 1968; Schwartz et al., 1985), but it has not been included in most recent measurements of psychological control.

Other descriptors of parental control strategies that can be considered to be manipulative but that are less commonly used in the literature are *excluding outside influence* and *deifying* (Schaefer & Bell, 1958), and *isolating child from parent, appeals to pride and guilt, expressions of disappointment*, and *shaming* (Becker, 1964).

Constraining

Although, not typically included in earlier explicit characterizations of psychological control, the constraint of children/adolescents' verbal expression has been often identified as a negative aspect of parental behavior, and one that appears to fit the criteria of psychologically controlling behavior. Parents who stifle their child's verbal behavior inhibit the child's discovery and expression of self. Initially, Schaefer and Bell had scales of *avoidance of communication* and *encouraging verbalization*, both designed to determine "whether the parent would permit or encourage the child to talk about his anxieties, conflicts, hostilities, and disagreements with parental policies" (1958, p. 347). Others have discussed the importance of verbal interchange between parents and children (Baumrind, 1966) and the importance of the child's self-expression (Swanson, 1988). Stierlin (1974), followed by Hauser (Best, Hauser, & Allen, 1997; Hauser, 1991; Hauser et al., 1984) have emphasized parental *binding* and *constraining* behaviors that either restrict verbal interactions to parental interests or excessively gratify, distract, withhold, or show indifference to the child. Such behaviors are seen to undermine the child's participation in family interactions and thereby discourage involvement with perceptions, ideas, and observations related to self and others. Because of the direct relevance of such behaviors to psychological control, Barber (1996) incorporated *constraining verbal interaction* in his measurement of psychological control.

Miscellaneous

Several other characterizations of parental attitudes or behavior are relevant to the discussion of psychological control either because, empirically, they have been correlated with psychological control, or because they are logically related to the underlying elements of the construct. Examples include *excessive parental expectations* of children, as in Baumrind's (1966) "absolute standard" of parents for children and Siegelman's (1965) *achievement demands*, wherein parents are described to insist that children make a special effort in anything they do, or that they get particularly good marks at school. Other examples are a series of behaviors related to disruption in the affective relationship between parents and children, such as *avoiding tenderness* and *ignoring* (Schaefer & Bell, 1958), *affective punishment* (Siegelman, 1965), and *rejection and hostile detachment* (Schludermann & Schludermann, 1970). Finally, Barber (1996), in addition to aspects of psychological control already discussed (constraining, invalidating, love withdrawal, guilt induction) included in his observational measure *personal attack on the child*, reflecting parental attacks on the place or worth of the child in the family, questioning family loyalty, and blaming the child for other family members' problems, and *erratic emotional behavior*, indexing parental vacillation between caring and attacking that may fundamentally confuse the child's appraisal of his or her acceptability to the parent.

PSYCHOLOGICAL CONTROL AND THE PARENTAL SELF

We interpret research to indicate that historical characterizations of psychological control describe parental behavior that fundamentally implicates the parent's psychological status in interactions with the child. Thus, in these cases, we judge that parents are not acting as neutral socializers administering control strategies for the benefit of their children, but are behaving in ways that protect or insure their own (parental) position in the family, and specifically their position in relationship to the child. To the extent that this interpretation is fair, it helps shift the understanding of psychological control away from one of a parenting behavior phenomenon to one of a characterization of the quality of the relationship between parents and children, in this case the parents concern and effort to manage the relationship to their own psychological advantage. Three types were discerned from the literature that appear to illustrate this position: (a) possessive, (b) dominant, and (c) enmeshing.

Possessive

Historically, parental attempts to infantilize their children, encourage their emotional and psychological dependence on the parent, and to restrict children to the psychological world of the parent has been labeled possessiveness. Early definitions of possessiveness included behaviors such as *babying the child, unduly emphasizing affectional bonds between parent and child, restricting the child's activities* to the family realm (Shoben, 1949), and *fostering dependency* on the parent (Schaefer & Bell, 1958; Shoben, 1949). Possessiveness was one of the secondary, empirical scales that defined psychological control in Schaefer's (1965b) original analysis, as it has been in many subsequent analyses using the longer versions of his Children's Report of Parent Behavior Inventory (CRPBI). This was the first instrument to explicitly measure parental psychological control. Various revised versions of the CRPBI are still commonly used in research on parent–child/adolescent relations. (Armentrout & Burger, 1972; Droppleman & Schaefer, 1963; Schwartz et al., 1985). Items tapping possessiveness have not been maintained in the 30-item version of the CRPBI (Schludermann & Schludermann, 1988; personal communication), nor in adaptations of it (e.g., the Psychological Control Scale-Youth Self-Report (PCS-YSR); Barber, 1996).

Dominant

Similar to possessiveness, parental dominance over the child has been a concern from the earliest formulations of parenting practices. Shoben (1949) described dominant behaviors such as *placing the child in a subordinate role* needing to conform completely to parental wishes under penalty of severe punishment. Other similar characterizations included the *ascendancy of the mother* (Schaefer & Bell, 1958) and *power* (insisting child receives parental permission for everything, parents want to know exactly how child spends money; Siegelman, 1965). *Parental direction* has been a central scale in some analyses of the CRPBI (Droppelman & Schaefer, 1963; Schaefer, 1965a, 1965b). In addition, Baumrind (1966, 1978, 1987) has regularly discussed parental dominance in her descriptions of authoritarian parents (e.g., parents do not willingly share power and responsibility; parent believes in keeping the child in place; parent attempts to shape, control, and evaluate the behavior and attitudes of the child according to an absolute standard of conduct).

Enmeshing

Related to both possessiveness and dominance is the concept of en-meshing, or blurring individual psychological boundaries in favor of a family identity. Schaefer and Bell (1958) discussed how their measure *excluding outside influence*—a scale designed to measure "family ethnocentrism"—may be related to parental control and authoritarian attitudes. Barber (Barber et al., 1994; Barber & Buehler, 1996; Barber & Shagle, 1992) has also made this same link, suggesting that *enmeshment* is the family-system-level analogue to psychological control in the parent–child dyad. At either level, behaviors intended to enmesh or psychologically control the child force the child into the parent's psychological world, encourage dependency, and inhibit individuation. Related concepts in other studies are *parental anxious emotional involvement* (Becker, 1964) and *permeability* and *mutuality* in family relationships (Groteveant & Cooper, 1986).

PSYCHOLOGICAL CONTROL AND THE CHILD SELF

A final way to view the various historical characterizations of parental psychological control is to attend to the aspects of the child that have been linked conceptually and theoretically to parental psychological control. This strategy makes it clear that the essential impact of parental psychological control of the child is to violate the self-system of the child. Throughout the literature, most aspects of child development that this form of parental behavior is thought to target or affect deal with the child's psychological self.

Aspects of the child's psychological self that have been implicated are many and varied. They include controlling the child's *self-will* (Baumrind, 1966; Schaefer & Bell, 1958), interference in the child's *self-regulation* (Baumrind, 1991; Grotevant & Cooper, 1986), not fostering child *self-reliance* (Barber & Buehler, 1996; Hauser, 1991; Steinberg et al., 1989), interference in *self-discovery* (Costanzo & Woody, 1985), and *ego development* (Best et al., 1997; Hauser, 1991; Hauser et al., 1984).

Interference in child *self-expression* has been implicated in psychological control, including expression of opinions (Barber, 1996; Kurdek, Fine, & Sinclair, 1995; Shulman, Collins, & Dital, 1993) and expression of emotions (Barber, 1996; Kuczynski & Kochanska, 1995). Handicapping child *decision-making* (Grolnick, Weiss, McKenzie, & Wrightman, 1996; Kurdek et al., 1995; Steinberg & Dornbusch, 1991; Steinberg, Fegley, & Dornbusch, 1993) and *autonomy* of choice in daily activities (Kurdek et al., 1995) are other similar elements.

Also, numerous elements of the child's *self-in-relation-to-parent* have been discussed as being compromised by psychological controlling behaviors, such as *individuality* (Goldin, 1969; Kurdek et al., 1995; Litovsky & Dusek, 1985; Schaefer, 1965a, 1965b; Steinberg, Lamborn, Dornbusch, & Darling, 1992); *individuation* (Barber et al., 1994; Barber & Shagle, 1992; Costanzo & Woody, 1985; Goldin, 1969; Smetana, 1995; Steinberg & Silverberg, 1986; Wakschlag, Chase-Landsdale, & Brooks-Gunn, 1996); *independence* (Barber, 1992); *identity* (Grotevant & Cooper, 1986; Hein & Lewko, 1994; Steinberg et al., 1989), *degree of psychological distance between parents and children* (Barber et al., 1994); *emotional autonomy* (Steinberg & Silverberg, 1986); and *threatened attachment to parents* (Barber, 1996; Becker, 1964).

CHILD AND ADOLESCENT CORRELATES OF PARENTAL PSYCHOLOGICAL CONTROL

In this second half of the chapter, we review the empirical studies that have linked parental psychological control (or variables similar to it) to indexes of child and adolescent functioning. The section ends with a brief presentation of the cross-cultural applicability of such findings. We located 71 empirical studies that we have divided into three categories: (a) studies that have measured psychological control via the few existing instruments that explicitly measure psychological control, or adaptations of them; (b) studies that have measured constructs not specifically labeled psychological control but that are conceptually similar to psychological control; and (c) studies that have used typologies of parental behaviors, one part of which was psychological control or a conceptually similar construct. This division is made for the sake of precision. At this early stage of evaluating the conceptual and empirical nature of the psychological control construct, it is important to have in mind clearly what is being discussed or measured so that any variance in findings can be appropriately attributed. One example that will be discussed in the final chapter of this volume is the frequent, and problematic, equating of psychological control and psychological auton-omy, as if they were opposite ends of the same continuum. The logic of separating out studies that have used psychological control as part of an aggregated parenting typology is that, once aggregated, one cannot be certain what role psychological control has played in the observed effects of the typology.

Before proceeding with the review of these studies, four general com-ments will be made. First, it is noteworthy that only 5 of the 71 studies

(7%) were published before 1990. This makes clear that although discussion of parental psychological control has existed since the 1950s, explicit attempts to measure its impact on child development are very recent. This burst of interest in linking psychological control to elements of child functioning might have several explanations. First, it coincides with efforts to disaggregate parental typologies so that more precise information can be gained about the nature and effects of the common typologies' constituent parts. Beginning in the 1960s, Diana Baumrind's exacting work in constructing ecologically valid constellations of parental behaviors—typologies—has dominated the parent–child research agenda. Indeed, this methodological trend in conceptualizing and measuring parental behaviors in the aggregate may be in large part the reason why explicit attention to the specific parenting dimension of psychological control was overlooked for some decades.

The voluminous work over the ensuing three decades after Baumrind's methods began to dominate the field has provided consistent evidence for the validity and salience to child development of a basic, yet evolving, set of typologies of parenting (e.g., authoritative, authoritarian, permissive, etc.). Beginning around the 1990s, a trend has begun among some researchers to extend this work by disaggregating these typologies to better specify the effects of parents on children's development. Because a parent's involvement in the psychological world of her or his child has always been a fundamental part of Baumrind's conceptualization and measurement (as pointed out earlier in this chapter), it is not, therefore, surprising that disaggregation would include a focus on psychological control or autonomy.

Second, another possible reason for the recent attention to psychological control might be the increasing presence of child self-reported data in published studies over the past 15 years or so. In contrast to earlier periods, it has become quite common since the mid-1980s to see published studies that rely completely or in part on child reports of parenting behavior. Because versions of Schaefer's CRPBI are among the most widely used child-reported indexes of parenting behaviors, and because psychological control is one of the three dimensions of these inventories, it is natural to see increased attention to this construct.

Third, as noted at the beginning of this chapter, in 1990 Laurence Steinberg articulated a critical conceptual distinction between behavioral and psychological control. This conceptual isolation of the construct of psychological control apart from other forms of parental control essentially re-legitimized the explicit study of psychological control, and it has been a significant source of inspiration for many of the studies that have been published in the past decade.

The second general comment about the studies linking parental psychological control to child functioning regards the predominant focus in these studies on adolescents. Eighty-three percent of the published studies reviewed investigated parenting of children in the second decade of life. One reason for this predominant attention to adolescents is that they, more than younger children, can adequately complete self-reported assessments of parental behavior. However, the theoretical relevance of autonomy processes to adolescence is certainly another reason why most researchers have studied parental psychological control of adolescents rather than younger children. As is commonly known, the period of adolescence, more than any other phase in the life-cycle, is thought to be characterized by issues of independence, identity formation, and realignment of emotional relationships with parents. Included in all of these psychosocial processes is the element of psychological autonomy, that which is violated by psychological control. Adolescence, therefore, is an ideal time to study psychological control and its effects (see chapters 3 and 4, this volume, for extensions of the work on adolescents).

The third comment is that the large majority of studies have used child or adolescent self-reports of parental psychological control (81%). Twenty-four studies (34%) used parent reports of psychological control, and 19 studies (27%) used observational measures of psychological control. (A few studies used multiple sources of information.) Because the first and still most prominently used measure of psychological control—Schaefer's CRPBI—is a self-reported survey instrument, it is not surprising that most studies investigating this concept have used a child-report methodology (Schaefer, 1965a, 1965b; Schludermann & Schludermann, 1970; personal communication, 1988). The Psychological Control Scale (Barber, 1996), another child-report measure that is being used, is in part an adaptation of the CRPBI.

In theory, there is also good reason to opt for child-reported data on psychological control. Simply, children may be the best informants on their psychological self, which is the aspect of their functioning and development that is the target of parental psychologically controlling behavior. Validation of self-reported findings by alternative methodologies certainly enhance the validity of the findings (see chapters 4 through 8, this volume, for examples of studies that use alternative measurement strategies), but for this basic reason, psychological control and its effects will likely always be measured in part by the recipients of it.

The fourth comment is that there are seemingly ubiquitous effects of psychological control. In all but four studies reviewed, researchers found significant associations between parental psychological control—however measured, and often controlling for other relevant parenting variables—and a variety of aspects of child functioning, regardless of methodology or sample size. The various ways in which this growing literature should be expanded and validated will be discussed in the final chapter of this volume, but at this point in the short but concentrated history of attention to the effects of parental psychological control, it appears that it is an aspect of the parent–child relationship that is significant and consistent in its effect.

Studies Explicitly Measuring Psychological Control

Table 2-1 summarizes the 34 studies that explicitly measured psychological control. Data for most of these studies were obtained by way of the various versions of the CRPBI or the PCS. A few of the studies measured psychological control by adapting other instruments and calling the measure *psychological control*. The specific aspects of child or adolescent functioning or development found in these studies to be associated with parental psychological control can be divided roughly into five main types: (a) self-processes, (b) internalized problems, (c) externalized problems, (d) academic achievement, and (e) miscellaneous.

Self-Processes

Consistent with theory and conceptualization, a number of studies have linked parental psychological control with elements of the child's psychological self. These include self-esteem (Litovsky & Dusek, 1985), self-worth (Garber et al., 1997), self-derogation (Comstock, 1994), self-confidence (Conger et al., 1997), self-reliance (Shulman et al., 1993), self-expression (Bronstein, 1994), and psychosocial maturity (e.g., self-reliance, identity, work orientation; Steinberg et al., 1989). With one exception, these studies showed parental psychological control to be associated with lower levels of self well-being. Although these studies have not covered all aspects of the self that have been postulated to be harmed by psychological control, they are consistent with the conceptualizations reviewed earlier relative to the negative impact of psychological control on the child's psychological self, and as a set, therefore, they provide some empirical validation for the postulated effects.

The one exception to this pattern was Bronstein's (1994) study of Mexican families in which she found that daughters of psychologically controlling parents tended to be higher in "assertive self-expression," as measured by giving opinions, acting expressively, laughing, and showing off. Should such an isolated finding be validated, it could suggest that there may be variation in how some cultures interpret parental behaviors that index psychological control.

Internalized Problems

Numerous studies tested the association between psychological control and internalized problems of children and adolescents, a link that was highlighted in some theorizing about the effects of parental psychological control (Barber, 1992). Internalized problems were measured either with global scoring (as in the Child Behavior Checklist; Achenbach & Edelbrock, 1987) or by more specific indexes of problems. With the exception of a

TABLE 2-1
Overview of Studies Measuring Psychological Control

Article	N	Age	Sample Characteristics	Measures	Source	Correlates
Teleki et al., 1984	59	7 to 11	Second-born child	CRPBI (56)	Child report Parent report	Lower self-esteem
Litovsky & Dusek, 1985	130	13 to 15	White, intact family	CRPBI (56)	Child report	Lower self-esteem
Steinberg et al., 1989	120	11 to 16	First-born child, diverse socioeconomic status, working, predominantly White	CRPBI (56)	Child report	Lower grades (longitudinal) Lower psychosocial maturity
Eastberg & Johnson, 1990	56	College	Freshmen women	CRPBI (108)	Child report	Higher social reticence
Fauber et al., 1990	97	11 to 14	Divorced/nondivorced	CRPBI (30) PC-Behaviors (3)	Child report Observational	Higher internalized problems
Barber & Shagle, 1992	473	Mean 13	White, mid-income	CRPBI (30) PC (10)	Child report	Higher internalized problems Lower school performance
Lyon et al., 1992	131	13 to 18	Incarcerated males, 75 in gang, 56 not, 44% Hispanic American	CRPBI (30)	Child report	{NS} Gang status, delinquency
Forehand & Nousiainen, 1993	70	11 to 17	Biological parents	CRPBI (30)	Parent report	{NS} Internal and external factors
Shulman et al., 1993	192	9 and 11	Israel, mid to upper socio-economic status	CRPBI (77)	Child report	Lower self-reliance (9-year-olds)
Barber et al., 1994	524	10 to 15	White, mid-income	CRPBI (30) PC (10)	Child report Parent report	Higher internalized problems
Bronstein, 1994	78	7 to 12	Central Mexico	PC Behaviors (5)	Observational	Higher assertive self-expression (females) Higher defiant behavior Higher passive resistance Higher inattentive obedience (punitive)
Comstock, 1994	473	Mean 13	White, mid-income	CRPBI (30)	Child report	Higher self-derogation Higher depression Higher eating disorders (males) Higher suicidal ideation Higher delinquency Higher aggression

(continued)

Article	N	Age	Sample Characteristics	Measures	Source	Correlates
Imbimo, 1995	96	17 to 25	Urban colleges, divorced mother-custody	CRPBI (108)	Child report	Higher identity status (females)
Barber, 1996	581 221	10 to 15	White, mid-income, low-income, 58% African American	CRPBI (30)	Child report	Higher depression
Barber, 1996 Barber, 1996	158 933	Mean 12 10 to 14	95% White 16% Hispanic	PC Behaviors (6) PCS	Observational Child report Parent report	Higher depression (females; mother) Higher depression Higher delinquency
Barber & Olsen, 1997	925	10 to 14	16% Hispanic, mid socio-economic status	PCS	Child report	Higher antisocial behavior Higher depression
Bogenscheider et al., 1997	666 510	14 to 18 14 to 18	Mother–adolescent pair Father–adolescent pair White, Midwest	Adapted	Child report Parent report	Higher parenting competency (parent report)
Conger et al., 1997	388	12 to 14	Mid- to lower-mid socioeconomic status, White, Iowa	Adapted	Child report Observational Sibling	Higher internalization (longitudinal) Lower self-confidence Parent change in psychological control positively to change in females' self-confidence Mothers' change in psychological control negatively to change in females' internalizing Higher external behavior problems (longitudinal) Parent change in psychological control negatively to change in externalizing
Garber et al., 1997	240	11 to 12	Depressed mothers, African American (14%)	CRPBI (108)	Child report Parent report	Higher depression Lower self-worth
Jensen, 1997	204	Mean 13	Females, Hispanic (16%)	PCS	Child report	Higher bulimia Higher drive for thinness
Litchfield et al., 1997 Bean, 1998	992 202	11 to 15 12 to 16	LDS African American (58%)	Adapted PCS	Child report Child report	{NS} Religiosity and deviance Higher depression (mother PC) Higher delinquency (mother PC)
Bean, 1998	933	12 to 16	Hispanic (16%)	PCS	Child report	Higher depression (bivariate only) Higher delinquency (bivariate only) Lower grades (bivariate only)

Study	N	Age	Sample	Measure	Report	Findings
Hart et al., 1998	207	3 to 6	Russia	Adapted	Parent report	Higher overall aggression (mothers' PC) (bivariate only)
Knowlton, 1998	450	11 to 18	Clinical sample	PCS	Child report	Mothers' PC high and fathers' connection low, more internalizing (females); Higher internalizing (males, both parents' PC); Higher externalizing
Knowlton, 1998	524	11 to 18	Community sample	PCS	Child report	Higher internalized problems (males; mothers' PC); Higher externalized problems (mothers' PC)
Mills & Rubin, 1998	459	4 to 9	Withdrawn, aggressive, control, with mothers	Adapted	Observational	More withdrawn-internalizing children had psychologically controlling mother (mostly boys)
Wells, 1998	555	3 to 6	White, 8% Latino, educated, LDS	Adapted PCS (8) PCS (16)	Parent report	Higher internalized problems (mothers' PC); {NS} internalized problems (fathers' PC); Higher externalized problems
Barber, 1999	6923	14	Palestinians (West Bank, Gaza)	PCS	Child report Parent report	Higher depression; Higher aggression; Higher antisocial behavior (males); Lower grades
Pettit et al., 2001 Rodgers, 1999	375	14 to 18	White, sexually active	CRPBI (30) 5-item Subscale	Child report	Higher risky sexual behavior (females; fathers' PC)
Morris et al. (chapter 5, this volume)	63	5 to 8		Puppet interview	Child report	More internalized problems (mother–children with angry temperment); More externalized problems (mother–sons with angry temperment)
Nelson & Crick (chapter 6, this volume)	127	3rd grade	70% White, 16% Black, 15% other	PCS (adapted)	Parent report	Higher physical aggression (mother–daughter); Higher relational aggression (father–son)
Olsen et al. (chapter 8, this volume)	194	3 to 5	U.S. White	PCS (adapted)	Mother report	More internalized problems (girls); More externalized problems (girls)
	190	3 to 6	Russian	PCS (adapted)	Mother report	More externalized problems (boys)
	248	3 to 6	Chinese	PCS (adapted)	Mother report	More internalized problems (girls); More externalized problems (boys)

(continued)

TABLE 2-1
Overview of Studies Measuring Psychological Control (*Continued*)

Article	N	Age	Sample Characteristics	Measures	Source	Correlates
Pettit & Laird (chapter 4, this volume)	456	13 to 14	80% White, 18% Black	PCS	Child report Mother report	More delinquency (low delinquency in middle childhood; low parental involvement) Less delinquency (high parental involvement) Higher anxiety
Holmbeck et al. (chapter 7, this volume)	136	8 to 9	82 to 91% White, 68 spina bifida, 68 without physical challenges	CRPBI (108) Video observation	Child report Parent report	Video observation More internalized problems More externalized problems Lower social competence Lower school grades Lower intrinsic motivation Fewer activities (spina bifida group)
Stone et al. (chapter 3, this volume)	337	10 to 15	White	PCS	Child report	More internalized problems More externalized problems
Stone et al. (chapter 3, this volume)	555	9 to 15	75% White, 12% Hispanic	CRPBI PCS	Child report	More internalized problems More externalized problems

Note: CRPBI = Children's Report of Parental Behavior Inventory (Schaefer, 1965b); NS = nonsignificant; PC Behaviors = psychologically controlling behaviors; PCS = Psychological Control Scale (Barber, 1996).

nonsignificant association between psychological control (parent-reported data) and internalized problems (Forehand & Nousianen, 1993), all other studies found psychological control to be positively related to problems, including internalized problems generally (Barber & Shagle, 1992; Conger et al., 1997; Fauber et al., 1990; Knowlton, 1998), depression (Barber, 1996, 1999; Barber & Olsen, 1997; Barber et al., 1994; Bean, Barber, & Crane, 2001; Garber et al., 1997), suicidal ideation (Comstock, 1994), withdrawn behavior (Mills & Rubin, 1998), eating disorders (Jensen, 1997), and passive resistance (Bronstein, 1994).

Externalized Problems

Findings for externalized problems were similar to those for internalized problems, although somewhat less consistent. Where significant, all relationships between psychological control and externalized problem behaviors were positive, including externalized problems generally (Conger et al., 1997; Knowlton, 1998), aggression (Comstock, 1994; Hart et al., 1998), delinquency (Barber, 1996; Bean et al., 2001; Comstock, 1994), antisocial behavior (Barber, 1999; Barber & Olsen, 1997), and defiance (Bronstein, 1994). Psychological control was not significantly related to gang membership (Lyon, Henggeler, & Hall, 1992), rebelliousness or compliance (Shulman et al., 1993), or deviance (Litchfield, Thomas, & Li, 1997). The several findings linking parental psychological control to externalized problems in children and adolescents underscores the relevance of this form of parenting. The relative lesser consistency of these findings compared to those for internalized problem behaviors might suggest that externalized effects, compared to internalized effects, are more contingent on other aspects of children, parents, or the broader socializing environment. Potential directions for future research on this issue are discussed briefly in the final chapter of this volume.

Academic Achievement

In all cases (U.S. majority and minority youth, Palestinian youth, disabled and able-bodied youth), psychological control was related to lower achievement (Barber, 1999; Barber & Shagle, 1992; Beau, 1998; Steinberg et al., 1989; chapter 7, this volume).

Miscellaneous

One study tested the longitudinal association between psychological control and adolescent religiosity. It found no association between a three-item, adapted measure of psychological control and religiosity (Litchfield et al., 1997).

Studies Measuring Concepts Similar to Psychological Control

Table 2-2 summarizes the 21 studies that have tested the relationship between parenting constructs that appear to be conceptually or theoretically related to psychological control and indexes of child or adolescent functioning. These studies can be grouped roughly into the same five types as before.

Self-Processes

Hauser's work (Best et al., 1997; Hauser et al., 1984) has demonstrated that parent–child interactions characterized by constraining (devalue, judge, excessively gratify, etc.) are negatively related to adolescent ego development. In contrast, this same work, plus that by Allen, Hauser, Eickholt, Bell, and O'Connor, 1994, has demonstrated that parent–child interactions that encourage autonomy and relatedness are positively associated with ego development. One finding contrary to this trend was the study by Crockenberg and Litman (1990), who found parental negative control to be associated with self-assertion in 2-year-olds, a finding, once validated, that may raise questions as to the developmental parameters to parental psychological control and its effects (see the final chapter of this volume for a brief discussion of this issue).

Internalized

Four studies tested the association between constructs similar to psychological control and internalized forms of problems in children and adolescents. Eccles, Early, Frasier, Belansky, and McCarthy (1997) found parent support for autonomy to be negatively related to depression in a sample of predominantly Black adolescents, whereas Barber and Buehler (1996) found family enmeshment to be positively related to depression and withdrawn behavior among adolescents. Herman, Dornbusch, Herron, and Herting (1997) found parental psychological autonomy to be negatively related to both psychological and somatic symptoms in adolescents. Gottman, Katz, and Hooven (1997) found parental derogation of children to be positively related to young children's negative affectivity and to physical illness (at the bivariate level only).

Externalized

Several studies have linked constructs similar to psychological control to various forms of externalized problems in children. Crockenberg and Litman (1990) found parental negative control to be associated with higher levels of defiance in 2-year-olds. Dobkin, Tremblay, and Sacchitelle (1997) found that mothers' promotion of autonomy was associated with less

TABLE 2-2

Overview of Studies Using Constructs Similar to Psychological Control

Article	N	Age	Sample Characteristics	Measures	Source	Correlates
Hauser et al., 1984	27 34	14–15	Psychiatric hospital Suburban high school	Constraining (cognitive and emotional)	Observational	Lower ego development Withdrawing from conversation
Crockenberg & Litman, 1990	95	23 to 26 mo	White, working/non-working	Negative control	Observational	Higher self-assertion Higher defiance
Allen et al., 1994	49 47	Mean 14	Psychiatric hospital High school freshmen	Inhibiting (autonomy–relatedness)	Observational	Higher depressive mood (mothers, Time 2) Higher externalizing symptoms (mothers, longitudinal)
Baumrind, 1991	139	15	Middle-class White, educated	Authoritarian–directive	Parent report Observational	Lower individualism Higher internalizing Lower social consciousness Lower autonomy Higher external locus of control Lower drug use Higher restrictiveness Lower achievement
Campbell et al., 1991	108	2 to 4	ADDH boys and controls	Negative control	Observational	Higher externalizing symptoms (mothers, longitudinal) bivariate Higher externalizing symptoms (initial symptoms controlled, parent referred group)
Steinberg & Dornbusch, 1991	5300	14 to 18	65% White, 13% Asian	Autonomy from parents	Child report	More work hours
Kurdek & Fine, 1993	911	10 to 14	90% White, two parents	Authoritarian	Child report	Higher authoritarian parenting from a divorced father
Steinberg & Darling, 1994	2000	14 to 18	Diverse ethnicity socioeconomic status Family structures Community	Psychological autonomy	Child report	Higher peer substance use Higher grade point average Higher work orientation
Nielsen & Metha, 1994	30	13 to 17	Clinical; White (86%) Biological parents (40%)	Autonomy-granting (CRPBI-56)	Child report	Lower social self-esteem (females) Lower (father) social self-esteem (males; controlling for family) all above bivariate

(continued)

TABLE 2-2
Overview of Studies Using Constructs Similar to Psychological Control (Continued)

Article	N	Age	Sample Characteristics	Measures	Source	Correlates
	165	14 to 17	Nonclinical; White (85%) Biological parents (89%)	Autonomy-granting (CRPBI-56)	Child report	Higher competence, comparative worth and social self-esteem (females) Higher (father) virtue and comparative worth, self-esteem (males) Higher (father) social self-esteem (males; controlling for family) all above bivariate
Kurdek et al., 1995	223	Mean 11	Midwest, White Family structures	Autonomy-granting	Child report	More parent transitions Lower achievement when supervision low Positive supervision to achievement correlation when autonomy low
Barber & Buehler, 1996	471	Mean 13	White, Mid-income	Enmeshment	Child report	Higher depression Higher aggressive behavior Higher delinquency
Mason et al., 1996	106	12 to 14	African American Urban Seattle	Restrictiveness	Parent report	Quadratic interaction with peer problem behavior {NS} Problem behavior with few problem peers Strong positive curvilinear problem behavior with more problem peers
Yau & Smetana, 1996	120	12 to 19	Hong Kong Laborers	Control	Observational	More youth–parent conflict More serious conflicts
Best el al., 1997	40	25	Psychiatric hospital Mid-upper socioeconomic status	Constraining (autonomy–relatedness)	Child report Observational	Higher resiliency, far more talkative Lower resiliency, less talkative Lower competencies Lower educational attainment
Best et al., 1997	39	25	High school Mid-upper socioeconomic status	Constraining (autonomy–relatedness)	Child report Observational	{NS} Ego resiliency Lower educational attainment
Bogenscheider et al., 1997	666 510	14 to 18 14 to 18	Mother–adolescent pair Father–adolescent pair White, Midwest	Parental sensitivity	Child report Parent report	Higher parenting competency (parent report)

Study	N	Age	Sample	Construct	Report	Outcomes
Dobian et al., 1997	20 21 22 19	13	French Canadian Low socioeconomic status, mother and son SOMA, disruptive SOMA, nondisruptive nonSOMA, disruptive nonSOMA, nondisruptive	Promotes autonomy	Observational	Higher substance use with hard task and disruptive group Autonomy, disruptive group, and task interaction
Eccles et al., 1997	1387	13 to 15	African American (60%)	Support for psychological autonomy (PC reverse scored)	Child report Parent report	Higher depression More problem behavior Higher academic alienation Lower grade point average
Gondoli & Silverberg, 1997	94	13	Nondivorced, single mother, Hispanic (17%)	Responsiveness (psychological autonomy) (CRPBI-30)	Child report Parent report Observational	Higher depression Higher anxiety More overwhelmed feelings (above all bivariate: mother and adolescent report)
Gottman et al., 1997	56	4 to 8	Varied parent marital satisfaction	Derogation	Parent report	Higher negative affectivity Lower academic achievement Higher physical illness (bivariate only)
Herman et al., 1997	2850	12 to 18	Diverse ethnicity 22% Asian	Psychological autonomy (PC reverse scored)	Child report	More somatic symptoms More psychological symptoms More substance use Higher delinquency Lower grades Lower expectations Lower grades Lower expectations
Gray & Steinberg, 1999	8700	14 to 18	Diverse ethnicity	Psychological autonomy (PC reverse scored)	Child report	Higher psychosomatic symptoms Higher internal distress

Note: CRPBI = Children's Report of Parental Behavior Inventory (Schaefer, 1965b); SOMA = sons of male alcoholics.

disruptiveness (especially while performing a hard task) in their adolescent sons of alcoholic fathers. Herman et al. (1997) found parental psychological autonomy to be negatively related to adolescent substance use and delinquency. Eccles et al. (1997) found parental promotion of autonomy to be negatively related to adolescent problem behaviors. Barber and Buehler (1996) found family enmeshment to be positively associated with adolescent aggression. Yau and Smetana (1996) found parental autonomy-related control to be associated with more, and more serious, conflicts between adolescents and their parents. Mason, Cauce, Gonzales, and Hiraga (1996) found parental restrictiveness to be associated with adolescent problem behavior in interaction with peer problem behavior.

Academic Achievement

Parental behavior related to psychological control has also often been linked to academic achievement in children. In longitudinal analyses of adolescent to young adult development, Best et al. (1997) found parent–child constraining interaction to be associated with lower educational attainment, and parent–child autonomy/relatedness to be positively associated with educational attainment. Kurdek et al. (1995) found parental autonomy-granting to predict achievement scores positively (when parental supervision was low), but otherwise not related to other forms of academic achievement when tested in combination with parental transitions and peer norms. Eccles et al. (1997) found support for autonomy to be positively related to grade point average and negatively related to academic alienation.

Miscellaneous

Steinberg and Dornbusch (1991) found that a measure of autonomy from parents (including family decision making) was associated with longer work hours at their jobs for adolescents. Bogenschneider, Small, and Tsay (1997) found a measure of parental sensitivity to be predictive of adolescent reports of higher parental competence.

Studies Using Psychological Control (or Similar Construct) in a Typology

Table 2-3 summarizes 16 studies that combined measures of psychological control (or similar constructs) with other parenting dimensions into a typology of parenting, typically typologies labeled *authoritarian parenting*. We include these in the review because of the specific reference to psychological control or similar constructs. However, because these variables are mixed with other parenting variables, any effects of the typology cannot be

TABLE 2-3
Overview of Studies Using Psychological Control in a Typology

Article	N	Age	Sample Characteristics	Measures	Source	Correlates
Dornbusch et al., 1987	7836	14 to 18	San Francisco Diverse ethnicity and socioeconomic status	Authoritarian (Authoritarian)	Child report	Lower grades (Whites, Asians) Lower grades (Hispanic females)
Baumrind, 1991	139	15	Middle-class White, educated	Authoritarian–directive (instrusive)	Parent report Observational	Lower individuation Higher internalizing Lower social consciousness Lower autonomy Higher external locus of control Lower drug use Lower achievement
Steinberg et al., 1991	1000	14 to 18	Diverse ethnicity, socioeconomic status Family structure Community (16 ecological niches)	Nonauthoritative (psychological autonomy-granting)	Child report	Lower self-reliance Higher depression Higher delinquency Lower grades (except Asians and Blacks)
Steinberg et al., 1992	3500	14 to 18	Diverse ethnicity	Nonauthoritative (psychological autonomy-granting)	Child report	Lower school engagement Lower school performance (Both moderated by lower parental school engagement and involvement)
Boyes & Allen, 1993	141	15 to 20	Canada High school, college	Authoritarian (CRPBI-108)	Child report	Lower moral development
Lamborn & Steinberg, 1993	8700	14 to 18	Diverse ethnicity socioeconomic status, family, community	Ambivalent (emotional autonomy)	Child report	Lower internal distress Lower psychosocial development Lower behavior problems Lower academic competence Higher school deviance, drug/alcohol use
Taylor et al., 1993	165	14 to 18	African American	Nonauthoritative (CRPBI-30)	Child report	More problem behavior Lower self-reliance {NS} Kinship and adolescent adjustment

(continued)

TABLE 2-3
Overview of Studies Using Psychological Control in a Typology (Continued)

Article	N	Age	Sample Characteristics	Measures	Source	Correlates
Hein & Lewko, 1994	363	12 to 22	Canada, High achievers, High socioeconomic status, 85% White	Nonauthoritative (authoritarian)	Child report	Lower positive views of science (females); Lower involvement in science activities (females); Less science knowledge (males); Worse attitudes toward science (males); Lower image of scientists; Less science curiosity
Fletcher et al., 1995	4431	14 to 18	Diverse ethnicity	Nonauthoritative (psychological autonomy-granting)	Child report	Lower self-reliance; Lower self-esteem; More psychological symptoms; More somatic symptoms; Lower social competence; Higher delinquency (bivariate only); Higher drug/alcohol use (bivariate only); Lower academic competence; Higher peer susceptibility (bivariate only); Lower grade point average; Less time on homework; More school misconduct (bivariate only); Lower school orientation; Lower bonding with teachers; Lower work orientation
McIntyre & Dusek, 1995	140	17 to 20	Private university in New York	Authoritarian CRPBI (56)	Child report	Lower social support and problem-focused coping
Robinson et al., 1996	190	Preschool	United States	Authoritarian (directiveness)	Parent report	Higher externalizing; Higher internalizing
Robinson et al., 1996	198	Preschool	Australia	Authoritarian (directiveness)	Parent report	Higher externalizing (fathers); Higher hostility (fathers); Higher internalizing; Higher anxiety (fathers)
Robinson et al., 1996	208	Preschool	China	Authoritarian (directiveness)	Parent report	Higher externalizing (fathers); Higher hostility (fathers)

Study	N	Age	Population	Parenting measure	Report	Outcomes
Robinson et al., 1996	220	Preschool	Russia	Authoritarian (directiveness)	Parent report	Higher externalizing Higher hostility
Weiss & Schwarz, 1996	134	College	University of Connecticut	Authoritative-directive (Intrusive Control) (ERR); (CRPBI-108)	Child report Parent report Sibling	Less open to experience More neurotic/tempermental Lower SAT scores Lower grade point average (males) Higher maladjustment
Gondoli & Silverberg, 1997	94	13	Nondivorced Single mother 17% Hispanic	Responsiveness (PC behaviors-2); (CRPBI-30)	Child report Parent report Observational	Higher emotional distress (mother) (mother and youth report) Lower acceptance Lower parenting efficacy Lower parental perspective taking {NS} Emotional distress (mothers) (youth report, controlling for parental perspective taking)
Chapell & Overton 1998	120	11 to 18	Upper-mid socioeconomic status 11% African American	Authoritarian (psychological control)	Child report	{NS} Test anxiety
Mantzicopoulos et al., 1998	344 214	14 to 16 14 to 16	Korean American	Mixed parenting (psychological autonomy-granting)	Child report	Lower self-reliance Lower self-identity Lower work orientation {NS} Youth gender
Avenoli et al., 1999	1200	14 to 18	Diverse ethnicity, socio-economic status Family structure Community (16 ecological niches)	Authoritarian (psychological autonomy-granting)	Child report	Lower self-esteem Higher psychological distress More substance use Higher delinquency (depending on family structure) Lower grades (depending on family structure)

Note: CRPBI = Children's Report of Parental Behavior Inventory (Schaefer, 1965b).

attributed to psychological control. Notably, the findings from these 16 studies fit easily into the five types defined earlier.

Self-Processes

Authoritarian parenting has been linked to lower self-reliance (Mantzicopoulos & Oh-Hwang, 1998; Taylor, Casten, & Flickinger, 1993), lower self-identity (Mantzicopoulos & Oh-Hwang, 1998), lower individuation (Baumrind, 1991), lower autonomy (Baumrind, 1991), higher external locus of control (Baumrind, 1991), and less openness to experience (Weiss & Schwartz, 1996).

Internalized

Authoritarian parenting has also been linked to higher internalizing problems (Baumrind, 1991; Robinson et al., 1996), higher internalized distress (Fletcher, Darling, Steinberg, & Dornbusch, 1995; Robinson et al., 1996), higher anxiety, higher neurotic/temperamental behavior (Weiss & Schwartz, 1996), lower social consciousness (Baumrind, 1991), and lower psychosocial adjustment (Fletcher et al., 1995).

Externalized

Associations between authoritarian parenting and externalized problem behaviors include higher externalizing problems and hostility (Robinson et al., 1996) more problem behavior (Taylor et al., 1993), misconduct (Fletcher et al., 1995), and higher maladjustment (Weiss & Schwartz, 1996). Contrary to this trend of positive associations between authoritarian parenting and externalized problem behaviors is the Baumrind (1991) finding that authoritarian–directive parenting was linked to lower drug use by adolescents.

Academic

The associations between authoritarian parenting and academic achievement include lower scores on college entrance exams and grade point average (Dornbusch, Ritter, Leiderman, Roberts, & Fraleigh, 1987; Fletcher et al., 1995; Weiss & Schwartz, 1996), lower achievement (Baumrind, 1991; Fletcher et al., 1995), lower grades (Avenevoli et al., 1999; Steinberg, Mounts, Lamborn, & Dornbusch, 1991), lower school performance and engagement (Steinberg et al., 1992), lower academic competence (Fletcher et al., 1995; Lamborn & Steinberg, 1993), less time on homework, lower school orientation, lower bonding with teachers (Fletcher et al., 1995), and lower knowledge, curiosity, and attitudes about science (Hein & Lewko,

1994). Chapell and Overton (1988) found no relationship between authoritarian parenting and test anxiety.

Miscellaneous

Boyes and Allen (1993) found authoritarian parenting to be related with lower moral development. Mantzicopoulos and Oh-Hwang (1998) found authoritarian parenting to be associated with lower work orientation.

Evidence of the Cross-Cultural Salience of Psychological Control

An important issue when reviewing any process as fundamental to human development as is the parent/caregiver–child relationship is the extent to which elements of the process are valid among people of different cultures. Accordingly, we have searched the literatures for any evidence that addresses this issue. Despite the fact that empirical investigations of psychological control are relatively new, a surprising number of these reviewed studies have involved families other than the commonly studied middle-class European American family. This prevalence can be explained by the current *zeitgeist* in the study of child and adolescent development that is conscious of cultural diversity (Grotevant, 1998), by increasing numbers of studies of child development internationally in which psychological control has been included as a variable, and by explicit attempts to test the cross-cultural validity of parental psychological control.

The most extensive cross-cultural work in the United States has been conducted by Steinberg and Dornbusch and their colleagues in three analyses of parenting typologies using their large California and Wisconsin adolescent data sets. Dornbusch et al. (1987) found authoritarian parenting to be associated negatively with school grades among European Americans, Asian Americans, and Hispanic American females, but not for Hispanic American males or African American males or females. These initial findings were clarified with subsequent analyses. For example, Steinberg et al. (1991) grouped the sample into 16 ecological niches defined by ethnicity, socioeconomic status, and family structure. Nonauthoritative parenting was related across niches to lower self-reliance, higher depression, higher delinquency, and lower grades, with findings less strong for some niches. Using the same methodology of ecological niches but emphasizing more forms of parenting, Avenevoli, Sessa, & Steinberg (1999) found authoritarian parenting to be associated with higher psychological distress, lower self-esteem, and lower grade point average among European Americans, African Americans, Asian Americans, and Hispanic Americans. In some cases, these associations were contingent on social class and single versus intact parent structures (i.e., only related for single parents or intact parents of one ethnic group, or only related for middle-class or working-class families for a specific ethnic group). Authoritarian parenting was not associated consistently with delinquency or substance use for any of the ethnic groups.

Other evidence from relevant typological studies includes higher problem behavior and lower self-esteem for U.S. African American adolescents (Taylor et al., 1993); lower moral development among English speaking Canadians (Boyes & Allen, 1993); less positive orientation to science among Canadian adolescents from a variety of ethnic backgrounds (Hein & Lewko, 1994); lower self-esteem among Korean adolescents (Mantzicopoulos & Oh-Hwang, 1998); and higher internalized and externalized problems among Australian, Chinese, and Russian preschool children (Robinson et al., 1996).

A variety of unrelated studies have investigated psychological control as one of several discrete dimensions of parenting in different cultures. These studies have found psychological control (or a construct related to it) to be associated with lower self-reliance among preadolescent Israelis (Shulman et al., 1993); higher defiance, passive resistance, and inattentive obedience among preadolescent Mexicans (Bronstein, 1994); higher depression and delinquency among U.S. African Americans and Hispanic Americans (Bean et al., 2001); higher overt aggression among Russian preschool children (Hart et al., 1998); and higher depression, aggression, antisocial behavior, and lower grades among Palestinian adolescents (Barber, 1999, 2001). Olsen et al. (chapter 8, this volume) also found psychological control to be related to internalized or externalized problems in samples of U.S., Chinese, and Russian children.

Our own research program is in the midst of a systematic study of varying cultures regarding the role of psychological control. The intent is to test our hypothesis that the effects of parental psychological control are as ubiquitous as they have recently been shown to be because this behavior intrudes on a basic human drive for some form of psychological and emotional autonomy, and that therefore these negative effects should be found broadly across cultures. Though not yet complete, enough data is available now to support the existing evidence cited previously for the cross-cultural relevance of psychological control. Our methodology has been self-reported surveys from 14- and 17-year-old school-going, male and female adolescents in nations and ethnic groups varying on factors such as family size, degree of industrialization, collectivist versus individualistic orientation, religion, and exposure to social unrest (e.g., political violence). The same instrumentation was used in all cultures for all variables, with translation as necessary. The PCS-YSR (Barber, 1996) was the measure for psychological control.

Table 2-4 summarizes the results of analyses of the nine cultures for which data are now available. The coefficients are regression coefficients from structural equation analyses of invariance (AMOS) in which depression

TABLE 2-4
Descriptive Data and Standardized Regression Coefficients for Parental Psychological Control Predicting Adolescent Characteristics (Controlling for Parental Acceptance and Monitoring), by Culture

Culture	N	Language	Depression[a]	Antisocial Behavior[a]
United States: White	513	English	.23	.24
United States: Cheyenne	250	English	.17	.20
Colombia	642	Spanish	.21	.21
India	758	English	.20	.23
Gaza	465	Arabic	.19	.29
South Africa: White	230	English	.22	.27
South Africa: Black	290	Xhosa	.20	.23
South Africa: Coloured[b]	246	Afrikaans	.25	.24
Australia	240	English	.19	.25

Notes:
[a]All coefficients significant at the $p < .001$ level.
[b]"Coloured" is common terminology in South Africa and thus is retained here.

and antisocial behavior were regressed on parental psychological control (mother and father), controlling for parental acceptance and parental monitoring. The findings are consistent in showing that perceived psychological control is associated positively and significantly to both forms of problem behavior in all nine cultures (the exceptional negative association with antisocial behavior in Colombia needs further analysis). Particularly noteworthy is that these patterns hold in two relatively collectivist cultures—India and Gaza—in which less emphasis is placed on individual autonomy than it is in more individualistic cultures (see Yau & Smetana, 1996, for similar findings). These data will be analyzed more thoroughly, including important data breaks for sex of child and parent, yet for now they offer some support for the broad relevance of parental psychological control to child and adolescent development.

CONCLUSION

The purpose of this chapter was to provide a thorough assessment of the conceptualization, measurement, and correlates of parental psychological control. Such a treatment is warranted by the recent empirical interest in this aspect of parent–child/adolescent relationships, and it is hoped that it will serve as a useful resource for future research on the construct. Our review indicated that conceptualizations and measurement indexes of parental psychological control converge around a conceptualization of parental control that is psychologically intrusive in manipulating and constraining children. We have suggested that psychological control appears not to be an objective strategy for training children for healthy psychological and emotional development; rather, it reflects a type of interpersonal interaction in which the parent's psychological status and relational position to the child is maintained and defended at the expense and violation of the child's development of self. The empirical evidence is robust in establishing that this form of interaction is associated primarily with disturbances in the self-processes of children and adolescents, as well as with numerous forms of problem behavior and difficulties in school functioning. The dramatic increase in attention to this construct since 1990 and the consistency of findings across scores of studies using different methodologies and samples from a variety of cultures and subcultures indicates that this is an important and fruitful area of study for family socialization.

Chapters 3 through 8 illustrate how the study of parental psychological control is expanding to include novel designs and measurement. Specifically, the chapters extend the work on psychological control of adolescents (chapters 3 and 4) and psychological control of younger children (chapters 5 to 8). Chapter 9 provides suggestions about how this growing work can move forward and how the construct of psychological control can be understood beyond the parent–child dyad.

REFERENCES

Achenbach, T. M., & Edelbrock, C. (1987). *Manual for the youth self-report and profile*. Burlington: University of Vermont, Department of Psychiatry.

Allen, J. P., Hauser, S. T., Eickholt, C., Bell, K. L., & O'Connor, T. G. (1994). Autonomy and relatedness in family interactions as predictors of expressions of negative adolescent affect. *Journal of Research on Adolescence, 4*, 535–552.

Armentrout, J. A., & Burger, G. K. (1972). Children's reports of parental child-rearing behavior at five grade levels. *Developmental Psychology, 7*, 44–48.

Avenevoli, S., Sessa, F. M., & Steinberg, L. (1999). Family structure, parenting practices, and adolescent adjustment: An ecological examination. In E. M. Hetherington (Ed.), *Coping with divorce, single parenting, and remarriage: A risk and resiliency perspective* (pp. 65–90). Hillsdale, NJ: Erlbaum.

Barber, B. K. (1992). Family, personality, and adolescent problem behaviors. *Journal of Marriage and the Family, 54*, 69–79.

Barber B. K. (1996). Parental psychological control: Revisiting a neglected construct. *Child Development, 67*, 3296–3319.

Barber, B. K. (1997). Adolescent socialization in context—The role of connection, regulation, and autonomy in the family. *Journal of Adolescent Research, 12*, 5–11.

Barber, B. K. (1999). Political violence, family relations, and Palestinian youth functioning. *Journal of Adolescent Research, 14,* 206–230.

Barber, B. K. (2001). Political violence, social integration, and youth functioning: Palestinian youth from the Intifada. *Journal of Community Psychology, 29,* 259–280.

Barber, B. K., & Buehler, C. (1996). Family cohesion and enmeshment: Different constructs, different effects. *Journal of Marriage and the Family, 58,* 433–441.

Barber, B. K., & Olsen, J. A. (1997). Socialization in context: Connection, regulation, and autonomy in the family, school, and neighborhood, and with peers. *Journal of Adolescent Research, 12,* 287–315.

Barber, B. K., Olsen, J. A., & Shagle, S. (1994). Associations between parental psychological control and behavioral control and youth internalized and externalized behaviors. *Child Development, 65,* 1120–1136.

Barber, B. K., & Shagle, S. C. (1992). Adolescent problem behaviors: A social-ecological analysis. *Family Perspective, 26,* 493–515.

Baumrind, D. (1966). Effects of authoritative parental control on child behavior. *Child Development, 37,* 887–907.

Baumrind, D. (1978). Parental disciplinary patterns and social competence in children. *Youth and Society, 9,* 239–276.

Baumrind, D. (1987). A developmental perspective on adolescent risk taking in contemporary America. *New Directions for Child Development, 37,* 93–125.

Baumrind, D. (1989). Rearing competent children. In W. Damon (Ed.), *Child development today and tomorrow* (pp. 349–378). San Francisco: Jossey-Bass.

Baumrind, D. (1991). The influence of parenting style on adolescent competence and substance use. *Journal of Early Adolescence, 11,* 56–95.

Bean, R. A. (1998). *Academic grades, delinquency, and depression among ethnically diverse youth: The influences of parental support, behavioral control, and psychological control.* Doctoral dissertation, Brigham Young University, Provo, UT.

Bean, R. A, Barber, B. K., & Crane, D. R. (2001). *Academic grades, delinquency, and depression among ethnically diverse youth: The influences of parental support, behavioral control, and psychological control.* Manuscript under review.

Becker, W. C. (1964). Consequences of different kinds of parental discipline. In M. L. Hoffman & W. W. Hoffman (Eds.), *Review of child development research* (Vol. 1, pp. 169–208). New York: Russell Sage Foundation.

Best, K. M., Hauser, S. T., & Allen, J. P. (1997). Predicting young adult competencies: Adolescent era parent and individual influences. *Journal of Adolescent Research, 12,* 90–112.

Bogenschneider, K., Small, S. A., & Tsay, J. C. (1997). Child, parent, and contextual influences on perceived parenting competence among parents of adolescents. *Journal of Marriage and the Family, 59,* 345–362.

Boyes, M. C., & Allen, S. G. (1993). Styles of parent-child interaction and moral reasoning in adolescence. *Merrill-Palmer Quarterly, 39,* 551 570.

Bronstein, P. (1994). Patterns of parent-child interaction in Mexican families: A cross-cultural perspective. *International Journal of Behavioral Development, 17,* 423–446.

Campbell, S. B., March, C. L., Pierce, E. W., & Szumowski, E. K. (1991). Hard-to-manage preschool boys: Family context and the stability of externalizing behavior. *Journal of Abnormal Child Psychology, 19*(3), 301–318.

Chapell, M. S., & Overton, W. F. (1998). Development of logical reasoning in the context of parental style and test anxiety. *Merrill-Palmer Quarterly, 44,* 141–156.

Comstock, D. C. (1994). *Parental control and gender-specific etiology of internalized and externalized adolescent deviance.* Master's thesis, Department of Sociology, Brigham Young University, Provo, Utah.

Conger, K. J., Conger, R. D., & Scaramella, L. V. (1997). Parents, siblings, psychological control, and adolescent adjustment. *Journal of Adolescent Research, 12,* 113–138.

Constanzo, P. R., & Woody, E. Z. (1985). Domain-specific parenting styles and their impact on the child's development of particular deviance: The example of obesity proneness. *Journal of Social and Clinical Psychology, 3,* 425–445.

Crockenberg, S., & Litman, C. (1990). Autonomy as competence in 2-year-olds: Maternal correlates of child defiance, compliance, and self-assertion. *Developmental Psychology, 26,* 961–971.

Dobkin, P. L., Tremblay, R. E., & Sacchitelle, C. (1997). Predicting boys' early-onset substance abuse from father's alcoholism, son's disruptiveness, and mother's parenting behavior. *Journal of Consulting and Clinical Psychology, 65,* 86–92.

Dornbusch, S. M., Ritter, P. L., Leiderman, P. H., Roberts, D. F., & Fraleigh, M. J. (1987). The relation of parenting style to adolescent school performance. *Child Development, 58,* 1244–1257.

Droppleman, L. F., & Schaefer, E. S. (1963). Boys' and girls' reports of maternal and paternal behavior. *Journal of Abnormal and Social Psychology, 67,* 648–654.

Dusek, J. B., & Litovsky, V. G. (1988). *Maternal employment and adolescent adjustment and perceptions of child rearing.* Paper presented at the Biennial Meeting of the Society for Research on Adolescence, Alexandria, VA, March 26.

Eastburg, M., & Johnson, W. B. (1990). Shyness and perceptions of parental behavior. *Psychological Reports, 66,* 915–921.

Eccles, J. S., Early, D., Frasier, K., Belansky, E., & McCarthy, K. (1997). The relation of connection, regulation, and support for autonomy to adolescents' functioning. *Journal of Adolescent Research, 12,* 263–286.

Engels, M. L., & Moisan, D. (1994). The psychological maltreatment inventory: Development of a measure of psychological maltreatment in childhood of ruse in adult clinical settings. *Psychological Reports, 74,* 595–604.

Fauber, R., Forehand, R., Thomas, A. M., & Wierson, M. (1990). A mediational model of the impact of marital conflict on adolescent adjustment in intact and divorced families: The role of disrupted parenting. *Child Development, 61,* 1112–1123.

Fletcher, A. C., Darling, N. E., Steinberg, L., & Dornbusch, S. M. (1995). The company they keep: Relation of adolescents' adjustment and behavior to their friends' perceptions of authoritative parenting in the social network. *Developmental Psychology, 31,* 300–310.

Forehand, R., & Nousiainen, S. (1993). Maternal and paternal parenting: Critical dimensions in adolescent functioning. *Journal of Family Psychology, 7,* 213–221.

Garber, J., Robinson, N. S., & Valentiner, D. (1997). The relation between parenting and adolescent depression: Self-worth as a mediator. *Journal of Adolescent Research, 12,* 12–33.

Goldin, P. C. (1969). A review of children's reports of parent behaviors. *Psychological Bulletin, 71,* 222–236.

Gondoli, D. M., & Silverberg, S. B. (1997). Maternal emotional distress and diminished responsiveness: The mediating role of parenting efficacy and parental perspective taking. *Developmental Psychology, 33,* 861–868.

Gottman, J. M., Katz, L. F., & Hooven, C. (1997). *Meta-emotion: How families communicate emotionally.* Mahwah, NJ: Erlbaum.

Gray, M. R., & Steinberg, L. (1999). Unpacking authoritative parenting: Reassessing a multidimensional construct. *Journal of Marriage and the Family, 61,* 574–587.

Grolnick, W. S., Weiss, L., McKenzie, L. & Wrightman, J. (1996). Contextual, cognitive, and adolescent factors associated with parenting in adolescence. *Journal of Youth and Adolescence, 25,* 33–55.

Grotevant, H. D. (1998). Adolescent development in family contexts. In W. Damon (Ed.), *Handbook of child psychology Vol. 3: Social, emotional, and personality development* (N. Eisenberg, Vol. Ed.). New York: John Wiley & Sons.

Grotevant, H. D, & Cooper, C. R. (1986). Individuation in family relationships: A perspective on individual differences in the development of identity and role-taking skill in adolescence. *Human Development, 29,* 82–100.

Hart, C. H., Nelson, D. A., Robinson, C. C., Olsen, S. F., & McNeilly-Choque, M. K. (1998). Overt and relational aggression in Russian nursery-school-age children: Parenting style and marital linkages. *Developmental Psychology, 34,* 687–697.

Hauser, S. T. (1991). *Families and their adolescents.* New York: Free Press.

Hauser, S. T., Powers, S. I., Noam, G., Jacobson, A., Weiss, B., & Follansbee, D. (1984). Familial contexts of adolescent ego development. *Child Development, 55,* 195–213.

Hein, C., & Lewko, J. H. (1994). Gender differences in factors related to parenting style: A study of high performing science students. *Journal of Adolescent Research, 9,* 262–281.

Herman, M. R., Dornbusch, S. M., Herron, M. C., & Herting, J. R. (1997). The influence of family regulation, connection, and psychological autonomy on six measures of adolescent functioning. *Journal of Adolescent Research, 12,* 34–67.

Hoffman, M. L. (1963). Childrearing practices and moral development. *Child Development, 34,* 295–318.

Imbimbo, P. V. (1995). Sex differences in the identity formation of college students from divorced families. *Journal of Youth and Adolescence, 24,* 745–761.

Jensen, B. S. (1997). *Family interaction and adolescent female eating disorders: An analysis of family, marital, and parent–child level correlates.* Master's thesis, Department of Sociology, Brigham Young University, Provo, Utah.

Knowlton, S. S. (1998). *Connection, regulation, and autonomy: A comparison of nonclinical adolescents and adolescents in residential treatment.* Master's thesis, Department of Family Sciences, Brigham Young University, Provo, Utah.

Kuczynski, L., & Kochanska, G. (1995). Function and content of maternal demands: Developmental significance of early demands. *Child Development, 66,* 616–628.

Kurdek, L. A., & Fine, M. A. (1993). The relation between family structure and young adolescents' appraisals of family climate and parenting behavior. *Journal of Family Issues, 14*(2), 279–290.

Kurdek, L. A., Fine, M. A., & Sinclair, R. J. (1995). School adjustment in sixth graders: Parenting transitions, family climate, and peer norm effects. *Child Development, 66,* 430–445.

Lamborn, S. D., & Steinberg, L. (1993). Emotional autonomy redux: Revisiting Ryan & Lynch. *Child Development, 64,* 483–499.

Litchfield, A. W., Thomas, D. L., & Li, B. D. (1997). Dimensions of religiosity as mediators of the relations between parenting and adolescent deviant behavior. *Journal of Adolescent Research, 12,* 199–226.

Litovsky, V. G., & Dusek, J. B. (1985). Perceptions of child rearing and self-concept development during the early adolescent years. *Journal of Youth and Adolescence, 14,* 373–387.

Lyon, J. M., Henggeler, S., & Hall, J. A. (1992). The family relations, peer relations, and criminal activities of Caucasian and Hispanic-American gang members. *Journal of Abnormal Child Psychology, 20,* 439–449.

Mantzicopoulos, P. Y., & Oh-Hwang, Y. (1998). The relationship of psychosocial maturity to parenting quality and intellectual ability for American and Korean adolescents. *Contemporary Educational Psychology, 23,* 195–206.

Marcus, A. M., & Tisne, S. (1987). Perception of maternal behavior by elementary school children of alcoholic mothers. *The International Journal of the Addictions, 22,* 543–555.

Mason, C. A., Cauce, A. M., Gonzales, N., & Hiraga, Y. (1996). Neither too sweet nor too sour: Problem peers, maternal control, and problem behavior in African American adolescents. *Child Development, 67,* 2115–2130.

McIntyre, J. G., & Dusek, J. B. (1995). Perceived parental rearing practices and styles of coping. *Journal of Youth and Adolescence, 24*(4), 499–509.

Miller, K. A., Kohn, M. L., & Schooler, C. (1986). Educational Self-Direction and Personality. *American Sociological Review, 51,* 372–390.

Mills, R. S. L., & Rubin, K. H. (1998). Are behavioural and psychological control both differentially associated with childhood aggression and social withdrawal? *Canadian Journal of Behavioural Sciences, 30,* 132–136.

Minuchin, S., Montalvo, B., Guerney, B. G., Rosman, B. L., & Schumer, F. (1967). *Families of the slums*. New York: Basic Books.

Nielsen, D. M., & Metha, A. (1994). Parental behavior and adolescent self-esteem in clinical and nonclinical samples. *Adolescence, 29*(115), 525–542.

Parker, G., Tupling, H., & Brown, L. B. (1979). A parental bonding instrument. *British Journal of Medical Psychology, 52*, 1–10.

Pettit, G. S., Laird, R. D., Dodge, K. A., Bates, J. E., & Criss, M. M. (2001). Antecedents and behavior-problem outcomes of parental monitoring and psychological control. *Child Development, 72*, 583–598.

Renson, G. J., Schaefer, E. S., & Levy, B. I. (1968). Cross-national validity of a spherical conceptual model for parent behavior. *Child Development, 39*, 1229–1235.

Robinson, C. C., Hart, C. H., Mandleco, B. L., Olsen, S. F., Russell, A., Aloa, V., Jin, S., Nelson, D. A., & Bazarskaya, N. (1996, August). *Psychometric support for a new measure of authoritative, authoritarian, and permissive parenting practices: Cross-cultural connections*. Paper presented at the Biennial Conference of the International Society for the Study of Behavioral Development, Quebec City, Canada.

Rodgers, K. B. (1999). Parenting processes related to sexual risk-taking behaviors of adolescent males and females. *Journal of Marriage and the Family, 61*, 99–109.

Schaefer, E. S. (1965a). Children's reports of parental behavior: An inventory. *Child Development, 36*, 413–424.

Schaefer, E. S. (1965b). A configurational analysis of children's reports of parent behavior. *Journal of Consulting Psychology, 29*, 552–557.

Schaefer, E. S., & Bell, R. Q. (1958). Development of a parental attitude research instrument. *Child Development, 29*, 339–361.

Schludermann, E., & Schludermann, S. (1970). Replicability of factors in children's report of parent behavior (CRPBI). *The Journal of Psychology, 76*, 239–249.

Schwarz, J. C., Barton-Henry, M. L., & Pruzinsky, T. (1985). Assessing child-rearing behaviors: A comparison of ratings made by mother, father, child, and sibling on the CRPBI. *Child Development, 56*, 462–479.

Shoben, E. J., Jr. (1949). The assessment of parental attitudes in relation to child adjustment. *Genetic Psychology Monographs, 39*, 101–148.

Shulman, S., Collins, W. A., & Dital, M. (1993). Parent-child relationships and peer-perceived competence during middle childhood and preadolescence in Israel. *Journal of Early Adolescence, 13*, 204–218.

Siegelman, M. (1965). Evaluation of Bronfenbrenner's questionnaire for children concerning parental behavior. *Child Development, 36*, 163–174.

Smetana, J. G. (1995). Parenting styles and conceptions of parental authority during adolescence. *Child Development, 66*, 299–316.

Steinberg, L. (1990). Autonomy, conflict, and harmony in the family relationship. In S. S. Feldman & G. R. Elliott (Eds.), *At the threshold: The developing adolescent* (pp. 255–276). Cambridge, MA: Harvard University Press.

Steinberg, L., & Darling, N. E. (1994). The broader context of social influence in adolescence. In R. K. Silbereisen & E. Todt (Eds.), *Adolescence in context: The interplay of family, school, peers, and work adjustment.* New York: Springer Verlag.

Steinberg, L., & Dornbusch, S. M. (1991). Negative correlates of part-time employment during adolescence: Replication and elaboration. *Developmental Psychology, 27,* 304–313.

Steinberg, L., Elmen, J. D., & Mounts, N. S. (1989). Authoritative parenting, psychosocial maturity, and academic success among adolescents. *Child Development, 60,* 1424–1436.

Steinberg, L., Fegley, S., & Dornbusch, S. (1993). Negative impact of part-time work on adolescent adjustment: Evidence from a longitudinal study. *Developmental Psychology, 29,* 171–180.

Steinberg, L., Lamborn, S. D., Dornbusch, S. M., & Darling, N. (1992). Impact of parenting practices on adolescent achievement: Authoritative parenting, school involvement, and encouragement to succeed. *Child Development, 63,* 1266–1281.

Steinberg, L., Mounts, N. S., Lamborn, S. D., & Dornbusch, S. M. (1991). Authoritative parenting and adolescent adjustment across varied ecological niches. *Journal of Research on Adolescence, 1,* 19–36.

Steinberg, L., & Silverberg, S. B. (1986). The vicissitudes of autonomy in early adolescence. *Child Development, 57,* 841–851.

Stierlin, H. (1974). *Separating parents and adolescents.* New York: Quadrangle.

Swanson, K. A. (1988). *Childrearing practices and the development of prosocial behavior.* Doctoral dissertation, Biola University, La Mirada, CA.

Taylor, R. D., Casten, R., & Flickinger, S. M. (1993). Influence of kinship social support on the parenting experiences and psychosocial adjustment of African-American adolescents. *Developmental Psychology, 29,* 382–388.

Teleki, J. K., Powell, J. A., & Claypool, P. L. (1984). Parental child-rearing behavior perceived by parents and school-age children in divorced and married families. *Home Economics Research Journal, 13,* 41–51.

Wakschlag, L. S., Chase-Lansdale, P. L., & Brooks-Gunn, J. (1996). Not just "Ghosts in the Nursery": Contemporaneous intergenerational relationships and parenting in young African-American families. *Child Development, 67,* 2131–2147.

Weiss, L. H., & Schwarz, J. C. (1996). The relationship between parenting types and older adolescents' personality, academic achievement, adjustment, and substance use. *Child Development, 67,* 2101–2114.

Wells, M. E. W. (1998). *Psychological control and internalizing and externalizing behavior in early childhood.* Master's thesis, Brigham Young University, Provo, UT.

Yau, J., & Smetana, J. G. (1996). Adolescent-parent conflict among Chinese adolescents in Hong Kong. *Child Development, 67,* 1262–1275.

3

INTERPARENTAL CONFLICT, PARENTAL PSYCHOLOGICAL CONTROL, AND YOUTH PROBLEM BEHAVIOR

GAYE STONE, CHERYL BUEHLER, AND BRIAN K. BARBER

The indirect and insidious family patterns that disrupt the development of social and emotional competence in children and adolescents have interested clinicians for years (Bowen, 1989; Minuchin, 1974). Family systems therapies—especially psychoanalytic, object relations and structural family therapy—have emphasized the indirect, insidious elements of family interaction patterns (Bowen, 1989; Bray & Williamson, 1987; Haley, 1976; Minuchin, 1974). However, only recently have researchers documented empirically these basic clinical assumptions (Barber, 1996; Kerig, 1995; McHale, 1997). Most of those theoretical and empirical works have grappled with the interconnections among the marital and parent–child dyads, and to some but limited extent, how these connections shape children's development. The purpose of this chapter is to elaborate some of these family processes and to examine their connections to problem behavior in children and adolescents. Specifically, we focus on the linkages among interparental conflict styles, parents' use of psychological control with their children, and youth problem behavior (YPB).

The works presented in this volume address the role of parental psychological control in the socialization of children and adolescents. In this chapter we examine the interplay between parents' marital relations—with

The Knoxville study was supported, in part, by a Faculty Research Award from the University of Tennessee to C. Buehler. We would like to thank Dr. Sam Bratton of the Knox County School System for his support and the many youth and families who participated in this project. The Ogden study was supported by Grant R29-MH47067-03 from the National Institute of Mental Health to B. K. Barber. We thank the many administrators, teachers, parents, and students from the Ogden City School District for their participation.

a particular focus on conflict—and psychological control of their children. We conduct this examination by focusing on the existence of YPB as an indicator of socialization that has, to some extent, gone awry. Although few scholars have simultaneously examined the effects of interparental conflict and parental psychological control of their child (see Fauber, Forehand, Thomas, & Wierson, 1990, for an exception), extant research that has examined the predictors independently documents an association with YPB. Exposure to interparental conflict seems to be associated concurrently and prospectively with total scores of YPB, as well as with specific scales measuring externalizing and internalizing YPB (Buehler et al., 1997; Forehand, Neighbors, Devine, & Armistead, 1994; Grych, Seid, & Fincham, 1992; Harold, Fincham, Osborne, & Conger, 1997; Katz & Gottman, 1993; O'Brien, Margolin, & John, 1995). We focus on interparental conflict rather than general marital quality because existing research documents the salience of conflict for YPB (Cummings, Davies, & Simpson, 1994; Jouriles, Barling, & O'Leary, 1987; Jouriles et al., 1991; Katz & Gottman, 1993). Although prospective findings are limited, extant research also documents a concurrent association between parental psychological control and youth problems (Barber, 1996; Conger, Conger, & Scaramella, 1997; Garber, Robinson, & Valentiner, 1997; Herman, Dornbusch, Herron, & Herting, 1997; Linver & Silverberg, 1995; see also chapter 2, this volume, for an overview of studies that link parental psychological control to measures of youth functioning).

DEFINING STUDY TERMS

Before discussing some of the potential connections between interparental conflict, parental psychological control, and YPB, we define each of these concepts.

Youth Problem Behavior

Externalizing YPB is outer-directed behavior such as aggression, stealing, and lying that functions maladaptively in society by producing harm or distress to others. Internalizing YPB is inner-directed behavior such as anxiety, depressive affect, and excessive fear that functions maladaptively by producing harm or distress to self (Reynolds, 1992). These forms of maladjustment constitute primary reasons for referring youth to mental health services (Kazdin, 1995). Morever, evidence of problem behavior during adolescence might be linked to impaired later adult functioning, including poor mental health, substance abuse, and problematic social relationships (Farrington, 1991; Kovacs et al., 1984; Pine, Cohen, Gurley, Brook, & Ma, 1998; Robins & McEvoy, 1990).

Interparental Conflict

Interparental conflict is a multidimensional concept, and the specific aspects need to be differentiated and separately measured (Fincham, 1994). For example, the frequency of interparental disagreement should be assessed separately from conflict behaviors and emotion expressed during marital interaction. Conflict interactions between parents are denoted by behaviors, affect, or strategies used to express disagreements or oppositional interests between parents. *Conflict style* is the term used most frequently in the literature to denote ways of expressing disagreements, so we use *conflict styles* instead of *mode of expression*. In a recent meta-analysis, Buehler et al. (1997) reported that the average effect size of the association between the frequency of interparental disagreement and YPB (M = .19, SD = .19, number of effects = 32) was significantly smaller than that between parents' use of a hostile, overt conflict style and YPB (M = .35, SD = .36, number of effects = 126). It is important to note that hostile conflict expression seems to be independently and more strongly related to child maladjustment than is the frequency of disagreement (Buehler et al., 1998; Jenkins & Smith, 1991; Kempton, Thomas, & Forehand, 1989).

The literature points to two important hostile interparental conflict styles: overt (physical and verbal) and covert (Buehler et al., 1998; Camara & Resnick, 1988; Jenkins & Smith, 1991; McHale, 1997). An *overt conflict style* (overt conflict) is defined as hostile behaviors and affect that indicate direct manifestations of negative connections between parents. Identifying characteristics include belligerence, contempt, derision, screaming, insulting, slapping, threatening, and hitting (Buehler et al., 1997). Buehler et al. (1997) reported that the average effect size for the association between parents' use of an overt conflict style and YPB was .35 (SD = .36; p < .01; number of effects = 126). This average effect was greater statistically than the one for frequency of disagreement and YPB. An important point of distinction with this definition is that we focus in this study on overt conflict that is seen or heard by the youth. Emery (1982) suggested that this is an important point of reference. Harold et al. (1997) substantiated this argument empirically by finding that the association between parent-reported and videotaped marital conflict (recorded with the child outside of earshot) at time 1 and YPB two years later was completely mediated by adolescent perceptions of marital hostility (and adolescent perceptions of parent–youth hostility). By fighting in front of the child (or within earshot), the parents involve the child through observation but not necessarily through engagement. McHale (1997) also supported the idea that conflict between parents displayed in front of the child differs from "encapsulated conflict." He has suggested that overt conflict is part of the "coparenting relationship."

A *covert conflict style* (covert conflict) is defined as hostile behaviors and affect that reflect indirect ways of managing conflict between parents (Buehler & Trotter, 1990). One important aspect of covert interparental conflict is triangling children (Minuchin, 1974). This involves active recruitment (even though this activity might be fairly subtle) or implicit approval of child-initiated involvement in the parents' disputes. Identifying characteristics include trying to get the child to side with one parent; scapegoating the child; using the child to get information about the other parent when one does not want to ask the other parent directly; having the child carry messages to the other parent because one does not want to relay the information; denigrating the other parent in the presence of the child when the other parent is not present; denigrating the other parent to the child in the presence of the other parent, but acting as though the other parent is not present, and allowing continued involvement by a child who initiates involvement in the parental dispute (Buchanan, Maccoby, & Dornbusch, 1991; Buehler et al., 1997; Johnston, Gonzalez, & Campbell, 1987; Kerig, 1995; McHale, 1997; Stone & Buehler, 1997; Tschann, Johnston, Kline, & Wallerstein, 1989). Buehler et al. (1997) reported that the average effect size for the association between parents' use of a covert conflict style and YPB was .28 (SD = .38; p < .01; number of effects = 24).

Although interrelated by the presence of hostility between the parents, a covert conflict style is most distinct from an overt conflict style in that covert behaviors and affect reflect indirect ways of expressing hostility between parents, rather than the direct expressions characteristic of overt conflict (Buehler & Trotter, 1990). This distinction regarding the degree of directness is made at the level of marital behavior rather than parenting behavior. This is an important point because, although the conflict management between parents who use covert strategies is indirect (i.e., they do not process their disagreement and anger only with each other), their triangling behaviors with their child might be very direct. Thus, our use of the word *indirect* defines the marital interaction rather than the parenting interaction.

Several scholars who have discussed how and why interparental conflict affects YPB have suggested that hostile interparental conflict interactions disrupt parenting (Buehler at al., 1997; Crockenberg & Covey, 1991; Cummings & Davies, 1994; Emery, 1982; Erel & Burman, 1995). A recent meta-analysis empirically documented the association between interparental conflict and troubled parenting (Krishnakumar & Buehler, 2000). One-hundred and thirty-eight effect sizes from 39 studies were analyzed, and the average weighted effect was .62, indicating a fairly strong association. Using daily checklists to record tension, disagreement, or an argument between spouses and between parents and children, Almeida, Wethington, and

Chandler (1999) corroborated the findings from the meta-analysis by reporting that both mothers and fathers were more likely to have tense interactions with their children on the day after there had been some marital tension.

One of the limitations of the Krishnakumar and Buehler (2000) review is that the association between interparental conflict and parental psychological control could not be examined because there was so little existing research. Thus, this study extends the current research on the association between interparental conflict and troubled parenting by focusing on parental psychological control.

Parental Psychological Control

As mentioned earlier in the book, parental psychological control is defined as verbal and nonverbal behaviors that intrude on youth's emotional and psychological autonomy (Barber, 1996; Barber, Olsen, & Shagle, 1994). Identifying characteristics include constraining verbal expressions, invalidating feelings, personal attacks, guilt induction, love withdrawal, and inconsistent emotional expression (Barber, 1996). The central elements of psychological control are intrusion into the child's psychological world and self-definition and parental attempts to manipulate the child's thoughts and feelings through invoking guilt, shame, and anxiety. Psychological control is distinguished from behavioral control in that the parent attempts to control, through the use of criticism, dominance, and anxiety or guilt induction, the youth's thoughts and feelings rather than the youth's behavior (Barber, 1996). Parents who use psychological control discourage children's expression of personal thoughts and feelings (Baumrind, 1971, 1978; see also chapter 2, this volume, for a detailed description of the construct of parental psychological control.)

EXPLORING THE ROLE OF PARENTAL PSYCHOLOGICAL CONTROL

In theory, there are several ways through which covert and overt interparental conflict and parental psychological control might interrelate to explain YPB: (a) redundant effects, (b) independent–additive effects, (c) indirect effects, (d) mediating effects, and (e) moderating effects.

Redundant Effects

It might be that interparental conflict and parental psychological control are highly enough correlated that they explain similar portions of variance in YPB. Conceptually, a high correlation might exist because each construct is characterized by boundary intrusions and anxiety induction. Both overt and covert conflict represent potential boundary transgressions. Exposing children to or engaging them in parental fights places them in an uncomfortable, and potentially anxiety-producing situation, particularly if the disputes are left unresolved (Cummings & Davies, 1994). Perceptions of self-relevance and potential threat might serve to engage the child further in the parents' dispute (Grych & Fincham, 1990). Boundary intrusions also characterize parental psychological control (Barber et al., 1994; see also chapter 9, this volume).

The study of Fauber et al. (1990) is the only research we have found that has examined the association between interparental conflict and parental psychological control (assessed using the Children's Report of Problem Behaviors Inventory (CRPBI; Schludermann & Schludermann, 1970) and observers' ratings). The partialized correlation was .30 (based on a sample of 46 nondivorced families). This was statistically significant but is relatively small in magnitude (Cohen, 1977). Thus, although the existing evidence does not suggest the existence of redundant effects between interparental conflict and parental psychological control, we test for this in the present study because so little extant research exists.

Independent–Additive Effects

Overt and covert interparental conflict and psychological control might each explain unique aspects of YPB (i.e., independent effects), and the joint contribution of these three predictors might be greater than any one of the independent predictors (i.e., additive effects).

In theory, youth might be at risk for problem behavior when exposed to either hostile interparental conflict or psychological control by parents. As suggested by social learning theory, youth might learn through parental examples that conflict is handled by insulting, yelling, name calling, threatening, or recruiting a third party to ease conflictual tensions. Youth repeatedly exposed to anxious tension or lessons in hostile patterns of conflict management might not develop important relational and emotional regulation skills (Cummings & Davies, 1994).

Fauber et al. (1990) found independent–additive effects for the divorced sample of families but not for the married families. Likewise, Gerard and Buehler (1999) found support for the independent–additive model when examining the joint effects of overt conflict and a composite indicator of troubled parenting that included inadequate monitoring, harsh or inconsistent discipline, and low acceptance. The present study builds on this work by incorporating covert conflict and by focusing on psychological conflict within the parenting realm.

Indirect Effects

Parental psychological control might be associated with overt and covert conflict and with YPB, forming a causal pathway from conflict to psychological control to YPB. An indirect effect (versus a mediating effect) would indicate that the pathway is statistically significant but that a significant direct effect between conflict and YPB also exists and is not diminished by the existence of the statistically significant pathway through psychological control. In essence, this pattern of relationships also suggests independent–additive effects, but with causal pathways included in addition to individual predictors.

In theory, overt conflict and psychological control might be linked causally through increased parental tension, anxiety, and distraction. Frequent and sustained fighting between parents seems to leave many parents upset, anxious, preoccupied, and tired (Patterson, 1982). These feelings and states are not conducive to enacting some of the elements of good parenting that require vigilance and energy (e.g., monitoring, consistent discipline, involvement in the child's life). Rather, because for some parents it entails less energy, parents might try to gain compliance from their children using psychological manipulation. Almeida et al. (1999) provided support for the direct transmission of marital tension to parent–child tension (and much less support for the reciprocal effect of parent–child tension to marital tension), but they did not examine linking mechanisms such as specific parental or child behaviors. Harold and Conger (1997) found that overt conflict was associated with internalizing YPB and sons' externalizing YPB two years later through parental hostility toward the child (measured one year after interparental conflict and one year before YPB). However, they assessed neither covert conflict nor parents' use of psychological control with their children.

Covert conflict and psychological control might be linked through binding processes. Stierlin (1985) suggested that parents who have distressed marriages might bind their children to themselves or the family. Binding occurs (a) when the child's dependency needs are used by a parent to tie the child to the parent or family; (b) when the child's ability to differentiate his or her own feelings, thoughts, and goals from others is impinged on; or (c) when the child's loyalty to the parent and the family is questioned at a fundamental level. One of the risks of binding interactions is that they might lead to enmeshed parent–child relationships and parent–child alliances, particularly in the face of unresolved or hostilely resolved marital tension. The enmeshment and cross-generational coalition maintains a parent–child emotional alliance against the other parent (Haley, 1976; Minuchin, 1974). To maintain the child's support, the parent might become overly ingratiating, overly and inappropriately demanding and intrusive, and might relax expectations and demands for appropriate behavior from the child. Potentially, this manifests in psychologically controlling and inconsistent parenting.

These parenting interactions increase the chance that children will be exposed to an anxiety-provoking, uncertain, and disturbing family atmosphere, and subsequently might shape difficulties in children's development, as indicated by depression, anxiety, noncompliance, low self-confidence, eating disorders, and somatic complaints (Barber, 1996; Stierlin & Weber, 1989; Stierlin, Weber, Schmidt, & Simon, 1986; Stierlin, Wirshing, & Knauss, 1977; see also chapter 2, this volume). However, parental distraction and binding processes might not be the only explanation for YPB.

As mentioned previously, in the indirect model the direct association between interparental conflict and YPB remains statistically significant and relatively unchanged when psychological control is added to the model. In theory, this might indicate that interparental conflict also effects YPB through mechanisms other than parenting or that some of the effect on YPB is direct through modeling and emotional insecurity (Buehler, Krishnakumar, Anthony, Tittsworth, & Stone, 1994; Cummings & Davies, 1994; Davies & Cummings, 1998).

Mediating Effects

Mediating effects would be present to the extent that parental psychological control completely explains the association between interparental conflict and YPB. This would indicate that psychological control is a complete mediator (Baron & Kenny, 1986). As a partial mediator, psychological control would significantly reduce (statistically speaking) but not eliminate the association between interparental conflict and YPB. Although many researchers test for mediating effects using cross-sectional data, the antecedent, mediating, and outcome variables should be time-ordered.

Analyzing cross-sectional data, Fauber et al. (1990) found support for mediating effects. They used parent and youth-report measures of global interparental conflict. They measured psychological control using the CRPBI subscale (Schludermann & Schludermann, 1970) of psychological control versus autonomy. This youth-report measure focuses primarily on psychological methods of parental control used to change children's behavior (see chapter 2, this volume). Mothers' behavior with their youth also was observed and rated. In terms of the observational rating scale, psychological control was defined as "the degree to which the mother uses psychological tactics designed to induce anxiety, guilt, and/or shame as a method of controlling the adolescent" (p. 1115). Externalizing problems were measured by mother reports of behavioral deviance using the Revised Behavior Problem Checklist (RBPC; Quay & Peterson, 1983). Internalizing problems were measured by youth reports of depressive affect using the Children's Depression Inventory (CDI; Kovacs, 1981). They collected data from 97 families with adolescents, 51 from recently divorced families and 46 from nondivorced families.

They found that psychological control completely mediated the effects of interparental conflict on internalizing YPB in nondivorced families. Parental rejection and lax control also were included in the model. Psychological control was not associated with externalizing YPB. In divorced families, parental psychological control was a partial mediator between interparental conflict and internalizing YPB. Again, psychological control was unrelated to externalizing YPB.

Moderating Effects

Moderating effects would exist if interparental conflict is associated with YPB only when the levels of psychological control are high. In theory, in this case psychological control conditionalizes the association between interparental conflict and YPB. Gerard and Buehler (1999) tested for moderating effects between overt conflict and a general measure of parenting that did not include psychological control and found no supporting evidence. Therefore, we test for moderating effects in this study because the conditionalizing effect of psychological control has not been examined.

CONTEXTUALIZING THE ROLE OF PARENTAL PSYCHOLOGICAL CONTROL

As part of the testing of these five different ways in which interparental conflict and parental psychological might interrelate to explain YPB, the moderating effects of youth age, youth gender, parents' marital status, and family economic situation were examined. These moderating analyses provide information about the extent to which any given pattern among variables is consistent across youth and families with varying background characteristics. In other words, these analyses contextualize the findings.

The effects of age need to be considered because there are substantial developmental changes that occur between childhood and adolescence. For instance, the individuation process is more prominent during adolescence, therefore the models might fit differently with adolescents than with children (Barber et al., 1994). Children seem particularly vulnerable to conflicting loyalties to parents (Hodges, 1991) and show increased sensitivity to and involvement with others' conflicts as they grow older (Cummings, 1987; Fauber et al., 1990). Also, parental psychological control seems to have similar negative correlates with children as it does with adolescents as suggested by other studies in this volume (see chapters 5 through 8, this volume).

The effects of youth gender also must be considered because some researchers have suggested that boys and girls have different responses to interparental conflict (Cummings & Davies, 1994) and may experience different levels of parental psychological control (see chapter 2, this volume).

Family structure is a salient variable to consider in the context of interparental conflict styles and YPB (Amato, 1993). Some researchers have found differences in the association between hostile conflict styles and YPB for married and divorced families (Fauber et al., 1990; Forehand, Wierson, McCombs, Brody, & Fauber, 1989). Fauber et al. (1990) also found that the mediational path of psychological control in the relationship between interparental conflict and internalizing YPB was strongest in the married sample.

The links among interparental conflict, parental psychological control, and YPB should be examined to determine how socioeconomic status conditionalizes the associations. Economic status is associated with both interparental conflict and YPB (Hotaling & Sugarman, 1990), and there appears to be a trend toward higher levels of parental psychological control among lower social class families (see chapter 2, this volume).

COLLECTING THE DATA

This study was conducted using two different samples of youth. The first sample consisted of youth living in Knox County, Tennessee. The second sample consisted of youth living in Ogden, Utah. These sites were selected because they are near universities (within 60 miles) where research on socialization processes and youth adjustment was being conducted. We used two samples of families to provide data on the replicability of substantive findings and to inform measurement construct validity (Lykken, 1968)

Total YPB as well as assessments of internalizing and externalizing YPB were analyzed. Youth reported on their perceptions of interparental conflict, parental psychological control, and their own problem behavior. Theoretical and empirical evidence justifies the use of youth reporters. Researchers argue that youth reports of interparental conflict are better indicators of youths' experience than parent reports (Davies & Cummings, 1994; Grych et al., 1992). Youth have access to the whole range of their own emotions and behavior in an array of settings, so youth reports represent a better estimate of what the youth actually sees, hears, and feels; therefore, youth might be the best interpreters and reporters of their own problem behavior. Compared with other family members and teachers, youth have the most access to and greatest pool of knowledge about their own behavior problems. In support of the value of youth reports, Harold and Conger (1997) concluded that the negative impact of marital conflict on present and future YPB was explained completely by youth perceptions of marital conflict and the significance youth attach to the conflict. Furthermore, there is extensive literature documenting that youth can accurately and reliably report their parents' behaviors (Golden, 1969; Moscowitz & Schwarz, 1982) and their own adjustment (McCord, 1990; see also chapter 2, this volume, for further discussion of the relevance of youth reports).

Knox County Families

Youth in the sixth through eighth grade were recruited at this site because of the authors' interest in exploring how interparental conflict is associated with youth behavior during their transition into adolescence. The sample included youth with biological or adoptive parents who are married or divorced or separated (and living with the mother).

In this cross-sectional research design, specific schools were targeted to ensure socioeconomic diversity. Students in each school were randomly assigned to homerooms, which reduced many sources of possible teacher selection bias. Child permission forms were distributed through homerooms and sent home with each student. To facilitate follow-through, each student received a finger puppet for returning the form, regardless of a parent's decision regarding participation. Parental consent was received for 75% of the invited youth.

The sample consisted of 337 youth aged 10 to 15 (M = 12.40, SD = .99). There were 190 females (56%) and 147 males (44%). Based on reports from 255 (76%) of the youth, the average level of formal education attained by mothers and fathers was between "completed high school" and "completed some college." Youth who did not complete this question told us it was because they did not know their parents' education level. Eighty-seven percent reported married parents. Eighty-seven percent of the youth paid full prices for their school lunch, which we used as a socioeconomic indicator (3% received a partial subsidy and 10% received free lunch).

The representativeness of this sample was examined by comparing these average characteristics with 1989 and 1990 census data on families and individuals living in Knox County (Slater & Hall, 1996; U.S. Bureau of the Census, 1996). The sample was representative of families in Knox County in terms of parents' education, marital status, family economic well-being, and race (see Buehler et al., 1998, for details).

Procedures

Youth completed their questionnaire during school. They were given as much time as needed to complete the survey, and several trained assistants were available to answer questions. On completion, students were treated to a pizza party as a reward for participation.

The measures used in the Knox County study were similar to those used in the Ogden study. Although included in the survey instrument, the specific parenting behavior of psychological control was not a central construct in the Knox County project. As a consequence, the measures of aspects of fathers' and mothers' use of psychological control were shorter in the Knox County study than in the Ogden study.

Youth reported their perceptions of their parents' frequency of use of covert conflict using eight items, four written for this study and four adapted from Grych et al. (1992). Sample items were "How often do you feel caught in the middle when your parents fight?" and "How often do you feel you have to take sides when your parents argue?" The response format ranged from "never" (1) to "very often" (4). Cronbach's alpha for this scale was .84. Evidence of construct validity can be found in Buchanan et al. (1991), Buehler et al. (1998), and Grych et al. (1992).

Youth perceptions of the frequency of their parents' use of overt conflict were measured using five items written for this study. Youth reported how often their parents did any of the following in front of them (so they could see or hear): "call each other names," "tell each other to shut up," and "threaten each other." The response format ranged from "never" (1) to "very often" (4). Cronbach's alpha was .87. Evidence of construct validity can be found in Buehler et al. (1998).

The scale to measure interparental conflict was formed by combining items from the covert conflict and overt conflict scales (α = 88).

Youth reported their perceptions of their father's and mother's use of psychological control using eight items for each parent. Some items were selected from the Psychological Control Scale-Youth Self–Report (PCS-YSR; Barber, 1996) and others were adapted from the CRPBI (Schludermann & Schludermann, 1970). Sample items were, "My mother is a person who tries to change how I feel or think about things," and "My father is a person who finishes my sentences when I talk." The response format ranged from "not like her" (1) to "a lot like her" (3). Cronbach's alpha was .60 for mother psychological control and .63 for father psychological control. Evidence of construct validity can be found in Barber (1996).

The scale to measure parental psychological control was formed by combining items from the mother psychological control and father psychological control scales (α = .75).

Youth reports of their own problem behavior (YPB) were measured using the Child Behavior Checklist-Youth Self-Report (CBC-YSR; Achenbach, 1991). This questionnaire consisted of 112 statements that described the youth within the past six months. The response format was "not true" (0), "somewhat or sometimes true" (1), and "very true or often true" (2). Based on Achenbach's (1991) recommendations, 30 were used to measure internalizing problems (α = .92) and 31 were used to measure externalizing problems (α = .90). Examples of internalizing items were, "I feel worthless or inferior" and "I am unhappy, sad, or depressed." Examples of externalizing items were, "I lie or cheat" and "I disobey at school." A total problem behavior score was calculated by combining the internalizing and externalizing scales (α = .94).

These scales have extensive evidence of both reliability and validity and are the most commonly used assessment of children's behavior problems (Achenbach, 1991). However, it is important to note that the internalizing and externalizing scores often are highly correlated, as they were in this sample.

Four background variables were used as controls in the analyses. Youth age was coded "0" for children (youth aged 9 to 12) and "1" for adolescents (youth aged 13 to 15). Youth gender was coded "0" for boys and "1" for girls. Parents' marital status was coded "0" for married families (parents of the target child were not divorced or separated) and "1" for divorced or separated families (mother custody). Family poverty status was coded "0" for less poor youth (who paid full price for their school lunch) and "1" for more poor youth (who received free or reduced school lunch).

Ogden Families

Youth in fifth- and eight-grade classrooms were recruited at this site to participate in a study that focused on family interaction; personality; youth behavior; and peer, school, and neighborhood experiences. A stratified random sampling procedure was used to select classrooms, oversampling Hispanic youth. All of the youth in the selected classrooms took home permission forms. The parental permission rate was 90%, providing evidence of minimal bias because of subject selectivity. The sample of 935 youth was reduced for the present study by restricting the sample to youth who lived with both biological or adoptive parents or with divorced or separated mothers. The restricted sample provided data on youth who lived in similar family structures as those in the Knox County study, thus reducing the chance of finding group differences attributable to living in a step family.

After applying the inclusion criterion regarding residence and adjusting for youth with missing data, the sample of 545 youth consisted of 270 girls

(50%) and 275 boys aged 9 to 15 ($M = 12.21$, $SD = 1.58$). Seventy-five percent (402) were European American, 12% (67) were Mexican American, and the remaining 13% represented youth of African American, Latin American, or Asian American origin. Based on reports of 60% of the youth, the average formal education level obtained by mothers and fathers was between "some college, trade, or vocational school" and "graduated from college with a bachelor's degree." Eighty-four percent of the youth reported married parents. Fifty-two percent of the youth were Mormon, 15% were Catholic, 4% were Protestant, .4% were Jewish, 10% reported "other," and 18% reported "no preference." Youth reports of their family economic situation indicated that 1% believed they were a lot poorer than most families they know, 13% believed they were a little poorer than other families, 68% believed they were about the same as other families, 16% believed they were a little richer than other families, and 2% believed they were a lot richer than other families (see Pearlin, Lieberman, Menaghan, & Mullan, 1981, for information about this measure).

The representativeness of this sample was examined by comparing these average characteristics with data provided from the 1989 and 1990 census on families and individuals living in the city of Ogden, Utah (Slater & Hall, 1996; U.S. Bureau of the Census, 1996). The sample was representative of the city population in terms of parents' educational attainment, marital status, family economic standing, and race (see Buehler et al., 1998, for details).

Youth completed a questionnaire during school. They were given as much time as needed to complete the survey and were treated to a pizza party on completion.

The measures used in the Ogden study were similar to those used in the Knox County study. Although included in the survey instrument, interparental conflict was not a central construct in the Ogden project. As a consequence, the measures of interparental conflict styles were shorter in the Ogden study than in the Knox County study.

Youth reported their perceptions of frequency of their parents' use of a covert conflict style using three of the eight items used in the Knox County study. The response format for this variable was the same as that used in the Knox County sample. Cronbach's alpha was .79. Using the Knox County data, the correlation between the three items that were replicated in the Ogden study and the full six-item Knox County scale was .94 ($p < .001$).

Youth perceptions of frequency of their parents' use of an overt conflict style were assessed by responses to four of the items used in the Knox County study. Youth reported how often their parents engage in the following conflict behaviors: call each other names, threaten each other, yell at each other, and insult each other. The response format was the same as items for a covert conflict style. Cronbach's alpha was .87. The correlation between the four items used in the Ogden scale and the five items used in the Knox County scale was .98 ($p < .001$).

The scale measuring interparental conflict was formed by combining items from the covert conflict style and overt conflict style scales ($\alpha = .87$).

Youth reported their perceptions of their mother's and father's use of psychological control using 16 items, 5 from the revised CRPBI (Schaefer, 1965), and 11 items written to capture specific aspects of psychological control (Barber, 1996). The three-point response scale ranged from "not like her" (1) to "a lot like her" (3). Sample items were "My mother is a person who often interrupts me" and "My father is a person who is less friendly with me, if I do not see things his way." Cronbach's alpha for fathers' psychological control was .84 and mothers' psychological control was .85.

The scale that measured parental psychological control was formed by combining items from the mother psychological control and father psychological control scales ($\alpha = .88$).

YPB was measured with the same instruments used for the Knox County data. Youth reports of their internalizing and externalizing problem behavior were measured using the CBC-YSR (Achenbach, 1991), although the seven items for the somatic complaints syndrome scale were not included in the internalizing problem scale nor total problem behavior scale. Total YPB was assessed using a sum of the internalizing and externalizing items ($\alpha = .95$). The internalizing scale consisted of 22 items ($\alpha = .93$) and the externalizing scale consisted of 29 items ($\alpha = .92$).

Seven background variables were used as controls. Youth age, youth gender, parents' marital status, and family economic situation were coded the same as in the Knox County sample. Religious affiliation was coded "0" for non-Mormon and "1" for Mormon. Two variables represented ethnic heritage. European American was coded "0" for non-European American and "1" for European American. Mexican American was coded "0" for non-Mexican American and "1" for Mexican American.

DETAILING THE LINKS BETWEEN INTERPARENTAL CONFLICT, PARENTAL PSYCHOLOGICAL CONTROL, AND YOUTH PROBLEM BEHAVIOR

Zero-order correlations, means, and standard deviations for all variables used in this study are given in Table 3-1 for Knox County families and Table 3-2 for Ogden families. At the zero-order level, interparental conflict

TABLE 3-1
Correlations, Means, and Standard Deviations: Knox County

Variables	(1)	(2)	(3)	(4)	(5)	(6)	(7)	(8)	(9)	(10)	(11)	(12)	(13)
(1) Youth age	1.00												
(2) Youth gender	-.03	1.00											
(3) Parent's marital status	-.02	-.10	1.00										
(4) Poverty status	-.24	-.003	.22	1.00									
(5) Interparental conflict	-.05	-.01	.14	.26	1.00								
(6) Covert interparental conflict style	-.06	-.02	.09	.20	.86	1.00							
(7) Overt interparental conflict style	-.03	-.002	.15	.25	.90	.55	1.00						
(8) Parental psychological control	.001	.10	.01	.09	.40	.39	.25	1.00					
(9) Mother's psychological control	.03	.02	.07	.12	.37	.38	.28	.90	1.00				
(10) Father's psychological control	-.03	.16	-.07	.04	.27	.32	.17	.88	.58	1.00			
(11) Total YPB	.04	.07	.18	.12	.44	.44	.34	.43	.41	.36	1.00		
(12) Internalizing YPB	.03	-.08	.17	.12	.42	.45	.30	.37	.33	.33	.93	1.00	
(13) Externalizing YPB	.04	.16	.16	.12	.39	.36	.32	.43	.43	.34	.91	.70	1.00
Mean	.46	.44	.13	.13	1.42	1.38	1.47	1.55	1.61	1.48	21.47	10.39	11.12
Standard deviation	.50	.50	.33	.34	.51	.55	.62	.41	.47	.45	17.17	9.82	8.76

Note: Correlations are significant at the probability level of $p < .05$. Youth age: 0 = children, 1 = adolescents. Youth gender: 0 = male, 1 = female. Parent's marital status: 0 = married, 1 = divorced/separated. Family poverty status: 0 = less poor, 1 = more poor. YPB = youth problem behavior.

TABLE 3-2
Correlations, Means, and Standard Deviations: Ogden

Variables	(1)	(2)	(3)	(4)	(5)	(6)	(7)	(8)	(9)	(10)	(11)	(12)	(13)	(14)	(15)	(16)
(1) Youth age	1.00															
(2) Youth gender	.12	1.00														
(3) Parent's marital status	.05	.08	1.00													
(4) Religious affiliation	.06	-.02	-.04	1.00												
(5) Economic hardship	.02	-.01	.11	.02	1.00											
(6) European American	.15	-.04	-.01	.29	.01	1.00										
(7) Mexican American	-.03	.04	-.04	-.30	.04	-.63	1.00									
(8) Interparental conflict	.04	-.02	.06	-.15	.08	-.04	.09	1.00								
(9) Covert interparental conflict style	.04	-.06	.09	-.14	.10	-.04	.07	.88	1.00							
(10) Overt interparental conflict style	.04	.03	.04	-.13	.06	-.03	.09	.89	.56	1.00						
(11) Parental psychological control	-.02	-.13	-.03	-.11	.05	-.13	.12	.39	.42	.30	1.00					
(12) Mother's psychological control	.00	-.11	-.03	-.09	.05	-.11	.11	.36	.39	.26	.94	1.00				
(13) Father's psychological control	-.04	-.14	-.01	-.10	.07	-.11	.12	.41	.42	.31	.93	.74	1.00			
(14) Total YPB	.07	-.04	.03	-.10	.11	-.05	.08	.45	.43	.38	.39	.41	.41	1.00		
(15) Internalizing YPB	.03	.02	.02	-.07	.11	-.05	.08	.41	.39	.35	.36	.37	.37	.92	1.00	
(16) Externalizing YPB	.09	-.08	.03	.11	.09	-.05	.07	.43	.41	.36	.37	.39	.40	.95	.75	1.00
Mean	.49	.49	.21	.54	.14	.75	.12	1.53	1.53	1.53	1.45	1.45	1.45	19.19	8.43	10.78
Standard deviation	.50	.50	.41	.50	.35	.44	.32	.58	.68	.66	.40	.42	.42	16.48	7.99	9.61

Note: Correlations are significant at the probability level of $p < .05$. Youth age: 0 = children, 1 = adolescents. Youth gender: 0 = male, 1 = female. Parent's marital status: 0 = married, 1 = divorced/separated. Religious affiliation: 0 = non-Mormon, 1 = Mormon. Economic hardship: 0 = less poor, 1 = more poor. European American: 0 = other, 1 = European American. Mexican American: 0 = other, 1 = Mexican American. YPB = youth problem behavior.

was associated with all measures of YPB, with correlations ranging from .39 to .44 for Knox County and .41 to .45 for Ogden. Interparental conflict also was associated with parental psychological control (Knox County: $r = .40$; Ogden: $r = .39$). Parental psychological control was associated with all measures of YPB, with correlations ranging from .37 to .43 for Knox County and .39 to .43 for Ogden.

Redundant Effects

Evidence regarding redundant versus nonredundant effects was garnered from the correlations between interparental conflict and psychological control and from the factor analysis. These data suggested that interparental conflict (composite, covert, and overt) and parental psychological control were not measuring the same family phenomenon. Although the correlations between interparental conflict and psychological control for both samples (Knox County, $r = .40$; Ogden, $r = .39$) demonstrated that the two constructs were interrelated, the correlations were moderate enough to evidence discriminant validity (i.e., about 16% shared variance). Although psychological control and covert conflict share underlying characteristics, the correlations were higher between covert and overt conflict (Knox County: $r = .55$; Ogden: $r = .56$) than between covert conflict and psychological control (Knox County: $r = .39$; Ogden: $r = .42$) in both samples, providing additional evidence of discriminant validity and nonredundant conceptualization.

The results from factor analysis using maximum-likelihood extraction with oblimum (oblique) rotation also indicated that interparental conflict and parental psychological control are distinct concepts. Questionnaire items used to measure covert conflict, overt conflict, and psychological control were factor-analyzed together. Most of the items loaded on three factors that clearly represent covert conflict, overt conflict, and parental psychological control, providing additional evidence of adequate factorial validity. In the Knox County sample, four psychological control and two covert conflict items were dropped because they loaded on two factors. All of the retained items had primary loadings of at least .44. The difference between the primary and secondary factor loadings was at least .24, with the exception of one item for mother's psychological control, which was .12. This item was retained to keep the father's and mother's psychological control scales identical. In the Ogden sample, five psychological control items were dropped because they loaded on two factors. All of the retained items had primary loadings of at least .45 and the difference between the primary and secondary factor loadings was at least .15. These data suggest that interparental conflict and psychological control are measuring distinct family behaviors.

Independent–Additive Effects

The data support the independent–additive effects model. Ordinary least-squares regression was used to test for independent–additive effects. Interparental conflict and parental psychological control each uniquely explained variance in YPB (total, internalizing, and externalizing), and more variance was explained by including both interparental conflict and psychological control than if either one was considered on its own (see Table 3-3). This was true in both samples of youth.

We tested the independent–additive model by first using total YPB as the dependent variable. We entered the control variables in Block 1, interparental conflict in Block 2, and psychological control in Block 3. We conducted moderating analyses by examining the interaction between each background and predictor variable. These interaction terms were created by multiplying a centered form of the predictor variable by the background dummy variable as prescribed by Aiken and West (1991). We analyzed each background variable separately, and this interaction term was entered in Block 4 in each analysis. After testing the model using total YPB, we conducted follow-up analyses using internalizing and externalizing problem behavior subscales as the dependent variables (in separate analyses). Next we conducted follow-up analyses using separate covert and overt conflict scales with parental psychological control.

Total YPB was associated with interparental conflict (Knox County: $\beta = .31$, $p < .001$; Ogden: $\beta = .32$, $p < .001$) and parental psychological control (Knox County: $\beta = .31$, $p < .001$; Ogden: $\beta = .31$, $p < .001$) as evidenced by the partialized regression coefficients in Block 3 of Table 3-3. Interparental conflict accounted for variance in total YPB (Knox County: R^2 change = .16, $p < .001$; F change = 70.42, $p < .001$; Ogden: R^2 change = .19, F change = 126.87, $p < .001$). Parental psychological control explained additional variance in YPB (Knox County: R^2 change = .08, $p < .001$; F change = 39.03, $p < .001$; Ogden: R^2 change = .08, $p < .001$; F change = 57.49, $p < .001$). The association between interparental conflict and YPB was stronger for girls and less poor families in the Knox County sample and for children in the Ogden sample. The association between parental psychological control and YPB was similar for youth of all background characteristics in both samples, with the exception of a stronger effect for children in the Ogden sample.

This pattern of findings that supported independent and cumulative effects of interparental conflict and parental psychological control replicated when using internalizing YPB and externalizing YPB as dependent variables (see Tables 3-4 and 3-5). Similar findings replicated when separately examining maternal and paternal psychological control.

TABLE 3-3
Hierarchical Regression Analyses of Interparental Conflict (Composite Scale), Parental Psychological Control, and Total Youth Problem Behavior

	Knox County				Ogden			
Independent Variables	Background Variables	Interparental Conflict	Psychological Control	Interaction: IPC × PPC	Background Variables	Interparental Conflict	Psychological Control	Interaction: IPC × PPC
	Block 1	Block 2	Block 3	Block 4	Block 1	Block 2	Block 3	Block 4
Age	.07	.07	.06	.05	.09*	.06	.06	.06
Gender	.08	.09	.06	.06	-.04	-.04	-.001	-.001
Parent's marital status	.17**	.13*	.14	.15***	.03	.01	.02	.03
Religious affiliation					-.08	-.01	-.001	-.001
Economic hardship	.10	.00	-.01	-.01	.11*	.07	.06	.06
European American					-.01	-.04	-.02	-.02
Mexican American					.06	.02	.01	.01
Interparental conflict		.43***	.31***	.29***		.44***	.32***	.30***
Psychological control			.31**	.31***			.31***	.30***
Interaction: IPC × PPC				.05				.04
Total R^2	.05**	.22***	.30***	.30	.04*	.22***	.30***	.30
Adjusted R^2	.04	.21	.29	.29	.02	.21	.28	.28
F change	3.72**	70.42***	39.03***	.80	2.16*	126.87***	57.49***	.92
R^2 change	.05**	.16***	.08***	.002	.04*	.19***	.08***	.001

Note: Standardized regression coefficients are reported. Youth age: 0 = children, 1 = adolescents. Youth gender: 0 = male, 1 = female. Parent's marital status: 0 = married, 1 = divorced/separated. Religious affiliation: 0 = non-Mormon, 1 = Mormon. Economic hardship: 0 = less poor, 1 = more poor. European American: 0 = other, 1 = European American. Mexican American: 0 = other, 1 = Mexican American. IPC = interparental conflict, PPC = parental psychological control.
*$p < .05$ **$p < .01$ ***$p < .001$

TABLE 3-4

Hierarchical Regression Analyses of Interparental Conflict (Composite Scale), Parental Psychological Control, and Youth Internalizing Problem Behavior

Independent Variables	Knox County				Ogden			
	Background Variables — Block 1	Interparental Conflict — Block 2	Psychological Control — Block 3	Interaction: IPC × PPC — Block 4	Background Variables — Block 1	Interparental Conflict — Block 2	Psychological Control — Block 3	Interaction: IPC × PPC — Block 4
Age	.05	.05	.04	.04	.04	.01	.01	.01
Gender	-.01	-.01	-.03	-.03	.02	.03	.06	.06
Parent's marital status	.15**	.11*	.12*	.13*	.01	-.01	.004	.01
Religious affiliation					-.05	.02	.03	.03
Economic hardship	.10	-.001	-.01	-.01	.12**	.08*	.07	.07
European American					-.01	-.03	-.01	-.01
Mexican American					.06	.03	.01	.02
Interparental conflict		.41***	.32***	.29***		.41***	.30***	.28***
Psychological control			.25**	.25***			.28***	.28***
Interaction: IPC × PPC				.06				.05
Total R^2	.04	.19***	.25***	.25	.03	.19***	.25***	.25
Adjusted R^2	.02	.18	.23	.23	.01	.17	.23	.23
F change	2.61	63.66***	24.14***	1.24	1.55	104.91***	44.16***	1.15
R^2 change	.04	.16***	.06***	.003	.03	.16***	.06***	.002

Note: Standardized regression coefficients are reported. Youth age: 0 = children, 1 = adolescents. Youth gender: 0 = male, 1 = female. Parent's marital status: 0 = married, 1 = divorced/separated. Religious affiliation: 0 = non-Mormon, 1 = Mormon. Economic hardship: 0 = less poor, 1 = more poor. European American: 0 = other, 1 = European American. Mexican American: 0 = other, 1 = Mexican American. IPC = interparental conflict, PPC = parental psychological control.
*$p < .05$ **$p < .01$ ***$p < .001$

CONFLICT, PROBLEM BEHAVIOR, AND PSYCHOLOGICAL CONTROL   73

TABLE 3-5

Hierarchical Regression Analyses of Interparental Conflict (Composite Scale), Parental Psychological Control, and Youth Externalizing Problem Behavior

Independent Variables	Knox County				Ogden			
	Background Variables Block 1	Interparental Conflict Block 2	Psychological Control Block 3	Interaction: IPC × PPC Block 4	Background Variables Block 1	Interparental Conflict Block 2	Psychological Control Block 3	Interaction: IPC × PPC Block 4
Age	.08	.07	.06	.06	-.12**	.10*	.09*	.10*
Gender	.18***	.18***	.15**	.15**	-.09	-.08*	-.05	-.05
Parent's marital status	.16***	.13*	.14***	.14***	.04	.02	.03	.04
Religious affiliation					-.10*	-.03	-.02	-.02
Economic hardship	.10	.01	.01	.01	.09	.06	.04	.04
European American					-.01	-.04	-.02	-.02
Mexican American					.05	.01	-.002	.002
Interparental conflict		.37***	.25***	.24***		.41***	.30***	.28***
Psychological control			.32***	.32***			.29***	.29***
Interaction: IPC × PPC				.03				.03
Total R^2	.07**	.20***	.29***	.29	.04**	.21***	.28***	.28
Adjusted R^2	.06	.18	.27	.27	.03	.19	.26	.26
F change	5.32***	50.94***	40.90***	.28	2.73**	109.65***	51.13***	.51
R^2 change	.07***	.12***	.09***	.001	.04**	.16**	.07***	.001

Note: Standardized regression coefficients are reported. Youth age: 0 = children, 1 = adolescents. Youth gender: 0 = male, 1 = female. Parent's marital status: 0 = married, 1 = divorced/separated. Religious affiliation: 0 = non-Mormon, 1 = Mormon. Economic hardship: 0 = less poor, 1 = more poor. European American: 0 = other, 1 = European American. Mexican American: 0 = other, 1 = Mexican American. IPC = interparental conflict; PPC = parental psychological control.
*p < .05 **p < .01 ***p < .001

Total YPB was associated with covert conflict (Knox County: $\beta = .37$, $p < .001$; Ogden: $\beta = .32$, $p < .001$), overt conflict (Knox County: $\beta = .12$, $p < .05$; Ogden: $\beta = .21$, $p < .001$), and parental psychological control (Knox County: $\beta = .30$, $p < .001$; Ogden: $\beta = .30$, $p < .001$) as evidenced by regression coefficients in Block 2 of Table 3-6. However, in the Knox County sample, when parental psychological control was entered in the equation, overt conflict became insignificant. The association between covert conflict and YPB was stronger for adolescents, girls, and less poor families in the Knox County sample and stronger for children in the Ogden sample. The association between overt conflict and YPB was not moderated by any background characteristic. As mentioned previously, the association between parental psychological control and YPB was similar for youth of all background characteristics in both samples, with the exception of a stronger effect for children in the Ogden sample.

These findings replicated when separately analyzing internalizing and externalizing YPB, with additional evidence that suggested that the association between covert conflict and internalizing YPB was particularly robust (see Tables 3-7 and 3-8). The pattern of findings also replicated when separately examining the effects of maternal and paternal psychological control.

In summary, with the exception of overt conflict in the Knox County sample, all interparental conflict variables and parental psychological control each uniquely explained variance in YPB (total, internalizing, and externalizing) and more variance was explained by including both interparental conflict and psychological control than if either one was considered on its own. Therefore, the evidence suggests that an independent–additive model fits the data.

Indirect Effects

In addition to the direct association between interparental conflict and YPB, we found that parental psychological control was associated both with interparental conflict and YPB, forming a pathway from interparental conflict to parental psychological control to YPB. In both samples of families, parental psychological control transmitted part of the effect of conflict to YPB.

The first half of the pathway of interest, from interparental conflict to psychological control, was tested first. We entered the background–control variables in Block 1 and interparental conflict in Block 2. We conducted follow-up moderating analyses by entering an interaction term between interparental conflict and a background variable (e.g., youth gender) in Block 3. After testing the model using interparental conflict and parental psychological control, we conducted follow-up analyses using separate covert and overt conflict scales.

TABLE 3-6
Hierarchical Regression Analyses of Covert and Overt Interparental Conflict, Parental Psychological Control, and Total Youth Problem Behavior

	Knox County				Ogden			
Independent Variables	Background Variables Block 1	Covert/Overt Conflict Block 2	Psychological Control Block 3	Interaction Terms Block 4	Background Variables Block 1	Covert/Overt Conflict Block 2	Psychological Control Block 3	Interaction Terms Block 4
Age	.07	.07	.06	.06	.08	.05	.05	.04
Gender	.08	.09	.06	.07	-.03	-.02	.01	.02
Parent's marital status	.17**	.14**	.15*	.14**	-.05	.02	.03	.03
Religious affiliation					-.05	.03	.03	.03
Economic hardship	.10	.01	.002	.02	.13**	.09*	.07	.06
European American					.04	.01	.02	.02
Mexican American					.08	.04	.02	.03
Conflict styles: Covert		.37***	.26***	.23***		.32***	.20***	.23***
Overt		.12*	.10	.10		.21***	.17***	.13*
Psychological control			.30***	.30***			.30***	.30***
Interactions: CC × PPC				.12				-.07
OC × PPC				-.08				.11*
Total R^2	.05**	.24***	.31***	.32	.04*	.24***	.31***	.32
Adjusted R^2	.04	.22	.29	.30	.02	.22	.29	.30
F change	3.72**	39.83***	34.59***	1.44	1.98*	65.62***	49.63***	2.29
R^2 change	.05**	.19***	.07***	.01	.04*	.21***	.07***	.01

Note: Standardized regression coefficients are reported. Youth age: 0 = children, 1 = adolescents. Youth gender: 0 = male, 1 = female. Parent's marital status: 0 = married, 1 = divorced/separated. Religious affiliation: 0 = non-Mormon, 1 = Mormon. Economic hardship: 0 = less poor, 1 = more poor. European American: 0 = other, 1 = European American. Mexican American: 0 = other, 1 = Mexican American. CC = covert conflict style, OC = overt conflict style, PPC = parental psychological control.
*$p < .05$ **$p < .01$ ***$p < .001$

TABLE 3-7
Hierarchical Regression Analyses of Covert and Overt Interparental Conflict, Parental Psychological Control, and Youth Internalizing Problem Behavior

Independent Variables	Knox County				Ogden			
	Background Variables	Covert/Overt Conflict	Psychological Control	Interaction Terms	Background Variables	Covert/Overt Conflict	Psychological Control	Interaction Terms
	Block 1	Block 2	Block 3	Block 4	Block 1	Block 2	Block 3	Block 4
Age	.05	.06	.05	.05	.03	-.001	.002	-.01
Gender	-.01	-.01	-.03	-.02	.03	.05	.08	.08*
Parent's marital status	.15**	.12*	.12*	.11*	.03	.002	.01	.01
Religious affiliation					-.02	.05	.05	.05
Economic hardship	.10	.01	.003	.03	.15**	.11**	.09*	.09*
European American					.06	.03	.04	.04
Mexican American					.09	.06	-.04	.04
Conflict styles: Covert		.41***	.32***	.28***		.30***	.20***	.22***
Overt		.07	.06	.05		.19***	.16***	.11*
Psychological control			.23***	.23***			.27***	.26***
Interactions: CC × PPC				.18*				-.06
OC × PPC				-.13				.12*
Total R²	.04*	.22***	.27***	.28*	.03*	.21***	.27***	.27
Adjusted R²	.02	.21	.25	.26	.02	.19	.25	.25
F change	2.61*	39.54***	19.63***	3.34*	1.87*	54.34***	35.77***	2.40
R² change	.04*	.19***	.04***	.02*	.03*	.18***	.05***	.01

Note: Standardized regression coefficients are reported. Youth age: 0 = children, 1 = adolescents. Youth gender: 0 = male, 1 = female. Parent's marital status: 0 = married, 1 = divorced/separated. Religious affiliation: 0 = non-Mormon, 1 = Mormon. Economic hardship: 0 = less poor, 1 = more poor. European American: 0 = other, 1 = European American. Mexican American: 0 = other, 1 = Mexican American. CC = covert conflict, OC = overt conflict, PPC = parental psychological control.
*p < .05   **p < .01   ***p < .001

TABLE 3-8
Hierarchical Regression Analyses of Covert and Overt Interparental Conflict, Parental Psychological Control, and Youth Externalizing Problem Behavior

	Knox County				Ogden			
Independent Variables	Background Variables Block 1	Covert/Overt Conflict Block 2	Psychological Control Block 3	Interaction Terms Block 4	Background Variables Block 1	Covert/Overt Conflict Block 2	Psychological Control Block 3	Interaction Terms Block 4
Age	.08	.08	.06	.06	.11*	.08	.08	.07
Gender	.18***	.18***	.15**	.15**	-.09	-.07	-.04	-.04
Parent's marital status	.16**	.13**	.14**	.14**	.06	.03	.04	.04
Religious affiliation					-.07	.01	.004	.01
Economic hardship	.10	.02	.01	.02	.10*	.06	.04	.04
European American					.02	-.003	.001	.002
Mexican American					.06	.03	.01	.01
Conflict styles: Covert		.27***	.15*	.14*		.30***	.19***	.21***
Overt		.15*	.14*	.13*		.20***	.17***	.13*
Psychological control			.32***	.32***			.30***	.30***
Interactions: CC × PPC				.03				.06
OC × PPC				-.002				.09
Total R^2	.07***	.20***	.29***	.29	.04*	.22***	.29***	.29
Adjusted R^2	.06	.19	.27	.27	.02	.20	.27	.27
F change	5.32***	26.46***	38.98***	.15	2.13*	56.24***	45.99***	1.56
R^2 change	.07***	.13***	.09***	.001	.04*	.18***	.07***	.01

Note: Standardized regression coefficients are reported. Youth age: 0 = children, 1 = adolescents. Youth gender: 0 = male, 1 = female. Parent's marital status: 0 = married, 1 = divorced/separated. Religious affiliation: 0 = non-Mormon, 1 = Mormon. Economic hardship: 0 = less poor, 1 = more poor. European American: 0 = other, 1 = European American. Mexican American: 0 = other, 1 = Mexican American. CC = covert conflict, OC = overt conflict, PPC = parental psychological control.
*p < .05 **p < .01 ***p < .001

The second half of the pathway, the leg from psychological control to YPB, was tested using hierarchical regression analyses and the results were presented in the previous section on independent–additive effects.

The final step involved integrating results from the first half of the pathway (psychological control regressed on interparental conflict) with the second half of the pathway (problem behavior regressed on the interparental conflict and parental psychological control variables). This was done by mathematically testing the significance of the indirect pathway using Sobel's test (Sobel, 1982). Sobel's test provides a t value that represents the entire pathway, which can be evaluated for statistical significance.

In both samples, the first half of the pathway was significant. Interparental conflict was associated with increased levels of parental psychological control (Knox County: $\beta = .36$, $p < .001$; F change = 45.64, $p < .001$; Ogden: $\beta = .38$, $p < .001$; F change = .38, $p < .001$), as evident by the second block on the left side of Table 3-9. Each point increase in the interparental conflict measure resulted in an increase (Knox County: $b = .29$; Ogden County: $b = .26$) in parental psychological control. This association was stronger for adolescents and married families in the Knox County sample, but was not moderated by any background characteristic in the Ogden sample. As previously detailed, the second half of the pathway was significant in both samples (see Table 3-3). Each point increase in the three-point scale of parental psychological control resulted in an increase of 12.94 YPB for the Knox County sample and 12.66 for the Ogden sample. The effect was consistent for youth with varying background characteristics, except the second half of the pathway was stronger for children in the Ogden sample. Follow-up analyses using Sobel's equation indicated that the pathway from interparental conflict to YPB through parental psychological control was significant (Knox County: $t = 3.63$, $p < .001$; Ogden: $t = 3.01$, $p < .001$). This pathway replicated when internalizing and externalizing YPB were analyzed as separate measures. This pattern of intervening effects of parental psychological control also replicated when separately analyzing maternal and paternal psychological control.

In summary, the data provide evidence that the association between interparental conflict and YPB is not only direct but also indirect through parental psychological control. This finding is consistent for both samples using the total YPB scale as well as the internalizing and externalizing subscales. (Refer to Table 3-9 for the first half of the pathway and Tables 3-3 through 3-5 for the second half of the pathway).

In both samples, covert conflict was associated with increased levels of parental psychological control (Knox County: $\beta = .37$, $p < .001$; Ogden County: $\beta = .34$, $p < .001$), as evident by regression coefficients in Block 2 on the right side of Table 3-9. Each point increase in the covert conflict measure resulted in an increase of .28 (Knox County) and .20 (Ogden) for

TABLE 3-9
Hierarchical Regression Analyses of Interparental Conflict and Parental Psychological Control

| | Composite Scale | | | | Separate Scales | | | |
| | Knox County | | Ogden | | Knox County | | Ogden | |
Independent Variables	Background Variables Block 1	Interparental Conflict Block 2	Background Variables Block 1	Interparental Conflict Block 2	Background Variables Block 1	Interparental Conflict Block 2	Background Variables Block 1	Interparental Conflict Block 2
Age	.03	.03	.02	−.001	.03	.04	.02	−.01
Gender	.09	.10	−.12**	−.12**	.09	.10*	−.13**	−.11**
Parent's marital status	.004	−.03	−.02	−.04	−.002	−.03	.01	−.02
Religious affiliation			−.08	−.03			−.07	−.004
Economic hardship	.10	.02	.06	.03	.10	.02	.10*	.06
European American			−.05	−.08			−.01	−.04
Mexican American			.07	.03			.09	.06
Interparental conflict		.36***		.38***				
Covert conflict						.37***		.34***
Overt conflict						.05		.12*
Total R^2	.02***	.14***	.04***	.18***	.02	.17***	.05*	.21***
Adjusted R^2	.01	.13	.03	.16	.01	.16	.03	.19
F change	1.56***	45.64***	2.68**	91.44***	1.55	29.79***	2.67*	51.92***
R^2 change	.02***	.12***	.04***	.14***	.02	.15***	.05*	.17***

Note: Standardized regression coefficients are reported. Youth age: 0 = children, 1 = adolescents. Youth gender: 0 = male, 1 = female. Parent's marital status: 0 = married, 1 = divorced/separated. Religious affiliation: 0 = non-Mormon, 1 = Mormon. Economic hardship: 0 = less poor, 1 = more poor. European American: 0 = other, 1 = European American. Mexican American: 0 = other, 1 = Mexican American.
$*p < .05$ $**p < .01$ $***p < .001$

parental psychological control. The association was similar for all background variables in both samples, except the path was stronger for adolescents and for less poor families in the Knox County sample. Parental psychological control also was associated with increased total YPB (see Table 3-6). Follow-up analyses using Sobel's equation indicated that the pathway from covert conflict to YPB through parental psychological control was significant (Knox County: $t = 3.67$, $p < .001$; Ogden: $t = 3.34$, $p < .001$). This pathway replicated when internalizing and externalizing YPB were analyzed as separate measures, as evident by Block 3 of Tables 3-7 and 3-8.

In summary, the data provide evidence that the association between covert conflict and YPB is not only direct but also indirect through parental psychological control. This finding is consistent for both samples using the total problem behavior scale as well as the internalizing and externalizing subscales. Follow-up analyses indicated that both maternal and paternal psychological control were significant intervening variables.

In the Knox County sample overt conflict was not associated with parental psychological control (first leg of pathway; $\beta = .05$, $p = .06$). Thus, no indirect association existed between overt conflict and YPB through parental psychological control. However, in the Ogden sample overt conflict was weakly associated with parental psychological control ($\beta = .12$, $p < .05$), as shown in Block 2 on the right side of Table 3-9. This association was similar for boys and girls, but was stronger for adolescents, youth from married families, and youth from more poor families. Follow-up analyses using Sobel's equation indicated that the pathway from overt conflict to YPB through parental psychological control was significant in the Ogden sample ($t = 2.20$, $p < .01$.) This pathway replicated when we analyzed internalizing and externalizing YPB as separate measures, as shown in Block 3 of Tables 3-7 and 3-8. Also in the Ogden sample, follow-up analyses with the separate indicators of maternal and paternal psychological control indicated that paternal psychological control was a significant intervening variable (albeit weak), whereas maternal psychological control was not a significant intervening variable.

In summary, evidence supporting the indirect association between overt conflict and YPB through parental psychological control is equivocal because the association between overt conflict and YPB is nonexistent in the Knox County sample and weak in the Ogden County sample. However, in both samples the indirect association between covert conflict and YPB through parental psychological control is robust, which indicates that parental psychological control transmits part of the effect of covert conflict on YPB.

Mediating Effects

The data do not support the mediating effects model. According to Baron and Kenny (1986), four conditions must be met if mediation exists.

First, a direct relationship must exist between the predictor variable, interparental conflict, and the dependent variable, YPB. Second, the predictor variable, interparental conflict, should be associated with the hypothesized mediating variable, parental psychological control, to provide evidence of the significance of the first half of the pathway. Third, the hypothesized mediating variable, parental psychological control, should be associated with YPB, even after controlling for the variance accounted for by the predictor variable, interparental conflict. Fourth, the previously significant direct association between the predictor variable, interparental conflict, and the dependent variable, YPB, should disappear (full mediation) or diminish statistically (partial mediation) when the hypothesized mediator, parental psychological control, is entered into the analysis.

The first condition of the mediating test was met: Interparental conflict was related to YPB in both samples (Knox County: $\beta = .43$, $p < .001$; Ogden: $\beta = .44$, $p < .001$), as shown in Table 3-3. The second condition of the mediating test was met in both samples: Interparental conflict was associated with parental psychological control (Knox County: $\beta = .39$, $p < .001$; Ogden: $\beta = .38$, $p < .001$), as shown in Table 3-9. The third condition of the mediational test was met: Parental psychological control was associated with YPB (Knox County: $\beta = .31$, $p < .001$; Ogden: $\beta = .31$, $p < .001$), as shown in Table 3-3. However, the fourth condition of the mediational test was not met. The significant direct association between the predictor variable, interparental conflict, and the dependent variable, YPB, remained significant when the hypothesized mediator, psychological control was entered into the analysis (Knox County: F change $= 30.03$, $p < .001$; Ogden: $\beta = 57.49$, $p < .001$), as shown in Table 3-3. Although the effect of interparental conflict on YPB was reduced (Knox County: $\beta = .43$, $p < .001$ to $\beta = .31$, $p < .001$; Ogden: $\beta = .44$, $p < .001$ to $\beta = .32$, $p < .001$) when we entered parental psychological control into the equation, there is no evidence that suggests this reduction is statistically significant. A similar pattern was evident when we did follow-up analyses on the association between interparental conflict and the internalizing and externalizing problem behavior subscales, as shown in Tables 3-4 and 3-5. This pattern also replicated when covert conflict and overt conflict were analyzed simultaneously and when maternal and paternal psychological control were analyzed separately.

Therefore, although the data suggest an indirect pathway from interparental conflict to YPB through parental psychological control, the direct pathway remained significant. The impact of marital conflict on youth is not only transmitted through parental psychological control, but also the direct effects do not diminish in strength. Therefore we conclude that parental psychological control does not mediate the association between interparental conflict and YPB.

Moderating Effects

The data do not support the mediating effects model. A series of hierarchical multiple regression equations were computed to test for moderating effects of parental psychological control, as suggested by Baron and Kenny (1986). For example, to examine the moderating role of parental psychological control in the association between interparental conflict and YPB, we entered variables in the following order. Block 1 contained the background variables. We entered interparental conflict in Block 2, parental psychological control in Block 3, and the interaction term between interparental conflict and parental psychological control in Block 4.

Parental psychological control did not moderate the association between interparental conflict and YPB (total, internalizing, or externalizing) as indicated by a statistically nonsignificant standardized regression coefficient of the interaction term and a statistically nonsignificant F change following the last block in which the interactive effect was tested (see Block 4 of Tables 3-3 through 3-5). Follow-up analyses of covert and overt conflict styles and the three measures of YPB replicated these results, with one exception (see Block 4 of Tables 3-6 through 3-8). There was some evidence that parental psychological control moderated the relationship between covert conflict and internalizing YPB (β = .18, p < .05; F change = 3.34, p < .05). However, when we examined the interaction between covert conflict and parental psychological control in a regression equation that excluded the interaction term between overt conflict and psychological control, the interaction between covert conflict and psychological control was no longer significant (β = .10, p = .09; F change = 3.07, p = .09).

In summary, the association between interparental conflict and YPB does not seem to depend on the level of parental psychological control used with the child.

CONTEXTUALIZING THE MODELS: DO BACKGROUND CHARACTERISTICS MAKE A DIFFERENCE?

Slope comparisons of the relationships between interparental conflict, parental psychological control, and YPB across the background variables reveal that group differences are limited and are, therefore, not easy to characterize. It is important to note that slope comparisons across groups examine differences in relationships rather than the more commonly reported mean differences between groups. As such, the results of comparisons of strength of pathways across youth age, youth gender, parental marital status, and family economic situation show that patterns of differences do not exist to any great extent. Background characteristics do not make a difference in the direct and indirect (through parental psychological control) associations of interparental conflict with YPB.

EXPLAINING THE ROLE OF PARENTAL PSYCHOLOGICAL CONTROL

The purpose of this study was to examine the role of parental psychological control in explaining the established relationship between interparental conflict and YPB. Parents' overtly hostile ways of managing their disagreements have been examined by researchers, but few studies have explored the more indirect processes among the marital and parent–child dyads, and how these connections shape children's development. We began our examination of the role parental psychological control plays in the connection between interparental conflict and YPB using a composite interparental conflict measure of covert and overt conflict. Next, we detailed the role of parental psychological control in relationship to covert conflict and overt conflict as distinct measures of interparental conflict. Thus, in addition to the popularly studied overt conflict, we elaborated two of the more indirect family processes—covert conflict and parents' use of psychological control with their child—and examined their connections to YPB. We tested five ways through which overt and covert conflict and parental psychological control could interrelate to explain YPB: redundant effects, independent–additive effects, indirect effects, mediating effects, and moderating effects.

The results of this study clearly support two specific roles played by parental psychological control in the context of interparental conflict. First, parental psychological control and interparental conflict have independent and cumulative effects on YPB. Thus, when parents use psychological control with their children and fight with each other in hostile ways, psychological control adds to the effects children experience from the marital conflict. This finding was consistent across youth with varying background characteristics, with few exceptions. Second, psychological control intervenes between interparental conflict and YPB. Therefore, parental psychological control transmits part of the effect of the marital conflict on YPB. This finding, in general, held for youth with varying background characteristics.

Independent–Additive Effects

When parents fight in hostile ways with each other and use psychological control with their children, these behaviors make independent and cumulative contributions to the atmosphere experienced by children. Although interparental conflict and parental psychological control are interdependent, each contributes uniquely to the explanation of YPB. The risk children experience when parents use psychological control with their children adds to the risk children face when exposed to interparental conflict. For example, youth might be exposed to shouting and name calling (overt conflict), might feel obliged to participate in a parent–child emotional alliance against the other parent (covert conflict), and might feel the stifling intrusion of parents' use of psychological control.

Youth confronted with a pile-up of distress from both the marital and parent–child relationship might be affected in at least two ways. First, in the short term, youth are exposed to an atmosphere that might be permeated with emotional tension and anxiety. Second, as suggested by social learning theory, youth might learn through parental example that relationships are handled by insulting, yelling, name calling, threatening, recruiting a third party to ease conflictual tensions, or intruding on the psychological space of another. Repeated exposure to psychological intrusion, anxiety, or lessons in hostile patterns of conflict management might prevent the development of important intrapersonal and interpersonal skills (Barber, 1996; Cummings & Davies, 1994).

It is important to note that the linkage between covert conflict and psychological control is more robust than that between overt conflict and psychological control. Because psychological control and covert conflict are stifling and intrusive, these family processes impinge on youth by consuming energy that would be better spent on attention to tasks needed for healthy development. The indirect behaviors of covert conflict and psychological control might result in confusing signals from parents. Youth, particularly children who have not ventured toward the increasing independence characteristic of adolescents, might experience internal disequilibrium and insecurity. Such a response might lead to frustration and poor emotional and behavioral regulation in the face of indirect messages from parents. Thus, indirectness from parents in either the marital relationship or parental relationship appears to be risk factors for developing internalizing as well as externalizing YPB. Indeed, symptoms of adolescent depression and anxiety might be masked with aggression and delinquent behavior (Kaplan & Sadock, 1996).

As a consequence, youth might act out aggressively as a means to release tension from the stifling atmosphere created by interparental conflict and parental use of intrusiveness and guilt induction. Furthermore, youth might compensate for feeling emotionally controlled by behaving aggressively. Aggressive behavior, then, provides a needed outlet for expressing anger and distress that arises from emotional constraint and control imposed by parents. When youth feel drawn into interparental conflict, whether covert or overt, and if the parent uses psychological control, behaving aggressively might be one way youth vent their anxiety, depression, or feelings of entrapment.

Finding that psychological control and interparental conflict have independent and cumulative effects on children and adolescents suggests that changes made in either the marital or parental relationship would benefit the child. Thus, if interventions could be made in only one dyad, either the marital relationship or the parent–child relationship, children would be better off than if no interventions were made. This is an important point for practitioners who are uncertain about the most effective point of entry to help conflictual families change entrenched interactional patterns. Because change in either dyad would likely benefit the child, the practitioner would be wisest to intervene in the area where the family demonstrates the least resistance and greatest chance for success.

Indirect Effects

Psychological control plays an intervening role in the association between interparental conflict and YPB by transmitting part of the effect of the marital conflict on YPB. The finding of indirect effects addresses one of the ways marital conflict affects children by suggesting that when parents fight in hostile ways, their parenting becomes disrupted. Indeed, the analyses reveal that variability in psychological control used by parents is not random but is linked to interparental conflict, particularly covert conflict. Higher levels of covert conflict in the marital relationship heightened the likelihood that parents would use psychological control with their children. This might be because both parental psychological control and covert conflict are anxiety-driven. They share defining characteristics, particularly the qualities of intrusiveness, indirectness, and manipulation. Thus, a parent who tends to be indirect in relationships might be indirect with his or her child as well as his or her spouse.

Psychodynamic and family systems theories help explain the interplay between interparental conflict, especially covert conflict, and psychological control. Psychodynamic theory suggests that parents embroiled in unresolved conflict might displace their negative emotions of anxiety, unhappiness, and dissatisfaction onto the youth (Haley, 1976). Family systems theorists and clinicians label this behavior triangulation and hold that triangles are basic to understanding the functioning of any family system (Bowen, 1971; Minuchin, 1974). The concept of triangles "describes the way any three people relate to each other and involve others in emotional issues between them" (Bowen, 1989, p. 306). In the anxiety-filled environment of conflict, a third person is triangulated, either temporarily or permanently, to ease the anxious feelings of the conflicting partners. By default, that third person is exposed to an anxiety-provoking and disturbing atmosphere. For example, a child might become the scapegoat or focus of attention, thereby transferring the tension from the marital dyad to the parent–child dyad. Unresolved tension in the marital relationship might spill over to the parent–child relationship through parents' use of psychological control as a way of securing and maintaining a strong emotional alliance and level of support from the child. As a consequence, the triangulated youth might feel pressured or obliged to listen to or agree with one parents' complaints against the other. The resulting enmeshment and cross-generational coalition would exemplify parents' use of psychological control to coerce and maintain a parent–youth emotional alliance against the other parent (Haley, 1976; Minuchin, 1974).

At least part of the effect of interparental conflict is indirect through parenting behavior, lending support to the spillover hypothesis. Such scenarios illustrate how difficult it might be for conflicting couples to keep healthy boundaries between the marital relationship and the parenting relationship. For example, in the midst of marital conflict, men often withdraw from interaction rather than engage in the conflict, distancing themselves from their wives (Gottman & Levenson, 1988) as well as their children—especially their daughters (Amato, 1986). Thus, children of conflicting parents might be vulnerable, especially when father's anxiety regarding the conflict is expressed through withdrawal or psychological control.

We also found the relationship between overt conflict and YPB was indirect through parental psychological control, although the linkages were less robust. Extending the argument for the spillover hypothesis, we note that Patterson (1982) reasoned that when parents become emotionally upset and distracted by their own conflict, they focus less attention on their children. Thus, parents might ignore their youth and their youth's misbehavior until that misbehavior escalates to a point that demands control. Patterson suggests that at this point parents are likely to behave in a controlling way with threats and harsh punishment. Patterson's argument can be extended to include parental psychological control along with or instead of behavioral control. When parents are embroiled in conflict, they might ignore their youth until needed for emotional support or until misbehavior occurs. At this point, because of reduced energy and feeling overwhelmed with their conflictual relationship, parents might use guilt induction with their youth, an emotional coercion that is at the heart of psychological control. Psychological control, such as inducing guilt or provoking shame for misbehavior or divergent opinions, might seem to parents to require less effort than consistent disciplinary practices or discussing opposing viewpoints.

CONCLUSION

Overall results provide evidence for two roles played by parental psychological control in the context of marital conflict. First, parental psychological control and interparental conflict each uniquely explain YPB. Second, we found not only a direct relationship in the association between interparental conflict and YPB but also an indirect effect through parental psychological control (particularly when explaining the association between covert conflict and YPB). These findings held for two diverse samples in terms of age, gender, marital status, economic situation, religious affiliation, ethnicity, and geographic locations.

Our second finding differs from the only other study to date that has examined psychological control in the context of marital conflict. Fauber et al. (1990) found through structural equation modeling that psychological control partially mediated the relationship between marital conflict and internalizing YPB for divorced families and fully mediated the relationship for married families. One reason that Fauber et al. found support for a full mediating effect when we did not might be that we used a broader measure of interparental conflict. Another reason might be that they also included measures of lax parenting and parental rejection in their model.

Despite the overall support for the findings of independent–additive and indirect effects of parental psychological control, there are limitations in the study and alternative explanations for the results that need to be considered. First, although it is tempting to conclude that it is conflict that triggers parents' use of psychological control, a causal role for conflict cannot be argued because of the correlational and contemporaneous nature of the data. Alternatively, one parent might have responded to dissatisfaction with the other parent's psychological control attempts with their child by initiating conflictual interactions in the marriage. Likewise, one must caution against assuming that interparental conflict and psychologically intrusive parenting cause behavior problems. It is possible that youth with behavior problems *provoke* higher levels of interparental conflict and more intrusive parenting behaviors. For example, clinical case studies detail that when parents are worried that their youth might be depressed or involved in alcohol or drug abuse, parents begin to afford their youth less physical and psychological privacy (Ambert, 1997). Thus, it might be that youth with high levels of problem behavior create an environment that leads parents to be conflictual or psychologically controlling in a way they would not be otherwise. Second, a final caution involves the limitations of these two samples. The variance on the conflict variables is limited. Based on the limited information available to us, clinic-referred families were not overrepresented in the study. Thus, the greater extremes in highly conflictual marriages and destructive family processes likely to occur among clinic populations might yield a different pattern of results than that obtained in this study.

One important point highlighted by Fauber et al.'s (1990) study is the need to examine other parenting behaviors besides parental psychological control. As evident from Fauber et al.'s research, additional parenting behaviors help explain the association between interparental conflict and YPB. The addition of low parental acceptance, inconsistency, harsh punishment, and inadequate behavioral monitoring, as well as alternative conflict styles, such as avoidance, withdrawal, and cooperation, will provide a more comprehensive understanding of the linkages among interparental conflict, psychological control, and YPB. Some researchers have suggested that parental depression might help explain the association between conflict styles and YPB (Buehler et al., 1994) as well as psychological control and YPB (chapter 9, this volume). An enhanced model that includes additional interparental conflict styles, parenting behaviors, and parental depression should help pinpoint strategic areas for intervention.

The results of this study might be enriched by examining more closely a global dimension of covert conflict. Global covert conflict is exemplified when unspoken resentments and tensions between parents are manifested in subtle, indirect behaviors and affect such as the "silent treatment," sarcasm, or veiled teasing (Jenkins & Smith, 1991; Stone & Buehler, 1997; Whittaker & Bry, 1991). This subtle aggression is expressed toward one's partner in indirect ways that do not involve the child. Global covert conflict has been explored only superficially and deserves further attention. Although Jenkins and Smith (1991) did not find a significant relationship between parents' silent tensions and YPB, a well-developed measure that taps all aspects of the global covert conflict construct should provide a more complete understanding of the role psychological control plays in the relationship between marital conflict and YPB.

In summary, we have examined the associations among covert and overt interparental conflict styles, parental psychological control, and YPB in two diverse samples of youth and found evidence of both additive and intervening effects of parental psychological control. In terms of independent–additive effects, both covert and overt interparental conflict and parental psychological control explain YPB. In terms of indirect effects, covert and overt interparental conflict partially explain YPB through fathers' and mothers' psychological control. The strongest linkages in the association between interparental conflict and YPB involve the processes of covert conflict and parental psychological control.

A key contribution of this study is the examination of the more covert and ambiguous processes of marital conflict and parenting behavior that seem to place children at risk by modeling specific patterns of boundary violations and by placing captivating and potentially exhaustive demands on children and adolescents. Such family interactions promote unhealthy roles for the child in the family and have detrimental effects on both the marital dyad as well as the mother–child and the father–child relationship (Osborne & Fincham, 1996). Overall, the findings reported buttress our understanding of parental psychological control in the larger family context by highlighting how parental psychological control effects youth functioning in an environment of hostile marital conflict.

REFERENCES

Achenbach, T. M. (1991). *Manual for the youth self-report and 1991 profile*. Burlington: University of Vermont Department of Psychiatry.

Aiken, L. S., & West, S. G. (1991). *Multiple regression: Testing and interpreting interaction*. Newbury Park, CA: Sage.

Almeida, D. M., Wethington, E., & Chandler, A. L. (1999). Daily transmission of tensions between marital dyads and parent-child dyads. *Journal of Marriage and the Family, 61*, 49–61.

Amato, P. (1986). Marital conflict, the parent-child relationship and child self-esteem. *Family Relations, 35*, 403–410.

Amato, P. (1993). Children's adjustment to divorce: Theories, hypotheses, and empirical support. *Journal of Marriage and the Family, 55*, 23–28.

Ambert, A.-M. (1997). *Parents, children, and adolescents: Interactive relationships and development in context*. New York: Haworth Press.

Barber, B. K. (1996). Parental psychological control: Revisiting a neglected construct. *Child Development, 67*, 3296–3319.

Barber, B. K., Olsen, J. A., & Shagle, S. C. (1994). Associations between parental psychological and behavioral control and youth internalized and externalized behaviors. *Child Development, 65*, 1120–1136.

Baron, R. M., & Kenny, D. A. (1986). The moderator-mediator variable distinction in social psychological research: Conceptual, strategic, and statistical considerations. *Journal of Personality and Social Psychology, 51*, 1173–1182.

Baumrind, D. (1971). Current patterns of parental authority. *Developmental Psychology Monographs, 4*, 1–102.

Baumrind, D. (1978). Parental disciplinary practices and social competence in children. *Youth and Society, 9*, 239–276.

Bowen, M. (1971). Family therapy and marital therapy. In H. Kaplan and B. Sadock (Eds.), *Synopsis of psychiatry* (pp. 480–484). Baltimore: Williams and Wilkins.

Bowen, M. (1989). *Family therapy in clinical practice*. New York: Jason Aronson.

Bray, J. H., & Williamson, D. S. (1987). Assessment of intergenerational family relationships. In A. J. Hovestadt & M. Fine (Eds.), *Family of origin therapy* (pp. 31–43). Rockville, MD: Aspen.

Buchanan, C. M., Maccoby, E. E., & Dornbusch, S. M. (1991). Caught between parents: Adolescents' experience in divorced homes. *Child Development, 62*, 1008–1029.

Buehler, C., Anthony, C., Krishnakumar, A., Stone, G., Gerard, J., & Pemberton, S. (1997). Interparental conflict and youth problem behaviors: A meta-analysis. *Journal of Child and Family Studies, 6*, 233–247.

Buehler, C., Krishnakumar, A., Anthony, C., Tittsworth, S., & Stone, G. (1994). Hostile interparental conflict and youth maladjustment. *Family Relations, 43*, 409–416.

Buehler, C., Krishnakumar, A., Stone, G., Anthony, C., Pemberton, S., Gerard, J., & Barber, B. K. (1998). Interparental conflict and youth problem behaviors: A two-sample replication study. *Journal of Marriage and the Family, 60*, 119–132.

Buehler, C., & Trotter, B. B. (1990). Nonresidential and residential parents' perceptions of the former spouse relationship and children's social competence following marital separation: Theory and programmed intervention. *Family Relations, 39*, 395–404.

Camara, K. A., & Resnick, G. (1988). Interparental conflict and cooperation: Factors moderating children's post-divorce adjustment. In E. M. Hetherington & J. D. Aratesh (Eds.), *Impact of divorce, single parenting, and step parenting on children* (pp. 169–196). Hillsdale, NJ: Erlbaum.

Cohen, J. (1977). *Statistical power analysis for the behavioral sciences.* New York: Academic Press.

Conger, K. J., Conger, R. D., & Scaramella, L. V. (1997). Parents, siblings, psychological control, and adolescent adjustment. *Journal of Adolescent Research, 12*, 113–138.

Crockenberg, S. B., & Covey, S. L. (1991). Marital conflict and externalizing behavior in children. In D. Cicchetti & S. Toth (Eds.), *Rochester Symposium on Developmental Psychopathology: Vol. 3. Models and integration* (pp. 235–260). Rochester, NY: University of Rochester Press.

Cummings, E. M. (1987). Coping with background anger in early childhood. *Child Development, 58*, 976–984.

Cummings, E. M., & Davies, P. (1994). *Children and marital conflict: The impact of family dispute and resolution.* New York: Guilford Press.

Cummings, E. M., Davies, P. T., & Simpson, K. S. (1994). Marital conflict, gender, and children's appraisals and coping efficacy as mediators of child adjustment. *Journal of Family Psychology, 8*, 141–149.

Davies, P. T., & Cummings, E. M. (1994). Marital conflict and child adjustment: an emotional security hypothesis. *Psychological Bulletin, 118*, 387–411.

Davies, P. T., & Cummings, E. M. (1998). Exploring children's emotional security as a mediator of the link between marital relations and child adjustment. *Child Development, 69*, 124–139.

Emery, R. E. (1982). Interparental conflict and the children of discord and divorce. *Psychological Bulletin, 92*, 310–330.

Erel, O., & Burman, B. (1995). Interrelatedness of marital relations and parent-child relations: A meta-analytic review. *Psychological Bulletin, 118,* 106–132.

Farrington, D. (1991). Childhood aggression and adult violence: Early precursors and later life outcomes. In D. J. Pepler & K. H. Rubin (Eds.), *The development and treatment of childhood aggression* (pp. 5–29). Hillsdale, NJ: Erlbaum.

Fauber, R., Forehand, R., Thomas, A. M., & Wierson, M. (1990). A mediational model of the impact of marital conflict on adolescent adjustment in intact and divorced families: The role of disrupted parenting. *Child Development, 61,* 1112–1123.

Fincham, F. D. (1994). Cognition in marriage: Current status and future challenges. *Applied and Preventive Psychology: Current Scientific Perspectives, 3,* 185–198.

Forehand, R., Neighbors, B., Devine, D., & Armistead, L. (1994). Interparental conflict and parental divorce: The individual, relative, and interactive effects on adolescents across four years. *Family Relations, 43,* 387–393.

Forehand, R., Wierson, M., McCombs, A., Brody, G., & Fauber, R. (1989). Interparental conflict and adolescent problem behavior: An examination of mechanisms. *Behaviour Research and Therapy, 27,* 365–371.

Garber, J., Robinson, N. S., & Valentiner, D. (1997). The relation between parenting and adolescent depression: Self-worth as a mediator. *Journal of Adolescent Research, 12,* 12–33.

Gerard, J. M., & Buehler, C. (1999). Multiple risk factors in the family environment and youth problem behaviors. *Journal of Marriage and the Family, 61,* 343–361.

Golden, P. (1969). A review of children's reports of parental behaviors. *Psychological Bulletin, 71,* 222–235.

Gottman, J., & Levenson, R. (1988). The social psychophysiology of marriage. In P. Noller & M. A. Fitzpatrick (Eds.), *Perspectives on marital interaction* (pp. 182–200). Clevedon, England: Multilingual Matters.

Grych, J. H., & Fincham, F. D. (1990). Marital conflict and children's adjustment: a cognitive-contextual framework. *Psychological Bulletin, 2,* 267–290.

Grych, J. H., Seid, M., & Fincham, F. D. (1992). Assessing marital conflict from the child's perspective: The Children's Perception of Interparental Conflict Scale. *Child Development, 63,* 556–572.

Haley, J. (1976). *Problem-solving therapy.* San Francisco: Jossey-Bass.

Harold, G. T., & Conger, R. P. (1997). Marital conflict and adolescent distress: The role of adolescent awareness. *Child Development, 68,* 333–350.

Harold, G. T., Fincham, F. D., Osborne, L. N., & Conger, R. D. (1997). Mom and dad are at it again: Adolescent perceptions of marital conflict and adolescent psychological distress. *Developmental Psychology, 33,* 333–350.

Herman, M., Dornbusch, S., Herron, M., & Herting, J. (1997). The influence of family regulation, connection, and psychological autonomy on six measures of adolescent functioning. *Journal of Adolescent Research, 12,* 34–67.

Hodges, W. F. (1991). *Intervention of children of divorce: Custody, access, and psychotherapy.* New York: John Wiley & Sons.

Hotaling, G. T., & Sugarman, D. B. (1990). A risk marker analysis of assaulted wives. *Journal of Family Violence, 5,* 1–13.

Jenkins, J. M., & Smith, M. A. (1991). Marital disharmony and children's behavior problems: Aspects of a poor marriage that affect children adversely. *Journal of Child Psychology, 32,* 793–810.

Johnston, J. R., Gonzalez, R., & Campbell, L. (1987). Ongoing postdivorce conflict and child disturbance. *Journal of Abnormal Child Psychology, 15,* 493–509.

Jouriles, E. N., Barling, J., & O'Leary, K. D. (1987). Predicting child behavior problems in maritally violent families. *Journal of Abnormal Child Psychology, 15,* 165–173.

Jouriles, E. N., Murphy, C. M., Farris, A. M., Smith, D. A., Richters, J. E., & Waters, E. (1991). Marital adjustment, parental disagreements about child rearing, and behavior problems in boys: Increasing the specificity of marital assessment. *Child Development, 62,* 1424–1433.

Kaplan, H., & Sadock, B. (1996). *Pocket handbook of primary care psychiatry.* Baltimore: Williams & Wilkins.

Katz, L. F., & Gottman, J. M. (1993). Patterns of marital conflict predict children's internalizing and externalizing behavior. *Developmental Psychology, 29,* 940–950.

Kazdin, A. E. (1995). *Conduct disorders in childhood and adolescence* (2nd ed.). Thousand Oaks, CA: Sage.

Kempton, T., Thomas, A. M., & Forehand, R. (1989). Dimensions of interparental conflict and adolescent functioning. *Journal of Family Violence, 4,* 297–307.

Kerig, P. (1995). Triangles in the family circle: Effects of family structure on marriage, parenting, & child adjustment. *Journal of Family Psychology, 9,* 28–43.

Kovacs, M. (1981). Rating scales to assess depression in school-aged children. *Acta Paedopsychiatria, 46,* 305–315.

Kovacs, M., Feinberg, T. L., Crouse-Novak, M., Paulauskas, S. L., Pollock, M., & Finkelstein, R. (1984). Depressive disorders in childhood: II. A longitudinal study of the risk for a subsequent major depression. *Archives of General Psychiatry, 41,* 643–649.

Krishnakumar, A., & Buehler, C. (2000). Interparental conflict and parenting: A meta-analytic review. *Family Relations, 49,* 25–44.

Linver, M. R., & Silverberg, S. B. (1995). Parenting as a multidimensional construct: Differential prediction of adolescents' sense of self and engagement in problem behavior. *International Journal of Adolescent Medicine and Health, 8,* 29–40.

Lykken, D. T. (1968). Statistical significance in psychological research. *Psychological Bulletin, 70,* 151–159.

McCord, J. (1990). Problem behaviors. In S. Feldman & G. Elliot (Eds.), *At the threshold: The developing adolescent* (pp. 414–430). Cambridge, MA: Harvard University Press.

McHale, J. (1997). Overt and covert coparenting processes in the family. *Family Process, 36,* 183–201.

Minuchin, S. (1974). *Families and family therapy*. Cambridge, MA: Harvard University Press.

Moskowitz, D. S., & Schwarz, J. C. (1982). A validity comparison of behavior counts and ratings by knowledgeable informants. *Journal of Personality and Social Psychology, 42*, 518–528.

O'Brien, M., Margolin, G., & John, R. S. (1995). Relation among marital conflict, child coping, and child adjustment. *Journal of Clinical Child Psychology, 24*, 346–361.

Osborn, L. N., & Fincham, F. D. (1996). Marital conflict, parent-child relationships, and child adjustment: Does gender matter? *Merrill-Palmer Quarterly, 42*, 48–75.

Patterson, G. R. (1982). *Coercive family process*. Eugene, OR: Castalia.

Pearlin, L. I., Lieberman, M. A., Menaghan, E. G., & Mullan, J. T. (1981). The stress process. *Journal of Health and Social Behavior, 22*, 337–356.

Pine, D. S., Cohen, P., Gurley, D., Brook, J., & Ma, Y. (1998). The risk for early-adulthood anxiety and depressive disorders in adolescents with anxiety and depressive disorders. *Archives of General Psychiatry, 55*, 56–64.

Quay, H. B., & Peterson, D. R. (1983). *Interim manual for the revised behavior problem checklist*. Unpublished manuscript, University of Miami.

Reynolds, W. M. (1992). *Internalizing disorders in children and adolescents*. New York: Wiley.

Robins, L. N., & McEvoy, L. (1990). Conduct problems as predictors of substance abuse. In L. Robins & M. Rutter (Eds.), *Straight and devious pathways from childhood to adulthood* (pp. 182–204). Cambridge: Cambridge University Press.

Schaefer, E. (1965). Children's reports of parental behavior: An inventory. *Child Development, 36*, 413–424.

Schludermann, F., & Schludermann, S. (1970). Replicability of factors in children's reports of parent behavior (CRPBI). *The Journal of Psychology, 76*, 239–249.

Slater, C. M., & Hall, G. E. (Eds.). (1996). *County and city extra annual metro city and county data book*. Lanham, MD: Bernan.

Sobel, M. E. (1982). Asymptopic confidence intervals for indirect effects in structural equation models. In S. Leinhart (Ed.), *Sociological methodology* (pp. 290–312). San Francisco: Jossey-Bass.

Stierlin, H. (1985). Centripetal and centrifugal forces in the adolescent separation drama. In G. Handel (Ed.), *The psychosocial interior of the family* (pp. 339–366). New York: Aldine.

Stierlin, H., & Weber, G. (1989). *Unlocking the family door. A systemic approach to the understanding and treatment of anorexia nervosa*. New York: Brunner/Mazel.

Stierlin, H., Weber, G., Schmidt, G., & Simon, F. (1986). Features of families with major affective disorders. *Family Process, 25*, 325–336.

Stierlin, H., Wirsching, M., & Knauss, W. (1977). Family dynamics and psychosomatic disorders in adolescence. *Psychotherapy and Psychosomatics, 28*, 243–251.

Stone, G., & Buehler, C. (1997). *An observational measure of covert interparental conflict*. Paper presented at the annual conference of National Council on Family Relations.

Tschann, J. M., Johnston, J. R., Kline, M., & Wallerstein, J. S. (1989). Family process and children's functioning during divorce. *Journal of Marriage and the Family, 51*, 431–444.

U.S. Bureau of the Census. (1996). *County and city data books*. Washington, DC: U.S. Government Printing Office.

Whittaker, S., & Bry, B. (1991). Overt and covert parental conflict and adolescent problems: Observed marital interaction in clinic and nonclinic families. *Adolescence, 26*, 865–876.

4

PSYCHOLOGICAL CONTROL AND MONITORING IN EARLY ADOLESCENCE: THE ROLE OF PARENTAL INVOLVEMENT AND EARLIER CHILD ADJUSTMENT

GREGORY S. PETTIT AND ROBERT D. LAIRD

In this chapter we consider how parents' use of psychological control and parents' monitoring of their children's whereabouts and activities may be shaped, and their effects altered, by characteristics of the parent–child relationship. In line with Belsky's (1984) determinants of parenting model, we trace the roots of psychological control and monitoring in earlier parenting and child adjustment characteristics. In a departure from our earlier treatment of this issue (Pettit, Laird, Dodge, Bates, & Criss, 2001), and in contrast to the approach undertaken in some of the chapters in this volume, we consider not only main and additive effects but also moderators of parental psychological control and monitoring (see also chapter 5, this volume). The general thrust of our arguments and data presentation is that continuities in parenting behavior and the putative effects of parenting on child outcomes may be conditional in the sense that they may depend on certain child and parent–child relationship characteristics. That is, parents' use of a given control or regulatory strategy may hinge on whether the child is perceived negatively (e.g., as being difficult to manage) or positively, and whether the parent is positively involved in the child's social and academic life or disengaged from these spheres of the child's experience. Likewise, the extent to which parents' use of a given regulatory strategy predicts a

Preparation of this chapter and the research reported herein were supported by grants from the National Institute of Mental Health (MH 42498, MH 57095) and the National Institute of Child Health and Human Development (HD 30572) to G. S. Pettit, K. A. Dodge, and J. E. Bates. Appreciation is extended to Michael Criss for assistance in various phases of this undertaking.

given adjustment outcome in adolescence may depend on these same child and parenting factors.

The notion that the effects of specific parenting behaviors and styles are conditional has received a good bit of recent research attention (see Collins, Maccoby, Steinberg, Hetherington, & Bornstein, 2000). This research has, for the most part, focused on the extent to which differing parenting attributes may alter the effects of one another, or the extent to which child characteristics (e.g., temperament) may alter the impact of parenting behaviors in the prediction of child outcomes. Much less attention has been devoted to the ways in which parenting behaviors and attributes may moderate the effects of one another, or the ways in which parenting and child characteristics may moderate the effects of one another, in the prediction of subsequent *parenting* orientations. Moreover, little of the research examining interactions among parenting and child characteristics has been longitudinal. The reliance on cross-sectional data means that the actual processes giving rise to the moderated "effects" may be difficult to discern. That is, even if it is shown that the presence of high versus low levels of a given child behavior or characteristic alters the relationship between parental behavior and child outcomes, it remains unclear as to whether the "effect" is attributable to enduring individual differences in the child or to changes in parenting behavior, or to some combination. Such processes might be better understood through the use of longitudinal data. Of course, longitudinal data are necessary to examine whether the presence of high versus low levels of a child characteristic (e.g., externalizing behavior problems) or high versus low levels of a parenting behavior (e.g., involvement) alters the stability seen over time in other parenting behaviors (e.g., psychological control and monitoring).

Although there are numerous studies of relations among child adjustment and parenting behavior over time (e.g., Jang & Smith, 1997), typically only main effects are examined (e.g., whether parental supervision predicts change in child adjustment, or whether child adjustment predicts change in level of parental supervision). It would seem useful at this juncture to augment these main-effects models by considering moderated effects. In this manner it may be possible to ask not only whether early parenting predicts later child adjustment, controlling for early child characteristics, or whether early child characteristics predict later parenting, controlling for earlier parenting, but whether parenting and child characteristics moderate the effects of one another in the prediction of either later parenting or later child adjustment. Moreover, from a process-oriented perspective, it is of interest to ask whether moderated effects, either with respect to parenting characteristics or to parenting and child characteristics, are themselves associated with changes in parenting. If, for example, it were found that parents' use of psychological control with their children predicted adolescent anxiety more strongly for those adolescents who earlier had been relatively high in anxiety, questions arise about whether this effect is attributable to a vulnerability in the high-anxiety adolescents to the effects of psychological control or to an increase in parents' subsequent use of psychological control. Along these lines, if it were found that monitoring interacts with child characteristics observed earlier in predicting later adjustment outcomes such that monitoring is more "effective" when the adolescent previously was showing relatively low levels of behavioral maladjustment, then questions may be asked about whether this enhanced effectiveness is attributable to the susceptibility of the better-behaved adolescents to their parents' efforts at regulating and supervising their behavior or to a concomitant change (i.e., increase in effectiveness) in parents' monitoring and supervision.

Psychological control and monitoring are of particular interest in this context because each describes an important facet of parental control of adolescents. Although in the past the two forms of control often were combined in parenting-style typologies (e.g., Baumrind, 1966), more recent theoretical accounts and supporting empirical data (e.g., Barber, Olsen, & Shagle, 1994; Steinberg, Elmen, & Mounts, 1989) have highlighted their distinctiveness, both in terms of their socialization focus and in terms of their association with differing aspects of child and adolescent adjustment. By contrasting the two, we thought it possible to evaluate the generality of the interactive-effects formulation across two theoretically orthogonal yet empirically related parental control strategies.

In the following sections, we first briefly summarize research that has taken a "main effects" approach in examining the impact of psychological control and monitoring on adolescent adjustment and in considering the antecedents of psychological control and monitoring in earlier parenting and child adjustment. We then turn our attention to literature bearing on interaction effects (parenting × parenting or parenting × child characteristics), with special reference to evidence of such interactions in studies of psychological control and monitoring and related parenting constructs. To illustrate the operation of additive, main effects and interaction effects, we present data from our own ongoing longitudinal study.

PSYCHOLOGICAL CONTROL AND MONITORING AS DISTINCT CONSTRUCTS

For many contemporary socialization researchers, the case for the distinctiveness of psychological control and monitoring was made most compellingly by Steinberg (1990; Steinberg et al., 1989) and Barber (1996; Barber et al., 1994). Although it is possible to trace the psychological control construct back to earlier writing on parenting dimensions, most notably by

Schaefer (e.g., Schaefer, 1965), Steinberg and then Barber provide the most detailed description of the operation of psychological control and how it differs, both conceptually and empirically, from other forms of parental control. At the heart of this distinction is the notion that monitoring reflects parents' efforts to adapt and regulate children's behavior through guidance and supervision, whereas psychological control emanates from parents' motivations to inhibit the child's developing psychological autonomy, to keep the child dependent on the parent, and to help retain power in the relationship. Barber (chapter 1, this volume) and Barber and Harmon (chapter 2, this volume) focus on this distinction, review a large body of studies that have linked psychological control with anxious, internalizing problems, as well as externalizing problems.

Additional support for the distinctiveness of psychological control and monitoring would derive from studies of their broader correlates and antecedents. Data on the antecedents of psychological control and monitoring are scarce, and those studies that have attempted to identify such antecedents typically have taken a main-effects approach (e.g., Barber, 1996; Bogenschneider, Small, & Tsay, 1997). One main-effects conclusion is that monitoring and psychological control are anteceded by the very behavioral and psychological adjustment variables that they in turn predict—for example, high levels of anxiety–depression and delinquency antecede subsequent psychological control, and low levels of delinquency and externalizing problems antecede subsequent monitoring (Barber, 1996). To date, when earlier child adjustment characteristics, or parenting characteristics, have been examined as precursors (of parenting in general, or of psychological control and monitoring in particular), their possible interaction has not been considered.

PARENTING × PARENTING INTERACTIONS IN THE PREDICTION OF CHILD OUTCOMES

Two theoretical accounts of how aspects of parenting might moderate the impact of other aspects of parenting were published in 1993. Darling and Steinberg (1993) sought to distinguish between parenting practices, which were conceived as strategic behaviors used in the service of specific socialization goals, and parenting styles, which were viewed as more general indicators of the emotional climate of the family. Parenting style was thought to moderate the impact of parenting practices, such that practices would be effective in terms of achieving the desired outcome only if they were undergirded by a positive and supportive parent–child relationship. Evidence consistent with this premise was reported by Steinberg et al. (1989). These researchers were interested in the connection between parents' involvement in their children's school activities (e.g., ensuring that homework assignments were completed) and children's school performance. At first glance, parents' school-related involvement would seem to be desirable and generally promoting of positive school outcomes. However, such parental activities were positively correlated with children's school outcomes only in the context of an authoritative style. When parents' style was authoritarian, parents' involvement in school-related activities was associated with poorer academic performance. Thus, the meaning of a particular parenting behavior— involvement in school activities—appeared to change (or at least the direction of its relation with school performance changed) as a function of the general parenting style. Similar kinds of findings (i.e., in which parent–child relationship style or values moderated other parenting attributes) have been reported by Bogenschneider, Wu, Raffaelli, and Tsay (1998) and Mounts (1999).

Pettit and Mize (1993) also addressed the conceptual issue of how differing parenting characteristics might moderate the effects of one another, with special reference to young children's development of social skills and competencies. The distinction was drawn between parenting style, akin to the Darling and Steinberg (1993) construal, and the substance of parental teaching about social themes and issues. Pettit and Mize (1993) articulated a compensatory model, in which responsive parenting was conceived as providing a buffer against possible negative effects of deficiencies in social teaching, and where constructive social teaching was viewed as a possible buffer for those children whose parents were comparatively nonresponsive. These propositions were explored in a subsequent study (Mize & Pettit, 1997) in which independent assessments were made of mothers' positive relationship style and mothers' social coaching and used to predict preschool children's social competence. Relationship style and social coaching incrementally predicted peer competence; their interaction also made a significant predictive contribution. Further inspection of the interaction effect revealed that social coaching was associated with children's social competence only when relationship quality was comparatively low. Likewise, positive relationship style predicted competence only when social coaching was low in terms of rated effectiveness. In other words, one parenting attribute (e.g., positive style), if it occurred at a high level, compensated for the other parenting attribute (e.g., social coaching), if it occurred at a low level.

Regarding psychological control and monitoring, extant data are inconsistent with respect to whether their effects on child and adolescent adjustment are moderated by other forms of parenting. As pointed out by Barber (chapter 9, this volume), several studies have sought to identify such patterns for psychological control (e.g., Barber et al., 1994; Herman, Dornbusch, Herron, & Herting, 1997), but only one thus far has provided evidence that fits with an interactive-effects model. Gray and Steinberg (1999) found psychological control to interact with parental acceptance-involvement in predicting psychosocial development, internal distress, and academic competence. Specifically, autonomy-granting (i.e., lack of psychological control) predicted self-reliance and academic competence more strongly at low levels of parental acceptance-involvement. Thus, greater autonomy-granting appeared to compensate for low levels of parental acceptance.

Moderators of monitoring have not been studied in great detail, but at least one study has found evidence that its effects on child adjustment are moderated by other parenting factors. Bogenschneider et al. (1998) reported that parental monitoring was associated with lower levels of adolescent substance use, but that this effect was strongest among those adolescents whose fathers had values that were most disapproving of even casual substance use (mothers' values with respect to substance use did not moderate mothers' monitoring). This finding, though interesting, is difficult to evaluate in terms of parenting *behavior* as a moderator of monitoring. However, if one assumes that fathers who disapproved of substance use created a family climate consistent with their values, then the evidence fits with the Darling and Steinberg (1993) notion of style moderating the effects of specific parenting behaviors, the specific behaviors in this case reflecting monitoring and supervision.

CHILD CHARACTERISTICS × PARENTING INTERACTIONS IN THE PREDICTION OF CHILD OUTCOMES

Considerably more literature bears on the general issue of child characteristics—especially temperament and early adjustment characteristics—as moderators of parenting effects (Rothbart & Bates, 1998). Bates, Pettit, Dodge, and Ridge (1998) conducted one of the very few separate-sample replications of a conditional (moderating) effect of child characteristics on parenting. The question of interest was whether temperamental resistance to control in infancy, as perceived by mothers, interacted with observed restrictive control in early childhood in the prediction of children's schoolage externalizing problems. Although the main research focus was on whether parental control moderated the impact of early temperament (and findings revealed consistent evidence of this), it also was found that temperament moderated the impact of later control. Specifically, high levels of restrictive control were associated more strongly with later externalizing problems for children low in temperamental resistance to control than for children high in temperamental resistance to control. This finding runs counter to the presumption guiding much of the thinking about child temperament and parenting: that difficult-to-manage youngsters elicit harsher treatment, exacerbating their difficultness (Patterson, 1982). Instead, the pattern seems to suggest that high levels of control are unneeded and indeed inappropriate for children who are relatively easy to manage.

The work of Kochanska (1995) also has been important in documenting ways in which children's temperamental dispositions alter the impact of parental behavior. In this research, the outcome of interest is children's internalization of parental standards (i.e., "conscience"). Kochanska (1995) has shown that gentle discipline and reasoning are the most effective approaches to promoting conscience development among relatively fearful, anxious children. In contrast, manifestations of conscience development in relatively fearless children were predicted by parental responsiveness and a closer emotional bond with the child. These findings are consistent with models postulating interactions among parenting and child characteristics in the prediction of subsequent child outcomes.

A few studies have focused on child characteristics as moderators of monitoring and related parenting-behavior constructs. Wootton, Frick, Shelton, and Silverthorn (1997) examined whether a callous, unemotional (CU) child personality characteristic interacted with ineffective parenting (indexed in part as lack of supervision and monitoring) in the prediction of child conduct problems. It was found that ineffective parenting predicted conduct problems only for those children who were low in the CU trait; for those high in CU, ineffective parenting and conduct problems were unrelated, presumably because high CU children are less responsive to environmental events, including parenting. In contrast, low CU children are thought to be more sensitive to their parents' socializing efforts, and when parents are ineffective in this role, low-CU children show elevated levels of conduct problems. These findings fit with Belsky's (1997) notion that children differ in their susceptibility to parental influence.

Colder, Lochman, and Wells (1997) were interested in the extent to which schoolage children's fearfulness and activity levels interacted with poor monitoring and supervision in the prediction of aggression and depression. As expected, lack of monitoring was associated with higher levels of teacher-rated aggression only for those children who were rated by their parents as high in activity level. This finding suggests that preadolescent children who are highly active may be more likely to engage in risky activities that require adult supervision and monitoring (Pettit, Bates, Dodge, & Meece, 1999). In the absence of such monitoring, highly active children may become more aggressive. For similar reasons, it also was expected that children low in self-rated fearfulness would be at greater risk for aggressive behavior when monitoring was low, but this expectation did not receive empirical support.

INTERACTION EFFECTS IN THE PREDICTION OF PARENTING

We were unable to identify any literature pertaining specifically to interaction effects—whether in the form of one aspect of parenting interacting with another or in the form of parenting interacting with child characteristics—in the prediction of parenting. This is surprising given the long-standing interest in accounting for continuity and change in parenting behavior more generally (e.g., Pettit & Bates, 1984). Moreover, transactional processes involving interactions among child characteristics and parenting behavior have been posited to play key roles in the evolution of family relationship patterns, including coercive family systems (e.g., Patterson, 1982). Nonetheless, current accounts of the interplay of child characteristics and parenting behavior in the prediction of later parenting tend to stress their cumulative, additive effects rather than their moderating effects.

ANTECEDENTS AND CONDITIONAL EFFECTS OF PSYCHOLOGICAL CONTROL AND MONITORING: ILLUSTRATIONS FROM THE CHILD DEVELOPMENT PROJECT

We now turn our attention to an empirical demonstration of some of the additive and interactive models discussed in the preceding sections. Specifically, we use data collected as part of the ongoing Child Development Project (see Pettit, Bates, & Dodge, 1997) to document (a) antecedents of parental psychological control and monitoring in adolescence, both in terms of early childhood parenting and child characteristics and in terms of adjustment characteristics, (b) stability of psychological control and monitoring over one to two years and the extent to which such stability is moderated by adjustment or parental involvement, and (c) differential links between psychological control and monitoring and adolescent anxiety and delinquent behavior problems and the extent to which such links are moderated by earlier adjustment characteristics or parental involvement.

Participants and Background

The Child Development Project was initiated in 1987 as a longitudinal study of children's adaptation in a community sample selected at three geographical sites (Knoxville and Nashville, TN, and Bloomington, IN). Children and their families were recruited at spring registration for kindergarten and in-home assessments were conducted the summer before kindergarten. As part of these assessments, parents were interviewed and completed questionnaires, and children were administered a social–cognitive test battery. Subsequent yearly family follow-ups were made through questionnaire mail-outs and phone contacts. The children were followed through the elementary school years, with annual collection of teacher ratings. Home visits were conducted the summer before grade 6 (only mothers were interviewed at this time) and in grade 7 (only child participants were interviewed at this time). Both mothers and teenagers were interviewed in the home (and completed questionnaires) in the summer following grade 7 and again in the summer following grade 8.

At the initial assessment when the children were 5 years of age, 585 families participated, representing a range of family backgrounds (30% were single-parent families) and ethnicity (80% European American, 18% African American, 2% other ethnicity), with an almost equal split between boys and girls. Attrition has been relatively modest for such an assessment-intensive longitudinal study, with approximately 80% of the original sample ($N = 456$) still participating at the time of the most recent wave of data collection (1998 to 1999). Detailed analyses of attrited families compared to ongoing families has revealed little evidence of systematic attrition (see Pettit et al., 1997; Pettit et al., 1999), with the exception that lower socioeconomic status families have been somewhat more likely to drop out of the study compared to higher socioeconomic families.

Procedure and Measures

Data to be reported in this chapter are listed in Table 4-1 and come from the sources and years (child age) listed. For the sake of brevity, only abbreviated summaries are provided for measures that have been described in detail in published research reports.

1. *Early childhood antecedents* (age 5 years): Mothers' use of harsh discipline (i.e., extent to which mothers were severe, strict, and physical in their discipline) and mothers' proactive teaching and involvement (i.e., extent to which mothers espoused a planful, prevention-oriented approach to child misbehavior) were indexed with home interviewers' ratings (see Pettit et al., 1997). Mothers' perceptions of child behavioral adjustment were assessed with the externalizing problems scale of the Achenbach (1991) Child Behavior Checklist (CBC). Externalizing scores were dichotomized at the sample mean. Information on family socioeconomic and marital status also were collected during the home interview (Pettit et al., 1997).
2. *Behavioral and psychological adjustment in childhood* (ages 8, 9, and 10) was assessed with the Achenbach (1991) Teacher Report Form (TRF). As part of annual follow-ups, children's classroom teachers completed the TRF, a widely used behavior-

TABLE 4-1
Summary of Measures and Constructs

Category	Informant	Age	Construct
1. *Early childhood antecedents*	Mother	5	Harsh discipline
	Mother	5	Proactive teaching
	Mother	5	Externalizing behavior
2. *Behavioral and psychological*	Teacher	8 to 10	Delinquent behavior
adjustment in childhood	Teacher	8 to 10	Anxiety
3. *Parental involvement*	Mother	13	Parental involvement
	Adolescent	12	Parental involvement
4. *Psychological control and*	Adolescent	12	Psychological control
monitoring			
	Mother	13	Psychological control
	Adolescent	13	Psychological control
	Mother	11	Monitoring
	Adolescent	12	Monitoring
	Mother	13	Monitoring
	Adolescent	13	Monitoring
5. *Adolescent adjustment outcomes*	Teacher	14	Delinquent behavior
	Mother	14	Delinquent behavior
	Adolescent	14	Delinquent behavior
	Teacher	14	Anxiety
	Mother	14	Anxiety
	Adolescent	14	Anxiety

problem inventory. Cross-year childhood composite scores were created for the anxiety/depression subscale (within-year αs = .80 to .86; cross-year composite α = .88) and the delinquent behavior subscale (within-year αs = .71 to .74; cross-year composite α = .83). Conceptually, psychological control has been implicated as undermining autonomy and self-confidence and as contributing to feelings of personal distress and inadequacy (Barber, 1996; Steinberg, 1990). It therefore seemed appropriate to focus specifically on measures tapping anxiety and depression. Delinquency was of interest because of consistent findings linking monitoring with delinquency and related antisocial behaviors. Most models of monitoring stress its role in preventing young adolescents' "drift" toward antisocial peers and the concomitant increase in risk of delinquency (e.g., Dishion, Patterson, Stoolmiller, & Skinner, 1991).

3. *Adolescent parental involvement* (age 12 and 13) was assessed via home interviews with adolescents and mothers. As part of an extensive interview and questionnaire session at age 12, adolescents were asked to report how much time (in hours) they spent with their parents on a typical weekday and how

much time they spent with their parents on a typical weekend day ($r = .38$, $p < .001$, $\alpha = .49$). Mothers were asked to provide similar information approximately 16 months later (age 13). As part of an interview session mothers were asked to report (in hours) how much time they spent per week talking with their adolescent, and how much time per week they spent doing things with their adolescents that the adolescent enjoys (excluding watching TV and eating meals together; $r = .41$, $p < .001$, $\alpha = .58$). The adolescent and parent reports of parental involvement were not correlated with one another ($r = .04$, n.s.).

4. *Parental psychological control and monitoring* (ages 11, 12, and 13) were indexed through items administered during separate mother and child interviews over the course of a three-year span. At age 11, mothers only were interviewed and responded to a series of items designed to tap parents' awareness of their children's activities and companions and parents' judgments of the extent to which other adults would be available to provide supervision when their children were away at friends' homes (see Pettit et al., 1999). A 9-item monitoring composite scale was selected for use ($\alpha = .73$).

In the following school year (approximately age 12), adolescents only were interviewed and were asked to respond to a series of five items describing their parents' knowledge of their whereabouts and activities (e.g., "How much do your parents really know about who you spend time with in the after-school hours?") and six items describing the existence of family rules (e.g., "Does your family have rules about telling your parents where you are at all times?"). The knowledge items were adapted from items described by Brown, Mounts, Lamborn, and Steinberg (1993) and the family rules items were adapted from items described by Dishion et al. (1991). Because the two sets of items were scored on slightly different scales, the age 12 monitoring score was computed as the mean of the 11 standardized items ($\alpha = .64$). The adolescents also rated their parents' use of psychologically controlling behaviors using eight items adapted from Barber (1996; Barber et al., 1994; e.g., "Do your parents blame you for other family members' problems?"). The age 12 psychological control score is the mean of the eight items ($\alpha = .71$).

At age 13, mothers and their adolescents were interviewed in their homes. Embedded in the interviews were several questions pertaining to monitoring and psychological control (see

Pettit et al., 2001). Construct scores were computed as the mean of the respective items. The same five parent knowledge items ("How much do your parents really know. . . . ") used in the previous year were again used in the age 13 adolescent interview to index parental monitoring (α = .65). In the mother interview, monitoring was assessed through mothers' ratings of eight items (e.g., "If your child played with children who get in trouble, how often would you know it?"; α = .67). The 10 psychological control items embedded into the adolescent interview were adapted directly from Barber (1996; e.g., "My mother is always trying to change how I feel or think about things"; α =.76). Mothers were asked the same ten items, reworded slightly (α =.63).

5. *Adolescent adjustment outcomes.* Behavioral and psychological adjustment at age 14 was assessed through mother, teacher, and adolescent report. Mothers' completed the Achenbach (1991) CBC, teachers (nominated by school personnel as most familiar with the child) completed the Achenbach (1991) TRF, and the adolescents themselves completed the Achenbach (1991) Youth Self Report. Scale scores were derived from each instrument to index anxiety/depression (all αs > .84) and delinquent behavior problems (all αs > .73).

ANALYTIC APPROACH

Correlational techniques were used to assess both main effects and interactions. Based on the recommendations of Jaccard, Turisi, and Wan (1990) and Cohen and Cohen (1983), predictor variables were centered (i.e., the grand mean was subtracted from each participants' score) before creating multiplicative interaction terms. The dependent variable was then regressed on the centered predictors and the interaction term. Each interaction term was tested in a separate regression analysis. For all interactions involving continuous moderator variables, significant interactions were decomposed by computing the standardized beta (β) of the predictor variable at high (+1 SD) and low (−1 SD) values of the moderator.

Results and Discussion

Early Childhood Antecedents of Psychological Control and Monitoring

Main Effects Analyses. The first analysis focused on main-effect, early childhood antecedents of the age 13 indexes of psychological control and monitoring. These analyses are described more fully in Pettit et al. (2001). Each parenting measure served as a dependent variable in a series of regression analyses. Independent variables were measures representing family background (socioeconomic status, single-parent status), parenting (mothers' harsh discipline and proactive involvement), and perceived child adjustment (age 5 externalizing score). We controlled for the alternate parenting measure (e.g., in the prediction of mother-reported psychological control, mother-reported monitoring is the "alternate" measure and was entered first) because the constructs are known to overlap (Barber, 1996). There were 414 participants contributing complete data for the analyses with the mother-reported parenting variables and 413 for the analyses with the adolescent-reported parenting variables.

Both mother-reported and adolescent-reported indexes of psychological control were significantly predicted by earlier parenting (R^2 = .02 and .01, respectively). It is interesting to note, however, that adolescents' reports were associated only with early harsh discipline, whereas mothers' reports were significantly predicted by proactive parenting. Mothers' reports also were predicted by mothers' earlier ratings of their children's externalizing problems.

These findings suggest rather different antecedents for mother and adolescent reports. From the adolescent's point of view, mothers who are harsh and coercive in disciplinary encounters in early childhood come to be viewed years later as psychologically intrusive and manipulative, suggesting that in some families there is an enduring undercurrent of hostility and lack of respect for autonomy. With respect to mothers' reports, the connection between earlier proactive parenting and later psychological control may stem in part from some mothers' tendencies to control and manipulate their children in indirect, and perhaps nonobvious, ways. This tendency appears to co-occur with mothers' judgments that their children were difficult to control, as manifested in mothers' reports of heightened levels of early externalizing problems.

In contrast, mother-reported and adolescent-reported monitoring appear to have similar antecedents. Significant (p < .05) incremental predictions were found for the family background variables (R^2 = .08 and .02, respectively) and for the parenting variables (R^2 = .02 and .01). Both mother- and adolescent-reported monitoring was predicted by early proactive parenting. Mother-reported monitoring also was forecast by earlier family socioeconomic status, by childgender, and by marital status. These results likely indicate the comparative ease of monitoring in higher socioeconomic, intact families, compared to lower socioeconomic, single-parent families (Dishion & McMahon, 1998). The fact that preventive parenting in the early childhood years forecasts higher levels of parental monitoring in early adolescence may reflect a pervasive, prevention-oriented child-rearing philosophy in some mothers that expresses itself in developmentally relevant ways at different ages.

Moderator Analyses: Parenting × Child Characteristics Interactions. Given that proactive parenting predicted both later psychological control and later monitoring, and that early mother-rated adjustment problems predicted later psychological control (as reported by mothers), we thought it possible that the impact of early proactive parenting on later psychological control and monitoring might be moderated by mothers' judgments about their children's early adjustment and manageability. We therefore conducted an additional set of regressions, focusing only on mothers' reports of psychological control and monitoring. Of interest was whether proactive involvement interacted with mothers' ratings of age 5 externalizing problems in the prediction of later psychological control and monitoring. As in the main-effects analyses, the alternate form of parenting was controlled first. Proactive parenting and age 5 externalizing were entered next followed by the proactive parenting × age 5 externalizing interaction term.

The interaction was significant in the prediction of both psychological control, $R^2 = .01$, $p < .001$, and monitoring, $R^2 = .01$, $p < .001$. At low levels of child adjustment difficulty, early proactive involvement predicted later psychological control ($\beta = .21$) but not later monitoring ($\beta = .03$). At high levels of child adjustment problems, proactive parenting predicted later monitoring ($\beta = .25$) but not later psychological control ($\beta = -.03$). Thus, the presence or absence of mother-perceived child adjustment problems appears to alter the meaning of early proactive involvement. Proactive parenting when the child is seen as fairly well-adjusted may indicate an unneeded level of maternal planning and anticipating, and may translate into an inappropriate and intrusive form of later maternal involvement— or psychological control. On the other hand, proactive parenting with a hard-to-manage youngster may suggest an appropriate and necessary form of maternal anticipatory guidance, which may then be manifested in an age-appropriate version of proactive parenting in adolescence: namely, monitoring and distal supervision.

These interaction-effect findings help to make sense out of what might appear on the surface to be an anomaly: Namely, an early proactive parenting style predicts *both* later monitoring *and* later psychological control, as reported by mothers. These divergent pathways appear to be engendered by the match (or mismatch) between preschoolaged children's apparent need for close supervision (as indexed by their levels of behavior problems) and mothers' use of an anticipatory, prevention-oriented parenting approach. When the child and parent behavior were "matched" (i.e., with mothers reporting the use of proactive parenting with their difficult-to-manage youngsters) the mothers were more likely years later to engage in higher amounts of monitoring and supervision. When there was a "mismatch" between mothers' proactive parenting (high) and child behavior problems (low), mothers subsequently were more likely to use psychologically controlling behaviors with their adolescents.

Stability of Psychological Control and Monitoring

Main Effects Analyses. The second set of analyses focused on the stability of psychological control and monitoring during early adolescence and explored whether parental involvement or adolescents' history of behavior problems moderated this stability. Adolescent-reported psychological control at age 12 was significantly correlated with adolescent-reported psychological control at age 13 ($r = .50$, $p < .001$) and with parent-reported psychological control at age 13 ($r = .11$, $p < .05$). Adolescent-reported monitoring at age 12 was significantly correlated with adolescent-reported monitoring at age 13 ($r = .37$, $p < .001$) and parent-reported monitoring at age 11 was significantly correlated with parent-reported monitoring at age 13 ($r = .53$, $p < .001$). These results provide evidence of modest stability in parenting over a period of one to two years. Analyses were undertaken to determine whether this stability was influenced by the adolescents' history of adjustment problems or by patterns of parental involvement.

Moderator Analyses: Parenting × Parenting and Parenting × Child Characteristics Interactions. Given the modest stability in parenting, we thought it possible that parenting patterns may be more inconsistent when children have a history of behavior problems, perhaps because parents of problem children may be actively seeking effective parenting strategies or because parents find it easier to be consistent when children are less demanding (Pettit & Lollis, 1997). To test for this we conducted a series of regression analyses, with the age 13 parenting variables serving as dependent variables. The analogous age 11 or 12 parenting variables (e.g., for mother-reported monitoring at age 13, the analogous variable was mother-reported monitoring at age 11) were entered along with teacher-reported delinquent behavior and anxiety–depression in middle childhood. Interactions between earlier parenting and teacher-reported adjustment were entered last. There were 397 participants contributing complete data (for age 13 mother-reported parenting) and 387 (for age 13 adolescent-reported parenting). None of the interactions were significant, indicating that stability in psychological control or monitoring in early adolescence is not moderated by previous child adjustment history.

It also was of interest to determine whether stability in parenting was moderated by parental involvement. We reasoned that parents who are highly involved may be more consistent in their parenting behaviors than parents who are less involved. First, we tested whether adolescent- or parent-reported parental involvement interacted with adolescent-reported psychological control at age 12 to predicting adolescent-reported psychological control at age 13 (controlling for main effects). The interaction between adolescent-reported involvement and age 12 psychological control was significant ($R^2 = .01, p < .05$). There was greater stability in adolescent-reported psychological control at low levels than at high levels of parental involvement (βs = .54 and .40, respectively). A similar pattern was found when age 13 parent-reported psychological control was considered ($R^2 = .01, p < .05$), with greater stability in psychological control at low levels than at high levels of parental involvement (βs = .23 and .02, respectively). Collectively, these results suggest that parents who are relatively uninvolved in their children's lives are more consistent in their use of psychological control.

The extent to which stability in monitoring was moderated by parental involvement was tested in a similar fashion. First, we tested whether adolescent- or parent-reported parental involvement interacted with age 12 adolescent-reported monitoring to predict age 13 adolescent-reported monitoring (controlling for main effects). The interaction term for parent-reported involvement × age 12 monitoring was significant ($R^2 = .01, p < .05$). In contrast to the results for psychological control, there was greater stability in monitoring when parent involvement was high ($\beta = .47$) than when parent involvement was low ($\beta = .27$). An analogous set of analyses were conducted to determine whether involvement interacted with age 11 parent-reported monitoring to predict age 13 parent-reported monitoring. The term for the adolescent-reported involvement × age 11 monitoring interaction was marginally significant ($R^2 = .01, p < .10$). Again, there was somewhat greater stability in monitoring when parent involvement was high ($\beta = .59$) than when parent involvement was low ($\beta = .48$). From these results it appears that parents who are relatively involved in their adolescents' lives are more consistent in their use of monitoring.

To summarize thus far, an anticipatory parenting style appears to antecede both psychological control and monitoring, with the later manifestation determined by the parents' ability to adjust their practices to the behavior of their children. Moreover, it appears that parental reliance on psychological control is more stable when parents are relatively uninvolved in their children's lives. In contrast, monitoring is more stable when parents are highly involved. These findings suggest that parental insensitivity to children's needs underlies the use of psychological control whereas involvement and sensitivity underlie the use of monitoring.

Psychological Control and Monitoring as Predictors of Subsequent Anxiety–Depression and Delinquent Behavior

Main Effects Analyses. The third set of analyses examined age 13 psychological control and monitoring as predictors of age 14 anxiety–

depression and delinquent behavior. Bivariate correlations between age 13 psychological control and monitoring and the age 14 indexes of anxiety and delinquent behavior are shown in Table 4-2. This table also presents partial correlations controlling for the alternate parenting variable and the alternative adolescent adjustment variable. At the bivariate correlation level, little discriminative prediction was seen: Higher levels of psychological control, and lower levels of monitoring, tended to be associated modestly with lower levels of anxiety and with fewer delinquent behaviors. Somewhat more specific associations were found for the partial correlations, with psychological control being associated (positively) with anxiety–depression, and monitoring being associated somewhat more strongly (negatively) with delinquent behavior. This pattern of prediction is consistent with most published reports of the consequences of psychological control and monitoring (see chapter 2, this volume).

Moderator Analyses: Parenting × Child Characteristics Interactions. We next examined whether the associations between psychological control and monitoring and later adjustment outcomes varied as a function of children's previous behavior problems. One might speculate, for example, that psychological control is more detrimental among anxious children, perhaps owing to their propensity to be reserved and inward looking (Barber, 1996). Likewise, it might be speculated that parental monitoring would be more effective in preventing behavior problems among relatively well-adjusted children. To test these possibilities, regression analyses were conducted, with the age 14 anxiety–depression and delinquent behavior scores serving as dependent variables. The main effects of teacher-reported anxiety and delinquent behavior in middle childhood and of adolescent- and parent-reported parental involvement were entered as additional predictors. The interactions of interest were examined individually in a series of second steps. Complete data were available for 334 participants for the analyses predicting teacher-reported behavior problems and 342 participants for the analyses predicting adolescent- and parent-reported behavior problems.

The first analysis considered the extent to which teacher-reported delinquent behavior during middle childhood moderated the impact of parental psychological control on later delinquent behavior. The childhood delinquent behavior index interacted with adolescent-reported psychological control in the prediction of teacher-reported delinquent behavior ($R^2 = .02$, $p < .01$) and with mother-reported psychological control in the prediction of teacher-reported delinquent behavior ($R^2 = .01$, $p < .10$). Both interactions indicate that psychological control is associated more strongly with age 14 delinquent behavior when teachers reported lower levels of delinquent behavior during childhood (βs =.20 and .10, for adolescent- and mother-reported psychological control, respectively) than when teachers reported higher levels of delinquent behavior during childhood (βs =.01

TABLE 4-2
Correlations Between Psychological Control and Monitoring at Age 13 and Behavioral Adjustment Indexes at Age 14

| | Delinquent Behavior | | | | | | Anxiety | | | | | |
| | Adolescent | | Mother | | Teacher | | Adolescent | | Mother | | Teacher | |
	r	pr	r	pr	r	pr	r	pr	r	pr	r	pr
Psychological control												
Mother-reported	.06	-.01	.18***	.00	.05	-.02	.06	.05	.23***	.17***	.01	-.01
Adolescent-reported	.22***	.06	.17***	-.01	.18***	.08	.20***	.14**	.18***	.15**	.08	.02
Monitoring												
Mother-reported	-.20***	-.19***	-.30***	-.26***	-.32***	-.30***	-.06	.04	-.14**	.07	-.10+	.02
Adolescent-reported	-.36***	-.30***	-.24***	-.25***	-.25***	-.20***	-.13**	.05	-.03	.16***	-.08	.02

Note: N = 374 to 378. Correlations are denoted as r; partial correlations are denoted as pr; partial correlations for alternate behavior problem and parenting indexes.
+ $p < .10$, * $p < .05$, ** $p < .01$, *** $p < .001$

and -.02). That is, psychological control appears to be associated with an increase in the delinquent behavior of children who were exhibiting low levels of delinquent behavior in childhood.

The second set of interactions examined whether teacher-reported delinquent behavior during childhood moderated the impact of monitoring on later delinquent behavior. Teacher-reported delinquent behavior interacted with parent-reported monitoring in the prediction of adolescent-reported delinquent behavior ($R^2 = .01$, $p < .05$), adolescent-reported monitoring in the prediction of mother-reported delinquent behavior ($R^2 = .01$, $p < .05$), and adolescent-reported monitoring in the prediction of adolescent-reported delinquent behavior ($R^2 = .01$, $p < .10$). For all three interactions, higher levels of monitoring were associated more strongly with lower levels of age 14 delinquent behavior when childhood delinquent behavior was low (βs = -.23, -.21, and -.38, for mother-reported monitoring in predicting adolescent-reported delinquent behavior and adolescent-reported monitoring in predicting mother- and adolescent-reported delinquent behavior, respectively) than when childhood delinquent behavior was high (βs = -.07, -.07, and -.28).

From these results it appears that monitoring is most effective when adolescents have a history of engaging in comparatively low levels of delinquent behavior. However, given the association between monitoring and proactive parenting, discussed earlier, another consistent interpretation is that monitoring is more effective when parents have been proactive in preventing the development of delinquent behavior problems than when parents are reacting to the presence of behavior problems (Pettit et al., 1997).

The next set of interactions considered age 14 anxiety–depression, and the extent to which its links with parent- or adolescent-reported psychological control or monitoring were moderated by teacher-reported anxiety during childhood. None of the interactions were significant predictors of anxiety at age 14. The impact of parenting on anxiety does not appear to vary with children's history of anxious behaviors.

Moderator Analyses: Parenting × Parenting Interactions. As described earlier, stability in parenting is moderated by parental involvement, with less involved parents showing more cross-time consistency in psychological control and with highly involved parents showing more cross-time consistency (relative to other parents in the sample) in monitoring. Given the differences in levels of stability, it was of interest to determine whether the consequences of psychological control and monitoring vary as a function of parental involvement. Specifically, high levels of parental involvement may exacerbate the impact of psychological control because of repeated exposure of the child to the parents' psychological manipulation. Parental monitoring may be harder to maintain, but be most effective, when parents are less involved in their children's lives (i.e., providing less direct supervision; Pettit et al., 1999).

To test parental involvement as a moderator of relations between psychological control and monitoring and adolescent behavior problems a series of regression analyses were conducted with the age 14 indexes of delinquent behavior and anxiety again serving as dependent variables. The main effects of teacher-reported delinquent behavior and anxiety in middle childhood and of adolescent- and parent-reported parental involvement were retained as predictors. The interactions of interest were examined individually in a series of second steps. Multivariate Ns were 334 for analyses of teacher-reported behavior problems, and 342 for analyses of adolescent- and parent-reported behavior problems.

The first set of analyses examined whether parental involvement moderated the impact of psychological control on delinquent behavior or anxiety–depression at age 14. One interaction was significant. Adolescent-reported parent involvement interacted with parent-reported psychological control to predict teacher-reported delinquent behavior ($R^2 = .02$, $p < .05$). Higher levels of psychological control were associated with more delinquent behavior when involvement was low ($\beta = .14$) and with less delinquent behavior when involvement was high ($\beta = -.12$). This finding replicates the interaction reported by Gray and Steinberg (1999) but emphasizes the autonomy-threatening dimension of psychological control. Gray and Steinberg found that autonomy-granting predicted more positive developmental outcomes when parental involvement was low, whereas our data show that psychological control (i.e., lack of autonomy-granting) predicts more negative developmental outcomes when parental involvement is low. Psychological control is linked to increased delinquent behavior both among adolescents without a history of behavior problems and among adolescents whose parents are relatively uninvolved in their lives. Moreover, because relatively uninvolved parents may find it easier to use psychological control, and because the use of psychological control is most consistent among less involved parents, exposure to psychologically controlling parenting may be a pathway through which relatively well-adjusted children with uninvolved parents begin to exhibit behavior problems during early adolescence.

The final set of analyses tested interactions between parental involvement and monitoring in the prediction of delinquent behavior or anxiety–depression at age 14. Parent-reported involvement interacted with adolescent-reported monitoring in the prediction of delinquent behavior as reported by both the adolescent ($R^2 = .01$, $p < .10$) and the mother ($R^2 = .01$, $p < .05$). Higher levels of monitoring were associated more strongly with low levels of delinquent behavior problems when involvement was low ($\beta s = -.47$, and $-.35$ for adolescent- and mother-reported delinquent behavior, respectively) than when involvement was high ($\beta s = -.29$ and $-.11$). Parent involvement also interacted with parent-reported monitoring in the prediction of teacher-rated delinquent behavior (parent-reported involvement, $R^2 = .02$, $p < .05$; adolescent-reported parent involvement $R^2 = .01$, $p < .05$). Again, higher levels of monitoring predicted lower levels of delinquent behavior more strongly when parental involvement was low (βs = -.39, and -.40 for adolescent- and mother-reported parental involvement, respectively) than when involvement was high (βs = -.09, and -.24).

The interaction between monitoring and involvement in the prediction of delinquent behavior appears to be evidence of a compensatory process whereby high levels of monitoring can make up for a lack of parental involvement. In other words, high levels of monitoring *or* parental involvement appears to be sufficient for parents to have the knowledge of their early adolescents' activities and whereabouts needed to prevent delinquent behavior.

CONCLUSION

In this chapter we illustrate the role of parental involvement and earlier child adjustment as factors shaping the course and consequences of psychological control and monitoring in adolescence. A summary of the main findings is presented in Table 4-3. As a whole, the findings lend further support to arguments that psychological control and monitoring represent distinct socializing constructs (see chapter 1, this volume), and underscore the importance of conceptualizing parenting effects in conditional (i.e., interactive) terms, rather than simply as main and additive effects (Collins et al., 2000).

Although main effects were not chiefly of interest in this investigation, and are discussed in greater detail in a related report (Pettit et al., 2001), it is noteworthy that psychological control and monitoring appear to have somewhat different antecedents and patterns of correlates. Monitoring is linked most consistently with a proactive, anticipatory parenting style, which makes sense when one considers that monitoring reflects both an outcome— a parent's having knowledge of the teenager's activities and whereabouts— and a process through which this knowledge and information is acquired. The process itself is not well-understood (Dishion & McMahon, 1998), but likely reflects historical factors in the parent–child relationship, such as warmth and mutual respect, and earlier efforts on the part of the parent to read "early warning" signs of potential problems (i.e., that the child is gravitating toward a friendship that the parent disapproves of). The seeds of being skilled in reading these early signs likely are sown in the childhood

TABLE 4-3
Summary of Findings

Early Childhood Antecedents of Psychological Control and Monitoring
- More psychological control found when there is a history of harsh discipline and child behavior problems
- More psychological control found among more proactive parents but only when children had no history of behavior problems
- More monitoring found among higher socioeconomic status families, parents with daughters, and two-parent families
- More monitoring among more proactive parents but only when children had a history of behavior problems

Stability of Psychological Control and Monitoring
- Psychological control relatively stable from age 12 to 13, with greater stability at low levels of parental involvement
- Monitoring relatively stable from age 11–12 to age 13, with greater stability at high levels of parental involvement

Psychological Control and Monitoring as Predictors of Subsequent Adjustment
- Greater psychological control predicts greater anxiety
- Greater psychological control predicts more delinquent behavior problems, but only when there is no history of childhood delinquent behavior problems and when parental involvement is low
- Greater monitoring predicts lower anxiety
- Greater monitoring predicts fewer delinquent behavior problems, particularly when there is no history of childhood delinquent behavior problems and when parental involvement is low

years, when parents are in closer proximity to the child and have greater opportunities for arranging and controlling the child's environment.

The arranging and supervising of the child's life may, however, eventuate into a less healthy form of parental control, as shown by psychologically controlling and manipulating parenting. Our data suggest that psychological control is anteceded both by early harsh discipline (when adolescents' reports of psychological control are considered) and by a mix of proactive involvement and perceived child behavioral problems (when mothers' reports of psychological control are considered). The mother who is, perhaps, overly attentive to early signs of problems—or who responds to a nonproblem child in a manner that might be more suitable for a demanding or hard-to-manage child—may be setting in motion a series of events leading to later difficulties in negotiating autonomy and personal identity issues with her adolescent (Steinberg, 1990).

It is interesting that early proactive involvement predicted later psychological control when mothers rated their preschoolers as low in externalizing problems but that proactive involvement predicted later monitoring when mothers rated their preschoolers as high in externalizing problems. The latter suggests the prevention-oriented parenting style shown by mothers of demanding youngsters may stem in part from characteristics of the child (or, at least, mothers' perceptions of those characteristics), as well as, perhaps, from the mothers' own prevention-oriented parenting philosophy (Pettit et al., 2001). The finding that mothers who are proactive when their children show comparatively few problems are more likely to be psychologically controlling in the early adolescent years suggests a more mother-driven pattern, perhaps stemming from personality dispositions (e.g., hostility or depression) or from earlier experiences in the mothers' family of origin (e.g., problems in individuation or conflict with parents) (see chapter 2, this volume). It will be important for future research to examine intermediate events between early parent–child relationship factors and later displays of monitoring and psychological control. It may be, as some have argued, that social learning (e.g., Dishion & McMahon, 1998) or social control (e.g., Jang & Smith, 1997) processes best explain the reciprocal relationships between child characteristics and parenting orientations. To understand the operation of such processes it will be necessary to trace the evolution of the parent–child system across multiple time periods, with assessments of parent–child connectedness and child behavioral adjustment, as well as age-appropriate indexes of psychological control and monitoring.

We also sought to document the stability in psychological control and monitoring and the extent to which this stability was moderated by parent involvement and earlier child adjustment history. In some ways our data set was not ideally suited for examining stability issues because we did not always have identical measures across ages and constructs, and for some ages we did not have parallel measures for both teenage reports and mother reports. Nonetheless, the overall pattern of findings was strikingly consistent in showing that psychological control was relatively more stable at lower levels of parental involvement whereas monitoring was more stable at high levels of parental involvement. The greater stability of monitoring when involvement is higher seems reasonable because more involved parents have greater opportunities to solicit information that is essential to effective monitoring (Jang & Smith, 1997). It is less clear why psychological control might be more stable when involvement is low, but it may be that the need to use, or the motivation to use, psychological control increases when parent and child spend less time together. It therefore may be that a fairly small number of low-involved, highly controlling parents account for this stability.

We had expected that earlier adjustment history also might moderate the stability of psychological control and monitoring (e.g., with greater stability of monitoring when children were generally well-adjusted), but this expectation was not supported by our data. However, we did find some support for the expectation that earlier adjustment might moderate the impact of psychological control and monitoring on subsequent adjustment. These data may be used to address two related questions: Are parents' control attempts actually associated with a reduction in the level of problem behavior exhibited by the adolescents? Do the "effects" of these interventions vary as a function of the level of maladjustment previously shown by the adolescents? Both questions were, for the most part, answered in the affirmative. When there is little history of earlier behavior problems, monitoring is more effective in "preventing" later problems. As mentioned earlier, social learning and social control perspectives might be applied to explain this finding, with both perspectives stressing a lessening of the parent–child relationship bond in those families in which children exhibit higher levels of behavioral maladjustment, with a concomitant decrease in parents' motivations to socialize the child (i.e., less monitoring). On the other hand, when there are low levels of earlier behavior problems (at least delinquent behavior problems), psychological control is less effective in preventing later delinquent behavior. The term "preventing" may be a bit of a misnomer in this instance, however, because it seems unlikely that many parents would apply psychological control in such a strategic manner (see chapter 2, this volume). Nonetheless, this finding may indicate that fairly well-adjusted children, who perhaps are less likely than their poorly adjusted counterparts to seek social connections with peers, especially deviant peers (Laird, Jordan, Dodge, Pettit, and Bates, 2001), are especially susceptible to the pernicious effects of psychological control.

When parent involvement was considered as a moderator of the impact of psychological control and monitoring on later adolescent adjustment, evidence was found for both conditional effects (Darling & Steinberg, 1993) and compensatory effects (Pettit & Mize, 1993). The interaction between psychological control and involvement fits with the conditional effects model because the meaning of psychological control may vary as a function of the level of parent–adolescent involvement. When involvement is low but parents engage in high amounts of psychological control, adolescents may interpret the parents' behavior as intrusive and insincere. When involvement is high, the same kinds of parenting behaviors may be viewed differently, perhaps as manifestations of concern or interest. We can only speculate on these processes because we did not assess children's interpretations of their parents' controlling behavior. Future research could benefit from more detailed assessments of intervening social–cognitive events that lead children to respond in different ways to parenting behavior under differing circumstances or contexts (e.g., Smetana, 1995).

The interaction of monitoring and involvement in the prediction of delinquent behavior is consistent with a compensatory model. Higher levels of monitoring were associated with fewer delinquent behavior problems, especially when parent involvement was low. Additional analyses (not presented) also suggest that monitoring moderates the impact of involvement. Inspection of means suggests that the adolescents most at risk are those whose parents are low in both involvement and monitoring. When either monitoring or involvement occurs at a high rate, the level of delinquent behavior problems is lower. Thus, hands-on involvement and supervision can compensate for lack of overall knowledge of whereabouts and companions (monitoring) and monitoring can, to some extent, compensate for lack of direct supervision and involvement (Pettit et al., 1999).

In sum, we have illustrated ways in which earlier and later forms of parental involvement and child adjustment profiles may be implicated in shaping the continuities and effects of psychological control and monitoring. Important parenting constructs are likely to be linked with child adjustment outcomes in complex ways (Collins et al., 2000). This chapter has shown that this complexity emanates from both the broader parent–child relationship context as well as by early and continuing patterns of child adjustment.

REFERENCES

Achenbach, T. M. (1991). *Integrative guide for the 1991 CBCL14-18, YSR, and TRF profiles*. Burlington: University of Vermont, Department of Psychiatry.

Barber, B. K. (1996). Parental psychological control: Revisiting a neglected construct. *Child Development, 67*, 3296–3319.

Barber, B. K., Olsen, J. A., & Shagle, S. C. (1994). Associations between parental psychological and behavioral control and youth internalized and externalized behaviors. *Child Development, 65*, 1120–1136.

Bates, J. E., Pettit, G. S., Dodge, K. A., & Ridge, B. (1998). The interaction of temperamental resistance to control and restrictive parental discipline in the development of externalizing problems. *Developmental Psychology, 34*, 982–995.

Baumrind, D. (1966). Effects of authoritative parental control on child behavior. *Child Development, 37*, 887–907.

Belsky, J. (1984). The determinants of parenting: A process model. *Child Development, 55*, 83–96.

Belsky, J. (1997). Theory testing, effect-size evaluation, and differential susceptibility to rearing influence: The case of mothering and attachment. *Child Development, 68*, 598–600.

Bogenschneider, K., Small, S. A., & Tsay, J. C. (1997). Child, parent, and contextual influences on perceived parenting competence among parents of adolescents. *Journal of Marriage and the Family, 59*, 345–362.

Bogenschneider, K., Wu, M., Raffaelli, M., & Tsay, J. C. (1998). Parent influences on adolescent peer orientation and substance use: The interface of parenting practices and values. *Child Development, 69*, 1672–1688.

Brown, B. B., Mounts, N., Lamborn, S. D., Steinberg, L. (1993). Parenting practices and peer group affiliation in adolescence. *Child Development, 64*, 467–482.

Cohen, J., & Cohen, P. (1983). *Applied multiple regression/correlation analysis for the behavioral sciences* (2nd ed.). Hillsdale, NJ: Erlbaum.

Colder, C. R., Lochman, J. E., & Wells, K. C. (1997). The moderating effects of children's fear and activity level on relations between parenting practices and childhood symptomatology. *Journal of Abnormal Child Psychology, 25,* 251–263.

Collins, W. A., Maccoby, E., Steinberg, L., Hetherington, E. M., & Bornstein, M. (2000). Contemporary research on parenting: The case for nature and nurture. *American Psychologist, 55,* 218–232.

Darling, N., & Steinberg, L. (1993). Parenting style as context: An integrative model. *Psychological Bulletin, 113,* 487–496.

Dishion, T. J., & McMahon, R. J. (1998). Parental monitoring and the prevention of child adolescent problem behavior: A conceptual and empirical foundation. *Clinical Child and Family Psychology Review, 1,* 61–75.

Dishion, T. J., Patterson, G. R., Stoolmiller, M., & Skinner, M. L. (1991). Family, school, and behavioral antecedents to early adolescent involvement with antisocial peers. *Developmental Psychology, 27,* 172–180.

Gray, M. R., & Steinberg, L. (1999). Unpacking authoritative parenting: Reassessing a multidimensional construct. *Journal of Marriage and the Family, 61,* 574–587.

Herman, M. R., Dornbusch, S. M., Herron, M. C., & Herting, J. R. (1997). The influence of family regulation, connection, and psychological autonomy on six measures of adolescent functioning. *Journal of Adolescent Research, 12,* 34–67.

Jaccard, J., Turisi, R., & Wan, C. K. (1990). *Interaction effects in multiple regression.* Newbury Park, CA: Sage.

Jang, S. J., & Smith, C. A. (1997). A test of reciprocal causal relationships among parental supervision, affective ties, and delinquency. *Journal of Research in Crime & Delinquency, 34,* 307–336.

Kochanska, G. (1995). Children's temperament, mother's discipline, and security of attachment: Multiple pathways to emerging internalization. *Child Development, 66,* 597–615.

Laird, R. D., Jordan, K. Y., Dodge, K. A., Pettit, G. S., & Bates, J. E. (2001). Peer rejection in childhood, involvement with antisocial peers in early adolescence, and the development of externalizing behavior problems. *Development and Psychopathology, 13,* 337–354..

Mize, J., & Pettit, G. S. (1997). Mothers' social coaching, mother–child relationship style, and children's peer competence: Is the medium the message? *Child Development, 68,* 291–311.

Mounts, N. S. (1999, April). *Parenting style and parental management of peers: Contributions to friend selection and adjustment.* Paper presented as part of the symposium, " 'So, these are your friends?' Parental management of adolescents' peer relationships (N.S. Mounts & K. McCoy, Chairs), at the biennial meeting of the Society for Research in Child Development, Albuquerque, NM.

Patterson, G. R. (1982). *Coercive family processes.* Eugene, OR: Castalia Press.

Pettit, G. S., & Bates, J. E. (1984). Continuity of individual differences in the mother-infant relationship from six to thirteen months. *Child Development, 55,* 729–739.

Pettit, G. S., Bates, J. E., & Dodge, K. A. (1997). Supportive parenting, ecological context, and children's adjustment: A seven-year longitudinal study. *Child Development, 68,* 908–923.

Pettit, G. S., Bates, J. E., Dodge, K. A., & Meece, D. W. (1999). The impact of after-school peer contact on early adolescent externalizing problems is moderated by parental monitoring, perceived neighborhood safety, and prior adjustment. *Child Development, 70,* 768–778.

Pettit, G. S., Laird, R. D., Dodge, K. A., Bates, J. E., & Criss, M. M. (2001). Antecedents and behavior-problem outcomes of parental monitoring and psychological control. *Child Development, 72,* 583–598.

Pettit, G. S., & Lollis, S. P. (1997). Reciprocity and bidirectionality in parent-child relationships: New approaches to the study of enduring issues. *Journal of Social and Personal Relationships, 14,* 435–440.

Pettit, G. S., & Mize, J. (1993). Substance and style: Understanding the ways in which parents teach children about social relationships. In S. Duck (Ed.), *Understanding relationship processes: Vol. 2. Learning about relationships* (pp. 118–151). Newbury Park, CA: Sage.

Rothbart, M. K., & Bates, J. E. (1998). Temperament. In W. Damon (Series Ed.) & N. Eisenberg (Vol. Ed.), *Handbook of child psychology: Vol. 3. Social, emotional, and personality development* (5th ed., pp. 105–176). New York: Wiley.

Schaefer, E. S. (1965). A configurational analysis of children's reports of parent behavior. *Journal of Consulting Psychology, 29,* 552–557.

Smetana, J. G. (1995). Parenting styles and conceptions of parental authority during adolescence. *Child Development, 66,* 299–316.

Steinberg, L. (1990). Interdependence in the family: Autonomy, conflict, and harmony in the parent-adolescent relationship. In S. S. Feldman & G. R. Elliott (Eds.), *At the threshold: The developing adolescent* (pp. 255–276). Cambridge, MA: Harvard University Press.

Steinberg, L., Elmen, J. D., & Mounts, N. S. (1989). Authoritative parenting, psychological maturity, and academic success among adolescents. *Child Development, 60,* 1424–1436.

Wootton, J. M., Frick, P. J., Shelton, K. K., & Silverthorn, P. (1997). Ineffective parenting and childhood conduct problems: The moderating role of callous-unemotional traits. *Journal of Consulting & Clinical Psychology, 65,* 292–300.

5

MEASURING CHILDREN'S PERCEPTIONS OF PSYCHOLOGICAL CONTROL: DEVELOPMENTAL AND CONCEPTUAL CONSIDERATIONS

AMANDA SHEFFIELD MORRIS, LAURENCE STEINBERG,
FRANCES M. SESSA, SHELLI AVENEVOLI, JENNIFER S. SILK,
AND MARILYN J. ESSEX

Widespread clinical anecdote links parenting that is psychologically controlling and intrusive in nature to emotional and behavioral problems in children, particularly in the development of internalizing disorders such as anxiety and depression (Barber, Olsen, & Shagle, 1994; Hetherington & Martin, 1986; Minuchin, 1974). However, few studies have examined the relationship between psychological control and child adjustment empirically. Existing research on psychological control has focused primarily on middle childhood and adolescence, and little is known about the effects of psychological control on young children. Because psychological control is an intrusion into the child's self-expression (Barber, 1996), and because psychologically controlling parents tend to create an environment in which love and acceptance are contingent on the child's behavior, it is likely that this type of parental control is harmful for children of all ages. Indeed, there is some emerging research suggesting that psychological control is harmful to schoolage and preschool children (Hart, Nelson, Robinson, Olsen, & McNeilly-Choque, 1998; Mills & Rubin, 1998; Morris, 1999; Morris et al., 2000; chapters 6, 7, 8, this volume).

This chapter discusses the literature on psychological control and children, with particular emphases on the importance of assessing the *child's*

This research was supported by the John D. and Catherine T. MacArthur Foundation Research Network on Psychopathology and Development. We would like to thank Abbe Garcia Marrs for her helpful comments in the preparation of this manuscript, and Michael D. S. Morris for his invaluable support and statistical advice.

perspective of psychological control and on examining the interaction between child temperament and psychological control. We present a new methodology for evaluating children's subjective experience of psychological control and discuss preliminary analyses on the relationship between children's perceptions of psychological control and emotional and behavioral problems. This research places the child at the center of the study of psychological control. We argue for the assessment of psychological control from the child's perspective, and we also provide evidence that child characteristics, specifically temperament, interact with psychological control in the prediction of child adjustment. Although psychological control is likely harmful to all children, children with specific temperamental vulnerabilities are especially susceptible to the deleterious impact of psychological control. In the final section of this chapter, new thoughts on the construct of psychological control and its measurement are discussed, and a new model examining specific domains through which parents exert psychological control is presented.

PSYCHOLOGICAL CONTROL AND CHILD ADJUSTMENT

Psychological control is related to several constructs in psychology literature (e.g., overprotectiveness, enmeshment) and has been operationalized in various ways (see chapter 2; this volume, for a review). The definition of *psychological control* adhered to in most current research, and in this chapter, comes from Barber's (1996) review of the history and empirical work on the construct. Barber defined psychological control as a type of intrusive parental control in which parents attempt to manipulate their children's behavior, identity, and psychological development. Psychologically controlling parents typically use strategies such as excessive criticism, contingent affection, guilt induction, restrictive communication, and invalidation of feelings in an attempt to control their children.

Although early scholars of parenting warned against the harmful effects of psychological control (e.g., Baumrind, 1965; Becker, 1964; Schaefer, 1959), little empirical research focused on this construct until a recent resurgence of interest in the last decade of the twentieth century (e.g., Barber, 1996; Barber et al., 1994; Fauber, Forehand, Thomas, & Wierson, 1990; Gray & Steinberg, 1999; Steinberg, 1990; Steinberg, Elmen, & Mounts, 1989; Steinberg, Lamborn, Dornbusch, & Darling, 1992; Steinberg, Mounts, Lamborn, & Dornbusch, 1991). This recent research has reintroduced psychological control back into the study of socialization, but, as noted in chapter 1 of this volume, most of the resulting work has focused on preadolescents or adolescents. Very few studies of young children have examined the impact of psychological control independent of other parenting behaviors (for exceptions see Hart et al., 1998; chapters 6, 7, and 8, this volume), studying psychological control, instead, as part of an aggregate measure of overall parenting style (Baumrind, 1965, 1966, 1971) or "negative parenting" (Campbell, March, Pierce, Ewing, & Szumowski, 1991; Crockenberg & Litman, 1990).

Despite this limitation, research does provide some evidence that psychological control, at least when aggregated with other aspects of negative parenting, has a negative impact on young children's adjustment. For example, Campbell et al. (1991) found that preschool boys with externalizing problems have mothers who are more intrusive, punitive, and negative in tone during a clean-up task, compared to mothers of boys without externalizing problems. Maternal negative control also predicted externalizing behaviors one year later. In a similar study, Crockenberg and Litman (1990) found that negative maternal control (high power assertion) was more likely to elicit defiance from toddlers in a clean-up task. In contrast, guidance (low power assertion) was more related to compliance and children's self-assertion. These studies aggregated psychological control and punitive control, but nevertheless provide evidence that intrusive control contributes to the development of problem behaviors in preschool children.

In one of the few research programs to examine the effects of psychological control on young children independent of other parenting constructs, Hart and colleagues found deleterious effects of psychological control among preschool children in different cultures. In a sample of Russian preschool children, mother reports of maternal psychological control were correlated with teacher reports of children's overt, hostile aggression with peers (Hart et al., 1998). Olsen et al. (chapter 8, this volume) found that maternal reports of psychological control was related to internalizing or externalizing problems in samples of U.S., Russian, and Chinese preschool children, with similar factor structures of psychological control across the cultures. This research suggests that psychological control is a salient construct across cultures and that psychological control may be related to both internalizing and externalizing behaviors in young children.

Research on older children diagnosed with an anxiety disorder further supports the link between parental psychological control and children's emotional problems. Stark, Humphrey, Crook, and Lewis (1990) examined the perceived family environments of children diagnosed with anxiety disorders, depression, mixed anxiety and depression, and nondiagnosed children ages 9 to 14. They found that children from all three groups diagnosed with internalizing disorders perceive their families as less democratic and more enmeshed compared with controls. In addition, depressed children report more enmeshment and lower levels of autocracy compared to anxious children. Messer and Beidel (1994) compared the family environments of three groups of children in the third through sixth grade: children with test anxiety, children diagnosed with an anxiety disorder, and children who were nonanxious. Results indicate that children with anxiety disorders describe their families as more controlling and promoting less independence than the children with test anxiety or children who are nonanxious. Finally, Siqueland, Kendall, and Steinberg (1996) examined family interactions and parenting in families with a preadolescent child diagnosed with an anxiety disorder versus families with a nonanxious child. Observers rated parents of children with anxiety disorders as less likely to grant autonomy and more psychologically controlling than parents of children who did not have anxiety disorders. In addition, children with anxiety disorders rated their parents as less accepting and warm. In summary, then, past research suggests that parental psychological control likely has a generally negative impact on children's emotional and behavioral adjustment, and may be linked to anxiety and depression in middle childhood and adolescence.

Although many studies consistently link psychological control to behavior problems, observed effect sizes are typically small to moderate, similar to other dimensions of parenting, with correlations between parenting and adjustment in the .2 to .4 range (Bates, Pettit, Dodge, & Ridge, 1998). One reason for the small effect sizes typically reported in parenting research is that researchers often fail to take into account the fact that children with different temperaments are likely to be differentially susceptible to different types of parenting. As a result, strong effects of parenting among some children are averaged with weak or negligible effects of parenting among others, resulting in the sorts of small effect sizes that are ubiquitous in the literature. Recent research on the impact of parenting on child development stresses the importance of examining the interplay between parenting practices and child characteristics (Rubin & Mills, 1991; Thomas, 1984). Although parenting sometimes has direct effects on children, child characteristics, such as temperament, often interact with parenting to influence children's development (Kochanska, 1993, 1994; Thomas, 1984; chapter 4, this volume). Thus, the purpose of this study is to examine whether the deleterious influence of psychologically controlling parenting is accentuated among children with particular types of temperamental vulnerabilities.

PSYCHOLOGICAL CONTROL AND CHILD TEMPERAMENT

Because psychological control is an intrusion into the development of the child's self-expression and identity, it is likely that the child's temperament moderates the effects of psychological control on developmental outcomes. Psychologically controlling parents often manipulate, invalidate, and ignore children's feelings, presumably damaging children's ability to learn how to interpret and manage their emotions. Accordingly, children with a predisposition to strong negative emotional arousal may be more reactive to intrusive parental control and more vulnerable to its effects precisely because of its interference with children's emotional expression. Rubin and Mills (1991) proposed that internalizing disorders develop in childhood as an interaction between child temperament, specifically temperamental wariness or fear, and socialization experiences in the family. Inhibited children may actually elicit psychological control from their parents if their parents are attempting to protect a child they view as vulnerable.

In the past few years, several studies have examined the interactive effects of temperamental and family characteristics on children's socio-emotional adjustment (e.g., Ackerman, Kogos, Youngstrom, Schoff, & Izard, 1999; Belsky, Hsieh, & Crnic, 1998; Kochanska, 1991; Park, Belsky, Putnam, & Crnic, 1997; Rubin, Hastings, Chen, Stewart, & McNichol, 1998; Rubin & Mills, 1991). Promising results from these studies suggest that parenting accounts for considerably more variance in child outcomes when temperamental characteristics of the child are taken into consideration. Yet, this area represents a relatively new domain of inquiry in psychological research (Bates et al., 1998).

This study focuses on one important dimension of temperament that is prominent in the formulation of several contemporary models of temperament: negative reactivity (Goldsmith et al., 1987; Goldsmith, Buss, & Lemery, 1997; Kochanska, 1999; Rothbart, Ahadi, & Hershey, 1994; Rothbart & Bates, 1998).[1] Negative reactivity (also called negative affectivity) represents the child's tendency to react to stressors with high degrees of emotional lability, including anger, irritability, fear, or sadness (Rothbart & Ahadi, 1994). Children who are high in negative reactivity are at risk for developing both externalizing and internalizing problems. For example, Bates and colleagues have shown that a dimension of temperament assessed in infancy labeled "difficultness" (which reflects the mother's perception of the child's negative emotionality) predicts behavior problems at age 2 and externalizing behavior in early childhood (Bates, 1987; Bates, Bayles, Bennett, Ridge, & Brown, 1991; Lee & Bates, 1985). Maternal and paternal ratings of negative reactivity also predict both externalizing and internalizing

---

[1] In factor analyses of the Child Behavior Questionnaire (CBQ) and the Temperament Battery Assessment Questionnaire (TBAQ), negative reactivity has repeatedly emerged as clear factor, with a second factor labeled effortful control and a third factor labeled surgency/extraversion. These dimensions of temperament are believed to represent broad temperamental processes (Goldsmith & Rothbart, 1991; Rothbart & Ahadi, 1994). These factors have emerged in replications in the United States, Japan, and the People's Republic of China (Rothbart, 1999; Rothbart & Ahadi, 1994).

behaviors among preschool children (McClowry et al., 1994; Mun et al., 1999; Rothbart & Ahadi, 1994). Conversely, Eisenberg and colleagues found that children who demonstrate low negative reactivity are less likely to exhibit externalizing behaviors than other children (Eisenberg et al., 1996, 1997).

Although negative reactivity has been studied as a global higher order construct, recent findings on temperament and physiology suggest that sadness, anger, and fear are probably characterized by different neurological substrates and systems (Buss & Goldsmith, 1998; Rothbart & Bates, 1998). For example, anger appears to be regulated by an approach system, and fear is regulated by a withdrawal system (Derryberry & Rothbart, 1997). These systems are most likely related to different outcomes (Kagan, 1997). Rothbart et al. (1994) found that in 6- to 7-year-old children, the fear and sadness components of negative reactivity (*fearful distress*) were related to prosocial outcomes, whereas the anger component of negative reactivity (*irritable distress*) was predictive of aggression and antisocial activity. Research on the development of internalizing disorders suggests that temperamental inhibition (Kagan, 1997) and fearful wariness (Rubin & Mills, 1991) make children particularly susceptible to environmental stressors, such as psychological control. For these reasons, it is advisable to distinguish between these two types of negative reactivity (Rothbart & Ahadi, 1994; Rothbart & Bates, 1998).

It seems reasonable to suspect that children with a predisposition toward negative reactivity are especially harmed by psychological control. Children's predisposition toward irritable distress, anger, and frustration makes them especially likely to experience intrusive, coercive interchanges as highly aversive (McClowry et al., 1994; Rothbart & Ahadi, 1994; Wahler, 1990). Research also suggests that psychological control may be particularly harmful for children prone to fearful distress (Rubin & Mills, 1991). Yet, these same reactive or dysregulated children may not develop problems when their parents are sensitive and responsive to their emotional liabilities. Although there is likely a level of psychological control at which nearly all exposed children will develop socioemotional problems, at lower levels the effect of exposure to psychological control likely depends somewhat on the temperament of the child.

In addition to examining the role of child temperament in the relationship between psychological control and children's social and emotional development, we believe that researchers should also assess children's perceptions of psychological control. Indeed, it is only when researchers put the child back into the study of parenting that we will gain a better understanding of the ways in which child characteristics affect adjustment and interact with parenting.

THE IMPORTANCE OF ASSESSING THE CHILD'S PERCEPTION OF PSYCHOLOGICAL CONTROL

Because psychological control is in the "eye of the controlled," it is especially crucial that any assessment of this construct take into account the child's subjective experience. Despite an abundance of research on young children and families, few researchers have actually asked young children *themselves* about their experience of psychological control in particular or their own perceptions of their families in general. This is surprising in light of the prominent role of the parent–child relationship in the etiology of behavioral and emotional problems (Maccoby & Martin, 1983; Parke & Buriel, 1998). This dearth of research is in part a result of a lack of developmentally sensitive methods to assess children's perceptions of their environment.

Research attempting to link family processes and psychopathology in young children has ignored the child's perception of the parent–child relationship, and has instead relied on reports and observations by trained observers or parents (Sessa, Avenevoli, Steinberg, & Morris, 2001). This is largely because of concerns about young children's ability to provide reliable and valid reports of their experiences. Although research conducted earlier concluded that before age 8, young children tend to describe the behaviors of themselves and others using external, situational, unstable characteristics (Barenboim, 1981; Livesley & Bromley, 1973; Peevers & Secord, 1973; Scarlett, Press, & Crockett, 1971; Secord & Peevers, 1974; Shantz, 1983), more recent reviewers and researchers have questioned these previously accepted conclusions (Miller & Alois, 1989; Ridgeway, Waters, & Kuczaj, 1985). A more contemporary perspective suggests that developmental researchers have historically underestimated younger children's social cognitive competencies and their ability to report on their own experiences, mainly because of the methods used to assess children's beliefs and social understanding (Hart & Damon, 1986; Miller & Alois, 1989). For example, most early research on young children's perceptions of people used open-ended interview techniques, which require extensive verbal production and expressive skills. Because young children's verbal comprehension skills are better than their verbal expressive skills (Kuczaj, 1986), observed age-related differences in children's use of dispositional terms in their descriptions of others likely reflect linguistic immaturity rather than the absence of psychological constructions of others (Furman & Bierman, 1983; Rotenberg, 1982; Ruble & Rholes, 1981). The demand characteristics of the standard interview research situation (i.e., being questioned by an unfamiliar adult) have also likely inhibited young children's ability to provide psychologically meaningful information. When children have been interviewed by more "benign" interviewers, such as puppets, children as young as 3½ years old have been able to provide general descriptions of the internal states and emotions of themselves and others with adequate reliability (Eder, 1989, 1990; Eder, Gerlach, & Perlmutter, 1987). Indeed, there is ample evidence that suggests young children are capable of reporting on their social relationships and giving psychological descriptions of others; however, the challenge researchers face is devising assessment methods that reliably measure children's perceptions of the family while remaining developmentally appropriate.

Despite the difficulties inherent in this endeavor, researchers must recognize that children actively construct their environment, and as a result of their perceptions and interpretations, children make decisions about behaviors and learn about their social world (Grych, Seid, & Fincham, 1992). As Bronfenbrenner (1979) wrote, "The aspects of the environment that are most powerful in shaping the course of psychological growth are overwhelmingly those that have meaning to the person in a given situation" (p. 22). Certainly both objective and subjective reports of parenting provide important information about the child's social context; however, it may be the child's personal subjective interpretation of the family context that is most influential in shaping the child's social and emotional development (Boyce et al., 1998; Schaefer, 1965; Steinberg et al., 1992). We developed an age-appropriate interview to assess children's perceptions of their exposure to psychological control, because we believe only by evaluating parenting through the child's subjective experience can researchers truly understand the impact of the social context on children's psychosocial adjustment.

THIS STUDY

The primary purpose of this investigation is to examine the relationship between psychological control and young children's internalizing and externalizing problems and the role of temperament as a potential moderator of this connection. One strength of the current investigation is that we obtained reports on all constructs of interests from different informants. We obtained the child's own report of maternal psychological control. Children's temperament was assessed via maternal report, and, to avoid contamination between reports of temperament and reports of internalizing and externalizing problems, information on children's emotional and behavioral problems was obtained from their teachers.

Based on previous research, it was expected that children's report of psychological control would be related to their teachers' reports of internalizing and externalizing behaviors in school. Past research suggests a stronger link between internalizing behaviors and psychological control (Barber et al., 1994; Siqueland et al., 1996), which we expected. However, we also believed children who reported high parental psychological control would display more externalizing behaviors than their peers, given the high comorbidity of internalizing and externalizing found in young children (Garber, Quiggle, Panak, & Dodge, 1991). It also was hypothesized that irritable distress would be associated with externalizing problems, and to a lesser degree internalizing problems, and fearful distress would be associated with internalizing problems, and to a lesser degree externalizing problems.

The primary hypothesis of this study was that psychological control would have a more deleterious impact on children with more negative reactivity, including both irritable and fearful distress. More specifically, we hypothesized that psychological control would interact with irritable distress in the prediction of externalizing problems, and to a lesser extent internalizing problems, and that psychological control would interact with fearful distress in the prediction of internalizing problems, and to a lesser extent externalizing problems. Interactions for both internalizing and externalizing were expected for both temperament dimensions because of high comorbidity of internalizing and externalizing at this age (Garber et al., 1991) and difficulties in assessing internalizing in young children. We also examined the possibility of gender differences in the effects of psychological control, irritable and fearful distress, and their interaction, because there is a substantial amount of research suggesting boys at this age are more susceptible to risk factors for problem behaviors (Eme & Kavanaugh, 1995; Keenan & Shaw, 1997; Webster-Stratton, 1996).

Forty children (16 girls, 24 boys) and their mothers and teachers participated in this study. The children and their families were participating in a larger study examining contextual influences on child adjustment. This sample is a subset of the larger study and includes children with data on all constructs of interest.[2] Children were recruited from urban public schools, an advertisement in a free local parent's magazine, and paycheck inserts at a large urban university. Children's ages ranged from 6 years, 1 month, to 9 years, 8 months (M = 7 years, 7 months). Mothers ranged in age from 24 to 51 years (M = 37 years, SD = 7 years). All mothers except one were the biological mothers of the target children. Approximately 51% of the children resided in two-parent homes (40% of the parents were married and 11% of the parents reported that they were in steady marriage-like relationships). Forty-eight percent of the children lived in single-parent

---

[2] Exact numbers differ slightly in analyses because some of the children did not provide complete data on all measures.

homes (23% of the mother were separated, divorced, or widowed, and 25% had never been married).

The families came from diverse ethnic and socioeconomic backgrounds. Approximately 60% of the children were African American; 35% were Caucasian; and the remaining 5% were from other or mixed ethnic groups. Eight percent of the mothers had some high school education; 10% had completed high school or the equivalent; 38% had some college education; 15% had completed college; and 28% had some post college education or a professional degree. Income to needs ratios for this sample based on the 1998 poverty threshold ranged from .51 to 10.28, with a median ratio of 2.64. According to income to needs general guidelines (Klebanov, Brooks-Gunn, McCarton, & McCormick, 1998),[3] 23% of the sample was poor (ratio of 0 to 1.5), 35% was middle income (ratio of 1.5 to 3.0) and 30% was affluent (ratio > 3.0). Five mothers did not provide information on family income.

Data were gathered during 1½–2-hour visits in the homes of participating families. During the visit, children were administered the Child Puppet Interview—Parenting Scale (CPI-P; Sessa et al., 2001) and mothers completed a series of questionnaires about their children and their child's home environment. With parental permission, teachers were mailed questionnaires to assess the child's behavior in school. Families were paid $40 for their time and teachers were paid $5 for completing the questionnaires. All procedures comply with APA ethics guidelines and were reviewed and approved by the university's human subjects committee.

Psychological Control Scale of the Child Puppet Interview—Parenting Scales (CPI-P)

Children's report of maternal psychological control was obtained using the Psychological Control Subscale of the CPI-P, a measure developed at Temple University in collaboration with the MacArthur Foundation Research Network on Psychopathology and Development (Sessa et al., 2001). The interview was administered to children individually, and children's responses were videotaped for later coding. This interview was strengthened by the methodological work of Eder (1987, 1989, 1990), who used a puppet interview to assess self-concept, and Measelle, Ablow, Cowan, and Cowan

---

[3] The income-to-needs ratio is a particularly useful measure of income because it provides an index of the family's socioeconomic status relative to current national averages and to the current threshold of poverty, and it also takes into account the number of adults and children living in the household. The income-to-needs ratio is calculated by dividing the pre-tax yearly household income by the official U.S. poverty threshold for a household of the specified size for the year during which data were collected (Duncan, Brooks-Gunn, & Klebanov, 1994). Poverty is defined as an income-to-needs ratio at or below 1.5 (Klebanov, Brooks-Gunn, McCarton, & McCormick, 1998) and an income-to-needs ratio above 3.0 designates affluence (J. Brooks-Gunn, personal communication, March 30, 1998).

(1998), who developed the Berkeley Puppet Interview to assess children's perceptions of marital conflict, emotional well-being, and self-competence.

Using an opposing statements format similar to that used by Harter (1982), two identical puppets present a series of statements that assess parental behavior. For example, one puppet says, "When I am bad, my mom ignores me," and the other says, "When I am bad, my mom does not ignore me." The child is asked to choose the puppet that is more like him or her by either pointing to the puppet, repeating what the puppet said, or putting the statement in his or her own words. To ensure that interviewers do not inadvertently reinforce certain choices, children's responses are always validated by one of the puppets (e.g., after each response, the puppet selected by the child indicates acknowledgement and agreement with the child—"My Mom does that too"). Children who have better verbal skills or who are more comfortable with verbal expression often expand on the item they select and spontaneously offer more descriptive details about their parent. More important, children who are not adept at or comfortable with verbal expression can simply point to the puppet that is more like him- or herself. When a child provides a response that is unclear or does not match either puppet's statement, the interviewer uses the puppets to probe for clarification by asking, "Which one of us is more like you?" Probing is kept to a minimum so that children do not feel as though they provided the "wrong" answer with their first response. In this study, children reported on maternal behavior because so many of the parents in our study were single mothers. However, it is possible to use the Child Puppet Interview to gather information on paternal behavior as well.

The CPI-P was developed through a series of pilot studies with more than 100 children in the Northeast and Southwest with diverse socioeconomic and racial backgrounds. Initially, a test-development study was conducted on 27 4- to 5-year-old children to evaluate the wording, syntax, and comprehensibility of 82 item pairs designed to assess the mother–child relationship (Sessa et al., 2001). These items were generated from a review of existing parent–child measures and by preschool teachers, daycare providers, developmental psychologists, and graduate students familiar with the parenting literature. Sample items for the original psychological control scale (6 items) included, "When I get dressed, I/my mommy picks out the clothes"; "My mommy lets/doesn't let me get washed by myself"; "When I am bad, my mommy stops/doesn't stop talking to me." Items in this scale reflected both autonomy granting and emotional control and manipulation.

Initial analyses indicated that preschool children were only able to reliably differentiate three dimensions of the mother–child relationship: structure, warmth/responsiveness, and hostility (Sessa et al., 2001). Despite our belief that children this age could reliably report on psychological control, our results suggested otherwise. Item analysis and Cronbach's alpha ($\alpha = .42$) for the preschool sample suggest that children of this age may not be capable of providing reliable reports of psychological control. We suspect children's inability to reliably report on this dimension of parenting is in part a result of the complexity of this dimension. This same sample of preschoolers gave internally consistent responses for parental responsiveness, structure, and hostility scales, and results of a one-month test–retest study indicate that preschoolers' perceptions of these parenting dimensions are stable over time (Sessa et al., 2001).

The revised psychological control subscale was developed later to determine whether first- and second-grade children could provide reliable information on this parenting construct. The psychometric analyses of the current scale suggest that it is a reliable and valid measure when used with children ages 6 to 9 (Morris, 1999; Morris et al., in press). Using a sample of 63 children in first and second grade from diverse backgrounds, we found that children of this age can give internally consistent responses ($\alpha = .73$) when asked about their parent's use of psychological control. The different results for preschoolers and first and second graders are not surprising given the more advanced cognitive abilities of first- and second-grade children compared to preschool children (Piaget, 1959). Indeed, first and second graders have a better understanding of emotions, the perspectives of others, and the causes of behavior compared with preschoolers (Siegler, 1991; Thompson, 1991).

Item pairs for the current version of the psychological control subscale, which was used in this study, were also generated from a review of the parenting literature and of existing parent report and adolescent report measures of psychological control. The current scale differs from the original in several important ways. First, it focuses specifically on psychological control, and any items reflecting autonomy-granting were eliminated. Second, some of the items reflect more complex parental behaviors, which older children can more easily understand. Sample items include, "My mom gets mad/doesn't always get mad whenever I disagree with her"; "My mom likes/does not like to hear my ideas about things." The entire set of items is listed in appendix 5A.

The CPI-P is coded on a 3-point scale, with a "1" given for an answer indicating that the mother is low on the parenting dimension being assessed and a "3" given for an answer indicating that the mother is high on that dimension. A "2" is given when the child indicates that both responses equally apply to him or her. All videotapes were coded twice by trained research assistants (interrater agreement was 98%), and discrepancies were resolved by an advanced graduate student. A mean score ranging from "1" to "3" was calculated using all the scale items, with higher scores indicating greater maternal psychological control.

There is also evidence for the validity of the psychological control subscale of the CPI-P. Children's reports of psychological control have been found to correlate with teacher reports of emotional and behavioral problems

(Morris, 1999). Further, correlations among psychological control and other CPI-P parenting scales suggest that these dimensions of parenting are perceived as conceptually distinct, despite related dimensions being somewhat correlated. Pearson correlations between responsiveness and psychological control ($r = -.24$, $p < 10$) and hostility and psychological control ($r = .40$, $p < .01$) are moderate, but appear to represent distinct scales. The correlation between structure–demandingness and psychological control ($r = -.13$) is low (Morris et al., in press; Sessa et al., 2001).

Child Behavior Questionnaire (CBQ)

Maternal report of child temperament was assessed using the Child Behavior Questionnaire (CBQ; Goldsmith & Rothbart, 1991), a widely used parent report measure of child temperament. The CBQ has been demonstrated to exhibit adequate reliability and validity (Goldsmith & Rothbart, 1991; Rothbart, 1999). The version of the CBQ used in this study is a shortened 99-item version consisting of 12 scales (Askan et al., 1999). This study uses information from two scales: anger and fear. Each item on the CBQ is rated on a 7-point Likert-type scale, ranging from "extremely untrue" (1) to "extremely true" (7). Internal consistency estimates for the CBQ scales range from .64 to .94 (Goldsmith & Rothbart, 1991). Based on the work of Rothbart and colleagues (Rothbart, 1999; Rothbart et al., 1994), the scales were designed to assess the following temperament dimensions:

- *Irritable distress*. The irritable distress component of negative reactivity (conceptualized as distinct from fearful distress) was assessed using the anger scale of the CBQ. The anger scale taps the amount of negative affect related to the interruption of ongoing tasks or goal-blocking. Sample items include, "Gets quite frustrated when prevented from doing something s/he wants"; "Gets mad when provoked by other children"; and "Gets angry when s/he can't find something s/he wants to play with."
- *Fearful distress*. The fearful distress component of negative reactivity was assessed using the fear scale of the CBQ. The fear scale taps the amount of negative affect, including worry, unease, or nervousness, related to anticipated pain or distress in threatening situations. Sample items for the fear scale (6 items) include "Is afraid of loud noises"; "Is frightened by nightmares"; and "Is afraid of the dark."

Ontario Child Health Study Scales (OCHS)

Teacher report of problem behavior was assessed via a modified version of the internalizing and externalizing scales of the Ontario Health Study

Scales (OCHS). The OCHS assesses problem behavior symptoms associated with *DSM-III* childhood psychiatric disorders (American Psychiatric Association, 1980; Boyle et al., 1987; Boyle, Offord, Racine, Szatmari, & Sanford, 1993) and contains items adapted from the Child Behavior Checklist (CBCL) (Achenbach & Edelbrock, 1981). The OCHS has good internal consistency, test–retest reliability, and agreement with psychiatrists' diagnoses, and has the advantage of being much shorter than the CBCL (Offord, Boyle, & Racine, 1991). The modified OCHS contains 35 symptom items rated on a Likert-type scale (0 = "rarely applies," 1 = "applies somewhat," 2 = "certainly applies"). Broadband scales are computed to assess internalizing (e.g., worries about things in the future; needs to be told over and over that things are okay) and externalizing (e.g., kicks, bites, or hits other children; defiant, talks back to adults) symptoms. Cronbach's alphas in this sample were .95 for the externalizing scale and .78 for the internalizing scale.

RESEARCH FINDINGS

Means and standard deviations for the major variables are presented in Table 5-1. In preliminary analyses, sex differences were examined with respect to the indicators of negative reactivity, the externalizing and internalizing composites, and psychological control. There were no significant sex differences in mean scores on any of the variables.

Interaction of Psychological Control and Irritable Distress in the Prediction of Externalizing and Internalizing Problems

Relations among constructs are presented in Table 5-2. Teacher reports of externalizing and internalizing problems were moderately correlated, sug-

TABLE 5-1
Means and Standard Deviations of Variables

Variable	Min	Max	Mean	SD
Psychological control[a]	1.00	2.54	1.61	.38
Irritable distress[b]	2.44	6.67	4.46	1.01
Fearful distress[b]	1.67	5.67	3.66	.97
Externalizing[c]	.00	1.65	.42	.48
Internalizing[c]	.07	1.07	.45	.27

[a]Possible scores range from 1 to 3.
[b]Possible scores range from 1 to 7.
[c]Possible scores range from 0 to 2.

TABLE 5-2
Correlation Matrix of Variables

Variable	1	2	3	4	5
1. Psychological control	1.00				
2. Irritable distress	.03	1.00			
3. Fearful distress	.04	.53***	1.00		
4. Externalizing	.22	.42*	.04	1.00	
5. Internalizing	.11	.42*	−.05	.44**	1.00

⁺p < .10; *p < .05; **p < .01; ***p < .001.

gesting some comorbidity of distinct constructs. Irritable distress and fearful distress were moderately correlated. Despite this correlation, these dimensions were kept separate in the analyses because of research suggesting different physiological underpinnings for irritable and fearful distress as well as differential associations with adjustment outcomes (Rothbart et al., 1994). As predicted, irritable distress was directly related to teacher reports of externalizing and internalizing behaviors. Contrary to expectations, fearful distress was not significantly related to internalizing or externalizing behaviors in school. Relations between psychological control and externalizing problems and psychological control and internalizing behaviors were weaker than expected.

A series of stepwise regression equations were computed to explore whether child report of maternal psychological control and mother report of child temperament interacted to predict teacher-reported emotional and behavioral problems. Regressions predicting externalizing and internalizing problems were computed by entering maternal control and one of the temperament dimensions (irritable distress, fearful distress) on the first step and the interaction between psychological control and the temperament dimension on the second step. Each of the independent variables and their interactions were centered (M = 0) before including them in the regression equations to minimize multicollinearity (Aiken & West, 1991). For all regression with interactions, separate regressions were run separately for boys and girls to see if similar patterns held for both genders.

As expected, psychological control did interact with irritable distress to predict internalizing behaviors (see Table 5-3). Following Aiken and West's (1991) procedures for interpreting and graphing interactions, unstandardized betas (slopes) were calculated for children scoring high (75th percentile) and low (25th percentile) in irritable distress to examine the relationship between maternal psychological control and internalizing behaviors at different levels of irritable distress. The Wald test (STATA, 1997) was used to test the significance of the slope for psychological control at high and low levels of irritable distress. These analyses show that among children

TABLE 5-3
Regression Analyses Predicting Internalizing Behaviors From
Psychological Control, Irritable Distress, and Their Interaction

	Internalizing		Internalizing With Interaction	
	B	β	B	β
Psychological control	.07	.10	.08	.12
Irritable distress	.10*	.36*	.10*	.36*
Psychological control Irritable distress			.28*	.34*
R^2 for equation	.15		.26	
F for equation	$F_{(2, 36)} = 3.06^+$		$F_{(3, 35)} = 4.12^*$	

Note: B is the unstandardized coefficient and β is the standardized coefficient.
$^+p < .10$, $^*p < .05$

high in irritable distress, children's reports of psychological control predicted teacher reports of internalizing behaviors (slope = .28, $F_{(1.35)} = 4.11$, $p < .05$); but among children low in irritable distress, psychological control did not predict internalizing behaviors (slope = −.08; see Figure 5-1). Separate regressions for girls and boys examining the interaction between psychological control and irritable distress in the prediction of internalizing indicated similar patterns for both groups.

Analyses of externalizing behaviors did indicate different patterns among girls versus boys, however. Specifically, the combination of high psychological control and high irritable distress had a much stronger impact on externalizing behavior among boys (see Table 5-4). Using the procedure defined previously for examining children high and low in irritable distress, we found that among boys with high levels of irritable distress, psychological control predicted externalizing (slope = .97, $F_{(1.20)} = 11.39$, $p < .01$). However, among boys with low irritable distress, psychological control did not significantly predict externalizing (slope = .32; see Figure 5-2). The relation between psychological control and externalizing was not significant among girls, regardless of their level of irritable distress.

Interaction of Psychological Control and Fearful Distress in the Prediction of Internalizing and Externalizing Problems

Although it was hypothesized that fearful distress would interact with psychological control to predict internalizing behaviors, this was not found to be the case (β = .29, $p = .10$; $F_{(3, 35)} = 1.17$, $p = .34$), even after examining groups high (slope = .20) and low (slope = −.16) in fearful distress. Nonsignificant results were found for both girls and boys when regressions were run separately. As expected, fearful distress did interact, at

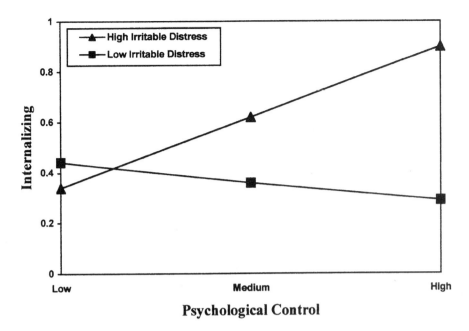

Figure 5-1. The Relationship Between Internalizing and Psychological Control for Children High (75th Percentile) and Low (25th Percentile) in Irritable Distress. Low, medium, and high psychological control correspond to scores of 1, 2, and 3 on the psychological control scale. *Note:* Although figure may suggest that psychological control has a positive effect on adjustment for children with temperamental vulnerabilities (low irritable/fearful distress), the slopes for these subgroups were minimal and not statistically significant.

the trend level, with psychological control to predict externalizing problems (see Table 5-5). Unstandardized betas (slopes) were calculated for children scoring high (75th percentile) and low (25th percentile) on fearful distress to examine the relationship between maternal psychological control and externalizing problems at high and low levels of fearful distress (Aiken & West, 1991). Among children high in fearful distress, children's reports of psychological control predicted teacher reports of externalizing behaviors (slope = .45, $F(1.36) = 4.76$, $p < .05$); but among children low in fearful distress, psychological control was not predictive of internalizing behaviors (slope = −.21; see Figure 5-3). Again, analyses of externalizing behaviors did indicate different patterns among girls versus boys, with boys indicating a similar pattern to the entire sample (see Table 5-5). Among boys high in fearful distress, psychological control predicted externalizing (slope = .65, $F(1,20)$ β = 4.83, $p < .05$). However, among boys low in fearful distress, psychological control did not significantly predict externalizing (slope = −.42). The relationship between psychological control and externalizing was not significant among girls, regardless of their level of fearful distress.

TABLE 5-4
Regression Analyses Predicting Externalizing Behaviors From
Psychological Control, Irritable Distress, and Their Interaction

	Externalizing		Externalizing With Interaction	
	B	β	B	β
Psychological control	.27	.21	.28	.22
Irritable distress	.19*	.39*	.19*	.40*
Psychological control Irritable distress			.18	.12
R^2 for equation	.20		.21	
F for equation	$F(2, 37) = 4.58^*$		$F(3, 36) = 3.25^*$	
Regression for girls				
Psychological control	.07	.07	.05	.05
Irritable distress	.04	.12	.05	.13
Psychological control Irritable distress			−.07	−.06
R^2 for equation	.03		.03	
F for equation	$F(2, 13) = .19$		$F(3, 12) = .13$	
Regression for boys				
Psychological control	.66*	.47*	.63*	.45*
Irritable distress	.37**	.67**	.37***	.67***
Psychological control Irritable distress			.52+	.27+
R^2 for equation	.47		.54	
F for equation	$F(2, 21) = 9.19^{**}$		$F(3, 20) = 7.74^{**}$	

Note: B is the unstandardized coefficient and β is the standardized coefficient.
$^+p \le .10$, $^*p < .05$, $^{**}p < .01$, $^{***}p < .001$

CONCLUSION

Psychological theories about the developmental pathway of internalizing disorders have pointed to the potentially deleterious impact of exposure to psychologically controlling parents. The results of the present analyses suggest, however, that exposure to psychological control may have stronger effects among some children than others. In particular, this study indicates that children with temperamental biases toward negative reactivity are more likely to experience emotional and behavioral problems in the face of parental psychological control than are children exposed to similar parenting practices but with a less vulnerable temperament. More specifically, children prone to experience irritable distress are more likely to display internalizing behaviors when their parents are psychologically controlling. Among boys with this temperamental vulnerability, psychological control is also associated with higher levels of externalizing problems. Children with a temperamental vulnerability toward fearful distress are more likely to display exter-

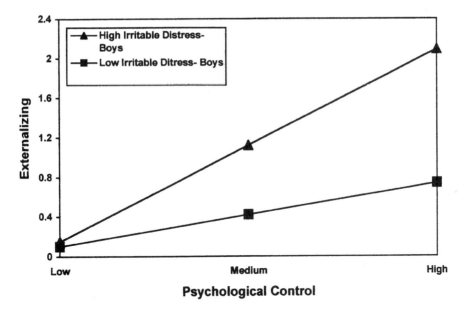

Figure 5-2. The Relationship Between Externalizing and Psychological Control for Boys With High (75th Percentile) and Low (25th Percentile) Irritable Distress. Low, medium, and high psychological control correspond to centered scores of 1, 2, and 3 on the psychological control scale.

nalizing problems when their parents are psychologically controlling, and this relationship is particularly strong among boys. These findings are in line with past research that suggests that boys are more at risk for developing problem behaviors than girls and at significantly greater risk for externalizing problems in particular behaviors (Eme & Kavanaugh, 1995; Keenan & Shaw, 1997; Webster-Stratton, 1996). However we must caution against over-interpreting these sex differences for girls because of the small number of girls when the sample was split by gender. Nevertheless, it would appear that among boys, exposure to psychological control is a nonspecific stressor that may be associated with very different types of problems.

This is the first research, to our knowledge, that assesses young children's perceptions of parental psychological control. Our initial findings suggest that preschool children younger than age 6 are not capable of providing internally consistent reports of maternal psychological control. However, results with older children (ages 6 to 9) indicate that children can reliably report on this and other dimensions of their parents' behavior, provided the assessment is done in a developmentally sensitive fashion. These results are in line with cognitive developmental literature that suggests children's cognitive abilities develop considerably as children shift from preschool to early elementary school (Piaget, 1959; Siegler, 1991). Our

TABLE 5-5
Regression Analyses Predicting Externalizing Behaviors From Psychological Control, Fearful Distress, and Their Interaction

	Externalizing		Externalizing With Interaction	
	B	β	B	β
Psychological control	.28	.22	.18	.14
Fearful distress	.01	.03	.05	.11
Psychological control			.48[+]	.32[+]
Fearful distress				
R^2 for equation	.05		.14	
F for equation	$F(2, 37) = .94$		$F(3, 36) = 1.95$	
Regression for girls				
Psychological control	.25	.24	.24	.23
Fearful distress	−.11	−.29	−.01	−.27
Psychological control			.07	.05
Fearful distress				
R^2 for equation	.09		.09	
F for equation	$F(2, 13) = .66$		$F(3, 12) = .42$	
Regression for Boys				
Psychological control	.40	.29	.17	.12
Fearful distress	.11	.20	.12	.22
Psychological control			.72*	.45*
Fearful distress				
R^2 for equation	.10		.27	
F for equation	$F(2, 21) = 1.16$		$F(3, 20) = 2.48^{+}$	

Note: B is the unstandardized coefficient and β is the standardized coefficient.
[+]$p \leq .10$, *$p < .05$

research also suggests that the Child Puppet Interview can be used within an economically and ethnically diverse sample for children of the appropriate age. We agree with Boyce et al. (1998) that researchers have not paid sufficient attention to the child's subjective experience of the social context in the study of psychopathology, and hope that the findings of this study will encourage other researchers to assess children's perceptions of the environment, with particular care in creating developmentally appropriate measures.

The direct links between temperament and symptomatology found in this study are consistent with previous research. Mother-reported irritable distress was related to teacher report of both externalizing and internalizing behaviors. This is consistent with findings that negative emotionality in infancy and middle childhood is linked to behavioral and emotional problems in children (Bates, 1987; Bates et al., 1991; Earls & Jung, 1987; Eisenberg et al., 1997; Lengua, West, & Sandler, 1998; McClowry et al., 1994; Mun et al., 1999; Rothbart et al., 1994). Although previous studies

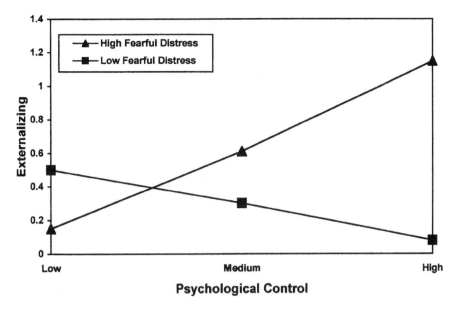

Figure 5-3. The Relationship Between Externalizing and Psychological Control for Children High (75th Percentile) and Low (25th Percentile) in Fearful Distress. Low, medium, and high psychological control correspond to centered scores of 1, 2, and 3 on the psychological control scale. *Note:* Although figure may suggest that psychological control has a positive effect on adjustment for children with temperamental vulnerabilities (low irritable/fearful distress), the slopes for these subgroups were minimal and not statistically significant.

have tended to combine irritable and fearful distress into a construct of negative reactivity, our findings were in accordance with the work of Rothbart et al. (1994), who found that these components of negative reactivity differentially predicted child outcomes, with irritable distress predicting externalizing behaviors and fearful distress predicting prosocial outcomes. The lack of strong associations between fearful distress and outcomes in this study, including internalizing behaviors, may indeed suggest that this component of negative reactivity is not related to child adjustment. However, it may be the case that the effects of fearful distress are only apparent in extreme groups, as Kagan, Reznick, and Gibbons (1989) have demonstrated in their research on inhibited children. Indeed, Kagan and colleagues have found that children classified as highly inhibited (in the top 15 to 20%) are likely to display internalizing symptoms, whereas children not in this group display few, if any, internalizing symptoms (Kagan, 1997, 1998; Kagan et al., 1989).

Contrary to expectations, no significant direct links were found between child report of maternal psychological control and teacher report of problem behavior. The relationship between maternal psychological control and internalizing and externalizing problems was only found among children high in negative reactivity. Rather than concluding that psychological control does not have a negative impact on children without these temperamental vulnerabilities, there are several likely reasons why we did not find main effects for psychological control. First, the limited number of children in our sample limits power for detecting small and moderate effects. Second, research suggests that psychological control may be more related to internalizing than externalizing problems (Rubin & Mills, 1991; Siqueland et al., 1996; Stark et al., 1990). Internalizing problems are difficult to detect at this age, and teachers, who reported on emotional and behavioral problems in this study, are arguably less likely to take note of withdrawn and anxious behaviors than aggressive and antisocial behaviors. Future research using parents' or clinicians' reports of internalizing behaviors may prove more sensitive to such effects.

The findings of this study provide support for the general proposition that child temperament interacts with family socialization in the development of internalizing (e.g., Barber, 1992; Rubin & Mills, 1991; Stark, Humphrey, Laurent, Livingston, Christopher, 1993) and externalizing disorders (Belsky et al., 1998; Rubin, et al., 1998). Our findings suggest that children with a temperamental predisposition toward irritable distress are particularly at risk for developing emotional and behavioral problems in the face of psychological control. These findings are in accordance with the work of Rothbart et al. (1994), who found that children with a predisposition toward irritable distress displayed more social and emotional problems compared to children with other temperamental vulnerabilities. We hypothesized that among children high in fearful or irritable distress, psychological control would be associated with externalizing and internalizing behaviors. However, we expected the strongest relationships between fearful distress and internalizing problems and irritable distress and externalizing problems. Our results paint a somewhat different picture. Among children high in fearful distress, psychological control is related to externalizing problems, especially among boys; and among children high in irritable distress, psychological control is related to internalizing problems and also externalizing problems among boys. There are several possible reasons for these findings. There is high comorbidity among internalizing and externalizing in our sample, as found in other research on children this age (Garber et al., 1991). Further, fearful distress and irritable distress are moderately correlated (see Table 5-2), suggesting that fearful children are also angry and vice versa, and display a variety of emotional and behavioral problems.

We believe that adolescents with a predisposition or personality characterized by wariness and fear, or high in negative reactivity, also will be more susceptible to the deleterious effects of psychological control. To date, most research on temperament is typically done in infancy and early childhood because temperament in adolescence and adulthood is difficult to assess and tends to be called personality (Rothbart & Bates, 1998). However, future research should consider examining adolescent characteristics and psychological control, and would likely benefit from assessing personality and physiological indicators of temperament.

Research on psychological control of children and adolescents should also explore the relationship between parent and family characteristics and psychological control. Although not part of a current investigation, in our sample we found that child report of psychological control was also associated with maternal report of her own behavioral inhibition ($\rho = .27$, $p < .05$), assessed via the Behavioral Inhibition, Behavioral Activation Scale (BIS/BAS, Carver & White, 1994). The behavioral inhibition system is linked to anxiety proneness, is sensitive to signals of punishment and novelty, and inhibits behavior that may lead to negative or painful outcomes (Gray, 1982); sample items include, "Even if something bad is about to happen to me, I rarely experience fear or nervousness" (reverse-coded); "If I think something unpleasant is going to happen I usually get pretty 'worked up'"; "I worry about making mistakes." This finding is in line with research suggesting that psychologically controlling parents are likely to be more overprotective and anxious compared to nonpsychologically controlling parents (Hetherington & Martin, 1986). Factors such as parents' personality as well as other contextual variables, such as stress, may also affect parental psychological control. Barber (1992) posed a model of psychopathology in which family stress affects parenting, specifically psychological control, and in turn has a negative affect on children's development. This model is in line with other research (e.g., Fauber et al., 1990) and should be examined empirically in relation to parental psychological control and children's emotional and behavioral problems. Indeed, a family systems approach to assessing psychological control in the family and its relationship to family interaction patterns and characteristics may shed light on the ways in which psychological control is exacerbated and maintained within the family system.

One important strength of this study is its use of independent informants for all of the major constructs of interest. Teachers are an important source of information about child symptomatology because they are presumably less biased than parents and because they possess a larger comparison base against which they can judge the behavior of different children. We also believe that the child is an essential informant of parenting behavior because it is the child's own experience of this behavior that is likely to have the greatest impact on the child's subsequent development. We must mention that it is possible that children prone to irritable and fearful distress describe their parents as more psychologically controlling because of their temperamental bias. However, there are several reasons to believe that this is not the case. First, the correlations between irritable and fearful distress and child report of psychological control are near zero ($r = .03$, $r = .04$, respectively). Second, the reports of temperament and psychological control come from independent sources. Nevertheless, it would be valuable to replicate the findings of this study using different informants. Kagan (1998), for example, warned against the exclusive use of parent report of temperament. He argued that parent report ignores the physiological correlates of temperament, and that parents do not have the expertise or training of researchers who observe temperamental patterns. Although this view is not held by all researchers (see Rothbart & Bates, 1998, for a different viewpoint), using multiple informants and assessment techniques in measuring temperament would strengthen this type of research.

Multimethod assessments of temperament also would reduce the likelihood that observed associations between temperament and symptomatology may be a result of item overlap in assessment measures. There may be minimal content overlap among irritable distress items and externalizing items used in this study, but fearful distress is not predictive of internalizing behaviors, suggesting that item overlap is not a problem for this construct. Although the issue of item overlap is always a concern in cross-sectional research on temperament and child outcomes, Lengua et al. (1998) have found that temperament and child adjustment remain correlated even after the removal of similar items on temperament and symptomatology questionnaires.

As in most nonexperimental studies of family relationships, the direction of parent–child effects cannot be determined, and definitive claims about causality cannot be drawn. It is known that children exert influences on parenting, and to some extent it is likely that problem behaviors preceded and elicited maternal negative behaviors in our sample (Anderson, Lytton, & Romney, 1986; Lytton, 1990). It may well be the case that children who have emotional and behavioral problems and who exhibit irritable and fearful distress elicit more psychological control from their parents. Relevant longitudinal designs are needed to address issues of causality. Also, caution should be taken in assuming that effects were not detected in the current study (such as direct effects of psychological control, effects for fearful distress, or the prediction of internalizing problems in general) would not be found with a larger sample.

Despite these limitations, this study offers additional evidence that child temperament likely moderates the relationship between parenting practices and children's externalizing and internalizing behaviors. Our suspicion is that children prone to negative reactivity are more susceptible to many different environmental stressors, of which parental psychological control is just one (see Steinberg & Avenevoli, 2000). The findings of this study suggest that the next generation of research attempting to predict child adjustment from contextual variables should examine the interaction of context and temperament, rather than examine either one of these factors alone.

FUTURE DIRECTIONS FOR THE STUDY OF PSYCHOLOGICAL CONTROL

Inconsistencies in our two psychological control scales and our evaluation of the literature on psychological control and other related parenting dimensions lead us to a reevaluation of psychological control and to some new ideas on ways to assess this construct in future research. We wondered if including both autonomy-granting and psychological control items in the preschool scale, whereas the first- and second-grade scale contained only psychological control items, contributed to some of the reliability problems with the measure. Indeed, Barber, Bean, and Erickson (chapter 9, this volume) caution against assessing these two dimensions as opposite ends of a continuum. Also, psychological control is measured in many studies with adolescents and older children in a variety of ways (e.g., intrusiveness, negative parenting, overprotectiveness, enmeshment, the absence of psychological autonomy), causing confusion in the literature.

We suggest that psychological control is a type of coercive, passive–aggressive control that is hostile toward the child. Psychological control is manifested primarily through covert strategies (invalidating feelings, making a child feel guilty, taking away a child's freedom to make decisions). In examining these covert strategies, different domains over which parents exhibit psychological control become evident. We suggest that there are three primary domains through which parents exert psychological control, control over *cognitions, emotions,* and *behaviors,* each of which may have different effects on children's development. It is likely that these three domains of psychological control are related, but we posit that they may be manifested in differing degrees and that it is possible for them to occur independently. The result of each of these three domains of psychological control is still dependency and control over children's psychological development. A brief analysis of these three domains follows.

First, the cognitive domain reflects parents' psychological control over children's cognitive development and expression of thoughts. This view of psychological control can be seen as the absence of autonomy and democracy (e.g., Steinberg, 1990), and emphasizes parents' control over children's identity development. This domain of psychological control is often reflected in parental attempts to constrain verbal and individual expression, and results in a lack of children's independent thinking and expression of opinions and ideas. This type of psychological control is especially harmful during adolescence, when adolescents are becoming more independent and individ-uated from their families (Steinberg, 1990). Second, the emotional domain reflects parents' control and manipulation of children's emotions. Parents exert this type of psychological control by withdrawing their love from children and manipulating their own emotional responses toward the child or by constraining children's emotional expressions and invalidating children's emotions. Early research on love withdrawal suggests that it may be less harmful than other emotional manipulation if it is in combination with parental warmth and responsiveness (Becker, 1964). However, other forms of emotional control or children's belief that parental love is contingent on their behavior are likely to be associated with emotional and behavioral problems, particularly overregulation of emotional responses because of fear of invalidation or rejection. Third, the behavioral domain reflects psycholog-ical control exerted through the restriction of children's behaviors, and is seen primarily as overprotectiveness in the literature (Bowen, Vitaro, Kerr, & Pelletier, 1995; Hetherington & Martin, 1986). It is important to distinguish between behavioral control and psychological control via behavioral manip-ulation. Steinberg (1990) defined *behavioral control*, which is associated with adolescent adjustment, as the level of monitoring and limit-setting that parents maintain. The goals of behavioral control are socialization and behavioral regulation. In contrast, psychological control via behavioral con-straint is reflected in parents' exclusion of children from outside influences and opportunities, resulting in dependency. This lack of outside influence and opportunity restricts children's social interactions and their ability to learn social skills, limiting their behavioral experience (Hetherington & Martin, 1986). Because many of the behaviors parents restrict may be similar in behavioral control and psychological control, researchers must assess the parents' goals for restricting behavior. In addition, it is important to assess the reasons children believe they are being restricted, and children's beliefs about their parents' goals may affect adjustment.

We did not examine these components of psychological control in this investigation because our measure of psychological control was not designed to capture these elements of control separately. We did conduct some post-hoc exploratory analyses examining these domains using the current psychological control scale of the CPI-P, and our results were inclusive.[4]

---

[4] Items were categorized conceptually according to their control domain and alphas for the resulting scales were examined. Five items (1, 3, 4, 7, 9; see appendix 5A for items) were labeled as reflecting the emotional domain of psychological control, and eight items were categorized as reflecting the cognitive domain of psychological control (2, 5, 6, 8, 10, 11, 12, 13; see appendix 5A for items). There were no items in this scale that reflected the behavioral domain. Cronbach's alpha for the cognitive items suggest adequate internal consistency ($\alpha = .62$), whereas the internal consistency for the emotional items was not acceptable ($\alpha = .44$). Associations between the cognitive domain and child adjustment were weaker than with the entire scale, but were very similar with respect to pattern and direction.

However, we believe that these domains of control are worth exploring in future research with measures designed to specifically capture these specific domains, and with larger samples in which items reflecting these domains can be examined factor analytically.

An examination of the effects of psychological control on children and new conceptualizations of psychological control highlight the deleterious impact of this type of parental control on children's psychosocial development. In future research, interactive effects of psychological control and family and child characteristics should be explored to create a clearer picture of the specific ways in which psychological control impedes psychological and emotional adjustment. This chapter also indicates that future research endeavoring to examine children and adolescents' subjective experience of psychological control may prove fruitful in increasing our understanding of the development of emotional and behavioral problems. It is believed that a more thorough assessment of the processes that surround psychological control, and its specific domains, will shed light on the ways in which psychological control affects children and adolescents' social and emotional development.

REFERENCES

Achenbach, T. M., & Edelbrock, C. S. (1981). Behavioral problems and competencies by parents of normal and disturbed children aged four through sixteen. *Monographs of the Society for Research on Child Development, 46* (188).

Ackerman, B. P., Kogos, J., Youngstrom, E., Schoff, K., & Izard, C. (1999). Family instability and the problem behaviors of children from economically disadvantaged families. *Developmental Psychology, 35,* 258–268.

Aiken, L. S., & West, S. G. (1991). *Multiple regression: Testing and interpreting interactions.* Newbury Park, CA: Sage.

American Psychiatric Association. (1980). Diagnostic and statistical manual of mental disorders. Washington, D.C.: Author.

Anderson, K. E., Lytton, H., & Romney, D. M. (1986). Mothers' interactions with normal and conduct-disordered boys: Who affects whom? *Developmental Psychology, 22,* 604–609.

Askan, N., Goldsmith, H. H., Smider, N. A., Essex, M. J., Clark, R., Hyde, J. S., Klein, M. H., & Vandell, D. L. (1999). Derivation and prediction of temperamental types among preschoolers. *Developmental Psychology, 35,* 958–971.

Barber, B. K. (1992). Family, personality, and adolescent problem behaviors. *Journal of Marriage and the Family, 54,* 69–79.

Barber, B. K. (1996). Parental psychological control: Revisiting a neglected construct. *Child Development, 67,* 3296–3319.

Barber, B. K., Olsen, J. A., & Shagle, S. C. (1994). Associations between parental psychological and behavioral control and youth internalized and externalized behaviors. *Child Development, 65,* 1120–1136.

Barenboim, C. (1981). The development of person perception from childhood to adolescence: From behavior comparisons to psychological constructs to psychological comparisons. *Child Development, 52,* 129–144.

Bates, J. E. (1987). Temperament in infancy. In J. D. Osofsky (Ed.), *Handbook of infant development* (2d ed., pp. 1101–1149). New York: Wiley.

Bates, J. E., Bayles, K., Bennett, D. S., Ridge, B., & Brown, M. M. (1991). Origins of externalizing behavior problems at eight years of age. In D. J. Pepler (Ed.), *The development and treatment of childhood aggression* (pp. 93–120). Hillsdale, NJ: Erlbaum.

Bates, J. E., Pettit, G. S., Dodge, K. A., & Ridge, B. (1998). Interaction of temperamental resistance to control in the development of externalizing behavior. *Developmental Psychology, 34,* 982–995.

Baumrind, D. (1965). Parental control and parental love. *Children, 12,* 230–234.

Baumrind, D. (1966). Effects of authoritative parental control on child behavior. *Child Development, 37,* 887–907.

Baumrind, D. (1971). Current patterns of parental authority. *Developmental Psychology Monograph, 4.*

Becker, W. C. (1964). Consequences of different kinds of parental discipline. In M. L. Hoffman & W. W. Hoffman (Eds.), *Review of child development research* (Vol. I: pp. 169–208). New York: Russell Sage Foundation.

Belsky, J., Hsieh, K.-H., & Crnic, K. (1998). Mothering, fathering, and infant negativity as antecedents of boys' externalizing problems and inhibition at age 3 years: Differential susceptibility to rearing experience? *Development and Psychopathology, 10,* 301–319.

Bowen, F., Vitaro, F., Kerr, M., & Pelletier, D. (1995). Childhood internalizing problems: Prediction from kindergarten, effect of maternal overprotectiveness, and sex differences. *Development and Psychopathology, 7,* 481–498.

Boyce, W. T., Frank, E., Jensen, P. S., Kessler, R. C., Nelson, C. A., & Steinberg, L. (1998). Social context in developmental psychopathology: Recommendations for future research from the MacArthur Network on Psychopathology and Development. *Development and Psychopathology, 10,* 143–164.

Boyle, M. H., Offord, D. R., Hoffmann, H. G., Catlin, G. P., Byles, J. A., Cadman, D. T., Crawford, J. W., Links, P. S., Rae-Grant, N. I., & Szatmari, P. (1987). Ontario Child Health Study: I. Methodology. *Archives of General Psychiatry, 44,* 826–831.

Boyle, M. H., Offord, D. R., Racine, Y. A., Szatmari, P., & Sanford, M. (1993). Evaluation of the revised Ontario Child Health Study scales. *Journal of Child Psychology and Psychiatry and Allied Disciplines, 34,* 189–213.

Bronfenbrenner, U. (1979). *The ecology of human development*. Cambridge, MA: Harvard University Press.

Buss, K. A., & Goldsmith, H. H. (1998). Fear and anger regulation in infancy: Effects on the temporal dynamics of affective expression. *Child Development, 69*, 359–374.

Campbell, S. B., March, C. L., Pierce, E. W., Ewing, L. J., & Szumowski, E. K. (1991). Hard to manage preschool boys: Family context and the stability of externalizing behavior. *Journal of Abnormal Child Psychology, 19*, 301–318.

Carver, C. S., & White, T. L. (1994). Behavioral inhibition, behavioral activation, and affective responses to impending reward and punishment: The BIS/BAS scales. *Journal of Personality and Social Psychology, 67*, 319–333.

Crockenberg, S., & Litman, C. (1990). Autonomy as competence in 2-year-olds: Maternal correlates of child defiance, compliance, and self-assertion. *Developmental Psychology, 26*, 961–971.

Derryberry, D., & Rothbart, M. K. (1997). Reactive and effortful processes in the organization of temperament. *Development and Psychopathology, 9*, 633–652.

Duncan, C. G., Brooks-Gunn, J., & Klebanov, P. K. (1994). Economic deprivation and early childhood development. *Child Development, 65*, 296–318.

Earls, F., & Jung, K. G. (1987). Temperament and home environment characteristics as causal factors in the early development of childhood psychopathology. *Journal of the American Academy of Child & Adolescent Psychiatry (BIO), 26*, 491–498.

Eder, R. A. (1989). The emergent personologist: The structure and content of 3 1/2-, 5 1/2-, and 7 1/2-year-olds' concepts of themselves and other persons. *Child Development, 60*, 1218–1228.

Eder, R. A. (1990). Uncovering young children's psychological selves: Individual and developmental differences. *Child Development, 61*, 849–863.

Eder, R. A., Gerlach, S. G., & Perlmutter, M. (1987). In search of children's selves: Development of the specific and general components of the self-concept. *Child Development, 58*, 1044–1050.

Eisenberg, N., Fabes, R. A., Guthrie, I. K., Murphy, B. C., Maszk, P., Holmgren, R., & Suh, K. (1996). The relations of regulation and emotionality to problem behavior in elementary school children. *Development and Psychopathology, 8*, 141–162.

Eisenberg, N., Guthrie, I. K., Fabes, R. A., Reiser, M., Murphy, B. C., Holgren, R., Maszk, P., & Losoya, S. (1997). The relations of regulation and emotionality to resiliency and competent social functioning in elementary school children. *Child Development, 68*, 295–311.

Eme, R. F., & Kavanaugh, L. (1995). Sex differences in conduct disorder. *Journal of Clinical Child Psychology, 24*, 406–426.

Fauber, R., Forehand, R., Thomas, A. M., & Wierson, M. (1990). A mediational model of the impact of marital conflict on adolescent adjustment in intact and divorced families: The role of disrupted parenting. *Child Development, 61*, 1112–1123.

Furman, W., & Bierman, K. L. (1983). Developmental changes in young children's conceptions of friendship. *Child Development, 54*, 549–556.

Garber, J., Quiggle, N. L., Panak, W., & Dodge, K. A. (1991). Aggression and depression in children: Comorbidity, specificity, and social cognitive processing. In D. Cicchetti & S. L. Toth (Eds.), *Internalizing and externalizing expressions of dysfunction* (Vol. 2, pp. 225–264). Hillsdale, N.J: Erlbaum.

Goldsmith, H. H., Buss, A. H., Plomin, R., Rothbart, M. K., Thomas, A., & Chess, S. (1987). What is temperament? Four approaches. *Child Development, 58*, 505–529.

Goldsmith, H. H., Buss, K. A., & Lemery, K. S. (1997). Toddler and childhood temperament: Expanded content, stronger genetic evidence, new evidence for the importance of environment. *Developmental Psychology, 33*, 891–905.

Goldsmith, H. H., & Rothbart, M. K. (1991). Contemporary instruments for assessing early temperament by questionnaire and in the laboratory. In A. Angleitner & J. Strelau (Eds.), *Explorations in temperament* (pp. 249–272). New York: Plenum Press.

Gray, J. A. (1982). *The neuropsychology of anxiety: An inquiry into the functions of the septo-hippocampal system.* New York: Oxford University Press.

Gray, M. R., & Steinberg, L. (1999). Unpacking authoritative parenting: Reassessing a multidimensional construct. *Journal of Marriage and the Family, 61*, 574–587.

Grych, J. H., Seid, M., & Fincham, F. D. (1992). Assessing marital conflict from the child's perspective: The children's perception of interpersonal conflict scale. *Child Development, 63*, 558–572.

Hart, C. H., Nelson, D. A., Robinson, C. C., Olsen, S. F., & McNeilly-Choque, M. K. (1998). Overt and relational aggression in Russian nursery-school-age children: Parenting style and marital linkages. *Developmental Psychology, 34*, 687–697.

Hart, D., & Damon, W. (1986). Developmental trends in self-understanding. *Social Cognition, 4*, 388–407.

Harter, S. (1982). The perceived competence scale for children. *Child Development, 55*, 1969–1982.

Hetherington, E. M., & Martin, B. (1986). Family factors and psychopathology in children. In H. C. Quay & J. S. Werry (Eds.), *Psychopathological Disorders of Childhood* (3rd ed., pp. 332–390). New York: Wiley & Sons.

Kagan, J. (1997). Temperament and the reactions to unfamiliarity. *Child Development, 68*, 139–143.

Kagan, J. (1998). Biology and the child. In W. Damon (Series Ed.) & N. Eisenberg (Vol. Ed.), *Handbook of child psychology: Vol. 3, Social, emotional and personality development* (5th ed., pp. 117–236). New York: Wiley.

Kagan, J., Reznick, S., & Gibbons, J. (1989). Inhibited and uninhibited types of children. *Child Development, 60*, 838–845.

Keenan, K., & Shaw, D. (1997). Developmental and social influences on young girls' early problem behavior. *Psychological Bulletin, 121*, 95–113.

Klebanov, P. K., Brooks-Gunn, J., McCarton, C., & McCormick, M. C. (1998). The contribution of neighborhood and family income to developmental test scores over the first three years of life. *Child Development, 69*, 1420–1436.

Kochanska, G. (1991). Socialization and temperament in the development of guilt and conscience. *Child Development, 62*, 1379–1392.

Kochanska, G. (1993). Toward a synthesis of parental socialization and child temperament in early development of conscience. *Child Development, 64*, 325–347.

Kochanska, G. (1994). Beyond cognition: Expanding the search for the early roots of internalization and conscience. *Developmental Psychology, 30*, 20–22.

Kochanska, G. (1999, April). *Applying a temperament model to the study of social development*. Paper presented at the biennial meeting for the Society for Research in Child Development, Albuquerque, NM.

Kuczaj, S. A. (1986). Thoughts on the intentional basis of early object word extension: Evidence from comprehension and production. In S. A. Kuczaj & M. D. Barrett (Eds.), *The development of work meaning: Progress in cognitive development research* (pp. 99–120). New York: Springer-Verlag.

Lee, C. L., & Bates, J. E. (1985). Mother-child interaction at age two years and perceived difficult temperament. *Child Development, 56*, 1314–1325.

Lengua, L. J., West, S. G., & Sandler, I. N. (1998). Temperament as a predictor of symptomatology in children: Addressing contamination of measures. *Child Development, 69*, 164–181.

Livesley, W. J., & Bromley, D. B. (1973). *Person perception in childhood and adolescence*. London: Wiley.

Lytton, H. (1990). Child and parent effects in boys' conduct disorder: A reinterpretation. *Developmental Psychology, 26*, 683–697.

Maccoby, E. E., & Martin, J. (1983). Socialization in the context of the family: Parent-child interaction. In P. H. Mussen (Series Ed.) & E. M. Hetherington (Vol. Ed.), *Handbook of child psychology: Vol. 4, Socialization, personality, and social development* (4th ed., pp. 1–101). New York: Wiley.

McClowry, S. G., Giangrande, S. K., Tommasini, N. R., Clinton, W., Foreman, N. S., Lynch, K., & Ferketich, S. L. (1994). The effects of child temperament, maternal characteristics, and family circumstances on the maladjustment of school-age children. *Research in Nursing and Health, 17*, 25–35.

Measelle, J., Ablow, J. C., Cowan, P. A., & Cowan, C. P. (1998). Assessing young children's views of their academic, social, and emotional lives: An evaluation of the self-perception scales of the Berkeley Puppet Interview. *Child Development, 69*, 1556–1576.

Messer, S. C., & Beidel, D. C. (1994). Psychosocial correlates of childhood anxiety disorders. *Journal of the American Academy of Child and Adolescent Psychiatry, 33*, 975–983.

Miller, P. H., & Alois, P. A. (1989). Young children's understanding of the psychological causes of behavior: A review. *Child Development, 60*, 257–285.

Mills, R. S. L., & Rubin, K. H. (1998). Are behavioural and psychological control both differentially associated with childhood aggression and social withdrawal? *Canadian Journal of Behavioural Sciences, 30*, 132–136.

Minuchin, S. (1974). *Families and family therapy*. Cambridge, MA: Harvard University Press.

Morris, A. S. (1999, April). *Child report of psychological control: Links to temperament and internalizing and externalizing in school*. Paper presented at the biennial meeting for the Society for Research in Child Development, Albuquerque, NM.

Morris, A. S., Silk, J. S., Steinberg, L., Sessa, F. M., Avenevoli, S., & Essex, M. J. (in press). Temperamental vulnerability and negative parenting as interacting predictors of child adjustment. *Journal of Marriage and the Family*.

Mun, E., Poon, E., Fitzgerald, H. E., von Eye, A., Puttler, L. I., & Zucker, R. A. (1999, April). *Specificity of temperament in predicting externalizing and internalizing behavior problems in children*. Paper presented at the biennial meeting for the Society for Research in Child Development, Albuquerque, NM.

Offord, D. R., Boyle, M. H., & Racine, Y. A. (1991). The epidemiology of antisocial behavior in childhood and adolescence. In D. J. Pepler & K. H. Rubin (Eds.), *The development and treatment of childhood aggression* (pp. 31–54). Hillsdale, NJ: Erlbaum.

Park, S. Y., Belsky, J., Putnam, S., & Crnic, K. (1997). Infant emotionality, parenting, and 3-year inhibition: Exploring stability and lawful discontinuity in a male sample. *Developmental Psychology, 33*, 218–227.

Parke, R. D., & Buriel, R. (1998). Socialization in the family: Ethnic and ecological perspectives. In W. Damon (Series Ed.) & N. Eisenberg (Vol. Ed.), *Handbook of child psychology: Vol. 3, Social, emotional and personality development* (5th ed., pp. 463–552). New York: Wiley.

Peevers, B. H., & Secord, P. F. (1973). Developmental changes in attribution of descriptive concepts to persons. *Journal of Personality and Social Psychology, 27*, 120–128.

Piaget, J. (1959). *The language and thought of the child*. (3rd ed.). London: Routledge & Kegan Paul.

Ridgeway, D., Waters, E., & Kuczaj, S. A. (1985). The acquisition of emotion descriptive language: Receptive and productive vocabulary norms for ages 18 months to 6 years. *Developmental Psychology, 21*, 901–908.

Rotenberg, K. J. (1982). Development of character constancy of self and other. *Child Development, 53*, 505–515.

Rothbart, M. K. (1999, April). *Developing a model for the study of temperament*. Paper presented at the biennial meeting of the Society for Research in Child Development. Albuquerque, NM.

Rothbart, M. K., & Ahadi, S. A. (1994). Temperament and the development of personality. *Journal of Abnormal Psychology, 103*, 55–66.

Rothbart, M. K., Ahadi, S. A., & Hershey, K. L. (1994). Temperament and social behavior in childhood. *Merrill-Palmer Quarterly, 40*, 21–39.

Rothbart, M. K., & Bates, J. E. (1998). Temperament: In W. Damon (Series Ed.) & In N. Eisenberg (Ed.), *Handbook of child psychology: Vol. 3. Social, emotional and personality development* (5th ed., pp. 105–176). New York: Wiley.

Rubin, K. H., Hastings, P., Chen, X., Stewart, S., & McNichol, K. (1998). Intrapersonal and maternal correlates of aggression, conflict, and externalizing problems in toddlers. *Child Development, 69*, 1614–1629.

Rubin, K. H., & Mills, R. S. L. (1991). Conceptualizing developmental pathways to internalizing disorders in childhood. *Canadian Journal of Behavioral Science, 23*, 300–317.

Ruble, D. N., & Rholes, W. S. (1981). The development of children's perceptions and attributions about their social world. In J. H. Harvey, W. Ickes, & R. E. Kidd (Eds.), *New directions in attribution research*, (Vol. 3; pp. 3–36). Hillsdale, NJ: Erlbaum.

Scarlett, H. H., Press, A. N., & Crockett, W. H. (1971). Children's descriptions of peers: A Wernerian developmental analysis. *Child Development, 42*, 439–453.

Schaefer, E. S. (1959). A circumplex model for maternal behavior. *Journal of Abnormal and Social Psychology, 59*, 226–235.

Schaefer, E. S. (1965). Children's reports of parental behavior: An inventory. *Child Development, 36*, 413–424.

Secord, P. F., & Peevers, B. H. (1974). The development of attribution and person concepts. In W. Mischel (Ed.), *Understanding other persons* (pp. 117–142). New Jersey: Rowman & Littlefield.

Sessea, F. M., Avenevoli, S., Steinberg, L., & Morris, A. S. (2001). Correspondence among informants on parenting: Preschool children, mothers, and observers. *Journal of Family Psychology, 15*, 53–68.

Shantz, C. U. (1983). Social cognition. In J. H. Flavell & E. M. Markman (Eds.), *Handbook of child psychology: Vol. 3. Cognition development* (pp. 495–555). New York: Wiley.

Siegler, R. S. (1991). *Children's thinking.* (2nd ed.). Englewood Cliffs, NJ: Prentice-Hall.

Siqueland, L., Kendall, P. C., & Steinberg, L. (1996). Anxiety in children: Perceived family environments and observed family interaction. *Journal of Clinical Child Psychology, 25*, 225–237.

Stark, K. D., Humphrey, L. L., Crook, K., & Lewis, K. (1990). Perceived family environments of depressed and anxious children: Child's and maternal figure's perspectives. *Journal of Abnormal Child Psychology, 18*, 527–547.

Stark, K. D., Humphrey, L. L., Laurent, J., Livingston, R., & Christopher, J. (1993). Cognitive, behavioral, and family factors in the differentiation of depressive and anxiety disorders during childhood. *Journal of Consulting and Clinical Psychology, 61*, 878–886.

STATA. (1997). *Stata reference manual release 5: Vol. 3.* College Station, TX: STATA Press.

Steinberg, L. (1990). Autonomy, conflict, and harmony in the family relationship. In S. S. Feldmann & G. R. Elliot (Eds.), *At the threshold: The developing adolescent* (pp. 255–276). Cambridge, MA: Harvard University Press.

Steinberg, L., & Avenevoli, S. (2000). The role of context in the development of psychopathology: A conceptual framework and some speculative propositions. *Child Development, 71,* 66–74.

Steinberg, L., Elmen, J. D., & Mounts, N. S. (1989). Authoritative parenting, psychosocial maturity, and academic success among adolescents. *Child Development, 60,* 1424–1436.

Steinberg, L., Lamborn, S. D., Dornbusch, S. M., & Darling, N. (1992). Impact of parenting practices on adolescent achievement: Authoritative parenting, school involvement, and encouragement to succeed. *Child Development, 63,* 1266–1281.

Steinberg, L., Mounts, N. S., Lamborn, S., & Dornbusch, S. M. (1991). Authoritative parenting and adolescent adjustment across varied ecological niches. *Journal of Research on Adolescence, 1,* 19–36.

Thomas, A. (1984). Temperament research: Where we are, where we are going. *Merrill-Palmer Quarterly, 30,* 103–109.

Thompson, R. A. (1991). Emotional regulation and emotional development. *Educational Psychology Review, 3,* 269–307.

Wahler, R. G. (1990). Who is driving the interactions? A commentary on "Child and parent effects in boys' conduct disorder." *Developmental Psychology, 26,* 702–704.

Webster-Stratton, C. (1996). Early onset conduct problems: Does gender make a difference? *Journal of Consulting and Clinical Psychology, 64,* 540–551.

APPENDIX 5A

Psychological Control Items from the CPI-P; Alpha = .73

1. My mom gets mad whenever I disagree with her.
   My mom doesn't always get mad when I disagree with her.

2. My mom always tells me what to do.
   My mom does not always tell me what to do.

3. When I cry, my mom does not get mad at me.
   When I cry, my mom gets mad at me.

4. My mom wishes I were a different kid.
   My mom does not wish I were a different kid.

5. My mom likes to hear what I have to say.
   My mom does not like to hear what I have to say.

6. My mom tells me what to play.
   My mom does not tell me what to play.

7. My mom does not say that I do not love her enough.
   My mom says that I do not love her enough.

8. My mom tells me I have good ideas.
   My mom does not tell me I have good ideas.

9. When I am bad, my mom ignores me.
   When I am bad, my mom does not ignore me.

10. My mom likes it when I ask a lot of questions.
    My mom does not like it when I ask a lot of questions.

11. Sometimes my mom says, "I wish you would just grow up."
    My mom never says, "I wish you would just grow up."

12. My mom likes to hear my ideas about things.
    My mom does not like to hear my ideas about things.

13. My mom tells me, "grown-ups are always right."
    My mom does not tell me, "grown-ups are always right."

6

PARENTAL PSYCHOLOGICAL CONTROL: IMPLICATIONS FOR CHILDHOOD PHYSICAL AND RELATIONAL AGGRESSION

DAVID A. NELSON AND NICKI R. CRICK

Children who experience difficulties with peers also tend to experience both concurrent social–psychological difficulties and long-term negative developmental outcomes. Specifically, a significant amount of research has identified peer rejection and isolation as significant precursors to academic troubles and socially deviant behavior (DeRosier, Kupersmidt, & Patterson, 1994; Kupersmidt, Coie, & Dodge, 1990; Parker & Asher, 1987; Parker, Rubin, Price, & DeRosier, 1995). Substantial research and intervention efforts have consequently been dedicated to an understanding of the problem behaviors commonly identified as correlates or antecedents of peer rejection. Childhood aggression is one of the most significant predictors of peer rejection, and has accordingly engendered a significant amount of relevant research (see Coie & Dodge, 1998, for a review).

Earlier research has also sought to identify the contexts in which social interaction difficulties may develop. The parent–child relationship has understandably received a significant amount of attention as one of these contexts (Hart, DeWolf, & Burts, 1993; Hart, Olsen, Robinson, & Mandleco, 1997; Ladd, 1992; Maccoby & Martin, 1983). It is not unreasonable to assume that through repeated, familiar parent–child interactions, children acquire social–behavioral orientations that carry over into peer relationships (Hartup, 1979; Pettit & Harrist, 1992). Thus, certain forms

This research was supported by a Child Psychology Training Grant Fellowship from the National Institute of Mental Health (#T32MH15755) to the first author, and a FIRST award from the National Institute of Mental Health (#MH53524) and a Faculty Scholars Award from the William T. Grant Foundation to the second author. Special thanks are extended to the parents and children of Project KIDS who participated in this research.

of parenting behavior may hinder children's acquisition of social competence (Dekovič & Janssens, 1992; Ladd, 1992; MacDonald, 1987; MacDonald & Parke, 1984; Pettit & Harrist, 1992; Putallaz & Heflin, 1990).

One aspect of the parent–child relationship that can influence children's social development is the nature of parents' disciplinary control strategies. During the past several decades, parental control has received significant attention and its conceptual treatment has grown increasingly sophisticated. One important distinction assessed in recent research is the possibly unique consequences of behavioral versus psychological forms of control for child and adolescent development (Barber, 1992, 1996; Steinberg, 1990; Steinberg, Elmen, & Mounts, 1989).

In this chapter we provide a conceptual framework and cite initial research findings regarding the possible ways in which parental psychological or coercive control (as a form of excessive behavioral control) may be differentially related to peer interaction difficulties embodied in subtypes of childhood aggression. We will give special emphasis to a relational form of childhood aggression that has received relatively little attention in the psychological literature, especially in the context of possible parenting antecedents or correlates.

We first provide an overview of current conceptualizations of childhood aggression, with emphasis on the newly emerging research regarding relational aggression. This is followed by a limited review of conceptualizations of parental control strategies (e.g., behavioral control and psychological control) and past research showing their general relation to childhood aggression. In accordance with the objectives of this volume, we give special attention to psychological control as a possible antecedent of relational forms of aggression. We present results of initial work that illuminates some of the possible parental (maternal and paternal) psychological control connections for aggression in children (both boys and girls). Finally, we conclude with a discussion of these connections and propose directions for future research.

CONCEPTUALIZATIONS OF CHILDHOOD AGGRESSION

Childhood aggression is the best known behavioral predictor of children's concurrent and future social difficulties (Coie, Dodge, & Kupersmidt, 1990; Crick, 1996; Parker & Asher, 1987). Accordingly, as mentioned earlier, it has garnered a substantial amount of empirical attention. However, although many important advances have been made in understanding the developmental trajectory and consequences of childhood aggression, research findings have been limited because of a traditional focus on forms of aggression most characteristic of boys (Crick, 1996;

Crick & Grotpeter, 1995). Specifically, childhood aggression has typically been described in terms of physical aggression, such as hitting, pushing, or verbal threats of physical harm (Berkowitz, 1993; Block, 1983; Parke & Slaby, 1983).

Gender differences in these sorts of behaviors emerge early in life (i.e., in preschool; Loeber & Hay, 1993; Maccoby & Jacklin, 1980) and, before adulthood, widen substantially across development, so that by adolescence, boys far exceed girls in their commission of delinquent or violent, aggressive acts (e.g., Elliott, Ageton, Huizinga, Knowles, & Canter, 1983; Elliott, Huizinga, & Morse, 1987; Snyder et al., 1987). This exclusive focus on physical aggression (and related behaviors) in boys has consequently generated little information about the nature of aggression in girls (Crick & Dodge, 1994; Robins, 1986). Underlying this dearth of research related to female aggression is the implicit assumption that girls are somehow nonaggressive (Bjorkqvist & Niemela, 1992) and therefore do not encounter the ill effects of aggressive interaction in their peer relationships as do boys.

In recent research, however, a relational form of aggression has been identified that has been shown to be relatively more characteristic of girls (Crick & Grotpeter, 1995). Relational aggression differs from physical forms of aggression in that it focuses on harming others through purposeful manipulation or damage to their peer relationships or feelings of inclusion (Crick, 1996; Crick, Bigbee, & Howes, 1996; Crick & Grotpeter, 1995). Relational aggression includes acts such as the "silent treatment," social exclusion, or threatening to end a friendship; behaviors that may all be used as a form of retaliation or as a means of getting one's way. When this form of aggression is considered, in addition to physical aggression, the prevalence of aggression in girls begins to approach that of boys (Crick & Grotpeter, 1995). Therefore, a gender-balanced assessment of aggression is necessary, which incorporates relationally aggressive behaviors (Crick, Werner, et al., 1999). Further, systematic exploration of the construct is needed to understand its effects for the development of children (especially girls).

Because of its overt, negative consequences, physical aggression has received a substantial amount of theoretical and empirical attention (e.g., Bandura, 1973; Berkowitz, 1993; Coie & Dodge, 1998; Dodge, 1980; Grych & Fincham, 1990; Patterson, 1982). In contrast, research efforts have only recently begun to demonstrate the relevance of relationally aggressive behaviors for the social development and peer relations of young children. For example, children tend to view these behaviors as mean, hostile acts that inflict injury (Crick, 1995; Crick, Casas, & Ku, 1996). This is especially true for girls, who cite relational forms of aggression as the most common angry, harmful behavior enacted in girls' peer groups. In contrast, physical aggression is the most commonly cited form of aggression in boys' peer groups (Crick, Werner, et al., 1996).

Furthermore, past studies have indirectly shown that relational aggression may inflict significant harm. For example, girls report that they would experience significant emotional distress if they were targeted by relationally aggressive peers (Crick, 1995; Crick, Grotpeter, & Bigbee, 2000). In addition, children who are recurrent victims of relational aggression have been shown to experience significantly more adjustment problems (e.g., depression, peer rejection, problematic friendships, loneliness, low self-esteem, and emotional distress) than their nonvictimized peers (Crick & Bigbee, 1998; Crick et al., 1999; Crick & Grotpeter, 1996; Grotpeter, Geiger, Nukulkij, & Crick, 1999).

Finally, research evidence suggests that relational aggression may not only be detrimental for its recipients but also for its initiators. Specifically, relationally aggressive children report significantly higher levels of loneliness, depression, and negative self-perceptions than their nonaggressive peers (Crick & Grotpeter, 1995). In addition, similar to physical aggression, relational aggression has been shown to be significantly related to both concurrent and future peer rejection for its initiators, regardless of gender (Crick, 1996; Crick & Grotpeter, 1995; Crick et al., 1999).

Taken together, these studies demonstrate that relational aggression is a salient and potentially harmful activity in children's peer relationships, especially those of girls. However, studies of relational aggression are still few in number and much further work is needed. One substantial limitation of existing research is the lack of attention to parenting factors that may contribute to the development of relational aggression. Accordingly, we now turn our attention to certain forms of parental control and their demonstrated or hypothesized associations with subtypes of childhood aggression.

CONCEPTUALIZATIONS OF PARENTAL CONTROL

Parental control strategies have received widespread empirical attention over the past few decades (see Maccoby & Martin, 1983; Peterson & Hann, 1999; Peterson & Rollins, 1987; Rollins & Thomas, 1979, for reviews). To date, psychological control has been effectively contrasted with behavioral control (e.g., Barber, 1996; Barber, Olsen, & Shagle, 1994; Steinberg, 1990; Steinberg et al., 1989), and this distinction is adopted in this chapter. The primary distinction between these forms of control is that behavioral control specifically focuses on the control of behavior, whereas psychological control is centered on the control of the child's psychological world. Furthermore, behavioral control tends to be defined quantitatively, as the consequences of such control vary significantly according to the overall level of control being exercised, given the demands of a particular context. For example, an appropriate amount of behavioral control (e.g., firmness, maturity demands) is viewed positively as a strategy for gaining compliance, and is commonly associated with competent child and adolescent outcomes (e.g., Baumrind, 1967, 1971; Steinberg, 1990). In contrast, parental behavioral control which is, given the specific setting, inadequate (e.g., insufficient behavioral regulation and monitoring) or excessive (e.g., punitiveness and unqualified power assertion) is commonly reported in tandem with negative child and adolescent developmental outcomes (Coie & Dodge, 1998).

Specifically, inadequate or permissive behavioral control is commonly associated with numerous behavioral regulation problems in children and adolescents, including impulsivity, aggression, delinquency, drug use, and sexual precocity (see Barber, 1996, for a review). Singling out childhood aggression for the purposes of this chapter, probably the most outstanding evidence of an association with inadequate behavioral control, is found in the work of Patterson (1982, 1995). Patterson has demonstrated that children who frequently engage in physical aggression and other disruptive behaviors are inadvertently trained in these behaviors at home by their parents. Specifically, parents provide negative reinforcement for these undesirable behaviors via inconsistent discipline (i.e., dropping demands for compliance when the child reacts aversively). Thus, parents in these situations fail to provide sufficient behavioral control to counteract the development and maintenance of aggressive or disruptive child behaviors. Furthermore, from this viewpoint, aggressive or disruptive children generalize their experiences with parents to the peer group, expecting that their misbehavior will continue to help them achieve desired outcomes and avoid unwanted consequences.

There is also a substantial amount of empirical research that posits that excessive behavioral control, in the form of punitive and power-assertive discipline, is associated at least to some degree with childhood and adolescent physical aggression (see Coie & Dodge, 1998, for a recent perspective). Decades ago, Hoffman (1960) warned parents against the use of unqualified power assertion (commands, threats, deprivations, and physical force), declaring that such methods evoked feelings of opposition and hostility toward parents that would interfere with the proper internalization of control. Furthermore, from a social-learning perspective, parents' use of power assertion may serve as a model that the child might use in relationships with others (e.g., peers). In fact, findings from relevant studies affirm this hypothesis, showing that children reared in a power-assertive manner are more likely to expect that aggressive strategies will help them get their way with peers (e.g., Hart, DeWolf, & Burts, 1992; Hart, Ladd, & Burleson, 1990). Thus, childhood aggression (only physical aggression has been studied) has commonly been reported in past research as a correlate or consequence of maladaptive forms of parental behavioral control.

In contrast to behavioral control, psychological control has, from its inception as a construct (e.g., Schaefer, 1959, 1965a, 1965b), almost exclusively been construed as a negative form of control, interfering with the developing child's need for psychological autonomy. Parallel with Schaefer's work, the idea of parental intrusion on the psychological and emotional development of children is also found in the early typological work of Baumrind (1966), who specifically warned against the use of guilt-induction and manipulation of the love relationship with the child. However, psychological control has only recently received focused attention, beginning with the work of Steinberg and colleagues (Steinberg, 1990; Steinberg et al., 1989; Steinberg, Lamborn, Dornbusch, & Darling, 1992; Steinberg, Mounts, Lamborn, & Dornbusch, 1991), who have contrasted the adverse effects of psychological control with the positive effects of appropriate behavioral control on adolescent development. Steinberg (1990) described these seemingly paradoxical findings (opposite findings with two forms of control) as follows: "Adolescents appear to be adversely affected by psychological control—the absence of 'psychological autonomy'—but positively influenced by behavioral control—the presence of 'demandingness' " (p. 274). Finally, one of the most recent definitions of psychological control (Barber, 1996) clearly accentuates its negative effects by defining it as

> a rather insidious type of control that potentially inhibits or intrudes upon psychological development through manipulation and exploitation of the parent-child bond (e.g., love withdrawal and guilt induction), negative, affect-laden expressions and criticisms (e.g., disappointment and shame), and excessive personal control (e.g., possessiveness, protectiveness). (p. 3297)

Accordingly, a construct of such negative import certainly warrants further empirical attention to fully assess its impact on various facets of child development. Barber (1996) outlined two issues that are useful in theorizing about the effects of psychological control on child development: (a) how psychological control differs from other types of parental control, and (b) whether psychological control has unique relations to various child and adolescent outcomes. The evidence cited previously provides ample justification, at a conceptual level, for a distinction between behavioral and psychological control. This distinction is especially evident in the comparison of appropriate behavioral control with psychological control (e.g., Steinberg, 1990). Furthermore, in chapter 2 (this volume), Barber and Harmon note that numerous other research efforts have begun to probe for differential associations of psychological and varying levels of behavioral control with unique child and adolescent outcomes. One promising avenue of continued research is the possibly unique links between parental psychological control and variants of aggressive behavior.

Moreover, little is known about the unique effects of psychological control on the development of younger children. Barber (1996) hypothesized that the effects of psychological control may be most pronounced for adolescents (rather than younger children). This reasoning is based on the developmental need of adolescents to achieve greater autonomy as part of identity development (Erikson, 1968; Marcia, 1980), a developmental task that is hindered by high levels of parental psychological control. However, Barber (1996) also acknowledged that psychological control may be generally defined as "intrusion into the developing child's self-expression—whatever the form of expression that might be" (p. 3315). Accordingly, the psychological control construct deserves further empirical attention and exploration in work with younger children.

Finally, past studies have also demonstrated the possible moderating effect of the gender of the child or parent in the practice of psychological control (see chapters 8 and 9, this volume, for reviews). For example, Barber's (1996) series of studies found interactions between gender of parent and gender of child, wherein findings were obtained for certain parent–child dyads (e.g., mother–daughter, mother–son, father–daughter, father–son) but not for others. The inclusion of gender as a factor is especially important in the exploration of factors related to the development of physical and relational aggression, which tend to be uniquely related to gender norms.

EXPLAINING RELATIONAL AGGRESSION: THE CASE FOR PSYCHOLOGICAL CONTROL

The role of parenting styles and other family factors in the development of childhood physical aggression has received extensive empirical attention (see Coie & Dodge, 1998; Hart et al., 1997, for reviews). For example, in regard to parenting style dimensions, past research shows consistent associations between physical aggression and a lack of authoritative features, such as parental responsiveness, warmth, and involvement. In addition, physical aggression has also been linked to permissive (e.g., inadequate behavioral control, condoning of aggression) or authoritarian (e.g., coercive discipline in the form of physical punishment, verbal hostility, and lack of reasoning) parenting (see Hart, Nelson, Robinson, Olsen, & McNeilly-Choque, 1998; MacKinnon-Lewis et al., 1994, for reviews).

In contrast, very little research at this time suggests consistent associations between any particular parenting practices and the development of relational aggression. In addition, little research has specifically examined the possibly unique associations of different parenting variables to aggression subtypes (e.g., to physical versus relational; Crick, Werner, 1999). However, findings from a number of recent studies indicate that the study of parental psychological control may hold significant promise for enhancing our understanding of the development of relationally aggressive behavior patterns.

First, initial research regarding the nature of relationally aggressive children's dyadic peer and parent relationships suggests that the development of relational aggression may be associated with a relatively intense focus on the importance of relationships. For example, relationally aggressive children are more likely than their peers to characterize their dyadic friendships as relatively high in intimacy, jealousy, and desires for exclusivity (e.g., not wanting to "share" their friends with others; Grotpeter & Crick, 1996). Second, in contrast with developmental norms in which children begin to individuate themselves from their parents as they approach adolescence (Blos, 1962; Steinberg, 1990; Sullivan, 1953), Grotpeter, Crick, and O'Brien (1996) found that preadolescent (fifth- and sixth-grade) relationally aggressive children reported being significantly closer to their mothers (on intimacy and companionship dimensions) than their nonaggressive counterparts, and did not differ in this respect from younger (third- and fourth-grade) relationally aggressive or nonaggressive children. Finally, relative to their peers, relationally aggressive children report significantly higher levels of exclusivity with both their fathers and mothers (e.g., their parents would rather they stay home with them than do something with friends; Grotpeter, 1997). Taken together, these findings indicate that relationally aggressive children tend to describe their friendships and parent–child relationships as overly exclusive and perhaps enmeshed.

Based on these findings, we have hypothesized that, at an early age, relationally aggressive children, within the context of exclusive, enmeshed relationships with parents, may learn that close, intimate relationships are highly valued and, perhaps, that the manipulation of such relationships is an effective means for achieving one's goals (see Crick, Werner, et al., 1999). Such a hypothesis stresses that relationally aggressive children may have parents who manipulate their intense parent–child relationship in ways suggested by the psychological control construct (e.g., manipulation of the love relationship). Indeed, several of the theoretically relevant characteristics of psychological control (see Barber, 1996) closely resemble relationally aggressive behaviors. For example, love withdrawal and erratic emotional behavior are two dimensions of psychological control that may focus on manipulation of the love relationship ("love-oriented" control; Becker, 1964). These strategies may be most effective in a parent–child relationship that is overly exclusive or enmeshed. Love withdrawal strategies set a conditional tone for the relationship (e.g., being less friendly with the child when he or she does not see things your way), similar to the strategies relationally aggressive children use with their peers. Erratic emotional behavior is a fitting complement to such a relationship, whereby feelings may suddenly change according to compliance to demands. Thus, high levels of parental psychological control may be especially predictive of the development of relationally aggressive behaviors in children.

Studies of gender differences in children's social interactions indicate that this hypothesized association between psychological control and relational aggression may be most relevant for girls, who, following prescribed gender norms, are typically described as more invested in the development and maintenance of dyadic relationships (Block, 1983; Crick & Grotpeter, 1995). For example, Maccoby (1990) contrasted the peer interaction styles of boys and girls. Girls are described as having an "enabling" interactive style that contributes to the establishment and maintenance of dyadic interactions in which verbal give-and-take and positive affirmation are key elements. In contrast, boys are described as having a "restrictive" interactive style in that their peer interactions are defined by the establishment and maintenance of hierarchies (group-oriented focus). Accordingly, because of their sensitivity in regard to the maintenance of dyadic relationships, girls who are raised by psychologically controlling parents may be more vulnerable to the effects of such parenting (which threatens their dyadic ties with parents) and may be more likely to generalize their experiences to the peer group. Thus, we have hypothesized that parental psychological control may be uniquely related to the development of relational aggression and that this association might be most pronounced for girls.

Finally, as suggested earlier, this association may vary significantly for girls or boys, depending on the gender of the parent in question. This possibility is adequately demonstrated in previous research findings of psychological control (e.g., Barber, 1996). In short, appreciation of gender-differentiated parenting, and the corresponding particularities of father–son, father–daughter, mother–son, and mother–daughter relationships, may be necessary to fully understand family relationships and child outcomes (e.g., Collins & Russell, 1991; Cowan, Cowan, & Kerig, 1993; Dornbusch, 1989; Russell & Saebel, 1997; Steinberg, 1987, 1990).

EXPLORING PSYCHOLOGICAL CONTROL AND AGGRESSION SUBTYPES

Beyond our own preliminary, exploratory research with a middle childhood sample (third-grade children), which will be described below, to our knowledge only Hart and colleagues (e.g., Hart et al., 1998, 2000; Yang et al., 2001) have specifically evaluated the association between psychological control and subtypes of childhood aggression. These studies have also included various measures of behavioral control (conceptualized as coercion or excessive behavioral control) as a point of contrast. That work is also unique in that samples of Russian and Chinese preschool children and their parents have been the focus.

The results of the research with Russian preschoolers (Hart et al., 1998, 2000) showed that, contrary to our expectations, maternal psychological control was significantly related to overt (physical bullying and instrumental) aggression but not to relational aggression (for both boys and girls). Paternal psychological control was unrelated to aggression. Furthermore, maternal coercion was associated with overt aggression for boys and both overt and relational forms of aggression for girls. Paternal coercion was related to overt aggression for both boys and girls. These findings suggest that psychological control may not be uniquely tied to relational aggression in preschoolers, at least in the Russian culture.

In contrast, using similar measures but more sophisticated statistical analyses (e.g., structural equation modeling), Yang et al. (2001) found relationships between maternal and paternal psychological control and relational aggression in Chinese preschoolers. In particular, mothers' psychological control was associated with girls' physical and relational aggression and boys' physical aggression. In contrast, maternal coercion was unrelated to childhood aggression. Fathers' psychological control was also associated with girls' relational aggression. Finally, fathers' coercion was related to both girls' and boys' physical and relational aggression.

Results with the Chinese sample suggest that psychological control may indeed be related to the development of relationally aggressive tendencies, at least in preschool girls. However, firm conclusions cannot be established without further research. In any case, given the cultural contexts of these studies, it is uncertain whether any of the results will generalize to preschoolers in Western culture. Furthermore, different findings may be obtained with samples of children who are older (e.g., in middle childhood) than the preschoolaged children targeted by Hart and colleagues. In short, older children and adolescents may be the most vulnerable to the effects of psychological control, as the developmental need for autonomy increases, and more definitive findings may therefore be obtained by using such age groups in research design.

In this chapter, we share preliminary results of an initial attempt to explore the influence of psychological control on subtypes of aggression in a middle childhood, U.S. sample. Similar to previous studies, we rely on a unidimensional model of psychological control that includes several key theoretical characteristics that are likely related to relational aggression. In addition, we seek to further explore possibly unique effects of mothers versus fathers in the practice of psychological control. Based on previous research, wherein findings for psychological control varied according to the nature of the particular parent–child dyad (mother–daughter, mother–son, father–daughter, father–son; e.g., Barber, 1996), we speculate that psychological control by mothers and fathers may be differentially linked to aggression outcomes—both physical and relational—for boys and girls.

THE RESEARCH

The sample was composed of 115 third-grade children (58 boys, 57 girls) from two school districts in a large Midwestern city. These children constituted a normative sample drawn from a larger longitudinal study (beginning at third grade) of the development and consequences of physical and relational forms of childhood aggression. Approximately 69% of the sample was European American, 16% of the sample was African American, and the remaining 15% was a mix of other ethnicities (Hmong, Latino, Native American, Asian, Ethiopian, and biracial children). Mothers of all of these children participated in a home-based interview in which they completed a self-report measure of psychological control strategies they use with their child. More detail about this measure is given below. Numerous other measures were also completed during the interview but are not a part of this study. These interviews were led by trained graduate or undergraduate interviewers. Biological fathers also took part in 63 families and completed the psychological control measure. The socioeconomic status of participating families was varied, ranging from low to high.

Assessment of Aggression Subtypes

To obtain continuous aggression scores for each child in the study, a peer sociometric questionnaire was administered in participating children's elementary school classrooms. Written parental consent was obtained for each child before administering the sociometric. The particular sociometric instrument used was the Children's Social Behavior Scale-Peer Form (CSBS-P), a group-administered peer-nomination measure of aggression developed in past research (see Crick, 1997; Crick & Grotpeter, 1995) in which five items assess physical aggression (e.g., children who hit or kick others) and five items assess relational aggression (e.g., children who try to make kids not like a certain person by spreading rumors about him or her or talking behind his or her back). In addition, four items assess prosocial behavior (e.g., children who do nice things for others) and serve as positive filler items. Only the aggression items were used in the exploratory analyses.

During the administration of this instrument, children were instructed to name up to three classmates who best fit the description given for each item. A class roster was provided to assist them in this process. For each item, the number of nominations that each child received was standardized within each classroom. Finally, items belonging to separate subscales were summed to yield two subscale continuous scores for each child (physical aggression, relational aggression). Evidence for the internal consistency and test–retest reliability of this measure has been documented in previous studies (e.g., Crick, 1997). Finally, all of the children who participated in the classroom sociometric were extended the opportunity to participate with their families in the home interview portion of the study.

Assessment of Parental Behavioral and Psychological Control

Mothers and fathers independently completed a self-report parenting questionnaire that included items from the Parenting Practices Question-naire (PPQ; Robinson, Mandleco, Olsen, & Hart, 1995) and the Parental Psychological Control measure (PPC; Hart & Robinson, 1995). The items selected from the PPQ reflected dimensions of authoritative and authoritar-ian parenting styles. For the use of this study, we selected the authoritarian dimensions, made up of verbal hostility and corporal punishment, which are used as separate dimensions of coercive control in the analyses that follow. These control dimensions and their associated items are presented in appendix 6A. Parents responded to all of these items using a 5-point Likert-type response scale anchored by never (1) and always (5).

We used a parental self-report rather than a child-report measure to assess psychological control, based on Barber's (1996) speculation that younger research participants may not be mature enough to differentiate the types of control that might intrude on their psychological autonomy (see chapter 5, this volume, for an example of children's ability to report on parental behavior). The PPC was conceptualized based on dimensions of psychological control recently developed for adolescents by Barber (1996) and includes the items used in versions of Psychological Control Scale-Youth Self Report (PCS-YSR), except that those items have been adjusted to reflect a parent self-report rather than a child's report of parent behavior.

For the purposes of this chapter, we used an abbreviated list of the eight items that Barber (1996) cited in the final version of the PCS-YSR to form our psychological control variable. Of the original eight items, two represent the "constraining verbal expression" dimension and were not included in our questionnaire.[1] Another item reflecting love withdrawal was also not included in our analyses as it was copied incorrectly from the original measure and therefore did not adequately represent the original

---

[1] Based on a multidimensional view of psychological control, those dimensions that appeared conceptually most similar to the relational aggression construct were selected for use as part of a much larger study of childhood aggression. Accordingly, and also because of time constraints, we did not assess the "constraining verbal expression" items in our study.

item. Accordingly, we settled on a five-item scale of psychological control, which is presented in appendix 6A. This scale reflects the invalidating feelings, personal attack, and love withdrawal dimensions of psychological control. Finally, parents responded to the psychological control items with the same response scale described previously (5-point Likert-type response scale anchored by never (1) and always (5)).

Reliability was separately evaluated for mothers and fathers for each of these scales. For mother reports, Cronbach's alpha was .65, .84, and .68 for the psychological control, corporal punishment, and verbal hostility scales, respectively. For father reports, Cronbach's alpha was .54, .75, and .60 for the psychological control, corporal punishment, and verbal hostility scales, respectively.

In prelude to this and later sections it should be noted that, because of constraints imposed by the small size of the overall sample, the choice of analyses and results presented in this chapter constitute more of an exploratory and therefore limited test of the association between parental control and aggression subtypes. The limitations are especially apparent in the context of comparing parent–child dyads of different gender compositions, as cell sizes for the various dyads, especially father–child dyads, are small. Past research shows that the most appropriate manner to provide evidence for differences between the four parent–child dyads is to document a gender of parent by gender of child interaction (e.g., Jacklin, 1981). However, in a review of relevant research, Russell and Saebel (1997) noted that sample size is crucial to the detection of a possible gender interaction effect, with samples of less than 100 families typically showing no evidence of an interaction (and the inverse finding for most samples above this number). Accordingly, null or marginal findings must be interpreted with caution, because a restricted sample size can contribute to Type II errors.

Because direct comparison of mothers' and fathers' use of the psychological and coercive control strategies in this sample were based on small sample sizes ($n = 27$ for boys, $n = 33$ for girls), we did not anticipate a significant interaction. Consistent with our expectations, an exploratory 2 (gender of parent) × 3 (control type: psychological control, corporal punishment or verbal hostility) × 2 (gender of child) repeated measures ANOVA (in which gender of parent and control type served as within-subjects variables, gender of child was the between-subjects variable, and control scores served as the dependent variables) did not yield a significant interaction for psychological control or the separate components of coercive control.

However, some findings were gleaned from follow-up analyses. First, we conducted a 2 (gender of parent) × 2 (gender of child) repeated measures ANOVA (in which gender of parent served as the within-subjects variable, gender of child was the between-subjects variable, and psychological control

TABLE 6-1

Means, Standard Deviations, and Ranges for Parental Control Variables
by Parent–Child Dyad

| | Parent–Child Dyad | | | |
| | Mother–Son (n = 58) | Mother–Daughter (n = 57) | Father–Son (n = 28) | Father–Daughter (n = 35) |
Control Variable				
Psychological control				
Mean	1.59	1.51	1.63	1.66
(SD)	(0.58)	(0.37)	(0.53)	(0.38)
Corporal punishment				
Mean	1.62	1.25	1.44	1.40
(SD)	(0.61)	(0.36)	(0.43)	(0.39)
Verbal hostility				
Mean	2.22	2.09	2.04	2.06
(SD)	(0.68)	(0.58)	(0.61)	(0.31)

scores served as the dependent variables). A main effect for gender of parent revealed that fathers (M = 1.61; SD = 0.45) use significantly higher levels of psychological control than mothers (M = 1.46, SD = 0.36) with their offspring; $F(1, 58)$ = 6.4, $p <.$ 05, and no effect was found for gender of child, suggesting that boys and girls at this age may not differ in total exposure to parental psychological control.

Finally, to take advantage of full sample sizes to better detect mothers' possible differential use of control strategies with their children (to include mothers who were excluded from the repeated measures ANOVAs), we conducted a series of one-way ANOVAs in which child gender was the independent variable and maternal control strategies (psychological control, corporal punishment, verbal hostility) served as dependent variables. One significant finding emerged from these analyses. Mothers were found to use significantly more corporal punishment with sons than daughters: $F(1, 114)$ = 15.3, $p <.$ 001. Means and standard deviations for the control strategy scales for each parent–child dyad are provided in Table 6-1.

Correlational Analyses by Dyad

Following these analyses and the attendant concern over statistical power issues enumerated previously, we elected to conduct further analyses by dyad. Although this approach cannot firmly establish sex-related differences (Jacklin, 1981), it can suggest possible differences (Russell & Saebel, 1997). The first step in these analyses focused on intercorrelation matrices for all parent–child dyads, which are displayed in Tables 6-2 through 6-5. Verbal hostility and corporal punishment are listed separately as elements of coercive control. Beginning with Table 6-2, results showed that maternal corpo-

TABLE 6-2

Intercorrelations Between Boys' Aggression Subtypes and Maternal Psychological and Coercive Control

	Relational Aggression	Maternal Corporal Punishment	Maternal Verbal Hostility	Maternal Psychological Control
Physical aggression	.81***	.45***	.25+	.15
Relational aggression		.40**	.24+	.19
Maternal corporal punishment			.49***	.56***
Maternal verbal hostility				.48***

+$p < .10$; *$p < .05$; **$p < .01$; ***$p < .001$.

TABLE 6-3

Intercorrelations Between Girls' Aggression Subtypes and Maternal Psychological and Coercive Control

	Relational Aggression	Maternal Corporal Punishment	Maternal Verbal Hostility	Maternal Psychological Control
Physical aggression	.40***	.12	−.13	−.23+
Relational aggression		.20	.17	−.03
Maternal corporal punishment			.27*	.24+
Maternal verbal hostility				.25*

+$p < .10$; *$p < .05$; **$p < .01$; ***$p < .001$.

TABLE 6-4

Intercorrelations Between Boys' Aggression Subtypes and Paternal Psychological and Coercive Control

	Relational Aggression	Paternal Corporal Punishment	Paternal Verbal Hostility	Paternal Psychological Control
Physical aggression	.81***	−.43*	.15	.09
Relational aggression		−.38*	.15	.03
Paternal corporal punishment			.21	.16
Paternal verbal hostility				.45*

+$p < .10$; *$p < .05$; **$p < .01$; ***$p < .001$.

ral punishment was significantly and positively correlated with both physical and relational aggression in boys. There was also a trend for maternal verbal hostility to be associated with both forms of aggression in boys. In contrast, paternal corporal punishment was significantly and negatively related to both forms of aggression in boys (see Table 6-4).

TABLE 6-5
Intercorrelations Between Girls' Aggression Subtypes and Paternal Psychological and Coercive Control

	Relational Aggression	Paternal Corporal Punishment	Paternal Verbal Hostility	Paternal Psychological Control
Physical aggression	.40***	.36*	−.22	.30+
Relational aggression		.16	.01	.55***
Paternal corporal punishment			−.11	.12
Paternal verbal hostility				.00

+$p < .10$; *$p < .05$; **$p < .01$; ***$p < .001$.

For girls, maternal psychological control was marginally and negatively related to physical aggression (see Table 6-3). In comparison, girls' physical aggression was significantly and positively related to paternal corporal punishment and marginally and positively related to paternal psychological control. Finally, girls' relational aggression was moderately correlated with paternal psychological control (see Table 6-5). These contrasting findings suggest evidence of gender-differentiated effects of parent–child interaction and the need to separately consider the various combinations of parent–child dyads.

Hierarchical Regressions

In the next step of analysis, several sets of hierarchical regression analyses were conducted to evaluate the relative contributions of parental coercive control and psychological control to the prediction of concurrent levels of children's physical and relational aggression. These analyses were conducted separately for each of the possible parent–child dyads (mother–son ($n = 58$), mother–daughter ($n = 57$), father–son ($n = 28$), father–daughter ($n = 35$)). Physical and relational aggression continuous scores served as dependent variables and parental psychological control and coercive control (both verbal hostility and corporal punishment dimensions) scores served as independent variables. Each of the analyses were performed twice—the second set of equations had the order of entry of the independent variables reversed. This allowed for an assessment of the relatively unique contribution of maternal psychological control. All results are documented in Tables 6-6 through 6-9, but comment about findings of the second set of equations (after order of entry has been reversed) are only made if the findings were significantly different from those gained in the first set of equations.

TABLE 6-6
R^2 Values for Regression Equations Predicting Boys' Aggression Subtypes
From Maternal Psychological and Coercive Control

Dependent Variable	Maternal Psychological Control Entered at Step 1		Maternal Coercive Control Entered at Step 1	
	R^2 for Maternal Psychological Control	R^2 Change for Maternal Coercive Control	R^2 for Maternal Coercive Control	R^2 Change for Maternal Psychological Control
Physical aggression	.02	.19**	.20**	.02
Relational aggression	.04	.13*	.16**	.00

$+p < .10$; $^*p < .05$; $^{**}p < .01$; $^{***}p < .001$.

MATERNAL CONTRIBUTIONS TO PHYSICAL AND RELATIONAL AGGRESSION

In the first set of equations for mother–son dyads, maternal psychological control scores were entered at step one and maternal coercive control scores were entered as a block at step two. This allowed us to evaluate the degree to which maternal coercive control uniquely predicted physical or relational aggression beyond that predicted by maternal psychological control (see Table 6-6 for R^2 values). Results of step one analyses showed that maternal psychological control was unrelated to physical or relational aggression for boys. However, in step two analyses, maternal coercive control significantly predicted both physical aggression, $F(3, 54)$change = 6.7, $p < .01$; and relational aggression, $F(3, 54)$change = 4.3, $p < .05$; above and beyond maternal psychological control.

Next, in the first set of similar equations for mother–daughter dyads (see Table 6-7 for R^2 values), step one analyses showed that maternal psychological control was marginally related to physical aggression, $F(1, 55) = 3.1$, $p < .10$; and unrelated to relational aggression for girls. Maternal coercive control was also unrelated to both physical aggression and relational aggression for girls at step two in the analyses.

PATERNAL CONTRIBUTIONS TO PHYSICAL AND RELATIONAL AGGRESSION

In the first set of similar equations for father–son dyads (see Table 6-8 for R^2 values), step one analyses showed that paternal psychological control was unrelated to physical or relational aggression in boys. However, in step two

TABLE 6-7
R^2 Values for Regression Equations Predicting Girls' Aggression Subtypes From Maternal Psychological and Coercive Control

Dependent Variable	Maternal Psychological Control Entered at Step 1		Maternal Coercive Control Entered at Step 1	
	R^2 for Maternal Psychological Control	R^2 Change for Maternal Coercive Control	R^2 for Maternal Coercive Control	R^2 Change for Maternal Psychological Control
Physical aggression	.05+	.04	.04	.06+
Relational aggression	.00	.06	.05	.01

+$p < .10$; *$p < .05$; **$p < .01$; ***$p < .001$.

analyses, paternal coercive control significantly predicted physical aggression, $F(3, 24)$change = 3.7, $p < .05$; and marginally predicted relational aggression, $F(3, 24)$change = 2.9, $p < .10$; above and beyond paternal psychological control.

In the first set of similar equations for father–daughter dyads (see Table 6-9 for R^2 values), paternal psychological control entered at step one marginally predicted physical aggression, $F(1, 33) = 3.3$, $p < .10$, but significantly predicted relational aggression, $F(1, 33) = 14.1$, $p < .001$, for girls. Furthermore, at step two, paternal coercive control marginally added to the prediction of girls' physical aggression, $F(3, 31)$change = 2.9, $p < .10$, but failed to add to the prediction of relational aggression for girls. Finally, when the order of entry was reversed, findings were slightly different in that paternal psychological control no longer remained marginally predictive of girls' physical aggression.

TABLE 6-8
R^2 Values for Regression Equations Predicting Boys' Aggression Subtypes From Paternal Psychological and Coercive Control

Dependent Variable	Paternal Psychological Control Entered at Step 1		Paternal Coercive Control Entered at Step 1	
	R^2 for Paternal Psychological Control	R^2 Change for Paternal Coercive Control	R^2 for Paternal Coercive Control	R^2 Change for Paternal Psychological Control
Physical aggression	.01	.24*	.24*	.00
Relational aggression	.00	.19+	.19+	.00

+$p < .10$; *$p < .05$; **$p < .01$; ***$p < .001$.

TABLE 6-9
R^2 Values for Regression Equations Predicting Girls' Aggression Subtypes From Paternal Psychological and Coercive Control

Dependent Variable	Paternal Psychological Control Entered at Step 1		Paternal Coercive Control Entered at Step 1	
	R^2 for Paternal Psychological Control	R^2 Change for Paternal Coercive Control	R^2 for Paternal Coercive Control	R^2 Change for Paternal Psychological Control
Physical aggression	.09+	.14+	.16+	.07
Relational aggression	.30***	.01	.03	.28***

+p < .10; *p < .05; **p < .01; ***p < .001.

DISCUSSION

These findings, though limited in their scope and significance, do show that coercive control and psychological control, as conceptualized in this chapter, were relatively distinct in their links to childhood forms of aggression, with very little overlap displayed in the regression equation results. Further, where findings were obtained for coercive control, correlations showed that corporal punishment appeared to be the central influence in most of these findings, because verbal hostility was not significantly associated with aggression subtypes in any of the dyads.

In addition, unique findings were obtained for each of the parent–child dyads. Starting with mother–son dyads, maternal coercive control was significantly associated with both physical and relational forms of aggression. Correlations showed that higher levels of maternal corporal punishment were positively associated with more aggression of both forms in boys. In contrast, for father–son dyads, coercive control was significantly associated with physical aggression, but in a qualitatively different manner from the mother–son associations. Specifically, correlations clarified that higher levels of paternal corporal punishment were associated with *less* physical aggression in boys. Finally, for girls, the only significant finding was obtained for father–daughter dyads. Results showed that higher levels of paternal psychological control were positively associated with relational aggression in girls.

This chapter focuses on a fundamental problem—childhood aggression—and the possible influence of parental control strategies in the development of aggression subtypes (e.g., physical and relational aggression). In particular, we sought to explore the plausible relation between parental psychological control and childhood relational aggression, two constructs that have only recently begun to receive focused empirical attention. This is an important area to explore, as studies demonstrate that relational aggression, like physical aggression, is linked to social and psychological difficulties for perpetrators and their victims (see Crick, Werner, et al., 1999, for a review). Consequently, there is a significant need to understand the possible precursors to relational aggression. The definition of parental psychological control suggests an intuitive connection with relational aggression (Hart et al., 1998, 2000; Yang et al., 2001).

Indeed, elements of psychological control (e.g., love withdrawal, erratic emotional behavior) parallel the essence of relational aggression, in which relationships are manipulated or threatened. Accordingly, a child raised by psychologically controlling parents may be more likely to adopt relationally aggressive strategies in her interaction with peers. The fact that parents of schoolage children in this study acknowledge the practice of psychological control demonstrates that some parents may perceive these strategies to be effective in gaining compliance. Hence, this study provides further evidence that psychological control may influence child development from an early age. Furthermore, linking psychological control to relational aggression would suggest one more reason to consider this form of parental control as negative and therefore worthy of continued empirical attention. With these ideas as our framework, we explored our hypotheses with a sample of third-grade children and their parents. Consistent with our primary hypothesis, we found parental psychological control to be related to relational aggression in middle childhood, at least for girls.

In addition to this primary finding, we also found, consistent with past studies, that the association between various parental control strategies and childhood aggression varied by the gender composition of the particular parent–child dyad. These findings add further credence to the position, stated earlier, that appreciation of gender-differentiated parenting may further understanding of the influence of family relationships on various child outcomes (e.g., Cowan et al., 1993; Russell & Saebel, 1997). Such an emphasis also corresponds with surging interest in fatherhood research, which considers the possibly unique influence of fathers, relative to mothers, on their children (e.g., Lamb, 1997).

Speaking of fathers, we return to the main finding linking psychological control and relational aggression, which was unique to father–daughter dyads. This relatively strong finding suggests that fathers may contribute to the development or maintenance of relationally aggressive tendencies in their daughters. The strength of this finding was somewhat surprising, given the rather small number of father–daughter dyads ($n = 35$). Accordingly, because of small cell sizes, for this and other dyads, our analyses should be considered exploratory in nature. Indeed, sample size may be a significant factor in the rather limited findings for psychological control in other parent–child dyads. Still, consistent with findings of earlier studies, the results demonstrate that negative forms of parental control (both coercive and psychological control) are significantly associated with childhood aggression. Furthermore, we are confident that future studies will replicate and further define the link between psychological control and relational aggression.

In many ways, the finding for fathers and daughters is notable. First, in this and previous studies by Hart and colleagues (Hart et al., 1998, 2000; Yang et al., 2001), no link between parental psychological control and relational aggression was obtained for boys. There may be several explanations for this. One possible rationale was mentioned earlier: Girls are typically described as more focused on the development and maintenance of dyadic relationships (Block, 1983; Crick & Grotpeter, 1995). Accordingly, girls may be particularly sensitive to the effects of psychological control, a parenting style that may leave the impression that the parent–child relationship is constantly in a state of flux. Girls may also have greater difficulties establishing autonomy, given their greater sensitivity to relationship disturbances (Cross & Madsen, 1997; Leadbeater, Blatt, & Quinlin, 1995) and this may further heighten their susceptibility to the negative effects of psychological control.

The finding for fathers and daughters is also unique when one considers the research that consistently shows that fathers tend to be more involved with sons than with daughters (Parke, 1996; Pleck, 1997). Accordingly, past research on the role of fathers in child development has focused predominantly on father–son relationships, consistent with the emphasis in past years on sex-role development and identification with the same-sex parent (Biller & Kimpton, 1997). Gradually, however, the role of fathers in their daughters' lives has been taken more seriously, and empirical evidence to this end has accumulated (Biller & Kimpton, 1997). This study adds impetus to the study of father–daughter relationships and the possibly unique influences at work. In particular, the study of paternal influence may significantly contribute to our understanding of relationally aggressive girls.

It is also notable that, overall, fathers in this study were also found to be more psychologically controlling than mothers, a finding inconsistent with a trend indicating higher levels of maternal psychological control in the few studies that have tested parental sex differences (see chapter 9, this volume). Again, these findings collectively provide further evidence of a role for fathers in child maladjustment, a possibility that past developmental research has tended to neglect (Phares, 1997; Phares & Compas, 1992). More recent research shows that a father who is dominating and controlling in parent–child interaction constrains positive interaction and, accordingly, his child's ability to learn effective social skills (Biller & Kimpton, 1997). Relational aggression may be just one of the many manifestations of social difficulty related to improper control strategies used by fathers.

This study joins those studies presented in chapters 5, 7, and 8 (this volume) in showing linkages between parental psychological control and younger children's functioning. It also suggests further evidence for the impact of psychological control on childhood aggression, specifically. However, the meager amount of studies with early and middle-childhood samples (Hart et al., 1998, 2000; Yang et al., 2001) demonstrates a need for replication and further research in this area. Future studies should also incorporate a broader age range (e.g., adolescents) to examine how these associations may vary by parent and child gender as well as age of the child.

Furthermore, studies that incorporate larger samples, more sophisticated statistical approaches, and more complete models of possible variable relationships will be beneficial. For example, the recent study by Yang et al. (in press), noted earlier, used structural equation modeling to analyze how child temperament may interact with parental control strategies and childhood aggression outcomes (see chapter 5, this volume, for a similar approach). In short, there are many exciting possibilities for further research in this domain, which we hope will increase our understanding of the development of relational aggression and eventually suggest possible prevention or intervention strategies, such as parenting education, for better child social development outcomes.

REFERENCES

Bandura, A. (1973). *Aggression: A social learning theory analysis*. New York: Prentice-Hall.

Barber, B. K. (1992). Family, personality, and adolescent problem behaviors. *Journal of Marriage and the Family, 54*, 69–79.

Barber, B. K. (1996). Parental psychological control: Revisiting a neglected construct. *Child Development, 67*, 3296–3319.

Barber, B. K., Olsen, J. A., & Shagle, S. C. (1994). Associations between parental psychological and behavioral control and youth internalized and externalized behaviors. *Child Development, 65*, 1120–1136.

Baumrind, D. (1966). Effects of authoritative control on child behavior. *Child Development, 37*, 887–907.

Baumrind, D. (1967). Child care practices anteceding three patterns of preschool behavior. *Genetic Psychology Monographs, 75*, 43–88.

Baumrind, D. (1971). Current patterns of parental authority. *Developmental Psychology, 4*, 1–103.

Becker, W. C. (1964). Consequences of different kinds of parental discipline. In M. L. Hoffman & W. W. Hoffman (Eds.), *Review of child development research* (Vol. 1, pp. 169–208). New York: Russell Sage Foundation.

Berkowitz, L. (1993). *Aggression: Its causes, consequences, and control*. New York: Academic Press.

Biller, H. B., & Kimpton, J. L. (1997). The father and the school-aged child. In M. E. Lamb (Ed.), *The role of the father in child development* (3rd ed., pp. 143–161). New York: Wiley & Sons.

Bjorkqvist, K., & Niemela, P. (1992). New trends in the study of female aggression. In K. Bjorkqvist & P. Niemela (Eds.), *Of mice and women: Aspects of female aggression* (pp. 1–15). San Diego, CA: Academic Press.

Block, J. H. (1983). Differential premises arising from differential socialization of the sexes: Some conjectures. *Child Development, 54*, 1335–1354.

Blos, P. (1962). *On adolescence, a psychoanalytic interpretation*. New York: Free Press of Glencoe.

Coie, J. D., & Dodge, K. A. (1998). Aggression and antisocial behavior. In W. Damon (Series Ed.) & N. Eisenberg (Vol. Ed.), *Handbook of child psychology. Vol. 3: Social, emotional, and personality development* (5th ed., pp. 779–862). New York: Wiley & Sons.

Coie, J. D., Dodge, K. A., & Kupersmidt, J. A. (1990). Peer group behavior and social status. In S. R. Asher & J. D. Coie (Eds.), *Peer rejection in childhood* (pp. 309–337). New York: Cambridge University Press.

Collins, W. A., & Russell, G. (1991). Mother-child and father-child relationships in middle childhood and adolescence: A developmental analysis. *Developmental Review, 11*, 99–136.

Cowan, P. A., Cowan, C. P., & Kerig, P. K. (1993). Mothers, fathers, sons, and daughters: Gender differences in family formation and parenting style. In P. A. Cowan, D. Field, D. A. Hansen, A. Skolnick, & G. E. Swanson (Eds.), *Family, self, and society: Toward a new agenda for family research* (pp. 165–195). Hillsdale, NJ: Erlbaum.

Crick, N. R. (1995). Relational aggression: The role of intent attributions, feelings of distress, and provocation type. *Development and Psychopathology, 7*, 313–322.

Crick, N. R. (1996). The role of overt aggression, relational aggression, and prosocial behavior in the prediction of children's future social adjustment. *Child Development, 67*, 2317–2327.

Crick, N. R. (1997). Engagement in gender normative versus nonnormative forms of aggression: Links to social-psychological adjustment. *Developmental Psychology, 33*, 610–617.

Crick, N. R., & Bigbee, M. A. (1998). Relational and overt forms of peer victimization: A multi informant approach. *Journal of Consulting and Clinical Psychology, 66*, 337–347.

Crick, N. R., Bigbee, M. A., & Howes, C. (1996). Gender differences in children's normative beliefs about aggression: How do I hurt thee? Let me count the ways. *Child Development, 67*, 1003–1014.

Crick, N. R., Casas, J. F., & Ku, H. (1999). Relational and physical forms of peer victimization in preschool. *Developmental Psychology, 35*, 375–385.

Crick, N. R., & Dodge, K. A. (1994). A review and reformulation of social information-processing mechanisms in children's social adjustment. *Psychological Bulletin, 115*, 74–101.

Crick, N. R., & Grotpeter, J. K. (1995). Relational aggression, gender, and social-psychological adjustment. *Child Development, 66*, 710–722.

Crick, N. R., & Grotpeter, J. K. (1996). Children's treatment by peers: Victims of relational and overt aggression. *Development and Psychopathology, 8*, 367–380.

Crick, N. R., Grotpeter, J. K., & Bigbee, M. A. (2000). *Relationally and physically aggressive children's intent attributions and feelings of distress for relational and instrumental peer provocations.* Manuscript under review.

Crick, N. R., Werner, N. E., Casas, J. F., O'Brien, K. M., Nelson, D. A., Grotpeter, J. K., & Markon, K. (1999). Childhood aggression and gender: A new look at an old problem. In D. Bernstein (Ed.), *Nebraska symposium on motivation: Vol. 45. Gender and motivation* (pp. 75–141). Lincoln: Nebraska University Press.

Cross, S. E., & Madsen, L. (1997). Models of the self: Self-construals and gender. *Psychological Bulletin, 122*, 5–37.

DeRosier, M. E., Kupersmidt, J. B., & Patterson, C. J. (1994). Children's academic and behavioral adjustment as a function of the chronicity and proximity of peer rejection. *Child Development*, 1799–1813.

Deković, M., & Janssens, J. M. A. M. (1992). Parents' child-rearing style and child's sociometric status. *Developmental Psychology, 28*, 925–932.

Dodge, K. A. (1980). Social cognition and children's aggressive behavior. *Child Development, 51*, 162–170.

Dornbusch, S. M. (1989). The sociology of adolescence. *Annual Review of Sociology, 15*, 233–259.

Elliott, D. S., Ageton, S., Huizinga, D., Knowles, B., & Canter, R. (1983). *The prevalence and incidence of delinquent behavior: 1976–1980.* Boulder, CO: Behavioral Research Institute.

Elliott, D. S., Huizinga, D., & Morse, B. J. (1987). Self-reported violent offending: A descriptive analysis of juvenile violent offenders and their offending careers. *Journal of Interpersonal Violence, 1*, 472–514.

Erikson, E. E. (1968). *Identity: Youth and crisis.* New York: Norton.

Grotpeter, J. K. (1997). *Relational aggression, overt aggression, and family relationships.* Unpublished doctoral dissertation, University of Illinois at Urbana-Champaign.

Grotpeter, J. K., & Crick, N. R. (1996). Relational aggression, overt aggression, and friendship. *Child Development, 67*, 2328–2338.

Grotpeter, J. K., Crick, N. R., & O'Brien, K. M. (1996, April). *Relationally and overtly aggressive children's relationships with their mothers.* Paper presented at the biennial meeting of the Conference on Human Development, Birmingham, Alabama.

Grotpeter, J. K., Geiger, T., Nukulkij, P., & Crick, N. R. (1999). *Friendships of relationally and overtly victimized children: With friends like this, who needs enemies?* Manuscript submitted for publication.

Grych, J. H., & Fincham, F. D. (1990). Marital conflict and children's adjustment: A cognitive-contextual framework. *Psychological Bulletin, 108,* 267–290.

Hart, C. H., DeWolf, M., & Burts, D. C. (1992). Linkages among preschoolers' playground behavior, outcome expectations, and parental disciplinary strategies. *Early Education and Development, 3,* 265–283.

Hart, C. H., DeWolf, M., & Burts, D. C. (1993). Parental disciplinary strategies and preschoolers' play behavior in playground settings. In C. H. Hart (Ed.), *Children on playgrounds: Research perspectives and applications* (pp. 271–313). Albany: State University of New York Press.

Hart, C. H., Ladd, G. W., & Burleson, B. R. (1990). Children's expectations of the outcomes of social strategies: Relations with sociometric status and maternal disciplinary styles. *Child Development, 61,* 127–137.

Hart, C. H., Nelson, D. A., Robinson, C. C., Olsen, S. F., & McNeilly-Choque, M. K. (1998). Overt and relational aggression in Russian nursery-school-age children: Parenting style and marital linkages. *Developmental Psychology, 34,* 687–697.

Hart, C. H., Nelson, D. A., Robinson, C. C., Olsen, S. F., McNeilly-Choque, M. K., Porter, C. L., & Mckee, T. R. (2000). Russian parenting styles and family processes: Linkages with subtypes of victimization and aggression. In K. A. Kerns, J. M. Contreras, & A. M. Neal-Barnett (Eds.), *Family and peers: Linking two social worlds* (pp. 47–84). Westport, CT: Praeger.

Hart, C. H., Olsen, S. F., Robinson, C. C., & Mandleco, B. L. (1997). The development of social and communicative competence in childhood: Review and a model of personal, familial, and extra familial processes. In B. R. Burleson (Ed.), *Communication yearbook* (Vol. 20, pp. 305–373). Thousand Oaks, CA: Sage.

Hart, C. H., & Robinson, C. C. (1995). *Parental psychological control: An instrument for early childhood.* Unpublished manuscript.

Hartup, W. W. (1979). The social worlds of childhood. *American Psychologist, 34,* 944–950.

Hoffman, M. L. (1960). Power assertion by the parent and its impact on the child. *Child Development, 31,* 129–143.

Jacklin, C. N. (1981). Methodological issues in the study of sex-related differences. *Developmental Review, 1,* 266–273.

Kupersmidt, J. B., Coie, J. D., & Dodge, K. A. (1990). The role of poor peer relationships in the development of later disorders. In S. R. Asher & J. D. Coie (Eds.), *Peer rejection in childhood* (pp. 274–305). Cambridge: Cambridge University Press.

Ladd, G. W. (1992). Themes and theories: Perspectives on processes in family-peer relationships. In R. D. Parke & G. W. Ladd (Eds.), *Family-peer relationships: Modes of linkage* (pp. 3–34). New Jersey: Erlbaum.

Lamb, M. E. (1997). Fathers and child development: An introductory overview and guide. In M. E. Lamb (Ed.), *The role of the father in child development* (3rd ed.). New York: Wiley & Sons.

Leadbeater, B. J., Blatt, S. J., & Quinlin, D. M. (1995). Gender-linked vulnerabilities to depressive symptoms, stress, and problem behaviors in adolescents. *Journal of Research in Adolescence, 5,* 1–29.

Loeber, R., & Hay, D. F. (1993). Developmental approaches to aggression and conduct problems. In M. Rutter & D. F. Hay (Eds.), *Development through life: A handbook for clinicians* (pp. 488–516). Oxford, England: Blackwell.

Maccoby, E. E. (1990). Gender and relationships. *American Psychologist, 45,* 512–520.

Maccoby, E. E., & Jacklin, C. N. (1980). Sex differences in aggression: A rejoinder and reprise. *Child Development, 51,* 964–980.

Maccoby, E. E., & Martin, J. A. (1983). Socialization in the context of the family: Parent-child interaction. In E. M. Hetherington (Ed.) & P. H. Mussen (Series Ed.), *Handbook of child psychology, Vol. 4: Socialization, personality, and social development* (pp. 1-102). New York: Wiley.

MacDonald, K. (1987). Parent-child physical play with rejected, neglected, and popular boys. *Developmental Psychology, 23,* 705-711.

MacDonald, K., & Parke, R. D. (1984). Bridging the gap: Parent-child play interaction and peer interactive competence. *Child Development, 55,* 1265–1277.

MacKinnon-Lewis, C., Volling, B. L., Lamb, M. E., Dechman, K., Rabiner, D., & Curtner, M. E. (1994). A cross-contextual analysis of boys' social competence: From family to school. *Developmental Psychology, 30,* 325–333.

Marcia, J. E. (1980). Identity in adolescence. In J. Abelson (Ed.), *Handbook of adolescent psychology* (pp. 159–187). New York: Wiley.

Parke, R. D. (1996). *Fatherhood.* Cambridge, MA: Harvard University Press.

Parke, R. D., & Slaby, R. G. (1983). The development of aggression. In P. H. Mussen (Series Ed.) & M. Hetherington (Vol. Ed.), *Handbook of child psychology* (4th ed., Vol. 4, pp. 547–642).

Parker, J. G., & Asher, S. R. (1987). Peer acceptance and later personal adjustment: Are low accepted children "at risk"? *Psychological Bulletin, 102,* 357–389.

Parker, J. G., Rubin, K. H., Price, J. M., & DeRosier, M. E. (1995). Peer relationships, child development, and adjustment: A developmental psychopathology perspective. In D. Cicchetti & D. J. Cohen (Eds.), *Developmental psychopathology. Vol. 2: Risk, disorder, & adaptation* (pp. 96–161). New York: Wiley & Sons.

Patterson, G. R. (1982). *Coercive family processes.* Eugene, OR: Castilia Press.

Patterson, G. R. (1995). Coercion—A basis for early age of onset for arrest. In J. McCord (Ed.), *Coercion and punishment in long-term perspective* (pp. 81–105). New York: Cambridge University Press.

Peterson, G. W., & Hann, D. (1999). Socializing parents and children in families. In S. Steinmetz, M. Sussman, & G. W. Peterson (Eds.), Handbook of marriage and the family (rev. ed.; pp. 327–370). New York: Plenum Press.

Peterson, G. W., & Rollins, B. C. (1987). Parent-child socialization. In M. Sussman & S. K. Steinmetz (Eds.), *Handbook of marriage and the family* (pp. 471–507). New York: Plenum Press.

Pettit, G. S., & Harrist, A. W. (1992). Children's aggressive and socially unskilled playground behavior with peers: Origins in early family relations. In C. H. Hart (Ed.), *Children on playgrounds: Research perspectives and applications* (pp. 240–270). Albany: State University of New York Press.

Phares, V. (1997). Psychological adjustment, maladjustment, and father-child relationships. In M. E. Lamb (Ed.), *The role of the father in child development* (3rd ed., pp. 261–283). New York: Wiley & Sons.

Phares, V., & Compas, B. E. (1992). The role of fathers in child and adolescent psychopathology: Make room for daddy. *Psychological Bulletin, 111*, 387–412.

Pleck, J. H. (1997). Paternal involvement: Levels, sources, and consequences. In M. E. Lamb (Ed.), *The role of the father in child development* (3rd ed., pp. 66–103).

Putallaz, M., & Heflin, A. H. (1990). Parent-child interaction. In S. R. Asher & J. D. Coie (Eds.), *Peer rejection in childhood* (pp. 189–216). Cambridge: Cambridge University Press.

Robins, L. (1986). The consequences of conduct disorders in girls. In D. Olweus, J. Block, & M. Radke-Yarrow (Eds.), *Development of antisocial and prosocial behavior* (pp. 385–409). New York: Academic Press.

Robinson, C. C., Mandleco, B., Olsen, S. F., & Hart, C. H. (1995). Authoritative, authoritarian, and permissive parenting practices: Development of a new measure. *Psychological Reports, 77*, 819–830.

Rollins, B. C., & Thomas, D. L. (1979). Parental support, power, and control techniques in the socialization of children. In W. R. Burr, R. Hill, F. I. Nye, & I. L. Reiss (Eds.), *Contemporary theories about the family: Vol. 1. Research based theories* (pp. 317–364). New York: Free Press.

Russell, A., & Saebel, J. (1997). Mother-son, mother-daughter, father-son, and father-daughter: Are they distinct relationships? *Developmental Review, 17*, 111–147.

Schaefer, E. S. (1959). A circumplex model for maternal behavior. *Journal of Abnormal Social Psychology, 59*, 226–235.

Schaefer, E. S. (1965a). Children's reports of parental behavior: An inventory. *Child Development, 36*, 413–424.

Schaefer, E. S. (1965b). A configurational analysis of children's reports of parent behavior. *Journal of Consulting Psychology, 29*, 552–557.

Snyder, H., Finnegan, T., Nimick, E., Sickmund, D., Sullivan, D., & Tierney, N. (1987). *Juvenile Court Statistics, 1984.* Pittsburgh, PA: National Center for Juvenile Justice.

Steinberg, L. (1987). The impact of puberty on family relations: Effects of pubertal status and pubertal timing. *Developmental Psychology, 23*, 451–460.

Steinberg, L. (1990). Autonomy, conflict, and harmony in the family relationship. In S. S. Feldman & G. R. Elliot (Eds.), *At the threshold: The developing adolescent* (pp. 255–276). Cambridge, MA: Harvard University Press.

Steinberg, L., Elmen, J. D., & Mounts, N. S. (1989). Authoritative parenting, psychological maturity, and academic success among adolescents. *Child Development, 60,* 1424–1436.

Steinberg, L., Lamborn, S. D., Dornbusch, S. M., & Darling, N. (1992). Impact of parenting practices on adolescent achievement: Authoritative parenting, school involvement, and encouragement to succeed. *Child Development, 63,* 1266–1281.

Steinberg, L., Mounts, N. S., Lamborn, S. D., & Dornbusch, S. M. (1991). Authoritative parenting and adolescent adjustment across various ecological niches. *Journal of Research on Adolescence, 1,* 19–36.

Sullivan, H. S. (1953). *The interpersonal theory of psychiatry.* New York: Norton.

Yang, C., Hart, C. H., Nelson, D. A., Olsen, S. F., Robinson, C. C., & Jin, S. (2001). *Measuring mothers' and fathers' coercion and psychological control: Linkages with preschoolers' aggression in a Chinese sample.* Manuscript under review.

APPENDIX 6A
LIST OF CONTROL DIMENSIONS AND ASSOCIATED ITEMS

Corporal Punishment (3 items)

1. I use physical punishment as a way of disciplining my child.
2. I guide my child by physical punishment more than by reason.
3. I spank when my child is disobedient.

Verbal Hostility (3 items)

1. I explode in anger toward my child.
2. I argue with my child.
3. I yell or shout when my child misbehaves.

Psychological Control (5 items)

1. I try to change how my child feels or thinks about things.*
2. I blame my child for other family members' problems.**
3. I bring up my child's past mistakes when criticizing him/her.**
4. I am less friendly with my child when he/she does not see things my way.†
5. If my child has hurt my feelings, I stop talking to him/her until he/she pleases me again.†

---

*Invalidating feelings dimension
**Personal attack dimension
†Love withdrawal dimension

Source: Items adopted for use from "Parental Psychological Control: Revisiting a Neglected Construct," by B. K. Barber, 1996, Child Development, 62, p. 3316. Some items reproduced with permission of authors and publisher from: Robinson, C. C., Mandleco, B., Olsen, S. F., & Hart, C. H. Authoritative, authoritarian, and permissive parenting practices: Development of a new measure. Psychological Reports, 1995, 77, 819–830. © Psychological Reports 1995.

7

OBSERVED AND PERCEIVED PARENTING BEHAVIORS AND PSYCHOSOCIAL ADJUSTMENT IN PREADOLESCENTS WITH SPINA BIFIDA

GRAYSON N. HOLMBECK, WENDY E. SHAPERA, AND JENNIFER S. HOMMEYER

Few studies have examined conditions that produce variations in the level of parental psychological control *or* conditions (i.e., moderator variables) that affect the degree to which psychological control is associated with child and adolescent adjustment outcomes. Although the effects of psychological control appear to be negative regardless of cultural or demographic background, it appears that both the level and effects of psychological control may vary as a function of certain types of variables. A handful of studies have suggested that psychological control varies as a function of child and parent gender, socioeconomic status, and ethnicity (see chapter 9, this volume). A study by Gray and Steinberg (1999) has revealed that the impact of psychological control may vary as a function of other parenting variables (e.g., parental acceptance). In this volume, Morris et al. (chapter 5) investigated moderating

Completion of this manuscript was supported by Research Grants 12-FY93-0621, 12-FY95-0496, 12-FY97-0270, and 12-FY99-0280 from the March of Dimes Birth Defects Foundation and a Research Support Grant and paid leave from Loyola University of Chicago. The authors thank Ann Walsh Johnson, Caroline Anderson, Joy Ito, Pat McGovern, Pat Braun, David McLone, John Lubicky, the Illinois Spina Bifida Association, and the staff of the spina bifida clinics at Children's Memorial Hospital, Shriner's Hospital-Chicago Unit, and the Loyola University of Chicago Medical Center. We also thank Michelle Abdala, Sandra Alcala, Pam Bell, Mariana Belvedere, Rachael Bowers, Michelle Christensen, Ann Marie Czerwinski, Ken Davison, Carrie Donati, Sean Fischer, Lorin Gorey-Ferguson, Christine Gruse, Jane Holper, Sharon Johnson, Eva Kung, Eleanor Kwan, Mai Le, Wendy McKernon, Rachael Millstein, Tina Nikolopoulos, Lauren Paskiewicz, Anna Rosete, Jackie Ruba, Therese Skubic, Jennifer Uhler, Venette Westhoven, Christine Wienke, Raphael Ziegler, and Greer Zummo for help with data collection and data entry. Most important, we thank the parents and children who participated in our study.

191

effects of children's temperament, and Pettit and Laird (chapter 4) studied moderating effects of both parenting and child variables.

To date, studies in this literature have tended to focus on typically developing children, with a few investigators examining the effects of psychological control in children with psychological disturbances (e.g., Siqueland, Kendall, & Steinberg, 1996). Psychological control has not been examined in families that include children who demonstrate atypical developmental trajectories, such as those with compromising health problems. Indeed, there are reasons to believe that psychological control may be a particularly salient parenting construct in such populations. Because psychological control is expected to undermine children's level of self-reliance and autonomous functioning (see chapter 2, this volume) and because children with serious health concerns are expected to demonstrate difficulties with autonomy, it is likely that the level and effects of psychological control may differ in such populations from what is found in typically developing populations. Thus, this chapter examines the level of observed and perceived parenting behaviors (including parental psychological control) as well as the impact of parenting behaviors on psychosocial adjustment in preadolescents with a physical disability (spina bifida) compared with families that have preadolescents without physical challenges.

PAST RESEARCH ON PARENTING BEHAVIORS

For more than 60 years, researchers have investigated relationships between parenting behavior and child adjustment outcomes in typically developing children and adolescents (e.g., Baumrind, 1971; Becker, 1964; Darling & Steinberg, 1993; Gray & Steinberg, 1999; Holmbeck, Paikoff, & Brooks-Gunn, 1995; Maccoby & Martin, 1983; Rollins & Thomas, 1979; Schaefer, 1959, 1965b; Steinberg, 1990; Symonds, 1939). From this body of research, three parenting behaviors have emerged as significant predictors of child adjustment: parental acceptance, behavioral control, and psychological control. Schaefer (1965b) was the first to highlight the difference between behavioral and psychological control, defining *psychological control* as "covert, psychological methods of controlling the child's activities and behaviors that would not permit the child to develop as an individual apart from the parent" (Schaefer, 1965b, p. 555). In contrast, Schaefer (1965b) defined *behavioral control* as "the degree to which the parent makes rules and regulations, sets limits to the child's activities, and enforces these rules and limits" (p. 555). Finally, he defined *parental acceptance* as the degree to which the parent is affectionate, approving, emotionally supportive, and involved.[1]

---

[1] It is important to note that Schaefer (1965b) used the terms *acceptance, firm control,* and *psychological control* as anchors of three second-order parenting dimensions. We have chosen to use

Baumrind's (1967, 1971, 1973; see Darling & Steinberg, 1993, for a review) research in the 1960s and 1970s focused on typologies of parental control. Specifically, she identified three patterns of parental authority: authoritarian, authoritative, and permissive, which correspond to restrictive, firm, and lack of control, respectively (Baumrind, 1967, 1971). In the 1980s, Maccoby and Martin (1983) attempted to combine Baumrind's approach with several earlier schemes (including Schaefer's; also see Becker, 1964), proposing two higher order multidimensional parenting constructs: responsiveness and demandingness. Specifically, they defined demandingness as the degree to which parents supervise and discipline their offspring and have expectations for mature behavior. *Responsiveness* was defined as the level of parental sensitivity and adaptation exhibited in response to the child's concurrent needs, desires, and behaviors (Maccoby & Martin, 1983). Maccoby and Martin (1983) integrated responsiveness and demandingness into a 2 × 2 typology that included four global parenting styles: authoritative–reciprocal, authoritarian–autocratic, indulgent–permissive, and indifferent–uninvolved.

More recent operational definitions of these parenting styles have included acceptance and behavioral control in place of the more global responsiveness and demandingness constructs, with some investigators integrating parental psychological control as well (e.g., Barber, 1996; Barber, Olsen, & Shagle, 1994; Steinberg, 1990; Steinberg, Elmen, & Mounts, 1989). Despite the utility of the typological approach, a primary difficulty with this strategy is that researchers are unable to determine which specific parenting behaviors are associated with which child outcomes. In this study, parenting styles were "unpacked" into their component parts (i.e., acceptance, behavioral control, and psychological control) to examine behavior-specific correlates (see Gray & Steinberg, 1999; Steinberg et al., 1989; for examples of this strategy).

PARENTING BEHAVIORS AND CHILD AND ADOLESCENT ADJUSTMENT

Studies suggest that acceptance and behavioral control can facilitate positive psychosocial adjustment as assessed with measures of academic performance, social competence, and behavior problems (e.g., Barber, 1996;

---

these terms, except that *behavioral control* has been substituted for *firm control* in keeping with more recent work (Barber, 1996; Gray & Steinberg, 1999; Steinberg, 1990; Steinberg et al., 1989; see also chapter 2, this volume) and because the target of the parental control is more apparent for the term *behavioral control* than for the term *firm control*. There are, of course, numerous other terms that have been used interchangeably with the terms we have chosen (see Rollins & Thomas, 1979, for a review).

Lamborn, Mounts, Steinberg, & Dornbusch, 1991; Maccoby & Martin, 1983; Steinberg et al., 1989; Steinberg, Lamborn, Darling, Mounts, & Dornbusch, 1994; Weiss & Schwarz, 1996). Recently, Steinberg (1990; Gray & Steinberg, 1999) and Barber (1996; chapter 2, this volume) have revived an interest in psychological control. Reviews by these and other authors show that such control has been associated with negative psychosocial adjustment, particularly lower self-worth and internalizing problems.

Parental acceptance, behavioral control, and psychological control are particularly salient parenting behaviors during the transition to adolescence. The cognitive, social, and contextual changes associated with preadolescence (or middle childhood, ages 6 to 12) allow children to assume greater control over their daily lives (Collins, Harris, & Susman, 1995; Maccoby, 1984). The transfer of control from parent to child is a gradual process that begins in preadolescence and continues into young adulthood (Collins et al., 1995; Eccles et al., 1991; Hill & Holmbeck, 1986; Holmbeck, Belvedere, Gorey-Gerguson, & Schneider, 1995; Maccoby, 1984). Parents who are able to facilitate psychological autonomy in their child, while continuing to provide discipline, monitoring (e.g., behavioral control), warmth, and affection (e.g., acceptance) appear to facilitate the best adolescent adjustment outcomes (see chapter 2, this volume; see also Holmbeck et al., 1995; Maccoby & Martin, 1983; Steinberg, 1990, for reviews).

CHILDREN AND ADOLESCENTS WITH SPINA BIFIDA: THE RELEVANCE OF PARENTAL PSYCHOLOGICAL CONTROL

Spina bifida is a relatively common congenital physical disability, with an incidence of 1 in 1000 live births. It is caused by the incomplete closure of one or more vertebrae during the early weeks of pregnancy (Varni & Wallander, 1988). Children with spina bifida often have numerous medical problems, including urinary, bowel, weight, orthopedic, and neurological difficulties, requiring adherence to specific medical regimens (Charney, 1992; Lavigne, Nolan, & McLone, 1988; McLone & Ito, 1998). Many children with spina bifida use braces, crutches, or wheelchairs to ambulate (Charney, 1992; Varni & Wallander, 1988).

The task of parenting children with spina bifida requires the same types of parenting behaviors described earlier (Drotar, 1992). In addition, however, parents of children with spina bifida are also responsible for ensuring that their children adhere to complex medical regimens and learn effective self-care skills while at the same time facilitating their children's independent functioning (Anderson & Coyne, 1993; Drotar, 1992). When parents are unable or unwilling to grant increasing amounts of independence and autonomy to children with spina bifida, a process referred to as *miscarried helping* may unfold (Anderson & Coyne, 1993). Miscarried helping occurs when parents' investment in being supportive and in achieving a positive medical outcome for their children leads to parent–child interactions that become increasingly coercive over time and ultimately detrimental to the child's well-being and ability to function independently (Anderson & Coyne, 1993).

For parents who have a child with a physical disability, the unfolding of the miscarried helping process may begin before adolescence (Anderson & Coyne, 1993). Over the course of middle childhood (ages 6 to 12), children with pediatric conditions are often asked to become more involved in carrying out prescribed medical regimens (in the same way that typically developing children are granted more decision-making control with development; Holmbeck et al., 1995). The manner in which this transfer of responsibility occurs is critical. On the one hand, such a shift in responsibility requires that the parent give up control and that the child assume more control over self-care. On the other hand, considerable parental supervision may be necessary at the beginning of this process as the child learns to administer the treatments on his or her own. Depending on how the parent manages this transitional phase, the continued parental supervision and vigilance may cause the child to feel intruded on and deprived of the ability to make independent decisions (Anderson & Coyne, 1993). In some families, parents may become excessively concerned with achieving immediate and complete compliance from the child. In the final stage of this process, parental demands and child resistance increase until the helping process deteriorates. The child may feign incompetence or fail to comply with treatment in an effort to force parents to reduce their demands and to protect a sense of autonomy and control.

Anderson and Coyne's (1993) description of such overinvolved parenting is similar to descriptions of psychologically controlling parents (for example, see Barber & Harmon's emphasis on "intrusiveness" as a defining feature of psychological control, chapter 2, this volume). In other words, psychological control may be a particularly salient parenting dimension for some families of children with physical disabilities.

PARENTING BEHAVIORS AND CHILD ADJUSTMENT IN STUDIES OF PEDIATRIC POPULATIONS

Children with physical disabilities are at risk for displaying higher levels of internalizing and externalizing symptoms and lower levels of self-competence compared with their peers without physical challenges (e.g., Appleton et al., 1994; Borjeson & Lagergren, 1990; Lavigne & Faier-Routman, 1992; Thompson & Gustafson, 1996; Wallander & Thompson,

1995, for reviews). However, given the variability in psychosocial adjustment across children with pediatric conditions, investigators have also explored factors that may be associated with such variation (Lavigne & Faier-Routman, 1993; Thompson & Gustafson, 1996). One set of predictive factors that has received considerable attention includes the quality of family functioning and parental adjustment (Drotar, 1997; Kazak, Segal-Andrews, & Johnson, 1995; Thompson & Gustafson, 1996). On the other hand, parenting behaviors (and particularly *observed* parenting behaviors; e.g., Black, Hutcheson, Dubowitz, & Berenson-Howard, 1994; Pianta & Lothman, 1994), have received far less attention in this literature (Drotar, 1997; Kazak et al., 1995). In fact, no studies have examined parental acceptance, behavioral control, and psychological control in relation to child adjustment in a sample of children with physical disabilities. Instead, studies typically compare parents of chronically ill or physically handicapped children with those of either healthy or acutely ill children to determine if their parenting behaviors differ; such studies have yielded mixed findings (e.g., Davies, Noll, DeStefano, Bukowski, & Kulkarni, 1991; Hauser et al., 1986, 1989; Ievers, Drotar, Dahms, Doershuk, & Stern, 1994; Kazak, Reber, & Snitzer, 1988; Murch & Cohen, 1989; Spaulding & Morgan, 1986).

In some studies researchers have found no differences in parenting behavior between parents of children who have chronic illnesses or physical disabilities and their counterparts without physical challenges. For example, in a study comparing 19 children with spina bifida and 19 children without physical challenges and their parents, Spaulding and Morgan (1986) reported no differences on measures of parental attitudes, marital adjustment, and overall family functioning. Similarly, Davies et al. (1991) studied 24 families with a child who has cancer and 24 families with a healthy child and found that parents of children with cancer did not differ from parents of healthy children on measures of overprotection, discipline, and worry.

On the other hand, in a study that compared child-rearing practices of 42 acutely ill and 52 diabetic pre- and early adolescents and their parents, Hauser et al. (1989) found that parents of diabetic children placed greater emphasis on family organization, control, and system maintenance. Moreover, family orientation toward organization and independence predicted self-esteem for diabetic children, whereas family orientation toward achievement predicted self-esteem for acutely ill children (Hauser et al., 1989).

The inconsistent nature of these findings may be a result, in part, to significant methodological limitations. The majority of these studies: (a) fail to clearly define important components of parenting that are relevant to children with physical disabilities; (b) are insensitive to developmental issues (e.g., data are collected on samples with broad age ranges covering multiple developmental transition periods); (c) tend to rely exclusively on self-report data rather than direct observation; or (d) use one or two respondents, most often mother or child, and neglect other sources of information such as fathers (Kazak et al., 1995), thus making it difficult or impossible to rule out common method variance explanations for the findings. This study was designed to address these shortcomings.

HYPOTHESES AND OVERVIEW OF RESEARCH DESIGN

Levels of parenting behaviors as well as associations between parenting behaviors and child adjustment were examined in a sample of children with spina bifida and in a comparison sample of children without physical disabilities. The use of a comparison group allowed us to address an important unanswered question in the pediatric psychology literature: How do associations between parenting behaviors and child adjustment differ across pediatric and nonpediatric samples (Drotar, 1997)? With respect to group differences on the parenting variables, parents of children with spina bifida were expected to be as accepting as parents of children without physical challenges. However, given the salience of autonomy issues in children with physical disabilities during the transition to adolescence (e.g., Collins et al., 1996), parental behavioral control and psychological control were expected to be more highly used in families with children who have spina bifida. Regarding associations between parenting and child adjustment, parenting behaviors were expected to be more highly associated with adjustment outcomes in families of children with spina bifida, given that children with physical disabilities spend more time with their families (and less time with peers) than do children without such disabilities (Blum, Resnick, Nelson, & St. Germaine, 1991). Whereas acceptance and behavioral control were expected to be associated with positive outcomes in both groups, psychological control was expected to be associated with negative outcomes in both groups.

The design of this study is an improvement over past work because a specific age group was targeted (8- and 9-year-olds), multiple domains of child adjustment were assessed from multiple perspectives across multiple settings (e.g., child, mother, father, teacher), and observational data were used. Adjustment outcomes similar to those used in past research on parenting practices and parenting styles (e.g., chapter 2, this volume; Lamborn et al., 1991) and in recent studies of children with physical disabilities and chronic illnesses (Lavigne & Faier-Routman, 1992) were used. Specifically, this study focuses on child internalizing and externalizing symptoms, academic performance, and observed adaptive behavior. Past theorizing and empirical work suggest that psychological control undermines children's attempts to be self-reliant and is, as a result, most likely to be associated with internalizing symptoms (although psychological control has been found to be associated with a variety of outcomes; chapter 2, this volume). Lack of behavioral control has been linked with impulse control difficulties and, as a consequence, externalizing symptoms (Barber, 1996; Steinberg, 1990). Measures of academic performance and observed adaptive behavior allowed us to examine whether the parenting variables had an impact on adjustment across settings (i.e., behavior in the school and home environments). Common method variance was reduced by only examining associations among variables drawn from different sources. Finally, we examined gender differences with respect to levels of parenting behaviors across samples and in associations between the parenting variables and adjustment. Given that findings for both types of analyses have yielded mixed results, no hypotheses were advanced for these gender comparisons.

OVERVIEW OF SAMPLE, PROCEDURE, AND MEASURES

Participants were 68 families with 8- and 9-year-olds with spina bifida and a matched comparison group of 68 families with 8- and 9-year-olds without physical challengers who were part of a larger longitudinal study of the transition to adolescence in families with children who have spina bifida (Holmbeck et al., 1997, 1998; Hommeyer, Holmbeck, Wills, & Coers, 1999; McKernon et al., 2001). Complete demographic information for both groups is provided in Table 7-1. Although biological mothers from all families from both groups participated in the study, only 55 and 52 fathers or stepfathers participated in the group with spina bifida and comparison groups, respectively. As Table 7-1 shows, the groups were successfully matched on all demographic variables.

Information on a number of physical status variables for the group with spina bifida was obtained based on maternal report or from information gleaned from the child's medical chart: (a) *spinal lesion level:* 32% sacral, 50% lumbosacral or lumbar, 13% thoracic, 5% missing data; this variable indicates the point along the spinal column where the vertebrae were not completely closed; spinal lesion level is an indication of the degree of physical impairment that a child experiences; (b) *spina bifida type:* 82% myelomeningocele, 12% lipomeningocele, 6% missing or other; these terms refer to different types of spina bifida; lipomeningocele is a less severe form of spina bifida than myelomeningocele; (c) *shunt status:* 71% shunt, 29% no shunt; hydrocephalus, or an accumulation of cerebrospinal fluid in the ventricles of the brain, is experienced by 80 to 90% of children with myelomeningocele; shunts are inserted into the brain to drain fluid into the abdominal cavity, the heart, or the chest cavity; and (d) *ambulation:* 19% no assistance, 63% assistance with braces; 18% assistance with a wheelchair; many children with spina bifida have reduced mobility of the lower extremities, often requiring them to use braces or a wheelchair to ambulate (McLone

TABLE 7-1
Demographics: Comparisons Across Samples

Demographic Characteristics	Spina Bifida	Comparison	Statistical Tests
Child age M (SD)	8.34 (.48)	8.49 (.50)	$t\,(134) = -1.75$
Maternal age M (SD)	37.74 (5.19)	37.74 (4.84)	$t\,(134) = .00$
Paternal age M (SD)	41.02 (5.45)	40.63 (6.50)	$t\,(105) = .33$
Child gender			
% Male (n)	54.4 (37)	54.4 (37)	$x^2\,(1) = .00$
% Female (n)	45.6 (31)	45.6 (31)	
Child ethnicity			
% White (n)	82.4 (56)	91.2 (62)	$x^2\,(1) = 2.30$
% Other (n)	17.6 (12)	8.8 (6)	
Child birth order			
Mean birth order (SD)	2.12 (1.38)	2.06 (1.29)	$t\,(129) = .27$
Marital status			
% Two-parent intact (n)	80.9 (55)	69.1 (47)	$x^2\,(1) = 2.51$
% Nonintact (n)	19.1 (13)	30.9 (21)	
Maternal income M (SD)	5.75 (2.57)	5.73 (2.45)	$t\,(130) = .05$
Paternal income M (SD)	6.24 (2.50)	6.35 (2.22)	$t\,(105) = -.24$
Hollingshead socioeconomic status (SD)	43.12 (10.57)	46.46 (10.89)	$t\,(131) = -1.80$

Note: $N = 68$ for each sample. Marital status was collapsed to intact versus nonintact. Family income is rated on a scale from 1 to 11 with 1 < $10,000 . . . 5 = $40,000 to 49,999 . . . 10 = $90,000 to 99,999, and 11 > $100,000. The Hollingshead (1975) four factor index of socioeconomic status is based on a composite of maternal education, paternal education, maternal occupational status, and paternal occupational status. All statistics were nonsignificant.

& Ito, 1998). The average number of shunt surgeries among those with shunts was 2.50 ($SD = 2.91$). Medical chart interrater reliabilities for type of spina bifida, lesion level, and number of shunt surgeries were 83%, 92%, and $r = .97$, respectively.

As expected, a significant difference was found between the samples on a measure of receptive language (Peabody Picture Vocabulary Test, Revised; Dunn & Dunn, 1981): $M = 92.49$ ($SD = 18.49$) for the sample with spina bifida and $M = 108.97$ ($SD = 15.06$) for the sample with no physical challenges. This finding parallels results based on verbal IQ test scores insofar as children with spina bifida typically score in the low-average range (e.g., Wills, Holmbeck, Dillon, & McLone, 1990). Because lower receptive vocabulary scores were viewed as part of the symptom presentation in children with spina bifida (much like ambulation difficulties, for example) and because children with spina bifida are typically mainstreamed into classrooms with children without physical challenges, no attempt was made to match the samples on this variable and no statistical controls for PPVT-R scores were instituted.

Participating families in the group with spina bifida were recruited from lists provided by four sources: (a) a children's hospital, (b) a children's hospital that cares exclusively for youngsters with physical disabilities, (c) a university-based medical center, and (d) a statewide spina bifida association. A letter was sent to all parents of children within the 8- to 9-year-old range (and those who would reach this age within the following year). A total of 310 nonoverlapping names were gathered from the four sources. Of these, 72 families lived too far away (greater than 120 miles from the laboratory), 64 declined to participate, 56 could not be reached, 16 did not speak English, 14 children had turned 10 years old before a visit could be scheduled, 11 children did not have spina bifida, and 6 were excluded for miscellaneous reasons. Seventy-one families remained. One additional family was dropped following the family visit because the child was 13 years old (this family was selected because of an error on the original participant list), and two families were dropped to facilitate matching with the sample without physical challenges. A comparison of participating children with children from families that declined to participate (n = 64) revealed no differences with respect to lesion level, χ^2 (2)=.62, p > .05, or type of spina bifida (myelomeningocele vs. lipomeningocele), χ^2 (1)=1.63, p > .05.

Participating families from the comparison group were recruited by contacting schools where the children with spina bifida were enrolled. It proved unnecessary to contact all possible schools to obtain a comparison group the same size as the group with spina bifida. Therefore, schools were selected according to the average family income of the community (based on lists that were provided by state governments) for the first 42 children with spina bifida who participated in the study. Twenty-four of these schools were dropped: 12 were dropped because there was an overly high average family income in the community (the inclusion of these schools would have resulted in an imbalance in socioeconomic status for the two groups, particularly if numerous children without physical disabilities from these schools had agreed to participate), 5 schools were located too far away, 4 schools had a racial balance that would have produced difficulties with successful matching of the two groups, 2 schools were parochial or private, and 1 school had only special education programs. Twelve of the remaining 18 schools agreed to participate and were provided with informational letters (and self-addressed stamped envelopes) to be sent home with the children without physical challenges in our age range. Parents who wanted to participate returned a slip indicating their consent. Approximately 1700 letters were sent to obtain the control sample for this study. The longitudinal nature of the study, which was described in detail in the letter, may account for the low recruitment rate.

All family assessments were conducted by trained graduate and undergraduate research assistants during a three-hour home visit. After parents and child had signed informed consent forms, they were asked to complete a set of questionnaires and one hour of family interaction tasks that were videotaped and audiotaped, for which the family was paid $50. Child questionnaires were administered in an interview format, with all Likert scales printed on large laminated cards. Family interaction tasks consisted of (a) an unfamiliar board game requiring the family to make decisions regarding how to play the game on their own; (b) a structured family interaction task requiring the family to come to a collective decision in response to five multiple choice questions involving family activities (e.g., what to watch on television, family excursions; Ferreira, 1963); and (c) a conflict task requiring the family to discuss and resolve three issues, previously identified as contentious for the family with individually administered questionnaires (Robin & Foster, 1992; Smetana, Yau, Restrepo, & Braeges, 1991). Parents were also asked to sign release forms for the child's teacher, a health professional (the sample with spina bifida only), and a medical chart review (the sample with spina bifida only). After the family visit, questionnaire packets were sent to the child's teacher (return rate: 97% in sample with spina bifida; 84% in comparison sample) and a health professional (return rate: 98%), for which they were compensated $5 and $2, respectively. This study involves analyses of child, mother, father, and teacher questionnaire data, observer ratings of videotaped family interaction data, and observer ratings of child behavior in the home.

Measures of Parenting

Parental acceptance, behavioral control, and psychological control were assessed with questionnaire measures and observational coding. The questionnaire measure of parenting behavior used was the Child Report of Parental Behavior Instrument (CRPBI; Schaefer, 1965a; Schwarz, Barton-Henry, & Pruzinsky, 1985; Schuldermann & Schludermann, 1970). The CRPBI is one of the most widely used measures in the literature on parenting behavior. This version of the CRPBI is a 108-item scale that assesses maternal and paternal child-rearing behaviors. Mothers, fathers, and children completed this measure by rating individual items as "like," "somewhat like," or "not like" the parent. Parents completed self-reports of their own behavior, and children rated each parent. Items were reworded slightly to make them appropriate for use by mothers, fathers, and children (following the rewording procedure used by Schwarz et al., 1985).

Because of time considerations, only 44 items from the larger 108-item scale were administered. Sixteen items were used for the acceptance scale, 15 for the behavioral control scale, and 13 for the psychological control scale. Complete versions of the following subscales were used: acceptance (8 items; e.g., "my mother makes me feel better after talking over my worries with her") and rejection (8 items; reverse scored; e.g., "my mother almost always complains about what I do") as measures of *acceptance*; control (5 items; e.g., "my mother believes in having a lot of rules and sticking to them"), enforcement (5 items; e.g., "my mother sees to it that I obey when she tells me something"), lax discipline (5 items; reverse scored; e.g., "my mother lets me off easy when I do something wrong") as measures of *behavioral control*; and intrusiveness (5 items; e.g., "my mother asks me to tell her everything that happens when I am away from home") and hostile control (8 items; e.g., "my mother would like to be able to tell me what to do all the time") as measures of *psychological control*. Although these scales are similar to those used by other investigators (e.g., Barber et al., 1994), they do not cover all components of these parenting constructs because only a portion of the larger set of CRPBI items was used (i.e., the content validity of the scales would likely be improved by using all first-order subscales of the original CRPBI).

For the group with spina bifida, Cronbach's alphas were as follows: (a) child report for maternal acceptance, behavioral control, and psychological control were .60, .68, and .66, respectively; (b) child report for the three paternal parenting variables were .81, .77, and .71, respectively; (c) mother report for the three maternal parenting variables were .77, .78, and .67, respectively; and (d) father report for the three paternal parenting variables were .79, .79, and .69, respectively. For the group without physical challenges, alphas were as follows: (a) child report for the three maternal parenting variables were .83, .55, and .57, respectively; (b) child report for the three paternal parenting variables were .86, .76, and .74, respectively; (c) mother report for the three maternal parenting variables were .81, .80, and .65, respectively; and (d) father report for the three paternal parenting variables were .82, .75, and .61, respectively.

The three family interaction tasks were coded using a global method developed by Holmbeck et al. (1995), based on a system devised by Smetana et al. (1991). As is typically done with global coding systems, coders viewed an entire family interaction task and then provided 5-point Likert scale ratings on a variety of dimensions. The manual includes behavioral descriptions for each of the points along the Likert scale. Parental behavior was rated by two coders for all three tasks and across all families. These coders were undergraduate- and graduate-level research assistants who received 10 hours of training before beginning the coding process. All coders were blind to the specific hypotheses of this study.

This coding system contains five dimensions of parenting behavior, child behavior, and parent–child relationships (each of which includes multiple codes): (a) interaction style, (b) conflict, (c) affect, (d) control, and (e) child-centered and collaborative problem-solving. Several family atmosphere variables were coded as well. Scales for acceptance, behavioral control, and psychological control were formed rationally (as opposed to empirically) by selecting items from the complete list of codes that reflected the definitions of each parenting construct as discussed in the literature (e.g., Barber, 1996; Steinberg, 1990). The following codes were used in this study: listens to others, humor and laughter, warmth, anger (reverse-scored) and supportiveness as measures of maternal and paternal *acceptance*; overt power, nature of parental control–permissive (reverse-scored), and parental structuring of task as measures of maternal and paternal *behavioral control*; and pressures others to agree, nature of parental control–democratic (reverse-scored), tolerates differences and disagreements (reverse-scored), receptive to statements made by others (reverse-scored), and nature of parental control (overprotective) as measures of maternal and paternal *psychological control*. Given the focus of this volume, we have included a detailed listing of all coding criteria for the psychological control items in appendix 7A. Items were coded on a 5-point Likert scale for mothers and fathers separately and means of the two raters were used in data analyses. For single-parent families and for families in which a parent refused to participate, the behavior of only one parent was coded.

As noted earlier, there have been few attempts to assess psychological control with observational data. One exception is Barber's (1996) study of psychological control and child adjustment. His coding scheme included the following codes: constraining verbal expressions, invalidating feelings, personal attack on child, guilt induction, love withdrawal, and erratic emotional behaviors. Our coding system emphasizes the intrusive and constraining nature of psychological control. Thus, it overlaps most with Barber's (1996) codes that tap "constraining verbal expressions" and "invalidating feelings."

Satisfactory reliability was found between raters on their observations of maternal and paternal acceptance, behavioral control, and psychological control. For the group with spina bifida, intraclass interrater reliability correlations (Suen & Ary, 1989) for maternal acceptance, behavioral control, and psychological control were .79, .74, and .68, respectively. The intraclass rater reliabilities for the paternal parenting behaviors were .88, .87, and .80, respectively. For the sample without physical challenges, the rater reliabilities were .79, .85, and .69 for the maternal behaviors and .79, .85, and .79 for the paternal behaviors.

In addition, satisfactory scale reliability was established for these observational scales. In the group with spina bifida, Cronbach's alphas were .86, .66, and .71 for the maternal behaviors and .88, .68, and .76 for the paternal behaviors. For the group without physical challenges, Cronbach's alphas were .85, .85, and .73 for the maternal behaviors and .80, .78, and .76 for the paternal behaviors.

Measuring Psychological Adjustment

Internalizing and externalizing symptoms, academic performance, and observed adaptive behavior in the home were assessed with questionnaire data (from multiple sources) and observational coding. Mother, father, and teacher reports on the 113-item Child Behavior Checklist (CBCL; Achenbach, 1991a) were used to assess behavior problems. The parent version of this measure comprises three competence scales (activities, social competence, and school competence), eight problem scales, and two second-order problem scales representing internalizing and externalizing behavior problems. Given high correlations between mother and father report, the internalizing and externalizing problem behavior scales were averaged across parents for the data analyses (i.e., the correlations between mother and father report for internalizing and externalizing problems were .45 and .55, respectively, for the sample with spina bifida, and .41 and .61 for the sample without physical challenges). The teacher report version of this measure, the Teacher Report Form (TRF; Achenbach 1991b), was used to gather teacher-report information on the internalizing and externalizing problem scales described previously. Achenbach (1991a, 1991b) reported excellent reliability and validity data for this measure. In the sample with spina bifida, scale alphas were .82 and .85 for maternal report of internalizing and externalizing symptoms, .84 and .84 for paternal report of symptoms, and .90 and .92 for teacher report of symptoms. In the sample without physical challenges, scale alphas were .85 and .90 for maternal report of internalizing and externalizing symptoms, .80 and .89 for paternal report of symptoms, and .88 and .87 for teacher report of symptoms.

School grades were reported by teachers and were coded on a scale from 1 to 8, with high scores indicating better grades. A score of 8 indicated excellent performance (the letter grade "A"), a score of 4 represented satisfactory performance (the letter grade "B-/C+"), and a score of 1 indicated unsatisfactory performance (the letter grade "F"). Grade point averages were computed for four classes: science, social studies, English, and math. Cronbach's alphas indicated satisfactory internal consistency for ratings of grade point average (.85 for the group with spina bifida and .84 for the comparison group).

Child adaptive behavior was coded using 10 items from the 44-item Home Visit Report Form. Most items of this observational measure were developed for this study, with 17 items based on the work of another investigator (Judy Garber, personal communication, October 1993). This measure was used to assess child and parent behavior displayed during family home visits. The coding form was completed by trained research assistants who were present during the visits. Child adaptive behavior was rated on a 5-point Likert scale, with 1 corresponding to "not at all" and 5 corresponding to "very much." Items included "the child was cooperative with staff" and "the child was distrustful" (reverse-scored). Scale reliabilities were .76 and .75 for the group with spina bifida and comparison groups, respectively. The interrater reliability (i.e., intraclass correlation; Suen & Ary, 1989), based on ratings of two coders for 15 randomly selected families, was .70.

DATA ANALYSES

Preliminary analyses were conducted to determine the degree of association among the parenting constructs within and across methods. For the questionnaire data and across both samples, correlations between acceptance and behavioral control and between acceptance and psychological control were all less than $r = + .40$ for child report of maternal parenting, child report of paternal parenting, mother report of her own parenting, and father report of his own parenting. On the other hand, some correlations between behavioral control and psychological control exceeded .40 (range of r's = .19 to .53; M = .37).

Correlations among the three parenting constructs as assessed with observational data were higher than those for the questionnaire data. Across samples and maternal and paternal parenting, correlations between acceptance and behavioral control ranged from .27 to .61 (M = .42), correlations between acceptance and psychological control ranged from -.71 to -.80 (M = -.76), and correlations between behavioral control and psychological control ranged from -.18 to -.33 (M = -.24). Thus, for psychometric reasons, we expected that associations between parenting and adjustment would be more similar across the three parenting constructs for the observational data than for the questionnaire data (and particularly for findings related to observed parental acceptance and psychological control).

Child reports of parents were modestly associated with parents' reports of themselves, particularly for the sample without physical challenges. Specifically, the range of r's between child report of maternal parenting and mothers' reports of their own parenting on the same parenting constructs ranged from -.04 to .18 (M = .06) for the sample with spina bifida and from .20 to .31 (M = .24) for the sample without physical challenges. The same ranges for fathers' parenting were .09 to .23 (M = .16) for the group with spina bifida and .17 to .29 (M = .22) for the group without physical challenges.

Correlations between child report and observational measures for the same parenting constructs ranged from -.12 to .36 (M = .13). Correlations between mothers' and observers' reports of the same parenting constructs ranged from -.04 to .45 (M = .22). Correlations between fathers' and observers' reports of the parenting constructs ranged from -.14 to .27 (M = .09). Given that the observational measures were newly developed for this study, the positive correlations between methods (20 of 24 r's were positive) lend partial support to the construct validity of the observational data.

Preliminary analyses were also conducted to determine the degree of association among the adjustment outcome variables. Across all outcomes and across both samples, all r's were less than +.40, with three exceptions. Teacher report of school grades and teacher report of externalizing symptoms were negatively associated for the sample with spina bifida ($r = -.43$), parent report of externalizing symptoms and teacher report of externalizing symptoms were positively associated for the sample without physical challenges ($r = .43$), and parental internalizing and externalizing symptoms were positively associated for both samples ($r = .60$ in the sample with spina bifida, $r = .57$ in the sample without physical challenges).

Group Differences on Parenting Variables

Six one-way multivariate analyses of variance (MANOVAS) with univariate follow-up analyses were conducted to determine if parents of children with spina bifida would differ on measures of acceptance, behavioral control, and psychological control in comparison to parents of children without physical challenges. Separate MANOVAS were conducted for child report of mother, child report of father, mother report of self, father report of self, mother observational data, and father observational data. Initially, the analyses were run as two-way MANOVAs, with child gender as an additional between-subjects independent variable. Because no significant gender or gender × group effects emerged, these results for gender are not reported.

Analyses based on mothers' reports of maternal parenting revealed significant differences between the group with spina bifida and the group without physical challenges, $F (3, 129) = 3.74$, $p < .01$. As can be seen in Table 7-2, follow-up tests indicated that mothers in the group with spina bifida reported significantly higher levels of maternal psychological control, $F (1, 131) = 6.02$, $p < .01$, than mothers in the control sample. The groups also differed significantly on observers' ratings of mothers, $F (3, 131) = 4.47$, $p < .01$. Univariate follow-up tests again indicated that mothers in the group with spina bifida displayed higher levels of psychological control, $F (1, 133) = 6.29$, $p < .01$. In addition, significant group differences were found for fathers' reports of paternal parenting, $F (3, 101) = 4.24$, $p < .01$. Univariate follow-up tests indicated that fathers in the comparison group reported higher levels of paternal behavioral control, $F (1, 103) = 6.04$, $p < .01$.

Therefore, partial support was found for the hypotheses. Consistent with expectations, mothers of children with spina bifida demonstrated higher levels of psychological control based on both questionnaire and observational data. Furthermore, no differences were found between parents on measures

TABLE 7-2
Significant Group Differences on Parenting Variables

Variables	Spina Bifida M (SD)	Comparison M (SD)	Significance MANOVA F	Univar F
Child report of maternal parenting questionnaire			1.67	
Mother acceptance	2.54 (.26)	2.63 (.27)		3.90*
Mother behavioral control	2.21 (.33)	2.18 (.27)		.33
Mother psychological control	2.16 (.37)	2.09 (.30)		1.23
Child report of paternal parenting questionnaire			2.33	
Father acceptance	2.48 (.35)	2.53 (.36)		.44
Father behavioral control	2.21 (.37)	2.14 (.31)		1.38
Father psychological control	2.01 (.40)	1.82 (.37)		6.78*
Mother report of maternal parenting questionnaire			3.74**	
Mother acceptance	2.63 (.23)	2.64 (.24)		.06
Mother behavioral control	1.98 (.30)	2.04 (.32)		.97
Mother psychological control	1.95 (.31)	1.83 (.27)		6.02**
Father report of paternal parenting questionnaire			4.24**	
Father acceptance	2.60 (.25)	2.60 (.27)		.00
Father behavioral control	1.92 (.31)	2.06 (.29)		6.04**
Father psychological control	1.83 (.28)	1.77 (.27)		1.03
Maternal parenting observational			4.47**	
Mother acceptance	3.72 (.41)	3.76 (.36)		.47
Mother behavioral control	4.35 (.36)	4.23 (.46)		2.94
Mother psychological control	2.04 (.36)	1.90 (.30)		6.29**
Paternal parenting observational			1.07	
Father acceptance	3.66 (.52)	3.61 (.34)		.29
Father behavioral control	4.09 (.47)	4.04 (.52)		.28
Father psychological control	2.00 (.42)	1.95 (.35)		.42

Note: N varies for these analyses because of missing values.
*p < .05   **p < .01

of acceptance. However, contrary to expectations, fathers of children without physical challenges scored significantly higher on measures of perceived behavioral control.

Associations Between Parenting Behavior and Child Adjustment Outcomes

A series of hierarchical regression analyses were conducted to examine whether the nature and magnitude of associations between the parenting variables and the child adjustment outcomes differed as a function of group (spina bifida versus comparison) and gender. Analyses were run separately for different reporters of parenting and for each parenting variable. The findings for parental acceptance, behavioral control, and psychological control are included in Tables 7-3, 7-4, and 7-5, respectively.

TABLE 7-3
Multiple Regressions: Significant Associations Between Parental Acceptance and Preadolescent Adjustment

| | Preadolescent Adjustment Outcomes | | | | | | | | | | | | | | | | | |
| | Internalizing (P) | | | Externalizing (P) | | | Internalizing (T) | | | Externalizing (T) | | | School Grades (T) | | | Adaptive Behavior (Obs) | | |
Parenting variable	R	β	FΔ	R	β	FΔ	R	β	FΔ	R	β	FΔ	R	β	FΔ	R	β	FΔ
Mother acceptance (C)																		
Step 1: Group	.10	-.10	1.23	.03	-.03	.12	.34	-.34	16.05***	.22	-.22	5.91*	.33	.33	13.56***	.19	.19	4.90*
Step 2: Gender	.10	-.03	.12	.03	.01	.02	.35	.05	.40	.23	.08	.87	.33	-.02	.06	.19	.02	.08
Step 3: Acceptance	.14	-.09	1.11	.12	-.12	1.82	.36	-.08	.96	.23	-.01	.03	.38	.19	4.73*	.27	.20	5.31*
Step 4: Grp x Gen	.14	.02	.07	.13	-.04	.26	.36	-.00	.00	.23	-.01	.02	.39	.09	1.06	.28	.07	.72
Step 5: Acc x Grp	.16	-.09	.96	.19	-.14	2.43	.36	-.04	.23	.25	.09	.93	.39	.01	.01	.28	-.04	.22
Step 6: Acc x Gen	.16	-.00	.00	.21	-.10	1.22	.36	.01	.02	.25	.05	.25	.42	-.15	2.94	.31	-.12	1.90
Step 7: Acc x Grp X Gen	.21	-.14	2.27	.28	-.18	4.20*	.37	-.09	1.00	.27	-.11	1.43	.42	-.03	.12	.32	.10	1.41
Father acceptance (C)																		
Step 1: Group	.09	-.09	.99	.01	-.01	.01	.35	-.35	15.46**	.16	-.16	2.72	.28	.28	8.68**	.15	.15	2.92
Step 2: Gender	.09	-.01	.01	.01	.01	.01	.36	.09	.98	.21	.14	2.29	.28	-.04	.15	.15	-.01	.03
Step 3: Acceptance	.09	.01	.02	.09	-.09	.89	.36	.01	.02	.21	.04	.19	.36	.23	5.98*	.19	.11	1.51
Step 4: Grp x Gen	.09	-.01	.00	.09	-.03	.08	.36	-.02	.04	.23	-.08	.64	.38	.11	1.39	.20	.08	.73
Step 5: Acc x Grp	.09	.02	.06	.09	.02	.03	.36	.01	.02	.23	-.05	.27	.42	.20	4.51*	.20	.01	.02
Step 6: Acc x Gen	.10	.02	.07	.12	-.07	.55	.36	-.03	.13	.25	-.02	.05	.43	-.10	1.03	.21	.03	.08
Step 7: Acc x Grp x Gen	.26	-.25	7.35**	.22	-.19	4.08*	.38	-.13	1.87	xx	-.09	.74	.43	.03	.10	.21	-.06	.43
Mother acceptance (M)																		
Step 1: Group	—	—	—	—	—	—	.34	-.34	14.94***	.22	-.22	6.24**	.32	.32	12.39***	.19	.19	5.09*
Step 2: Gender	—	—	—	—	—	—	.34	.04	.22	.24	.07	.63	.32	-.03	.12	.20	.03	.70
Step 3: Acceptance	—	—	—	—	—	—	.39	.19	5.15*	.24	.02	.07	.40	.25	7.98**	.20	.03	.71
Step 4: Grp x Gen	—	—	—	—	—	—	.39	.02	.05	.24	-.00	.00	.42	.10	1.28	.20	.04	.64
Step 5: Acc x Grp	—	—	—	—	—	—	.40	-.08	.90	.25	-.08	.79	.44	.15	2.97	.25	.14	.10
Step 6: Acc x Gen	—	—	—	—	—	—	.42	.14	2.46	.25	-.01	.01	.46	.11	1.58	.26	-.08	.38
Step 7: Acc x Grp x Gen	—	—	—	—	—	—	.42	.04	.18	.25	.02	.03	.46	.07	.66	.26	-.00	.98

	R	β	FΔ	R	β	FΔ	R	β	FΔ	R	β	FΔ	R	β	FΔ	R	β	FΔ
Father acceptance (F)																		
Step 1: Group	—	—	—	—	—	—	.34	-.34	12.14***	.17	.17	2.89	.21	.21	4.13*	.19	.19	3.77
Step 2: Gender	—	—	—	—	—	—	.35	.09	.78	.19	.08	.71	.21	-.01	.01	.19	-.00	.00
Step 3: Acceptance	—	—	—	—	—	—	.35	.06	.34	.24	.14	1.91	.32	.24	5.40*	.19	.04	.19
Step 4: Grp x Gen	—	—	—	—	—	—	.35	.01	.01	.26	.09	.86	.33	.07	.48	.20	.07	.48
Step 5: Acc x Grp	—	—	—	—	—	—	.35	-.01	.01	.27	.08	.55	.33	.06	.34	.26	.17	2.96
Step 6: Acc x Gen	—	—	—	—	—	—	.36	.08	.59	.27	.00	.00	.33	-.02	.02	.30	-.14	2.05
Step 7: Acc x Grp X Gen	—	—	—	—	—	—	.37	-.07	.44	.27	.02	.02	.36	-.15	1.95	.31	-.08	.57
Mother acceptance (Obs)																		
Step 1: Group	.10	-.10	1.23	.03	-.03	.12	.34	-.34	16.05***	.22	-.22	5.91*	.33	.33	13.56***	.19	.19	4.90*
Step 2: Gender	.10	-.03	.12	.03	.01	.02	.35	.05	.40	.23	.08	.87	.33	-.02	.06	.19	.02	.08
Step 3: Acceptance	.10	.03	.10	.13	-.13	2.14	.37	.12	1.92	.23	-.03	.09	.37	.18	4.20*	.26	.19	4.86*
Step 4: Grp x Gen	.11	.03	.13	.13	-.02	.08	.37	-.00	.00	.23	-.01	.02	.38	.08	.76	.27	.04	.21
Step 5: Acc x Grp	.13	-.07	.70	.16	-.10	1.24	.40	.17	3.85*	.24	-.03	.13	.38	.00	.00	.29	-.11	1.82
Step 6: Acc x Gen	.29	.26	8.93**	.24	.18	4.32*	.41	.10	1.28	.31	.20	4.97*	.39	-.07	.62	.37	-.24	8.03**
Step 7: Acc x Grp x Gen	.29	.00	.00	.25	-.03	.13	.42	-.02	.08	.31	-.01	.02	.39	-.02	.03	.37	.01	.02
Father acceptance (Obs)																		
Step 1: Group	.14	-.14	2.07	.01	-.01	.02	.35	-.35	13.19***	.16	-.16	2.53	.21	.21	4.11*	.20	.20	4.11*
Step 2: Gender	.14	-.00	.00	.05	-.04	.21	.37	.12	1.50	.19	.10	1.06	.21	.01	.01	.20	-.01	.01
Step 3: Acceptance	.25	-.21	4.54*	.26	-.26	7.41**	.38	.08	.77	.22	-.10	.93	.23	.10	.87	.26	.17	3.05
Step 4: Grp x Gen	.25	-.03	.11	.28	-.09	.80	.38	-.02	.05	.24	-.11	1.14	.24	.05	.20	.27	.09	.81
Step 5: Acc x Grp	.26	-.07	.48	.28	-.06	.39	.38	.04	.17	.34	-.25	5.45*	.24	-.02	.04	.28	.08	.65
Step 6: Acc x Gen	.42	.34	13.22**	.41	.29	9.78**	.40	.03	.11	.34	.07	.41	.28	-.16	2.04	.33	-.18	3.23
Step 7: Acc x Grp x Gen	.44	-.15	2.07	.41	.08	.55	xx	-.14	1.52	.34	-.06	.25	.35	-.25	4.15*	.34	-.08	.60

Note: Both spina bifida and comparison groups were included in these analyses. Ns for these analyses vary somewhat because of missing values. R = Multible R; β = standardized beta coefficient; $F\Delta$ = F-change; P = parent-report; T = teacher-report; C = child-report; Obs = ratings of observers; Grp = group (spina bifida vs. comparison); Gen = gender; Acc = parental acceptance. — = not computed because predictors and outcomes were same method.
* $p < .05$ ** $p < .01$ *** $p < .001$

TABLE 7-4
Multiple Regressions: Significant Associations Between Parental Behavioral Control and Preadolescent Adjustment

	Preadolescent Adjustment Outcomes																	
	Internalizing (P)			Externalizing (P)			Internalizing (T)			Externalizing (T)			School Grades (T)			Adaptive Behavior (Obs)		
Parenting variable	R	β	FΔ	R	β	FΔ	R	β	FΔ	R	β	FΔ	R	β	FΔ	R	β	FΔ
Mother behavioral control (C)																		
Step 1: Group	.10	-.10	1.23	.03	-.03	.12	.34	-.34	16.05***	.22	-.22	5.91*	.33	.33	13.56***	.19	.19	4.90*
Step 2: Gender	.10	-.03	.12	.03	.01	.02	.35	.05	.40	.23	.08	.87	.33	-.02	.06	.19	.02	.08
Step 3: Behavioral Ctl	.14	.10	1.26	.14	.14	2.67	.35	.04	.20	.23	.02	.04	.33	-.04	.18	.21	.09	1.15
Step 4: Grp x Gen	.14	.03	.12	.15	-.04	.17	.35	-.00	.00	.23	-.01	.02	.34	.08	.87	.22	-.05	.29
Step 5: BC x Grp	.15	.05	.30	.15	-.03	.09	.35	.00	.00	.25	-.09	.95	.35	-.10	1.16	.24	-.10	1.23
Step 6: BC x Gen	.16	-.04	.19	.15	-.02	.04	.35	-.02	.06	.26	.06	.43	.36	-.08	.89	.24	-.01	.01
Step 7: BC x Grp x Gen	.19	-.11	1.54	.21	-.15	2.66	.35	.04	.19	.28	-.13	1.96	.37	.07	.56	.24	.00	.00
Father behavioral control (C)																		
Step 1: Group	.09	-.09	.99	.01	-.01	.01	.35	-.35	15.46***	.16	-.16	2.72	.28	.28	8.68**	.15	.15	2.92
Step 2: Gender	.09	-.01	.01	.01	.01	.01	.36	.09	.98	.21	.14	2.29	.28	-.04	.15	.15	-.02	.03
Step 3: Behavioral Ctl	.10	.05	.32	.17	.17	3.38	.36	.00	.00	.22	.04	.24	.31	-.12	1.67	.15	-.00	.00
Step 4: Grp x Gen	.10	-.01	.01	.17	-.04	.23	.36	-.02	.04	.23	-.08	.70	.33	.13	1.83	.17	.08	.81
Step 5: BC x Grp	.13	-.08	.68	.17	-.02	.07	.37	.08	.69	.23	-.04	.15	.34	-.07	.57	.18	-.05	.29
Step 6: BC x Gen	.17	-.12	1.55	.19	-.08	.77	.38	-.07	.60	.23	-.03	.09	.35	-.10	.94	.19	.07	.59
Step 7: BC x Grp x Gen	.18	-.06	.36	.20	-.04	.15	.38	.00	.00	.24	.04	.18	.35	-.03	.07	.20	.07	.59
Mother behavioral control (M)																		
Step 1: Group	—	—	—	—	—	—	.34	-.34	14.94***	.22	-.22	6.24**	.32	.32	12.39***	.19	.19	5.09*
Step 2: Gender	—	—	—	—	—	—	.34	.04	.22	.24	.07	.63	.32	-.03	.12	.20	.03	.15
Step 3: Behavioral Ctl	—	—	—	—	—	—	.34	.04	.22	.34	.25	8.03**	.33	-.08	.70	.23	-.11	1.72
Step 4: Grp x Gen	—	—	—	—	—	—	.34	.01	.03	.34	-.00	.00	.34	.09	1.04	.23	.04	.26
Step 5: BC x Grp	—	—	—	—	—	—	.36	-.10	1.37	.37	-.15	2.89	.35	.10	1.14	.29	.18	4.60*
Step 6: BC x Gen	—	—	—	—	—	—	.36	-.03	.12	.39	-.12	1.89	.35	-.01	.01	.36	.20	5.86*
Step 7: BC x Grp x Gen	—	—	—	—	—	—	.36	-.04	.23	.39	.03	.10	.38	.14	2.19	.36	.02	.09

Father behavioral control (F)

	R	β	Fx	R	β	Fx	R	β	Fx	R	β	Fx	R	β	Fx	R	β	Fx
Step 1: Group	—	—	—	—	—	—	.34	-.34	12.14***	.17	-.17	2.89	.21	.21	4.13*	.19	.19	3.77
Step 2: Gender	—	—	—	—	—	—	.35	.09	.78	.19	.08	.71	.21	-.01	.01	.19	-.00	.00
Step 3: Behavioral Ctl	—	—	—	—	—	—	.35	-.02	.04	.27	.19	3.50	.23	.08	.53	.20	-.06	.40
Step 4: Grp x Gen	—	—	—	—	—	—	.35	.00	.00	.28	-.09	.78	.23	.06	.27	.21	.07	.51
Step 5: BC x Grp	—	—	—	—	—	—	.37	.13	1.72	.29	-.07	.46	.31	.21	4.11*	.21	-.00	.00
Step 6: BC x Gen	—	—	—	—	—	—	.37	.04	.18	.31	-.10	.88	.34	.15	1.69	.27	.18	3.08
Step 7: BC x Grp x Gen	—	—	—	—	—	—	.38	.04	.12	.32	-.11	1.05	.36	.12	1.18	.27	-.01	.02

Mother behavioral control (Obs)

	R	β	Fx	R	β	Fx	R	β	Fx	R	β	Fx	R	β	Fx	R	β	Fx
Step 1: Group	.10	-.10	1.23	.03	-.03	.12	.34	-.34	16.05***	.22	-.22	5.91*	.33	.33	13.56***	.19	.19	4.90*
Step 2: Gender	.10	-.03	.12	.03	.01	.02	.35	.05	.40	.23	.08	.87	.33	-.02	.06	.19	.02	.08
Step 3: Behavioral Ctl	.14	.09	1.06	.03	-.01	.01	.35	-.01	.02	.25	-.09	.93	.34	-.08	.81	.23	.13	2.28
Step 4: Grp x Gen	.14	.04	.20	.05	-.03	.14	.35	-.00	.00	.25	-.02	.05	.35	.08	.74	.24	.06	.48
Step 5: BC x Grp	.14	-.03	.13	.05	.01	.01	.35	.03	.11	.25	.03	.11	.38	-.16	3.26	.29	-.18	4.24*
Step 6: BC x Gen	.14	.02	.05	.08	.07	.59	.35	.03	.03	.31	.19	4.47*	.40	-.13	2.03	.30	-.08	.81
Step 7: BC x Grp x Gen	.24	-.21	5.20*	.22	-.22	5.31*	.35	.06	.43	.36	-.20	4.48*	.40	.03	.13	.32	-.11	1.43

Father behavioral control (Obs)

	R	β	Fx	R	β	Fx	R	β	Fx	R	β	Fx	R	β	Fx	R	β	Fx
Step 1: Group	.14	-.14	2.21	.00	-.00	.00	.35	-.35	12.99***	.17	-.17	2.73	.22	.22	4.62*	.20	.20	4.49*
Step 2: Gender	.14	-.00	.00	.05	-.05	.28	.36	.11	1.38	.20	.11	1.14	.22	-.00	.00	.20	-.02	.03
Step 3: Behavioral Ctl	.19	-.11	1.37	.11	-.10	1.00	.37	.08	.68	.20	-.02	.06	.24	-.10	.96	.27	.18	3.71
Step 4: Grp x Gen	.19	-.02	.02	.13	-.07	.54	.37	-.03	.09	.22	-.10	.93	.24	.02	.03	.28	.07	.58
Step 5: BC x Grp	.19	-.05	.30	.14	.03	.11	.38	-.06	.34	.28	-.18	3.16	.27	.12	1.40	.30	.11	1.29
Step 6: BC x Gen	.24	.14	2.17	.22	.18	3.30	.38	-.01	.02	.29	-.02	.06	.30	-.12	1.26	.35	-.18	3.78
Step 7: BC x Grp x Gen	.34	-.24	6.11*	.24	-.09	.89	.40	-.14	2.05	.29	-.02	.04	.36	-.20	3.87*	.36	-.04	.15

Note: Both spina bifida and comparison groups were included in these analyses. Ns for these analyses vary somewhat because of missing values. R = Multible R; β = standardized beta coefficient; Fx = F-change; P = parent-report; C = child-report; T = teacher-report; Obs = ratings of observers; Grp = group (spina bifida vs. comparison); Gen = gender; BC = parental behavioral control. — = not computed because predictors and outcomes were same method.
* p < .05 ** p < .01 *** p < .001

TABLE 7-5
Multiple Regressions: Significant Associations Between Parental Psychological Control and Preadolescent Adjustment

	Preadolescent Adjustment Outcomes																	
	Internalizing (P)			Externalizing (P)			Internalizing (T)			Externalizing (T)			School Grades (T)			Adaptive Behavior (Obs)		
Parenting variable	R	β	FΔ	R	β	FΔ	R	β	FΔ	R	β	FΔ	R	β	FΔ	R	β	FΔ
Mother psychological control (C)																		
Step 1: Group	.10	−.10	1.23	.03	−.03	.12	.34	−.35	16.05***	.22	−.22	5.91*	.33	.33	13.56***	.18	.19	4.90*
Step 2: Gender	.10	−.03	.12	.03	.01	.02	.35	.05	.40	.23	.08	.87	.33	−.02	.06	.19	.02	.08
Step 3: Psycholog Ctl	.12	.06	.50	.23	.23	7.00**	.35	.00	.00	.35	.27	9.46**	.39	−.22	6.27**	.22	−.11	1.75
Step 4: Grp x Gen	.12	.04	.19	.23	−.01	.02	.35	.00	.00	.35	.01	.03	.40	.06	.44	.22	.04	.22
Step 5: PC x Grp	.14	.06	.51	.24	.09	.98	.35	−.00	.00	.36	−.05	.26	.40	.02	.05	.23	.06	.53
Step 6: PC x Gen	.14	.03	.13	.24	−.00	.00	.35	−.08	.76	.37	−.11	1.34	.40	−.01	.02	.25	.08	.88
Step 7: PC x Grp x Gen	.16	.08	.71	.25	−.03	.10	.36	.06	.38	.37	.08	.53	.41	−.10	.81	.25	−.03	.11
Father psychological control (C)																		
Step 1: Group	.09	−.09	.99	.01	−.01	.01	.35	−.35	15.46***	.16	−.16	2.72	.28	.28	8.68**	.15	.15	2.92
Step 2: Gender	.09	−.01	.01	.01	.01	.01	.36	.09	.98	.21	.14	2.29	.28	−.04	.15	.15	−.02	.03
Step 3: Psycholog Ctl	.10	.04	.16	.22	.23	6.31**	.37	−.06	.36	.28	.19	3.95*	.30	−.10	1.13	.19	−.11	1.45
Step 4: Grp x Gen	.10	−.01	.01	.23	−.05	.26	.37	−.02	.03	.29	−.08	.76	.32	.12	1.51	.21	.09	.95
Step 5: PC x Grp	.10	−.00	.00	.23	−.01	.02	.38	.12	1.72	.29	−.04	.24	.32	.03	.08	.21	.00	.00
Step 6: PC x Gen	.12	.06	.43	.23	.01	.01	.38	−.01	.01	.30	.08	.72	.38	−.20	4.29*	.21	−.03	.08
Step 7: PC x Grp x Gen	.12	.03	.11	.25	−.11	1.30	.39	−.05	.26	.30	.03	.10	.40	−.16	2.74	.22	−.09	.82
Mother psychological control (M)																		
Step 1: Group	—	—	—	—	—	—	.34	−.34	14.94***	.22	−.22	6.24**	.32	.32	12.39***	.19	.19	5.09*
Step 2: Gender	—	—	—	—	—	—	.34	.04	.22	.24	.07	.63	.32	−.03	.12	.20	.03	.15
Step 3: Psycholog Ctl	—	—	—	—	—	—	.34	−.02	.04	.33	.24	7.33**	.32	.02	.04	.30	−.24	7.69**
Step 4: Grp x Gen	—	—	—	—	—	—	.34	.02	.03	.33	−.01	.02	.33	.09	1.06	.31	.05	.33
Step 5: PC x Grp	—	—	—	—	—	—	.34	−.03	.15	.34	.05	.27	.34	.08	.82	.34	.16	3.44
Step 6: PC x Gen	—	—	—	—	—	—	.34	.04	.21	.34	−.07	.53	.34	−.03	.13	.35	.05	.29
Step 7: PC x Grp x Gen	—	—	—	—	—	—	.35	.08	.83	.34	.04	.20	.36	.11	1.33	.35	.03	.12

Father psychological control (F)

	R	β	FΔ	R	β	FΔ	R	β	FΔ	R	β	FΔ	R	β	FΔ	R	β	FΔ
Step 1: Group	—	—	—	—	—	—	.34	-.34	12.14***	.17	-.17	2.89	.21	.21	4.13*	.19	.19	3.77
Step 2: Gender	—	—	—	—	—	—	.35	.09	.78	.19	.08	.71	.21	-.01	.01	.19	-.00	.00
Step 3: Psycholog Ctl	—	—	—	—	—	—	.35	-.03	.09	.23	.14	1.75	.22	-.05	.27	.30	-.24	5.93*
Step 4: Grp x Gen	—	—	—	—	—	—	.35	.00	.00	.24	-.07	.48	.23	.05	.25	.30	.06	.35
Step 5: PC x Grp	—	—	—	—	—	—	.35	-.02	.06	.25	-.04	.14	.35	.27	6.67**	.30	.00	.00
Step 6: PC x Gen	—	—	—	—	—	—	.35	.04	.19	.30	-.18	3.01	.40	.22	4.16*	.32	.12	1.35
Step 7: PC x Grp x Gen	—	—	—	—	—	—	.35	-.02	.03	.31	.05	.25	.42	.11	1.01	.34	.10	.96

Mother psychological control (Obs)

	R	β	FΔ	R	β	FΔ	R	β	FΔ	R	β	FΔ	R	β	FΔ	R	β	FΔ
Step 1: Group	.10	-.10	1.23	.03	-.03	.12	.34	-.34	16.05***	.22	-.22	5.91*	.33	.33	13.56***	.19	.19	4.90*
Step 2: Gender	.10	-.03	.12	.03	.01	.02	.35	.05	.40	.23	.08	.87	.33	-.02	.06	.19	.02	.08
Step 3: Psycholog Ctl	.12	.06	.46	.20	.21	5.48*	.36	-.08	.94	.29	.17	3.72	.38	-.19	4.60*	.31	-.25	8.42**
Step 4: Grp x Gen	.12	.04	.16	.20	-.02	.08	.36	-.00	.00	.29	-.00	.00	.38	.07	.68	.31	.04	.21
Step 5: PC x Grp	.15	.09	1.07	.23	.11	1.54	.37	-.09	1.01	.29	.06	.42	.39	.03	.10	.33	.10	1.56
Step 6: PC x Gen	.23	-.18	3.73	.26	-.12	1.87	.37	.03	.09	.31	-.12	1.65	.39	.07	.59	.35	.14	2.45
Step 7: PC x Grp x Gen	.23	.02	.03	.26	.03	.14	.37	-.00	.00	.31	.01	.01	.40	.12	1.37	.35	.02	.04

Father psychological control (Obs)

	R	β	FΔ	R	β	FΔ	R	β	FΔ	R	β	FΔ	R	β	FΔ	R	β	FΔ
Step 1: Group	.14	-.14	2.21	.00	-.00	.00	.35	-.35	12.99***	.17	-.17	2.73	.22	.22	4.62*	.20	.20	4.49*
Step 2: Gender	.14	-.00	.00	.05	-.05	.28	.36	.11	1.38	.20	.11	1.14	.22	-.00	.00	.20	-.02	.03
Step 3: Psycholog Ctl	.25	.20	4.53*	.24	.23	5.86*	.38	-.11	1.32	.29	.21	4.64*	.32	-.23	5.29*	.26	-.16	2.90
Step 4: Grp x Gen	.25	-.02	.07	.25	-.08	.78	.38	-.03	.10	.31	-.10	1.11	.32	.04	.16	.27	.08	.62
Step 5: PC x Grp	.25	-.01	.02	.26	.04	.16	.39	-.06	.37	.34	.14	1.95	.34	.10	.94	.28	-.08	.63
Step 6: PC x Gen	.35	-.26	6.69**	.30	-.18	3.00	.39	-.00	.00	.35	-.11	1.02	.38	.18	2.81	.29	.08	.68
Step 7: PCx Grp x Gen	.37	.14	1.88	.30	.02	.04	.39	.03	.06	.35	.02	.05	.39	.10	.72	.30	.08	.62

Note: Both spina bifida and comparison groups were included in these analyses. *N*s for these analyses vary somewhat because of missing values. *R* = Multible *R*; β = standardized beta coefficient; *F*Δ = F-change; *C* = child–report; *T* = teacher–report; *P* = parent–report; *Obs* = ratings of observers; *Grp* = group (spina bifida vs. comparison); *Gen* = gender; *PC* = parental psychological control. — = not computed because predictors and outcomes were same method.
* *p* < .05 ** *p* < .01 *** *p* < .001

To reduce common method variance between predictors and outcomes, reporters of the parenting variables and the adjustment outcomes were never the same in any analyses (e.g., when parent report of parenting was the independent variable, all teacher- and observer-reported outcomes were used as dependent variables, but parent-reported dependent variables were not used; see Table 7-3). One special case is worth mentioning. Although parenting (an independent variable) and child adaptive behavior (a dependent variable) were assessed with observational ratings, these ratings were independent in the sense that the former were rated in the laboratory and were based on videotaped family interaction data and the latter were assessed with observations made during the home visit (but *not* during the family interaction; observers were not present for these family interaction sessions). By design, the coders who rated the videotapes were not the same individuals who completed the Home Visit Report Form during the home visit. Thus, analyses where both of these variables are included in the same regressions are reported.

Before running the regressions, all continuous independent variables (i.e., the parenting variables) were centered (Aiken & West, 1991; Holmbeck, 1997, in press). A variable is centered by simply subtracting the sample mean from all individuals' scores on the variable, thus producing a revised sample mean of zero ("group" and "gender" were dummy-coded as 0 and 1, where 0 = spina bifida and 1 = control for "group"; and 0 = male, and 1 = female for "gender"). This transformation reduces multicollinearity between the independent variables and the interactions between them and also facilitates the interpretation of significant interaction effects (whereby the significance of simple slopes is tested; see later discussion).

For all regressions, independent variables and interactions among the independent variables were entered in the following order: (a) group main effect, (b) gender main effect, (c) parenting main effect (acceptance, behavioral control, *or* psychological control), (d) group × gender two-way interaction (i.e., the product of the two main effects), (e) parenting variable × group two-way interaction, (f) parenting variable × gender two-way interaction, and (g) parenting variable × group × gender three-way interaction (Aiken & West, 1991; Holmbeck, 1997). Because group differences findings for the adjustment variables are provided in another report (Holmbeck et al., 2000), the significant findings for the group status variable will not be reported (this variable was entered in the regression equations so that interactions involving the group variable could be tested properly; Holmbeck, 1997).

Post hoc probing of all significant two-way (see Table 7-6) and three-way interactions (see Table 7-7) was conducted using methods described by Aiken and West (1991) and Holmbeck (in press). That is, when a significant interaction was found, simple slopes (and corresponding

TABLE 7-6
Post-Hoc Probing of Significant Two-Way Interactions

Parent (reporter of parenting)	Probing of Group × Parenting Interactions				Probing of Gender × Parenting Interactions			
	Comparison		Spina bifida		Females		Males	
	b	t	b	t	b	t	b	t
Mother (child)								
no significant 2-ways								
Father (child)								
Acc × Grp → School Grades (T)	1.45	3.21**	.10	.21			.01	.03
PC × Gen → School Grades (T)					-1.42	-2.81**		
Mother (mother)								
BC × Grp → Adapt Beh (Obs)	.08	.49	-.44	-2.50**				
BC × Gen → Adapt Beh (Obs)					.18	1.03	-.42	-2.47**
Father (father)								
BC × Grp → School Grades (T)	1.23	2.00*	-.51	-.87				
PC × Grp → School Grades (T)	1.08	1.60	-1.32	-2.17*				(ns)
PC × Gen → School Grades (T)					.84	1.00	-.87	-1.53
Mother (observational ratings)								
ACC × Grp → Internalizing (T)	8.69	2.41*	-.68	-.23				
BC × Grp → Adapt Beh (Obs)	-.01	-.07	.38	2.59**				
ACC × Gen → Internalizing (P)					7.91	2.48**	-4.62	-1.73
ACC × Gen → Externalizing (P)					2.04	.68	-6.34	-2.53**
ACC × Gen → Externalizing (T)					4.41	1.44	-3.84	-1.60
ACC × Gen → Adapt Beh (Obs)					-.06	-.37	.42	-3.38***
BC × Gen → Externalizing (T)					2.38	1.03	-5.26	-2.03*
Father (observational ratings)								
ACC × Grp → Externalizing (T)	-8.21	-2.54**	1.31	.61				(ns)
ACC × Gen → Internalizing (P)					3.65	1.41	-10.01	-4.22***
ACC × Gen → Externalizing (P)					1.34	.51	-10.40	-4.33***
PC × Gen → Internalizing (P)					-3.16	-.88	8.14	3.37***

Note: b = simple slope; t = signficance test for simple slope. Simple slopes represent the association between the parenting variable and the outcome at specific levels of group or gender. P = parent-report; C = child-report; T = teacher-report; Obs = ratings of observers; Grp = group (spina bifida vs. comparison); Gen = gender; ACC = parental acceptance; BC = behavioral control; PC = parental psychological control; ns = no significant simple slopes.
* $p < .05$ ** $p < .01$ *** $p < .001$

TABLE 7-7
Post-Hoc Probing of Significant Three-Way Interactions

Parent (reporter of parenting)	Comparison				Spina Bifida				
	Females		Males		Females		Males		
	b	t	b	t	b	t	b	t	
Mother (child)									
ACC × Grp × Gen → Externalizing (P)	−15.87	−3.05**	1.67	.28	4.33	.67	−1.76	−.33	
Father (child)									
ACC × Grp × Gen → Internalizing (P)	−4.30	−.94	5.41	1.27	6.76	1.41	−9.53	−1.74	(ns)
ACC × Grp × Gen → Externalizing (P)	−7.55	−1.78	3.43	.86	.60	.14	−.65	−1.27	(ns)
Mother (mother)									
no significant 3-ways									
Father (father)									
no significant 3-ways									
Mother (observational ratings)									
BC × Grp × Gen → Internalizing (P)	−1.08	−.33	4.93	1.32	8.64	2.00*	−3.84	−.81	
BC × Grp × Gen → Externalizing (P)	−1.63	−.54	2.01	.58	5.80	1.44	−8.03	−1.80	
BC × Grp × Gen → Externalizing (T)	−.49	−.16	−2.10	−.65	4.84	1.32	−11.70	−2.83**	(ns)
Father (observational ratings)									
ACC × Grp × Gen → School Grades (T)	−1.76	−1.86	1.08	1.70	.24	.54	.39	.79	(ns)
BC × Grp × Gen → Internalizing (P)	−3.74	−1.23	−1.74	−.57	8.12	2.04*	−6.26	−2.04*	
BC × Grp × Gen → School Grades (T)	−.83	−1.54	.74	1.54	−.23	−.36	−.75	−1.64	(ns)

Note: b = simple slope; *t* = significance test for simple slope. Simple slopes represent the association between the parenting variable and the outcome at specific levels of gender within groups. P = parent-report; C = child-report; T = teacher-report; Obs = ratings of observers; Grp = group (spina bifida vs. comparison); Gen = gender; ACC = parental acceptance; BC = behavioral control; PC = parental psychological control; ns = no significant simple slopes.
* *p* < .05   ** *p* < .01   *** *p* < .001

significance tests) were computed for associations between the parenting variable and the adjustment outcome for different levels of the group or gender variables. A summary of all significant parenting main effects is included in Table 7-8.

As Table 7-3 shows, child report of maternal acceptance was positively associated with teacher report of school grades and observer report of adaptive behavior during the home visit. Child report of maternal psychological control was positively associated with externalizing symptoms as reported by parents and teachers and negatively with teacher-reported school grades (see Table 7-5). A significant acceptance × group × gender interaction emerged in the prediction of parent report of externalizing symptoms (Table 7-3). As can be see in Table 7-7, maternal acceptance and externalizing symptoms were negatively associated for females in the control sample.

Child report of paternal acceptance was positively associated with teacher report of school grades (see Table 7-3). However, a significant paternal acceptance × group interaction effect was also found for teacher report of grades. As indicated in Table 7-6, paternal acceptance was positively associated with grades only for the control sample. Paternal psychological control as reported by children was positively associated with parent-reported and teacher-reported externalizing symptoms (see Table 7-5). There was also a significant psychological control × gender interaction for grades (see Table 7-5); psychological control was negatively associated with grades only for females (see Table 7-6). Acceptance × group × gender interactions also emerged for parent report of internalizing and externalizing symptoms. As revealed in Table 7-7, none of the subgroup simple slopes were significantly different from zero.

Contrary to the hypotheses, mother report of maternal acceptance was positively associated with internalizing symptoms as reported by teachers (see Table 7-3). Consistent with the hypotheses, maternal acceptance was positively associated with teacher-reported grades. As can be seen in Table 7-4, maternal behavioral control was positively associated with teacher report of externalizing symptoms. Maternal psychological control was positively associated with externalizing behavior as reported by teachers and negatively associated with observer report of child adaptive behavior (see Table 7-5). Significant maternal behavioral control × group and behavioral control × gender interaction effects were found for observer report of adaptive behavior (see Table 7-4). Maternal behavioral control was negatively associated with adaptive behavior for children with spina bifida and for all males (see Table 7-6).

Father report of paternal acceptance was positively associated with teacher-reported school grades (see Table 7-3). Paternal psychological control was negatively associated with observer report of adaptive behavior. A significant behavioral control × group interaction was found for grades; as

TABLE 7-8
Summary Matrix of Significant Main Effects Associations Between Parenting Variables and Child Psychological Adjustment

Parenting Variable	Preadolescent Adjustment Outcomes					
	Internalizing (P)	Externalizing (P)	Internalizing (T)	Externalizing (T)	School Grades (T)	Adapt Beh (Obs)
Acceptance						
Mother (C)					POS	POS
Father (C)					POS	
Mother (M)	—	—	POS		POS	
Father (F)	—	—			POS	
Mother (Obs)					POS	POS
Father (Obs)	NEG	NEG				
Behavior control						
Mother (C)						
Father (C)						
Mother (M)	—	—				
Father (F)	—	—		POS		
Mother (Obs)						
Father (Obs)						
Psychological control						
Mother (C)		POS		POS	NEG	
Father (C)		POS		POS		
Mother (M)	—	—		POS		NEG
Father (F)	—	—				NEG
Mother (Obs)		POS			NEG	NEG
Father (Obs)	POS	POS		POS	NEG	

Note. P = parent-report; T = teacher-report; C = child-report; Obs = ratings of observers; — = not computed because predictors and outcomes were same method. POS = positive main effect; NEG = negative main effect.

can be seen in Table 7-6, behavioral control was positively associated with school grades for the control sample. Significant paternal psychological control × group and psychological control × gender interactions were found for grades. Paternal psychological control was negatively associated with grades only in the group with spina bifida (see Table 7-6). The simple slopes for associations between psychological control and grades did not differ across gender.

As can be seen in Table 7-3, observed maternal acceptance was positively associated with grades and adaptive behavior. For adaptive behavior, there was also a significant acceptance × gender interaction, which suggested that acceptance was positively associated with adaptive behavior only for all males (see Table 7-6). Observed maternal psychological control was associated positively with parent-reported externalizing symptoms and negatively with grades and adaptive behavior.

A significant acceptance × group interaction emerged for teacher-reported internalizing symptoms; contrary to hypotheses, acceptance was positively associated with symptoms for the control sample (see Table 7-6). Significant acceptance × gender interactions were found for parent report of internalizing symptoms and parent and teacher report of externalizing symptoms. As can be seen in Table 7-6, acceptance was positively associated with internalizing symptoms for females and negatively associated with parent-reported externalizing symptoms for males. The simple slopes for teacher-reported externalizing symptoms were nonsignificant. A behavioral control × group interaction was found for adaptive behavior (behavioral control and adaptive behavior were positively associated for the sample with spina bifida; see Table 7-6) and a behavioral control × gender interaction was found for teacher-reported externalizing symptoms (behavioral control and symptoms were negatively associated for males; see Table 7-6).

Finally, 3 three-way behavioral control interactions were found for parent report of internalizing symptoms and parent and teacher report of externalizing symptoms. As revealed in Table 7-7, behavioral control was positively associated with internalizing symptoms for females in the sample with spina bifida and negatively associated with teacher-reported externalizing symptoms for males in the sample with spina bifida. The simple slopes for parent-reported externalizing symptoms were nonsignificant.

Observed paternal acceptance was negatively associated with parent-reported internalizing and externalizing symptoms (see Table 7-3). Paternal psychological control was positively associated with parent-reported internalizing and externalizing symptoms and teacher-reported externalizing symptoms. Observed psychological control was negatively associated with grades (see Table 7-5).

A significant acceptance × group interaction was found for teacher-reported externalizing symptoms such that acceptance was negatively associated with symptoms in the control sample. Acceptance × gender interactions were found for parent-reported internalizing and externalizing symptoms, with acceptance being negatively associated with symptoms in males. Similarly, a psychological control × gender interaction for parent-reported internalizing symptoms revealed that control was positively associated with symptoms only for males (see Table 7-6).

Three three-way interactions involving paternal observational data were found, with only one yielding a significant simple slope. Observed paternal behavioral control was positively associated with parent-reported internalizing symptoms for females in the sample with spina bifida and negatively with symptoms for males in the sample with spina bifida (see Table 7-7).

GENERAL CONCLUSIONS

The purpose of this study was to examine observed and perceived parenting behaviors in relation to child adjustment in samples of preadolescents with or without spina bifida. Group comparison analyses indicated that mothers of children with spina bifida exhibited significantly higher levels of psychological control than mothers of children without physical challenges across both questionnaire and observational data. Moreover, parental psychological control was associated with negative psychosocial outcomes across method and across group. Parental acceptance was significantly associated with positive outcomes in both groups, but such findings were somewhat less robust than for psychological control. Behavioral control was rarely associated with adjustment in either group (see Table 7-8).

Because of the nature our research design, we were able to rule out alternative explanations for our findings. Specifically, all relationships between predictors and adjustment outcomes in the regression analyses were assessed with variables based on different sources or methods, thus ruling out common method variance and response bias explanations for the findings. Moreover, other features of the design allowed us to expand the scope of our conclusions: (a) inclusion of two samples allowed us to examine whether certain parenting behaviors were more frequently used or more salient in certain contexts; (b) both questionnaire and observational measures of parenting were included; the consistency of the findings across method suggests that the findings do not apply only to *perceptions* of parenting; (c) inclusion of data on fathers allowed us to make statements about differences between parents in their parenting behaviors as well as statements about parental gender differences in associations between parenting and child outcome; indeed, reporting data *only* on mothers does not allow one to determine whether findings only apply to mothers exclusively or to both parents more generally; and (d) inclusion of reports of child adjustment from teachers allowed us to make conclusions about whether the effects of parenting "spill over" into the school setting. Finally, the collection of longitudinal data during a specific developmental period will allow us (in subsequent reports of our findings) to examine the impact of preadolescent parenting on future adjustment trajectories and also whether there is reciprocity between parenting behaviors and child adjustment (e.g., Rueter & Conger, 1998).

In the discussion that follows, we first review the findings for acceptance and behavioral control. Given the focus of this volume, we then devote the bulk of the discussion to a consideration of parental psychological control and the contributions of this study to the literature on this parenting construct.

Findings for Acceptance and Behavioral Control

The finding that parental acceptance was associated with positive adjustment across most outcomes used in this study is in line with past work (e.g., Armsden & Greenberg, 1987; Maccoby & Martin, 1983; B. Martin, 1975; Papini & Roggman, 1992), suggesting that the degree to which the parent is emotionally supportive, involved, and approving is a rather robust predictor of child adjustment during the preadolescent years. It is interesting to note that half of the significant findings for this parenting variable were for school grades. Perhaps acceptance, in this instance, is a proxy for parental involvement in the academic domain (Steinberg, Lamborn, Dornbusch, & Darling, 1992). The interaction analyses revealed that acceptance tended to be more highly associated with adjustment in the comparison group and for males in general, although probing of one three-way interaction revealed that the highest associations were for females in the comparison sample. On the other hand, the large number of main effects for acceptance suggests that this parenting variable is predictive of adjustment across both group and gender (see Table 7-8).

It is interesting to note that three findings for associations between maternal acceptance and child internalizing symptoms were contrary to the hypotheses, such that higher levels of acceptance from mothers was associated with more internalizing symptoms. Although these findings are somewhat counterintuitive, it is possible that maternal acceptance is actually a response to internalizing symptoms rather than the reverse. As noted previously, we will be able to examine this possibility when longitudinal data are available on these samples.

Findings for behavioral control were relatively sparse compared with those for acceptance and psychological control. Such findings run contrary to past work on this construct (e.g., Barber, 1996; Barber et al., 1994; Gray & Steinberg, 1999; Steinberg et al., 1989), which suggests that behavior control is associated with externalizing symptoms and school performance. One possibility is that our measures of behavioral control lack construct validity. It is possible that our use of only some of the CRPBI subscales may have undermined the quality of measurement for this parenting construct. On the other hand, the fact that behavioral control was not associated with adjustment for both questionnaire *and* observational measures of this construct would suggest that behavioral control had less utility in predicting adjustment than did the other parenting variables. Another possibility is that associations between behavioral control and adjustment do not appear until early or middle adolescence; indeed, the children in our sample were younger than in most other studies. A lack of behavioral control may only become predictive of externalizing symptoms (as tapped by the CBCL) only after there is an accumulation over time of impulse control difficulties and only after there are significant and repeated opportunities to engage in such externalizing behaviors. Finally, the three-way interaction findings for behavioral control suggest that observed control reduces risk for internalizing and externalizing symptoms in males but increases the risk for internalizing symptoms in females. That behavioral control would be protective for males is in line with other work, which suggests that boys' externalizing behavior problems decrease after parents are trained to use behavioral control (Martinez & Forgatch, in press).

Findings for Psychological Control

Results from our group differences analyses indicated that mothers of children with spina bifida scored significantly higher on observed *and* perceived measures of psychological control (e.g., behavior that limits the child's ability to express opinions and achieve psychological distance from parents). This finding supports speculations of others (e.g., Anderson & Coyne, 1993; Drotar, 1992). Specifically, Drotar (1992) suggested that a parents' need to protect their children from physical harm conflicts with their need to facilitate psychological independence in their offspring. This desire to protect the child with physical disabilities and help the child adhere to medical regimens can evolve into "miscarried helping" in some families (Anderson & Coyne, 1993). Such miscarried helping may be reflected in increased levels of psychologically controlling parenting behaviors. Although some studies have found few differences between parents of children with physical disabilities or children with chronic illnesses and their counterparts who are not physically challenged on measures of overprotectiveness, involvement, and worry (e.g., Davies et al., 1991; Ievers et al., 1994; Spaulding & Morgan, 1986), none of these studies examined observed family interactions. Moreover, the transition period between childhood and adolescence may be the opportune time to observe such group differences in psychological control.

It is surprising that there were no significant differences found between fathers of children with spina bifida and those of children without physical challenges on observed or perceived measures of psychological control. Such a lack of findings may have been a consequence of the smaller N (i.e., reduced power) for these analyses. Indeed, group differences for the variable means for paternal parenting were in the same direction as that for mothers, with one univariate finding reaching statistical significance in the absence of a multivariate effect (see Table 7-2). Additional findings indicated that fathers of children without physical disabilities scored significantly higher on measures of perceived behavioral control. As suggested by Murch and Cohen (1989), adolescents with spina bifida may feel pressure to achieve a level of independence that is beyond their capabilities if parents place a high value on such independence strivings. Thus, some parents of children with spina bifida may reduce their maturity demands to match their child's potential for independent functioning.

Perhaps most striking was the predictive utility of parental psychological control for child adjustment outcomes, findings that support past research and theorizing (Barber, 1996; Barber et al., 1994; Maccoby & Martin, 1983; Rohner, 1986; Steinberg, 1990; see also chapter 2, this volume). In general, most findings were main effects rather than interactions. Indeed, 15 of the 26 parenting main effects (see Table 7-8), but only 4 of the 27 interaction effects (see Tables 7-6 and 7-7), were for associations between psychological control and adjustment, suggesting that the adjustment correlates of this parenting variable were similar across the spina bifida and control samples and across gender. Moreover, psychological control was significantly associated with adjustment across all reports of parenting (i.e., child, mother, father, and observer ratings). This study adds to the growing body of literature that documents the negative impact of parental psychological control on children.

Although the general finding that psychological control is associated with maladjustment is consistent with the literature, the fact that the finding held for externalizing symptoms rather than internalizing symptoms is not (Barber, 1996; Gray & Steinberg, 1999). As noted by Barber and Harmon (chapter 2, this volume), it is not unusual to find that psychological control is associated with both internalizing and externalizing symptoms), but it is unusual to find associations only for externalizing symptoms. Our findings for externalizing symptoms suggest that the children in this study tend to respond to psychological control with defiance and resistance, rather than with depression and withdrawal (Anderson & Coyne, 1993). We would argue that this may be a consequence of the age of our sample. Their responses may represent early attempts to assert their independence in the face of psychologically controlling parenting. Perhaps as these children move into adolescence, internalizing symptoms may emerge if their early attempts to defy their parents produce no subsequent changes in parenting. It is interesting to note that Barber et al. (1994) found that a model of associations between parental control constructs (including psychological control and behavioral control) and internalizing and externalizing symptoms provided a better fit to the data for adolescents (8th and 10th graders) than for 5th graders (children that are close in age to those in this study). As suggested by Barber and colleagues, "for preadolescents, the individuation process characteristic of the adolescent transition has not typically begun. Therefore, the intrusive and inhibiting effects of psychological control may not be apparent at this earlier age" (p. 1129). Or alternatively, they may be apparent, but only for externalizing symptoms.

By studying a sample of children with physical disabilities, we have isolated a context in which parents are particularly at-risk for displaying high levels of psychological control (Anderson & Coyne, 1993)—a parenting behavior that appears to be universally associated with negative outcomes. Thus, one reason why children with spina bifida may be at-risk for behavior problems (e.g., Lavigne & Faier-Routman, 1992) is that parents in these families are more apt to exhibit higher levels of psychological control. Such findings of "cultural equivalence" with respect to associations between parenting and child adjustment, despite differences in levels of parenting behaviors, have emerged in other studies as well (Chiu, Feldman, & Rosenthal, 1992; Knight, Virdin, & Roosa, 1994; Steinberg, Mounts, Lamborn, & Dornbusch, 1991). In future work, it will be important to isolate other contexts in which psychological control is particularly prevalent.

What did we learn by including data on fathers, reports of adjustment from teachers, observational as well as questionnaire data, and analyses of gender and group interactions? The fact that the regression findings were similar across maternal and paternal parenting suggests that associations between parenting and child outcome are similar across parents for the dimensions of parenting assessed in this study. On the other hand, the group differences findings revealed different results across parents for levels of parenting behaviors. In future studies, it would be useful to examine the effects of congruence or incongruence in mothers' versus fathers' parenting and the impact of such discrepancies on child adjustment. Including data from teachers allowed us to demonstrate that the associations between psychological control and externalizing symptoms reported by parents were cross-validated with teacher reports of externalizing symptoms. These findings, in addition to those for grades, demonstrate the cross-situational impact of certain parenting behaviors. Similarly, the observational findings tended to cross-validate the questionnaire findings. With respect to the group and gender interaction findings, the *absence* of such interaction effects for psychological control allowed us to conclude that such parenting appears to have universally negative effects across gender and group.

Of course, this study is not without limitations. First, the small sample of children included in this study (*n* = 68 in each group) reduced the level of statistical power and may have rendered some otherwise significant results nonsignificant. Second, because of the cross-sectional nature of this study, no definitive statements can be made regarding the direction of associations between parenting behavior and child outcomes. Fortunately, this study is part of a larger longitudinal study and, therefore, prospective data will be forthcoming. Third, the generalizability of these findings is limited primarily to Caucasians. As noted earlier, however, this sampling strategy was done by design, given the typical racial distribution among children with spina bifida (although Spanish-speaking Latino children were underrepresented in our sample). Moreover, these findings cannot be generalized to all children with health-compromising conditions, given our exclusive focus on preadolescents with spina bifida. Fourth, there were moderately high correlations among some of the observational parenting constructs.

Given that psychological control was associated significantly with negative child adjustment and because levels of psychological control were higher among parents of children with spina bifida, it appears that these families are more at-risk than families with children without physical challenges for experiencing the negative outcomes of this form of parenting. Clinically, parents of children with physical disabilities would likely benefit from information on the negative impact of psychological control. Moreover, given that the onset of such behaviors appears to be a rather insidious process, it may also be helpful if such parenting is described to parents within a "miscarried helping" framework (Anderson & Coyne, 1993). Such efforts will serve to help these children navigate the adolescent developmental period as their parents strive to find a balance between encouraging independent functioning and managing the medical complexities of a significant physical disability.

REFERENCES

Achenbach, T. M. (1991a). *Manual for the child behavior checklist/4-18 and 1991 profile*. Burlington: University of Vermont Department of Psychiatry.

Achenbach, T. M. (1991b). *Manual for the teacher's report form and 1991 profile*. Burlington: University of Vermont Department of Psychiatry.

Aiken, L. S., & West, S. G. (1991). *Multiple regression: Testing and interpreting interactions*. Newbury Park, CA: Sage.

Anderson, B. J., & Coyne, J. C. (1993). Family context and compliance behavior in chronically ill children. In N. A. Krasnegor, L. Epstein, S. B. Johnson, & S. J. Yaffe (Eds.), *Developmental aspects of health compliance behavior* (pp. 77–89). Hillsdale, NJ: Erlbaum.

Appleton, P. L., Minchom, P. E., Ellis, N. C., Elliott, C. E., Boll, V., & Jones, P. (1994). The self-concept of young people with spina bifida: A population based study. *Developmental Medicine and Child Neurology, 36,* 198–215.

Armsden, G. C., & Greenberg, M. T., (1987). The inventory of parent and peer attachment: Individual differences and their relationship to psychological well-being in adolescence. *Journal of Youth and Adolescence, 16,* 427–454.

Barber, B. K. (1996). Parental psychological control: Revisiting a neglected construct. *Child Development, 67,* 3296–3319.

Barber, B. K., Olsen, J. A., & Shagle, S. C. (1994). Associations between parental psychological control and behavioral control and youth internalizing and externalizing behaviors. *Child Development, 65,* 1120–1136.

Baumrind, D. (1967). Child care practices anteceding three patterns of preschool behavior. *Genetic Psychology Monographs, 75,* 1120–1136.

Baumrind, D. (1971). Current patterns of parental authority. *Developmental Psychology Monograph, 4,* 1–103.

Baumrind, D. (1973). The development of instrumental competence through socialization. In A. D. Pick (Ed.), *Minnesota Symposia on Child Psychology* (Vol. 7, pp. 3–46). Minneapolis: University of Minnesota Press.

Becker, W. C. (1964). Consequences of different kinds of parental discipline. In M. L. Hoffman & L. W. Hoffman (Eds.), *Review of child development research* (Vol. 1, pp. 169–208). New York: Russell Sage Foundation.

Black, M. M., Hutcheson, J. J., Dubowitz, H., & Berenson-Howard, J. (1994). Parenting style and developmental status among children with nonorganic failure to thrive. *Journal of Pediatric Psychology, 19,* 689–707.

Blum, R. W., Resnick, M. D., Nelson, R., & St. Germaine, A. (1991). Family and peer issues among adolescents with spina bifida and cerebral palsy. *Pediatrics, 88,* 280–285.

Borjeson, M. C., & Lagergren, J. (1990). Life conditions of adolescents with myelomeningocele. *Developmental Medicine and Child Neurology, 32,* 698–706.

Charney, E. B. (1992). Neural tube defects: Spina bifida and myelomeningocele. In M. H Batshaw & Y. M. Perret (Eds.), *Children with disabilities: A medical primer* (pp. 471–488). Baltimore: Brookes.

Chiu, M. L., Feldman, S. S., & Rosenthal, D. A. (1992). The influence of immigration on parental behavior and adolescent distress in Chinese families residing in two western nations. *Journal of Adolescence, 2,* 205–239.

Collins, W. A., Harris, M. L., & Susman, A. (1995) Parenting during middle childhood. In M. Bornstein (Ed.), *Handbook of parenting* (Vol. 1, pp. 65–89). Mahwah, NJ: Erlbaum.

Collins, W. A., Susman-Stillman, A., Williams, F., Hyson, D., Alwin, J., Gleason, T., Sesma, A., & Steffes, M. (1996, March). Transitions in relationships between parents and adolescents with insulin-dependent diabetes mellitus. In J. G. Smetana (Chair), *Adolescent-parent relationships in diverse contexts*. Symposium conducted at the meetings of the Society for Research on Adolescence, Boston.

Darling, N., & Steinberg, L. (1993). Parenting style as context: An integrative model. *Psychological Bulletin, 113*, 487–496.

Davies, W. H., Noll. R. B., DeStefano, L., Bukowski, W. M., & Kulkarni, R. (1991). Difference in the child-rearing practices of parents of children with cancer and controls: The perspectives of parents an professionals. *Journal of Pediatric Psychology, 16*, 295–306.

Drotar, D. (1992). Integrating theory and practice in psychological intervention with families of children with chronic illness. In T. J. Akamatsu, M. A. Stephens, S. E. Hobfoll, & J. H. Crowther (Eds.), *Family health psychology* (pp. 175–192). Washington, DC: Hemisphere.

Drotar, D. (1997). Relating parent and family functioning to the psychological adjustment of children with chronic health conditions: What have we learned? What do we need to know? *Journal of Pediatric Psychology, 22*, 149–165.

Dunn, L. M., & Dunn, L. M. (1981). *Peabody Picture Vocabulary Test-Revised*. Circle Pines, MN: American Guidance Service.

Eccles, J. S., Buchanan, C. M., Flanagan, C., Fuligni, A., Midgley, C., & Yee, D. (1991) Control versus autonomy during early adolescence. *Journal of Social Issues, 47*, 53–68.

Ferreira, A. J. (1963). Decision making in normal and pathological families. *Archives of General Psychiatry, 8*, 68–73.

Gray, M. R., & Steinberg, L. (1999). Unpacking authoritative parenting: Reassessing a multidimensional construct. *Journal of Marriage and the Family, 61*, 574–587.

Hauser, S. T., Jacobson, A. M., Wertlieb, D., Weiss-Perry, B., Follansbee, D., Wolfsdorf, J. I., Hershowitz, R. D., Houlihan, J., & Rajapark, D. (1986). Children with recently diagnosed diabetes: Interactions within their families. *Health Psychology, 5*, 273–296.

Hauser, S. T., Jacobson, A. M., Wertlieb, D., Wolfsdorf, J. I., Hershkowitz, R. D., Vieyra, M. A., & Orleans, J. (1989). Family contexts of self-esteem and illness adjustment in diabetic and acutely ill children. In C. N. Ramsey (Ed.), *Family systems in medicine* (pp. 469–484). New York: Guilford Press.

Hill, J. P., & Holmbeck, G. N. (1986). Attachment and autonomy during adolescence. *Annals of Child Development, 3*, 145–189.

Hollingshead, A. A. (1975). *Four factor index of social status*. Unpublished manuscript, Yale University, New Haven, CT.

Holmbeck, G. N. (1997). Toward terminological, conceptual, and statistical clarity in the study of mediators and moderators: Examples from the child-clinical and pediatric psychology literatures. *Journal of Consulting and Clinical Psychology, 65*, 599–610.

Holmbeck, G. N. (in press). Post-hoc probing of significant moderational and mediational effects in studies of pediatric populations. *Journal of Pediatric Psychology.*

Holmbeck, G. N., Belvedere, M. C., Christiansen, M., Czerwinski, A. M., Johnson, S. Z., Kung, E., & Schneider, J. (1998). Assessment of adherence with multiple informants in pre-adolescents with spina bifida: Initial development of a multidimensional, multitask parent-report questionnaire. *Journal of Personality Assessment, 70,* 427–440.

Holmbeck, G. N., Belvedere, M., Gorey-Ferguson, L., & Schneider, J. (1995). *Family macro-coding manual-March of Dimes triadic version.* Unpublished manual, Loyola University of Chicago, Department of Psychology.

Holmbeck, G. N., Gorey-Ferguson, L., Hudson, T., Seefeldt, T., Shapera, W., Turner, T., & Uhler, J. (1997). Maternal, paternal, and marital functioning in families of preadolescents with spina bifida. *Journal of Pediatric Psychology, 22,* 167–181.

Holmbeck, G. N., Paikoff, R. L., & Brooks-Gunn, J. (1995). Parenting adolescents. In M. H. Bornstein (Ed.), *Handbook of parenting* (Vol. 1, pp. 91–118). Mahwah, NJ: Erlbaum.

Holmbeck, G. N., Westhoven, V., Bowers, R., Davison, K., Gruse, C., Nikolopoulos, T., & Wienke, C. (2000). *A multi-dimensional, multi-informant, and multimethod perspective on psychosocial adjustment in pre-adolescents with spina bifida.* Manuscript in preparation.

Hommeyer, J. S., Holmbeck, G. N., Wills, K., & Coers, S. (1999). Condition severity and psychosocial functioning in pre-adolescents with spina bifida: Disentangling proximal functional status and distal adjustment outcomes. *Journal of Pediatric Psychology, 24,* 499–509.

Ievers, C. E., Drotar, D., Dahms, W. T., Doershuk, C. F., & Stern, R. C. (1994). Maternal child-rearing behavior in three groups: Cystic fibrosis, insulin-dependent diabetes mellitus, and healthy children. *Journal of Pediatric Psychology, 19,* 681–687.

Kazak, A. E., Reber, M., & Snitzer, L. (1988). Childhood chronic disease and family functioning: A study of phenylketonuria. *Pediatrics, 81,* 224–229.

Kazak, A. E., Segal-Andrews, A., & Johnson, K. (1995). The role of families and other systems in pediatric psychology research and practice. In M. Roberts (Ed.), *Handbook of pediatric psychology* (2nd ed.; pp. 84–104). New York: Guilford Press.

Knight, G. P., Virdin, L. M., & Roosa, M. (1994). Socialization and family correlates of mental health outcomes among Hispanic and Anglo-American children: Consideration of cross-ethnic scalar equivalence. *Child Development, 65,* 212–224.

Lamborn, S. D., Mounts, N. S., Steinberg, L., & Dornbusch, S. M. (1991). Patterns of competence and adjustment among adolescents from authoritative, authoritarian, indulgent, and neglectful families. *Child Development, 62,* 1049–1065.

Lavigne, J. V., & Faier-Routman, J. (1992). Psychological adjustment to pediatric physical disorders: A meta-analytic review. *Journal of Pediatric Psychology, 17*, 133–157.

Lavigne, J. V., & Faier-Routman, J. (1993). Correlates of psychological adjustment to pediatric physical disorders: A meta-analytic review and comparison with existing models. *Developmental and Behavioral Pediatrics, 14*, 117–123.

Lavigne, J. V., Nolan, D., & McLone, D. G. (1988). Temperament, coping, and psychological adjustment in young children with myelomeningocele. *Journal of Pediatric Psychology, 13*, 363–378.

Maccoby, E. E. (1984). Middle childhood in the context of the family. In W. A. Collins (Ed.), *Development during middle childhood* (pp. 184–239). Washington, DC: National Academy Press.

Maccoby, E. E., & Martin, J. A. (1983). Socialization in the context of the family: Parent-child interaction. In P. H. Mussen (Eds.), *Handbook of child psychology* (Vol. 4, pp. 1–101). New York: Wiley & Sons.

Martin, B. (1975). Parent-child relations. In F. D. Horowitz (Ed.), *Review of child development research* (Vol. 4, pp. 463–540). Chicago: University of Chicago Press.

Martinez, C. R., & Forgatch, M. S. (in press). Preventing problems with boy's noncompliance: Effects of a parent training intervention for divorcing mothers. *Journal of Consulting and Clinical Psychology.*

McKernon, W. L., Holmbeck, G. N., Colder, C. R., Hommeyer, J. S., Shapera, W., & Westhoven, V. (2001). Longitudinal study of observed and perceived family influences on problem-focused coping behaviors of preadolescents with spina bifida. *Journal of Pediatric Psychology, 26*, 41–54.

McLone, D. G., & Ito, J. (1998). *An introduction to spina bifida.* Chicago: Children's Memorial Hospital Myelomeningocele Team.

Murch, R. L., & Cohen, L. H. (1989). Relationships among life stress, perceived family environment, and the psychological distress of spina bifida adolescents. *Journal of Pediatric Psychology, 14*, 193–214.

Papini, D. R., & Roggman, L. A. (1992). Adolescent perceived attachment to parents in relation to competence, depression, and anxiety. *Journal of Early Adolescence, 12*, 420–440.

Pianta, R. C., & Lothman, D. J. (1994). Predicting behavior problems in children with epilepsy: Child factors, disease factors, family stress, and child-mother interaction. *Child Development, 65*, 1415–1428.

Robin, A. L., & Foster, S. L. (1992). *Negotiating parent-adolescent conflict: A behavioral-family systems approach.* New York: Guilford Press.

Rohner, R. P. (1986). *The warmth dimension: Foundations of parental acceptance-rejection theory.* London: Sage.

Rollins, B. C., & Thomas, D. L. (1979). Parental support, power, and control techniques in the socialization of children. In W. R. Burr, R. Hill, F. I. Nye,

& I. L. Reiss (Eds.), *Contemporary theories about the family: Vol. 1. Research based theories* (pp. 317–364). New York: Free Press.

Rueter, M. A., & Conger, R. D. (1998). Reciprocal influences between parenting and adolescent problem-solving behavior. *Developmental Psychology, 34,* 1470–1482.

Schaefer, E. S. (1959). A circumplex model for maternal development. *Journal of Abnormal Social Psychology, 59,* 226–235.

Schaefer, E. S. (1965a). Children's reports of parental behavior: An inventory. *Child Development, 36,* 413–424.

Schaefer, E. S. (1965b). A configurational analysis of children's reports of parent behavior. *Journal of Consulting and Clinical Psychology, 29,* 552–557.

Schuldermann, E., & Schludermann, S. (1970). Replicability of factors in children's report of parent behavior. *Journal of Psychology, 76,* 239–249.

Schwarz, J. C., Barton-Henry, M. L., & Pruzinsky, T. (1985). Assessing child-rearing behaviors: A comparison of ratings made by mother, father, child, and sibling on the CRPBI. *Child Development, 56,* 462–479.

Siqueland, L., Kendall, P. C., & Steinberg, L. (1996). Anxiety in children: Perceived family environments and observed family interaction. *Journal of Clinical Child Psychology, 25,* 225–237.

Smetana, J. G., Yau, J., Restrepo, A., & Braeges, J. L. (1991). Adolescent-parent conflict in married and divorced families. *Developmental Psychology, 27,* 1000–1010.

Spaulding, B. R., & Morgan, S. B. (1986). Spina bifida children and their parents: A population prone to dysfunction? *Journal of Pediatric Psychology, 11,* 359–374.

Steinberg, L. (1990). Autonomy, conflict, and harmony in the family relationship. In S. S. Feldman & G. R. Elliott (Eds.), *At the threshold: The developing adolescent* (pp. 255–276). Cambridge, MA: Harvard University Press.

Steinberg, L., Elmen, J. D., & Mounts, N. S. (1989). Authoritative parenting, psychosocial maturity, and academic success among adolescents. *Child Development, 60,* 1424–1436.

Steinberg, L., Lamborn, S. D., Darling, N., Mounts, N. S., & Dornbusch, S. M. (1994). Over-time changes in adjustment and competence among adolescents from authoritative, authoritarian, indulgent, and neglectful families. *Child Development, 65,* 754–770.

Steinberg, L., Lamborn, S. D., Dornbusch, S. M., & Darling, N. (1992). Impact of parenting practices on adolescent achievement: Authoritative parenting, school involvement, and encouragement to succeed. *Child Development, 63,* 1266–1281.

Steinberg, L., Mounts, N. S., Lamborn, S. D., & Dornbusch, S. M. (1991). Authoritative parenting and adolescent adjustment across varied ecological niches. *Journal of Research on Adolescence, 1,* 19–36.

Suen, H. K., & Ary, D. (1989). *Analyzing quantitative behavioral observation data.* Hillsdale, NJ: Erlbaum.

Symonds, P. (1939). *The psychology of parent-child relationships*. New York: Appleton-Century-Crofts.

Thompson, R. J., & Gustafson, K. E. (1996). *Adaptation to chronic childhood illness*. Washington, DC: American Psychological Association.

Varni, J., & Wallander, J. (1988). Pediatric chronic disabilities. Hemophilia and spina bifida as examples. In D. K. Routh (Ed.), *Handbook of pediatric psychology* (pp. 190–221). New York: Guilford Press.

Wallander, J. L., & Thompson, R. J. (1995). Psychosocial adjustment of children with chronic physical conditions. In M. Roberts (Ed.), *Handbook of pediatric psychology* (2nd ed.; pp. 124–141). New York: Guilford Press.

Weiss, L. H., & Schwarz, J. C. (1996). The relationship between parenting types and older adolescents' personality, academic achievement, adjustment, and substance use. *Child Development, 67*, 2101–2114.

Wills, K. E., Holmbeck, G. N., Dillon, K., & McLone, D. G. (1990). Intelligence and achievement in children with myelomeningocele. *Journal of Pediatric Psychology, 15*, 161–176.

APPENDIX 7A
OBSERVATIONAL CODES FOR PSYCHOLOGICAL CONTROL

Codes A, B, and D are reverse-scored for psychological control. All codes are rated separately for mothers and fathers.

A. *Receptive to statements made by others.* Members are rated in terms of being open and permeable to other members' thoughts, ideas, and feelings. A receptive family member is willing to change his/her own opinion based on input from others. Openness and receptiveness can be indicated through verbal statements or nonverbal statements that indicate understanding and interest for other members in the family.

>   5. *Very receptive* = S is willing to consider other member's thoughts and reflect on them. S incorporates others' points of view into their own statements. S acknowledges others' points of view.
>   4. *Fairly receptive* = S acknowledges others' viewpoints several times during interaction. ONCE or TWICE, may not be as willing to change own views based on input from others.
>   3. *Somewhat receptive* = S considers others' thoughts, but without commentary (i.e., without accepting or rejecting them, or passively going along with rules suggested by others), or S seems distracted at some times when others are presenting their thoughts. May not be willing to change own views based on input from others MORE THAN TWO TIMES.
>   2. *Fairly unreceptive* = S tends to interrupt others' speeches, or disagrees with others' thoughts, or is rather uninterested. Does not seem as open to others' input.
>   1. *Very unreceptive* = S imposes own thoughts and ideas, rejected or does not consider others' feelings, thoughts or ideas. Will not alter own opinions based on input from others.

B. *Tolerates differences and disagreements.* The ability to be tolerant of disagreements during a family interaction and a willingness to engage in discussions about such differences. A tolerant S is one who is able to react nondefensively when others disagree with him/her. Can be indicated through verbal and nonverbal behaviors. VERBAL: S reacts nondefensively to disagreements, or S expresses a wish or a willingness to discuss a particular issue about which there is a disagreement, or S maintains the focus of conversation during a disagreement. NONVERBAL: S interacts with others during a disagreement, looks in direction of other family members who disagree with him/her. S does not look surprised about differences suggested.

5. *Almost always* = S is always tolerant of disagreements, reacts nondefensively when others disagree with him/her, is comfortable discussing disagreements.
4. *Usually* = S is comfortable discussing disagreements and typically reacts nondefensively. But S indicates on one or two occasions a wish not to discuss an issue during an interaction or reacts defensively on at least one occasion.
3. *Sometimes* = S is sometimes comfortable discussing disagreements and is sometimes tolerant of others disagreeing with him/her. But there are several instances where S reacts defensively or shows an unwillingness to discuss the disagreement.
2. *Rarely* = S is reluctant to discuss differences and disagreements. S often reacts defensively when others disagree with him/her. S frequently changes focus of issues discussed during a disagreement.
1. *Almost never* = S clearly does not want to discuss differences or disagreements, negates all problems or difficulties in relation to disagreements. S does not participate during disagreements, S frequently reacts defensively to others' disagreements.

C. *Pressures others to agree*. A family member pressures others to agree when he/she makes statements that implicitly or explicitly pressure another family member to change their mind by making it uncomfortable for them not to do so. Evidence of such pressuring include when a family member attempts to get another family member to change his/her mind, indirect pressure (other family member is made to feel stupid if he/she maintains his/her position), expressions of incredulity or condescension, impatience with the other family member's position, and ignoring the input of a family member who disagrees.

5. *Very often* = S applies direct or indirect pressure to other family members to change their positions throughout the interaction. Sometimes such pressuring comments are accompanied by anger or hostility. May appear condescending. Pressuring may also be more sporadic but very intense when it occurs.
4. *Frequent* = On several occasions, S pressures others to change their positions. Not hostile or angry, but person who is pressuring may appear annoyed or displeased during the discussion. Or, S may pressure others on a couple of occasions in a fairly intense manner.
3. *Some* = On a couple of occasions, S pressures others to change their positions. Pressure is mild with little displeasure during discussion. Or S may pressure on one occasion but somewhat intensely.

2. *Almost none or little* = S tends not to pressure others to change their opinions, tends to respect others' right to express their own points of view. But may on one occasion apply some pressure on others to change their positions. Very mild implied pressure. Pressuring may be mildly intense.
1. *None* = S never pressures others to change their opinions.

D. *Nature of parental control: Democratic*. DEMOCRATIC parents set expectations for their child and seem firm and consistent in enforcing their expectations. Unlike the authoritarian parent, the child's input is solicited—but the parents usually make the final decision.

1 = Not at all
2 = A little
3 = Somewhat
4 = Fairly much
5 = Very much

E. *Nature of parental control: Overprotective*. OVERPROTECTIVE parents are smothering and undermine the independent functioning of their offspring. Such parents infantilize or baby their children and they rarely let their child do things on his/her own. These parents are intrusive and do not allow their children to speak for themselves. Parents may be warm but condescending.

1 = Not at all
2 = A little
3 = Somewhat
4 = Fairly much
5 = Very much

Source: Holmbeck et al., 1995.

8

MATERNAL PSYCHOLOGICAL CONTROL AND PRESCHOOL CHILDREN'S BEHAVIORAL OUTCOMES IN CHINA, RUSSIA, AND THE UNITED STATES

SUSANNE FROST OLSEN, CHONGMING YANG, CRAIG H. HART,
CLYDE C. ROBINSON, PEIXIA WU, DAVID A. NELSON,
LARRY J. NELSON, SHENGHUA JIN, AND JIANZHONG WO

A growing body of Western literature has demonstrated the importance of three domains of socialization—connection with significant others, regulation of behavior, and the facilitation of psychological autonomy—in predicting outcomes in adolescents and children (Barber, 1997a, 1997b; Gray & Steinberg, 1999; Hart, Newell, & Olsen, in press; Nelson, 1997; Steinberg, Dornbusch, & Brown, 1992). Psychological control—parenting that does not allow children psychological autonomy, as has been defined elsewhere in this volume, has received increased attention in the past decade (for a discussion of definitions and research, see chapter 2, this volume).

Most of the earlier work regarding psychological control has focused on adolescents. The construct has been viewed as being more relevant to them than other age groups because adolescents strive to establish a sense of identity and transform their relationships with families and peers. It has been hypothesized, however, that the psychological control construct may be useful across the life course if it is conceptualized broadly as intrusion

We express our appreciation to the parents and teachers who participated in this study, as well as to Dr. Nina Bazarskaya, head of the Foreign Language Department, Voronezh Forestry Institute, Voronezh, Russia, for her assistance in providing access to the Russian sample. Support for this research was provided by the Kennedy Center for International Studies, the College of Family, Home and Social Sciences, the Camilla Eyring Kimball Endowment, and the Family Studies Center at Brigham Young University. We are also grateful to Dr. Joseph Olsen for his statistical consultation.

into the child's self-expression. Intrusion and violation of psychological autonomy may occur, even in children who are very young (Barber, 1996; see also chapter 2, this volume). Recent research indicates that components of psychological control may be linked to negative outcomes for schoolage children (Grotpeter, 1997; Mills & Rubin, 1998; Nelson, 1997; Shulman, Collins, & Dital, 1993), preschoolers (Gottman, Katz, & Hooven, 1997; Olsen, Wells, Hart, & Robinson, 2000; Wells, 1998), as well as younger children (Crockenberg & Litman, 1990).

Another limitation in previous work is that the majority of studies, with a few exceptions, have been conducted in the United States. As a result, research is only beginning to appear regarding the link between psychological control and child outcomes in cross-cultural settings (see chapter 2, this volume; for exceptions, see Hart, Nelson, Robinson, Olsen, & McNeilly-Choque, 1998). Steinberg, Mounts, Lamborn, and Dornbusch (1991) supported this type of research, recommending that more studies should attend to "process-by-context interactions," or the investigation of "the ways in which developmental processes vary as a function of the broader context in which they occur" (p. 20).

The purpose of our research is two-fold. Our first aim is to expand the study of psychological control and its related outcomes into the realm of younger children, specifically examining preschoolers. Our second purpose is to investigate these relations in three cultures, the United States, China, and Russia. We included three cultures, as recommended by Segal, Lonner, and Berry (1998), to make meaningful and interpretable cross-cultural comparisons.

PSYCHOLOGICAL CONTROL AND CHILDREN'S INTERNALIZING AND EXTERNALIZING BEHAVIOR

As mentioned previously, the relationship between psychological control and adolescents' problem behaviors has been documented in research literature for the past decade (e.g., Barber, 1996; Barber, Olsen, & Shagle, 1994; Gray & Steinberg, 1999; Steinberg, Elmen, & Mounts, 1989). A major focus of this research has been directed toward distinguishing between psychological control and behavioral control and how these constructs differentially relate to adolescent development (for distinctions between psychological control and behavioral control, see Steinberg, 1990; chapters 1 and 4, this volume).

In the literature regarding younger children, psychological control or some of its components (i.e., guilt induction, love withdrawal, etc.) has only recently been linked to schoolage and preschool child outcomes (Gottman et al., 1997; Grotpeter, 1997; Hart, Nelson, et al., 1998; Mills & Rubin, 1998;

Nelson, 1997; Olsen et al., 2000; Shulman et al., 1993; Wells, 1998; see also chapters 5–7, this volume). In the following section we briefly review research on psychological control and adolescents' internalizing and externalizing problems to provide a context for the research literature we review next regarding younger children.

Internalizing Behavior

In the adolescent literature, an extensive body of research has emerged supporting the relationship between psychological control and internalizing behavior. Studies have shown that psychological control is a significant predictor of internalizing problems, even after controlling for parenting variables such as connection and regulation or school and peer variables (Barber & Olsen, 1997; Eccles, Early, Frasier, Belansky, & McCarthy, 1997). These relationships have also been supported in longitudinal studies (see chapter 2, this volume).

In addition, preliminary findings of cross-cultural research conducted with adolescents in the United States, Colombia, Gaza, South Africa, India, and Australia indicate that psychological control is related to adolescent self-reported depression in these varied settings (chapter 2, this volume). In contrast, Bean (1997) found that after controlling for parental acceptance and monitoring, maternal and paternal psychological control was related to youth depression for African Americans but not for Hispanics in the United States.

Typically, work with adolescents has narrowly operationalized internalizing as including depression and psychological or somatic disorders; however, in studies of younger children internalizing behaviors have consisted of behaviors such as shyness, withdrawal, anxiety, sadness, loneliness, or poor self-esteem (e.g., Gresham & Elliott, 1990; Hart, Olsen, Robinson, & Mandleco, 1997). In addition, although much research with adolescents regarding psychological control has used Barber's (modified from Schaefer) conceptualization, research with young children has generally examined specific components of the psychological control construct (i.e., guilt induction, love withdrawal, etc.). Therefore, in reviewing the literature regarding young children, we must extrapolate in finding commonalities.

For example, Holden (1997) described "psychological maltreatment," which might be considered an extreme form of psychological control, as consisting of threatening to abandon the child and "ignoring the child's attempts and need for interaction" (p. 146). Baumrind (1966) also cautioned against manipulation of the love relationship as well as the use of guilt induction in relationships between parents and children. Besides these theoretical arguments, research has demonstrated possible linkages between components of psychological control and younger children's outcomes.

A line of research by Rubin and colleagues (e.g., Rubin, Bukowski, & Parker, 1998; Rubin, Nelson, Hastings, & Asendorpf, 1999; Rubin, Stewart, & Chen, 1995) has shown that psychological overcontrol (operationalized as overprotectiveness, overinvolvement and constraints on exploration and independence in earlier research) is related to social withdrawal in younger children. In addition, in a recent study of children in kindergarten, second, and fourth grades, psychologically controlling behavior, operationally defined as involving threats to the child's self esteem, was used more by mothers of withdrawn (i.e., internalizing) children than by mothers of average children (Mills & Rubin, 1998).

The literature indicates that children with severe internalizing problems such as neuroticism and anxiety disorders have family environments that include components of psychological control. For instance, descriptive research with younger children involving clinical records, case studies, and retrospective reports has characterized parents of children with neurotic or anxiety disorders as limiting their children's psychological autonomy by being invasive of their physical or psychological privacy (Siqueland, Kendall, & Steinberg, 1996). Also, children with anxiety and depressive disorders have rated their families as more enmeshed (interpersonally overinvolved) than children without anxiety disorders (Stark, Humphrey, Crook, & Lewis, 1990). Other researchers (Siqueland et al., 1996) found that observers rated parents of schoolage children with anxiety disorders as less granting of psychological autonomy than parents of children in the control group.

It has also been hypothesized that the use of love withdrawal may be related to anxiety (Maccoby & Martin, 1983) and neurotic, inhibited behaviors in younger children (Hoffman, 1983; Putallaz & Heflin, 1990). In addition, negative parental evaluative feedback, such as shaming of children, has been associated with preschoolers' expressions of being shamed, such as withdrawing from task situations or negative self-evaluations (Alessandri & Lewis, 1993).

Only a few studies with children have specifically examined the psychological control construct. Morriss et al. (chapter 5, this volume) found that for children who were rated as irritable and distressed by their mothers, maternal psychological control, as assessed by the children, predicted teacher assessments of child internalizing. Supporting some of the findings with adolescents and schoolage children, research with preschoolers indicated that psychological control was correlated with parent-reported child internalizing problems only when mothers described their spouse's use of psychological control; no associations existed when fathers reported about their wives (Olsen et al., 2000; Wells, 1998).

In sum, the body of research regarding the relationship between psychological control and adolescent internalizing behavior is more well-developed and in general supports the theory. Although less research has been performed with samples of children in preschool and middle childhood, the theory also appears to be supported.

Externalizing Behavior

Although psychological control was originally associated with adolescent internalizing behaviors, subsequent research demonstrated that it is also related to adolescent externalizing problems, such as delinquency or antisocial behavior (see chapter 2, this volume, for a review). Only a few studies, however, have investigated the linkage between psychological control and adolescent antisocial behavior with ethnically diverse samples or in cross-cultural settings. One example is Barber and Harmon (chapter 2, this volume), who found in cross-cultural research performed in the United States, Gaza, Colombia, South Africa, India, and Australia that psychological control was associated with adolescent antisocial behavior in all cultures.

Other research performed with Hispanics and African Americans in the United States has been less consistent. For example, Bean (1997) reported that maternal and paternal psychological control was unrelated to antisocial behavior for both Hispanics and African Americans. In contrast, in a longitudinal study of African American adolescents, maternal psychological control (measured somewhat differently than Barber's conceptualization) had a curvilinear relation with youth problem behaviors. When adolescents in the sample associated with problem peers, higher and lower levels of psychological control were related to higher levels of problem behaviors (Mason, Cauce, Gonzales, & Hiraga, 1996).

The linkage between psychological control and externalizing behaviors may also be applicable to younger age groups. For example, research conducted with both adolescents and schoolage children revealed that psychological control was a more salient predictor of delinquency among fifth-grade students than eighth-grade students (Barber, 1996). In addition, one aspect of psychological control (e.g., love withdrawal) has also been associated with externalizing behavior, such as overt aggression, in schoolage children (Grotpeter, 1997). Morris et al. (chapter 5, this volume) also found that when mothers rated their schoolage sons' temperament as high on either fearful or irritable distress, psychological control was related to teachers' ratings of the boys' externalizing behaviors. These relations were not significant for girls, however.

Although there is less research regarding psychological control and its relationship with younger children's externalizing behavior, Rubin, Coplan, Nelson, Cheah, and Lace-Seguin (1999) reported that parents who are disapproving and critical of their children, while also being permissive, have children who tend to be more aggressive with their peers. Wells (1998) noted that although not described as psychological control in Rubin's writing, these seemingly contradictory behaviors (disapproving and permissive or punitive and permissive) may demonstrate a tendency for erratic emotional behavior (one aspect of psychological control) on the part of parents.

Research with preschool children in the United States found that correlations existed between parents' assessments of their spouse's use of psychological control and their reports of their own child's externalizing behavior (Olsen et al., 2000; Wells, 1998). In contrast, in a study of preschoolers in Russia, mothers' psychological control was linked to teacher-reported overt aggression of boys and girls, but no association existed when fathers were reporting (Hart, Nelson, et al., 1998). In examining this data further, Hart, Nelson, et al. (2000) found preschool children whose mothers reported high levels of psychological control were rated as more overtly and proactively aggressive than children whose mothers reported low levels.

In sum, the patterns of findings regarding externalizing behavior are similar to those regarding internalizing. A larger and more highly developed body of research generally supports the hypothesis that psychological control is associated with adolescent externalizing; the extant literature for schoolage children and preschoolers is much less developed but indicates similar relationships.

CHINESE AND RUSSIAN CULTURE AND PSYCHOLOGICAL CONTROL

There is some evidence that differences may exist in cultural acceptance and parental use of psychological control. Parenting may vary across different ecologies because parents may have different goals, representing the cultural norms by which children are socialized (Darling & Steinberg, 1993; Hart, Nelson, et al., 2000). Thus, although psychological control has been viewed as uniformly negative in the United States (Barber, 1996), it may be more frequently used, and therefore more acceptable, as a means of regulating young children's behavior in other cultures, particularly in China (Wu et al., 2000).

China

Confucian values and teachings are still evident in patterns of socialization among Chinese people today, although many were denounced during the early years of the People's Republic (Miller, Wiley, Fung, & Liang, 1997; Wu, 1996, 1997). Even though Confucian values may permeate Chinese child-rearing, a number of authors (Bond, 1991; Ho, 1986, 1996) have proposed that there is no one predominant method of child socialization in Chinese society.

In addition, the pattern of Chinese socialization often changes as a function of the child's age. For example, Chinese parents typically are lenient or indulgent in their attitudes toward infants and young children, which is very different from the stricter discipline that they impose on older children (Garcia Coll, Meyer, & Brillon, 1995; Ho, 1986). Thus, following Confucian teachings, as soon as children are able to understand, obedience is more strongly emphasized (Wu, 1996). This change in attitude occurs when the child has reached the age of "understanding" or "reason," usually at around 4 to 6 years of age (Gorman, 1998; Ho, 1986).

In socializing their children, Ho (1986) reported that parents may use a variety of strategies, including threatening, scolding, punishing, and shaming. He emphasized, however, that these are not the only child-rearing methods being used. More recent empirical work (Chen, Dong, & Zhou, 1997) documenting the use of authoritarian and more positive authoritative parenting styles in the Chinese culture supports the view that a variety of parenting styles are present, including some that may be viewed negatively in the Western literature (see Wu et al., 2000).

Among some of the "negative" parenting styles that might be used by Chinese parents, the literature does support the notion that some components of psychological control are used by Chinese parents in socializing their children. For example, research conducted in the 1970s, reviewed by Ho (1986), indicated that compared to American mothers, Chinese mothers used more "love-oriented" methods of child-rearing, such as threat of withdrawal or actual withdrawal of love (a component of psychological control). Love withdrawal was used less frequently, however, than reasoning and induction. In addition, parents relied more on power assertion and love withdrawal when disciplining sons. Research conducted a decade later by Wu (1985) showed that many of the mothers who were interviewed reported that if a child misbehaved, she would scold him, ask him to apologize, and then "would assure the child that she would love him or her again as long as he or she was good" (p. 130).

More recent research (Fung, 1999) examined Chinese parents' beliefs and practices regarding shaming (another possible component of psychological control) and indicated that shaming was used to teach young children right from wrong. Shaming behaviors as measured by Fung ranged from explicit (where one of the persons made a specific reference to shame) to implicit. Although no single behavior defined shame, some "markers" of shaming included verbal techniques (name-calling, derogatory attributions, threats of abandonment, etc.), paralinguistic techniques (angry intonation, emphatic stress, etc.), as well as nonverbal techniques (displaying the shaming gesture, frowning, rolling the eyeballs, turning the whole body away from the child, etc.). Some of these behaviors (e.g., derogatory comments, threats of abandonment and turning away from the child) also seem akin to love withdrawal. For example, U.S. researchers (Rollins & Thomas, 1979) have described love withdrawal as including ignoring, isolating the child, indications of rejection, disappointment, or coldness in response to something the child has done that displeases the parent.

Fung (1999) also noted that not only did parents shame their children, but primary schools in Taiwan, for example, used shaming (including group ostracism or abandonment) as a principal moral training technique (see Wilson, 1970, 1981). Teachers manipulated the shaming to correct children's misbehavior as well as underscore the class' disapproval and the appropriateness of other children's behavior (Fung, 1999; Ho, 1986). It should be noted, however, that in one study neither parents nor children named shaming as a method used if a child misbehaved (Stevenson, Chen, & Lee, 1992).

Thus, some aspects of psychological control, particularly shaming, love withdrawal (i.e., threats of abandonment), and guilt induction seem to be a prevalent part of Chinese children's socialization, both at home and in the school. Chen, Rubin, Li, and Li (1996) pointed out that it is generally believed that awareness of shame may push a child to improve his or her performance. As a consequence, children who have behavioral or social problems may be humiliated, in private and in public, by parents, teachers, and peers.

Russia

Psychological control also may have been one means of parental and peer-group control encouraged in the Soviet Union when more positive types of socialization failed. For example, threat of ostracism from the group was one method used in the Russian educational system to encourage conformity to collectivistic ideals (Hart, Nelson, et al., 1998).

Bronfenbrenner (1970), writing about child-rearing in the former Soviet Union, described "love oriented" discipline as including love withdrawal (e.g., avoiding a child when she or he does not meet parental expectations) and guilt induction (e.g., telling a child that she or he may not be as good as other children). According to Bronfenbrenner, these two types of parenting "seem to apply rather well to patterns of child rearing in the Soviet family" (p. 71).

In addition, parenting patterns that provoke anxiety or guilt have also been reported to have been empirically measured in the Russian culture (Subbostskii, 1992). Research performed with adolescents in St. Petersburg demonstrated that parental granting of psychological autonomy was related to positive child outcomes such as self-reliance, but unrelated to antisocial behavior, substance abuse, and school misbehavior (Pallock & Lamborn, 1997). Alternately, a study conducted in Voronezh, Russia, with preschool-age children revealed that psychological control was related to overt aggression (Hart, Nelson, et al., 1998).

Once again, it should be mentioned that although Russian parents may use elements of psychological control in rearing their children, other parenting styles are also used (e.g., Bronfenbrenner, 1970; Marenko, 1937). For example, recent work with Russian parents of preschoolers has shown that authoritative, authoritarian, and permissive parenting can be empirically measured (Hart, Nelson, et al., 2000).

Thus, it appears that psychological control is a parenting style that has been used by parents in the United States, Russia, and China. In light of the growing empirical evidence suggesting that psychological control predicts negative outcomes in diverse cultural settings, we hypothesize that psychological control will be related to teacher perceptions of internalizing and externalizing behavior in preschool children in all three cultures.

THE STUDY

Parents and teachers of 632 children from three cultural contexts, China, Russia, and the United States, participated in the study. Sample 1 included mothers of 194 children (95 boys; 99 girls) attending a university or community-based early childhood program in the Provo-Orem area in Utah (response rate approximately 60%). Sample 2 consisted of mothers of 190 ethnic Russian children (88 boys; 102 girls) enrolled in 15 classrooms in three nursery schools in Voronezh, Russia (response rate above 75%). Voronezh is a provincial city of one million located approximately 250 miles south of Moscow. Soviet officials strictly regulated foreign visitors until 1990, when outsiders obtained free access to the city. Even today, Voronezh is unusual because it is relatively isolated from Western influence because of its location. Sample 3 included mothers of 248 children (129 boys; 119 girls) attending one of four nursery schools in Beijing, China (response rate over 80%). Beijing, with a population of approximately 10 million people, is the capital and cultural center of China.

Demographic statistics from the three samples, based on maternal reports, are presented in Table 8-1. Parents in all samples were relatively well-educated and were in their 30s. As expected, children in China had no siblings, as a result of the one-child policy. Russian families were smaller, compared to those living in Utah, where larger families are more the norm.

Data were gathered from parents and teachers in Utah, China, and Russia. Before collecting data, parental consent was obtained for all aspects of the study for the Utah sample. Russian and Chinese nursery schools act in loco parentis (in place of the parents), and as a result researchers were not allowed to obtain written parental permission. However, in group meetings

TABLE 8-1
Demographic Information for Samples from China, Russia, and the United States

	China			Russia			USA		
	M	*SD*	Range	*M*	*SD*	Range	*M*	*SD*	Range
Child age (months)	60.40	7.82	40 to 76	60.68	8.52	44 to 79	56.36	5.32	38 to 68
Mother's age (years)	32.60	2.92	26 to 43	30.52	5.34	21 to 45	30.17	4.13	20 to 55
Father's age (years)	34.95	3.53	28 to 52	32.40	7.09	22 to 62	32.53	5.85	21 to 53
Mother's education (in years)	13.39	2.40	5 to 20	14.88	2.37	9 to 17	13.84	1.93	9 to 20
Father's education (in years)	13.93	2.65	7 to 22	14.49	2.41	9 to 17	14.43	2.55	6 to 24
Children in family	1	0	1	1.33	.54	1 to 5	2.95	1.5	1 to 8

arranged by school administrators, parents were informed about the study, allowed to ask questions concerning the research, assured of the confidentiality of individual and parenting data that they or a teacher provided, and advised that they or their children could withdraw from voluntary participation at any time.

In Utah, parents individually completed the psychological control questionnaire in their homes. Researchers or teachers delivered the measures. In Russia and China, parents first attended an initial meeting held at the preschool. Chinese parents completed the psychological control questionnaire while at the preschool, and a member of the research team was available to respond to questions. After the initial meeting, Russian parents took questionnaires home to complete. In all cultures parents were asked not to consult with each other while completing the instruments. Questionnaires regarding children's externalizing and internalizing behavior were delivered to teachers in their classrooms in all three cultures. Teachers completed questionnaires at the preschool after school hours.

As we have discussed elsewhere (Hart, Nelson, et al., 1998; Hart, Yang, et al., 2000), a number of methodological issues are inherent in cross-cultural research, including the use of emic (arising from the culture) versus etic (comparison of similarities across cultures) approaches (Berry, 1989). Based on the literature reviewed and our experiences in the three cultures, we have hypothesized that there is *functional equivalence* in the psychological control, internalizing, and externalizing constructs being examined; that is, they seem to carry similar meanings and are "recurrent" in all three cultural settings (Berry, 1989).

Even though components of psychological control may be "recurrent" and "recognizable" in diverse cultural settings, there may be cultural nuances in the perceived meaning of the behaviors. For example, although psychological control may be equally identifiable in different cultures, it may be more prevalent in the Chinese and Russian cultures (Hart, Nelson, et al., 2000; Triandis, 1994; Wu et al., 2000). To examine this possibility, cultural comparative analyses were conducted to assess possible mean level differences or similarities in perceptions of psychological control.

Operating on the assumption that we do not have "imposed etics" (imposition of concepts originating in U.S. culture on other cultures), it is acceptable to use instruments that are *conceptually equivalent*, or in other words similarly understood by persons in the three cultures, even though they may carry somewhat different psychological meanings. Thus, items reflecting psychological control should be similarly understood by parents in U.S., Chinese, and Russian settings. Questionnaires were forward and back-translated to operationalize this, as well as to demonstrate translation equivalence.

We also wanted to examine whether results from the three cultures could be fit by a common statistical model. *Metric equivalence* exists when the psychometric properties of data from two or more cultures have similar factor structures (Hart, Yang, et al., 2000). Invariance of factor loadings across cultural groups are essential in cross-cultural studies (Little, 1997; Widaman & Reise, 1997).

All instruments were forward and back-translated by Chinese and Russian linguists who were fluent in both English and their native languages. Researchers were consulted on difficult to translate items. Back-translated items were comparable with the English version.

Parents in all three cultures completed a psychological control questionnaire that was an adaptation of Barber's (1996) measure, in which adolescents report on their parents' use of psychological control. Because our sample was made up of preschool children, the questionnaire was adjusted so that parents could fill out a self-report concerning their own parenting. A team of early childhood experts also added items to better reflect this construct for parents of preschoolers. This modification resulted in an item pool consisting of 16 items previously used by Barber and 17 additional items (Table 8-2). Items were designed to tap dimensions of psychological control and included constraining verbal expression, invalidating feelings, personal attack, erratic emotional behavior, love withdrawal, and guilt induction. Guilt induction, love withdrawal, and erratic emotional behavior were overrepresented in the item bank because of earlier research suggesting these constructs are often used with younger children (Eisenberg & Murphy,

TABLE 8-2
Psychological Control Item Bank

Constraining Verbal Expressions
(Bar)   Changes the subject whenever our child has something to say.
(Bar)   Interrupts our child when he/she is speaking.
(Bar)   Finishes our child's sentence whenever he/she talks.

Invalidating Feelings
(Bar)   Tries to change how our child feels or thinks about things.
(Bar)   Acts like he/she knows what out child is thinking or feeling.
(Bar)   Would like to tell our child how to feel or think about things.

Personal Attack
(Bar)   Brings up our child's past mistakes when criticizing him/her.
(Bar)   Tells our child that his or her hehavior was dumb or stupid.
(Bar)   Blames our child for other family member's problems.

Erratic Emotional Behavior
(New)   Shows impatience with our child.
(New)   Shows erratic emotional behavior around child.
(Bar)   Goes back and forth between being warm and critical toward our child.
(New)   Doesn't like to be bothered by our child.
(Bar)   Changes moods when with our child.
(New)   Loses temper easily with our child.

Love Withdrawal
(Sch)   Will avoid looking at our child when our child has disappointed him/me.
(New)   Ignores our child when he/she tries to get attention.
(Sc)   If our child has hurt our feelings, stops talking to our child until the child pleases him/me.
(Sch)   Is less friendly with our child if our child does not see things his/my way.
(New)   Doesn't pay attention when our child is speaking to us.

Guilt Induction
(Block)   Lets our child know when he/she has disappointed him/me.
(New)   Tells our child he/she is not as good as we were growing up.
(Block)   Lets our child know when we are angry with him/her.
(Block)   Makes our child aware of how much we sacrifice or do for him/her.
(Sch)   Says, if you really care for me, you would not do things that cause me to worry.
(Sch)   Tells our child of all the things he/I have done for him/her.
(New)   Acts disappointed when our child misbehaves.
(New)   Tells our child that he/she should be ashamed when he/she misbehaves.
(New)   Tells our child that we get embarrassed when he/she does not meet our expectations.
(New)   Makes our child feel quilty when our child does not meet our expectations.
(Block)   Informs our child that punishment will always find him/her when misbehavior occurs.
(Block)   Lets our child know how disappointed we are when he/she misbehaves.
(Bar)   Tells our child he/she is not as good as other children.

Note: Sch = Schaefer items used by Barber (1996); Bar = Barber items; New = new items developed by early childhood experts; Block = Block items.

1995; Hoffman, 1983). Parents rated their parenting behavior on the 33 Likert-scaled items anchored from (1) never to (5) always.

Preschool teachers in all three cultures rated children's internalizing and externalizing behaviors. Items used in this study have been included in measures successfully used with teachers of preschoolers in North American samples (Hart, Yang, et al., 1998; McNeilly-Choque, Hart, Robinson, Nelson, & Olsen, 1996; Nelson, Hart, Robinson, & Olsen, 1997) and were deemed by early childhood experts to be the most easily observed by preschool teachers in all three cultures. As described earlier, all items were forward-translated and then successfully back-translated by Russian and Chinese linguists. The items assessing internalizing and externalizing behaviors used a rating based on frequency or "how often" a social behavior occurs: (0) never, (1) sometimes, or (2) very often.

Traditionally, externalizing outcomes have been described as inappropriate, undercontrolled behaviors including verbal or physical aggression toward others, arguing, poor control of temper, or impulsive–disruptive and nonconforming behaviors (e.g., Gresham & Elliott, 1990; Hart et al., 1997). The five items used in this research reflect aggressive–disruptive behaviors that might be similarly identified by preschool teachers in the three cultures and included "becomes aggressive when rough housing with peers," "blames others," "disturbs ongoing activities," "is aggressive towards people or objects," and "gets into fights."

Internalizing outcomes have been defined as behaviors indicating shyness, withdrawal, anxiety, sadness, loneliness, or poor self-esteem (e.g., Gresham & Elliott, 1990; Hart et al., 1997). Internalizing items used in this research also consist of behaviors that preschool teachers could easily observe in all three cultures, and included "acts unhappy," "says nobody likes him or her," "pouts and sulks," and "appears lonely."

FITTING BARBER'S MODEL TO THE STUDY DATA

Initially, we used structural equation modeling (SEM) procedures (Arbuckle, 1997) to test whether psychological control items used with adolescents in previous research by Barber (1996) fit the cross-cultural data for mothers of preschoolers. Data from fathers was not used because of limitations in the sample size for fathers in some cultures.

We tested Barber's 8-item model (see Table 5 in Barber, 1996, for specific items) to assess whether the factor structure was comparable across cultures. Invariance of factor loadings was tested by comparing an unconstrained model with one whose factor loadings were constrained to be equivalent across the three cultures. The significant chi-square difference

$(\chi^2_{dif} = 26.97$ $[df_{dif} = 14]$, $p < .02)$ indicated that these items did not relate to the latent construct in the same way across the three cultures.

MATERNAL PSYCHOLOGICAL CONTROL MEASUREMENT MODEL

To find a model that was comparable across cultures, we next considered the Barber (1996) items as well as the additional psychological control items from the larger item bank, augmented by early childhood professionals. The relationships between these items and internalizing and externalizing behaviors were also explored, and items that were linked to these constructs in at least one culture were retained for further analysis. The final set of psychological control items were grouped conceptually into four of the dimensions previously identified by Barber (1996), including personal attack, erratic emotional behavior, guilt induction, and love withdrawal (see Table 8-3). Scores for items in each dimension were summed, and mean scores were calculated for each dimension to simplify the model in further analyses.

A measurement model of the psychological control latent construct was tested to assess invariances of factor loadings among six groups (Chinese, Russian, and U.S.; boys and girls), using the previously mentioned dimensions (Table 8-4). The chi-square difference was nonsignificant ($\chi^2_{dif} = 18.21$ $[df_{dif} = 15]$, $p < .25$), indicating that factor loadings were comparable (invariant) across the three cultures and across gender for this measurement model. Although the loading for erratic emotional behavior was relatively low

TABLE 8-3
Maternal Psychological Control Dimensions and Items
Used in Cross-Cultural Reseach

Dimension	Description
Personal attack	Brings up child's past mistakes when critizing him/her
	Tells our child that his/her behavior was dumb or stupid
Erratic emotional behavior	Shows impatience with our child
	Doesn't like to be bothered by our child
	Changes moods when with our child
Guilt induction	Acts disappointed when our child misbehaves
	Tells my child that he/she should be ashamed when he/she misbehaves
	Tells my child that we get embarrassed when he/she does not meet our expectations
	Tells our child that he/she is not as good as other children
Love withdrawal	If our child hurts my feelings, stops talking to our child until he/she pleases me again
	Am less friendly with our child when our child does not see things my way

TABLE 8-4
Maternal Psychological Control Measurement Model

	China		Russia		United States	
	Boys	*Girls*	*Boys*	*Girls*	*Boys*	*Girls*
Personal attack	.72	.67	.58	.62	.66	.70
Erratic emotional behavior	.41	.40	.40	.40	.36	.37
Guilt induction	.77	.70	.74	.82	.82	.72
Love withdrawal	.65	.51	.51	.54	.52	.70

Note: $\chi^2(27) = 46.72$, $\chi^2 df = 1.73$, Goodness of Fit Index = .97, Tucker Lewis Index = .94, Comparative Fit Index = .95.

across cultures and gender, we decided to retain it in the model because conceptually it is considered an aspect of psychological control.[1]

LATENT MEAN DIFFERENCES ACROSS CULTURES AND GENDERS FOR MATERNAL PSYCHOLOGICAL CONTROL

With factor loadings of the psychological control construct invariant across cultures and gender, differences among the latent means could be estimated using the SEM procedure to minimize measurement error. Cole, Maxell, Arvey, and Salas (1993) recommended this procedure over multiple analysis of variance if there is a possibility of cultural bias. For the measurement model to be identified, the intercepts (means of the observed variables) were constrained to be identical across groups, and the latent mean for U.S. boys was constrained to be zero. The means of other groups that are relative to this group (0) are listed in Table 8-5. Because the latent means are relative to one another, the differences among the means remain the same, regardless of which group mean was constrained to be zero. As a consequence, differences also remain invariant when the measure is rescaled in different units. Mothers of Russian girls had the highest mean and U.S. girls' mothers had the lowest mean. Means for the Chinese mothers were in the middle of the distribution.

The latent mean differences between boys and girls within cultures (Table 8-5), and between China, Russia, and the United States within gender (Table 8-6), as shown by the letters in parentheses, were tested by comparing the chi-square change of the model when the means of the two groups were constrained to be equal as opposed to when they were

---

[1] Subsequent analyses testing the relationship between psychological control and child outcomes in the three cultures were performed. A model that included erratic emotional behavior as an indicator was estimated first. Estimating the original model without erratic emotional behavior did not alter the previous findings.

TABLE 8-5
Latent Means and Difference for Maternal Psychological Control
Between Boys and Girls Within Culture

Culture	Group	Latent Mean	Within-Culture Difference Between Boys and Girls
United States	Boys[a]	0	(b & a = 0.06) $\chi^2_{dif} = 1.03\ p = 0.31$
	Girls[b]	−.06	
China	Boys[c]	0.89	(d & c = 0.05) $\chi^2_{dif} = 0.40\ p = 0.53$
	Girls[d]	0.94	
Russia	Boys[e]	1.24	(f & e = 0.01) $\chi^2_{dif} = 0.03\ p = 0.87$
	Girls[f]	1.25	

Notes: [a] U.S. boys
[b] U.S. girls
[c] Chinese boys
[d] Chinese girls
[e] Russian boys
[f] Russian girls

unconstrained. A significant change of chi square relative to the change of one degree of freedom suggests a significant difference in the means.

Within each culture, the nonsignificant chi-square difference suggests that mothers' psychological control toward boys is the same as it is toward girls (Table 8-5). However, the level of psychological control varied across

TABLE 8-6
Latent Mean Differences for Maternal Psychological Control Across
Cultures for Boys and Girls

	United States	China	Russia
United States		(d & b = 1.00) $\chi^2_{dif} = 129.63\ p = .00$	(f & b = 1.31) $\chi^2_{dif} = 158.59\ p = .00$
China	(c & a = 0.89) $\chi^2_{dif} = 116.64\ p = .00$		(f & d = 0.31) $\chi^2_{dif} = 12.06\ p = .00$
Russia	(e & a = 1.24) $\chi^2_{dif} = 132.19\ p = .00$	(e & c = 0.35) $\chi^2_{dif} = 14.33\ p = .00$	

Notes: Girls above the diagonal: boys below the diagonal.
[a] U.S. boys   (0).
[b] U.S. girls   (-.06).
[c] Chinese boys   (0.89).
[d] Chinese girls   (0.94).
[e] Russian boys   (1.24).
[f] Russian girls   (1.25).

the three cultures, as indicated by the significant chi-square differences for boys and girls across cultural groups (Table 8-6).

INTERNALIZING AND EXTERNALIZING MEASUREMENT MODEL

The cross-cultural comparability of the internalizing and externalizing constructs was also tested using the chi-square differences between a constrained measurement model and an unconstrained one. The fit of the unconstrained model was acceptable (χ^2 = 315.89 [df = 156], p < .00; Goodness of Fit Index (GFI) = .90; Comparative Fit Index (CFI) = .92; Tucker Lewis Index (TLI) = .89). When all the factor loadings were constrained to be equivalent across cultures and gender, the chi square increased significantly from that of an unconstrained model (χ^2_{dif} = 86.03 [df_{dif} = 35], p < .00), implying a variance in factor loadings across the six groups. Similar results were obtained even when substituting other possible internalizing and externalizing items from our item bank. Factor loadings of both constructs were found to be equivalent across gender in both the U.S. (χ^2_{dif} = 9.13 [df_{dif} = 7], p < .24) and Chinese samples (χ^2_{dif} = 10.73 [df_{dif} = 7], p < .15).

Factor-loading equivalence was found across gender only for the externalizing construct in the Russian sample (χ^2_{dif} = 5.55 [df_{dif} = 4], p < .24). The factor loadings of externalizing were also found to be equivalent across the three male groups (χ^2_{dif} = 7.08 [df_{dif} = 8], p < .53). Because of the differences in factor loadings across some groups, the internalizing and externalizing measurement models were not comparable, and the latent means may vary with ways to identify the model. Thus, additional tests of latent mean differences were not pursued.

PSYCHOLOGICAL CONTROL AND PRESCHOOLERS' INTERNALIZING AND EXTERNALIZING BEHAVIORS

Finally, the link between mothers' psychological control and children's internalizing and externalizing behaviors was assessed using structural equation modeling. Because of the variance in factor loadings in the outcome variables, the full structural model was estimated using a multiple sample approach without constraining any parameters to be equivalent across the three samples and the six groups. This is similar to estimating different models for each group, but with one set of indexes of goodness of fit.

Two sets of analyses were performed. First, models were tested in the three cultures using boys' and girls' combined data (Table 8-7). Uncon-

TABLE 8-7
Standardized Factor Loadings and Structural Coefficients for Confirmatory Factor Models of Psychological Control and Internalizing and Externalizing Behaviors Across Three Cultures

	China	Russia	United States
Psychological Control			
Personal attack	.70	.60	.68
Erratic emotional behavior	.41	.40	.37
Guilt induction	.72	.75	.75
Love withdrawal	.58	.52	.60
Externalizing			
Aggressive when rough-housing	.88	.73	.75
Blames others	.59	.58	.61
Disturbs ongoing activities	.79	.74	.72
Aggressive toward people	.89	.80	.89
Gets into fights	.82	.78	.73
Internalizing			
Acts unhappy	.51	.54	.66
Says nobody likes him/her	.33	.61	.56
Pouts and sulks	.55	.67	.75
Appears lonely	.70	.46	.55
Structural Coefficients			
Psychological Control → Exter	.13	.30*	.21*
Psychological Control → Inter	.11	.19	.22*

Note: $\chi^2(195) = 405.24$, $0^2/df = 2.08$, Goodness of Fit Index = .91, Tucker Lewis Index = .90, Comparative Fir Index = .92. *$p < .05$.

strained models were tested because the measurement models for internalizing and externalizing were not comparable across cultures. SEM revealed that for the U.S. data, psychological control was significantly related to both externalizing and internalizing behaviors. In China, no significant linkages were found. Psychological control was associated with externalizing behaviors only in the Russian sample. Model fit was acceptable ($\chi^2 = 354.35$ [$df = 183$], $p < .001$; GFI = .92; CFI = .93; TLI = .91).

In the second set of analyses, models were tested for boys and girls in each of the three cultures (Table 8-8). For U.S. girls, psychological control was again related to both internalizing and externalizing behaviors. Psychological control was linked to internalizing behaviors for Chinese girls and externalizing behaviors for Russian girls. Model fit was adequate ($\chi^2 = 271.56$ [$df = 180$], $p < .001$; GFI = .89; CFI = .93; TLI = .91).

No associations existed between psychological control and internalizing or externalizing behaviors for U.S. boys. Psychological control was related with externalizing behaviors for Chinese boys and with both externalizing and internalizing behaviors for Russian boys. Fit was adequate

TABLE 8-8
Standardized Factor Loadings and Structural Coefficients for Confirmatory
Factor Models of Psychological Control and Internalizing and Externalizing
Behaviors Across Three Cultures and Gender

	China		Russia		United States	
	Boys	*Girls*	*Boys*	*Girls*	*Boys*	*Girls*
Psychological Control						
Personal attack	.71	.75	.55	.68	.65	.74
Erratic emotional behavior	.44	.39	.42	.39	.39	.35
Guilt induction	.76	.51	.69	.76	.81	.67
Love withdrawal	.66	.65	.51	.54	.53	.67
Externalizing						
Aggressive when rough-housing	.87	.90	.79	.69	.72	.79
Blames others	.64	.48	.46	.54	.56	.64
Disturbs ongoing activities	.81	.66	.65	.80	.66	.82
Aggressive toward people	.91	.76	.84	.84	.93	.85
Gets into fights	.81	.76	.71	.81	.74	.76
Internalizing						
Acts unhappy	.48	.41	.70	.39	.86	.50
Says nobody likes him/her	.19	.52	.31	.84	.42	.66
Pouts and sulks	.62	.58	.59	.70	.64	.79
Appears lonely	.69	.60	.60	.27	.66	.54
Structural Coefficients						
Psychological Control → Exter	.28*	-.08	.34*	.31*	.04	.26*
Psychological Control → Inter	−.16	.51*	.33*	.17	−.02	.33*

Note: For boys: $\chi^2(180) = 277.16$, $0^2 df = 1.54$, Goodness of Fit Index = .89, Tucker Lewis Index = .90, Comparative Fit Index = .92.
For girls: $\chi^2(180) = 271.56$, $0^2 df = 1.51$, Goodness of Fit Index = .89, Tucker Lewis Index = .91, Comparative Fit Index = .93. *$p < .05$.

for this model ($\chi^2 = 277.16$ [$df = 180$], $p < .001$; GFI = .89; CFI = .92; TLI = .90).

CONNECTIONS WITH PREVIOUS RESEARCH, LIMITATIONS, AND FUTURE DIRECTIONS

The findings of this research are limited to maternal perceptions of psychological control and teachers' perceptions of children's externalizing and internalizing behavior in specific geographic locations within the three cultures and may be prone to type I error because of the number of correlation analyses. In addition, data is cross-sectional, based on mothers' self-reports of psychological control, and the research included measures of the dependent variable that may be considered limited in scope. Nevertheless, this research provides a starting point for an initial understanding of the relationships between psychological control and preschool children's internalizing and externalizing behaviors in three cultures.

The results indicated that the psychological control factor structure used in previous research with adolescents in the United States was not comparable for samples of Chinese, Russian, and U.S. preschoolers; however, after including items developed by early childhood professionals, it was possible to identify a factor structure for the maternal psychological control construct that was comparable across cultures. Triandis (1994) has noted that if in factor analysis the same items empirically cluster in each culture, this is an indication that in those cultures the latent construct may have the same meaning.

When comparing the latent means, within each of the three cultures mothers' use of psychological control with boys did not differ significantly from that of girls. However, when differences across cultures and genders were considered separately, there were significant differences among the latent means (U.S. mothers scored lowest and Russian mothers scored highest for both boys and girls). Psychological control may be more ingrained in Russian culture (Bronfenbrenner, 1970) and used more often by Chinese mothers because of its link to Confucian ideology (Ho, 1986). As a consequence, the use of psychological control or its components may be viewed as an effective means of obtaining parental goals for socialization of children in Russia and China. Thus, parents in these cultures may be inclined to use psychological control more often, which might explain why their latent means are higher than those in the United States.

Triandis (1994) provided another possible explanation for cross-cultural differences, noting that response sets to questions may vary across cultures. In some cultures people might mark moderate responses, whereas in other cultures individuals may mark extreme responses. As a consequence, parent measures used in different cultures may not reflect a common metric, because of differential reference points or response sets, reflecting societal norms. For example, in China, as in most Confucian cultures, there is the doctrine of the mean (*Zhong Yong Zhi Dao*) which promotes the avoidance of extremes. It may be possible that even though psychological control is a common parenting strategy in China, Chinese parents were more conservative than Russian parents in rating themselves because they felt it was improper to highlight their own behavior relative to societal norms. Further research is needed to address this issue.

A final purpose of this research was to assess whether or not the linkages between mothers' use of psychological control and preschool children's internalizing and externalizing behaviors were consistent with the literature and apply cross-culturally. Our results with preschool children partially support the findings of previous research conducted with adolescents and older schoolage children in the United States (chapter 2, this volume).

Specifically, results obtained with our sample of preschool children (boys and girls combined) in the United States were consistent with previous research findings in that preschoolers exposed to higher levels of maternal psychological control were perceived by teachers as displaying more internalizing and externalizing behaviors. This finding is also consistent with the cross-cultural evidence for psychological control of adolescents presented in chapter 2 of this volume, two of which cultures (Gaza and India) have authoritarian and collectivist characteristics. Findings from the other two samples in this study were less clear. In the Chinese sample, when male and female data were analyzed together, no linkages emerged between mothers' use of psychological control and children's internalizing and externalizing behaviors. When analyzing the combined male and female Russian samples, mothers' use of psychological control was related only to externalizing behaviors (a finding that was consistent with our earlier work from the same Russian sample; Hart, Nelson, et al., 1998). However, when we examined gender-differentiated linkages between maternal psychological control and child problems, a more refined, and complex, pattern of effects emerged. Specifically, psychological control was positively related to internalizing and externalizing for U.S. girls and Russian boys. The construct was positively associated with externalizing only for Russian girls and Chinese boys and with internalizing for Chinese girls.

The cross-cultural study of psychological control and its outcomes is a relatively new area of investigation. Although there has been some initial work with samples of adolescents of varied ethnicity in the United States (Bean, 1997; Mason et al., 1996) as well as in other cultures (chapter 2, this volume), none of these have separated samples by child gender when determining levels of parental psychological control. In addition, studies other than our own have not differentiated the effects of parental psychological control on boys versus girls. In general, the systematic study of the linkages between parenting and gender issues is more well-developed in western societies (see Hart et al., 1997; Russell & Russell, 1992; Russell et al., 1998; for reviews), but in China and Russia is relatively unexplored. Future research should continue to investigate the relationships between psychological control and preschool children's outcomes, taking into account both culture and gender.

In the future, researchers might investigate temperamental, social cognitive, or emotional mechanisms linking psychological control and preschooler's internalizing and externalizing behaviors (e.g., Hart, Nelson, et al., 2000). For example, research on parenting that is coercive and characterized by behavioral overcontrol indicates that children who are raised in this manner may exhibit disregulated emotion and be less likely to successfully encode social cues and consider appropriate consequences for their actions, which, in turn, may be related to aggression (e.g., Dodge, Bates, & Pettit,

1990; Dodge, Pettit, Bates, & Valente, 1995; Hart, Ladd, & Burleson, 1990). Because authoritarian parenting has also been linked to internalizing disorders (see Hart et al., 1997, for a review), and parental use of psychological control has been associated with both internalizing and externalizing, similar social–cognitive and emotional processes may be at work. Future research is needed to explore this possibility (see chapters 4 and 5, this volume, for efforts to account for child characteristics in the study of parental psychological control).

In generalizing findings, we must recognize the diversity of individuals living in China, the United States, and Russia. Cultures do not necessarily have "unitary orientations" (Yau & Smetana, 1996), and patterns of child-rearing may vary within cultures because of ethnic differences (Olson & Matskovsky, 1994). Stevenson-Hinde (1998) also reminded us that numerous differences may exist between rural and urban areas within a country, and as a consequence, "variation within countries may be as large as that between countries" (p. 699). Although these findings may apply to the sampled mothers in Beijing, Voronezh, and Provo-Orem, they may not be applicable to all ethnic groups or individuals in these three countries.

To improve the validity of cross-cultural findings, future research needs to include a multimethod approach (Triandis, 1994), possibly using ethnographic and qualitative methodologies to discover more precise cultural nuances associated with psychological control and its relationship to preschoolers' internalizing and externalizing in these cultures.

In sum, this research was a beginning foray into studying linkages between maternal psychological control and preschoolers' outcomes in different cultures. Links were found between psychological control and child outcomes in all three cultures; however, this research also raises new questions and avenues of study regarding child gender and its linkages to psychological control in non-Western settings that should prove to be a fruitful area of future inquiry.

REFERENCES

Alessandri, S. M., & Lewis, M. (1993). Parental evaluation and its relations to shame and pride in young children. *Sex Roles, 29,* 335–343.

Arbuckle, J. (1997). *Amos users' guide: Version 3.6.* Chicago: Smallwaters.

Barber, B. K. (1996). Parental psychological control: Revisiting a neglected construct. *Child Development, 67,* 3296–3319.

Barber, B. K. (1997a). Introduction: Adolescent socialization in context—Connection, regulation, and autonomy in multiple contexts. *Journal of Adolescent Research, 12,* 173–177.

Barber, B. K. (1997b). Introduction: Adolescent socialization in context—The role of connection, regulation, and autonomy in the family. *Journal of Adolescent Research, 12,* 5–11.

Barber, B. K., & Olsen, J. A. (1997). Socialization in context: Connection, regulation, and autonomy in the family, school, and neighborhood, and with peers. *Journal of Adolescent Research, 12,* 287–315.

Barber, B. K., Olsen, J. A., & Shagle, S. C. (1994). Associations between parental psychological and behavior control and youth internalized and externalized behaviors. *Child Development, 65,* 1120–1136.

Baumrind, D. (1966). Effects of authoritative control on child behavior. *Child Development, 37,* 887–907.

Bean, R. A. (1997). *Academic grades, delinquency, and depression among ethnically diverse youth: The influence of parental connection, regulation, and psychological control.* Unpublished doctoral dissertation, Brigham Young University, Provo, Utah.

Berry, J. W. (1989). Imposed etics-emics-derived etics: The operationalization of a compelling idea. *International Journal of Psychology, 24,* 721–735.

Bond, M. H. (1991). *Beyond the Chinese face: Insights from psychology.* Oxford: Oxford University Press.

Bronfenbrenner, U. (1970). *Two worlds of childhood: U.S. and U.S.S.R.* New York: Russell Sage Foundation.

Chen, X., Dong, Q., & Zhou, H. (1997). Authoritative and authoritarian parenting practices and social and school performance in Chinese children. *International Journal of Behavioral Development, 21,* 855–873.

Chen, X., Rubin, K. H., Li, B., & Li, D. (1996, August). *Adolescent outcomes of social functioning in Chinese children.* XXVI International Congress of Psychology, Montreal, Quebec, Canada.

Cole, D. A., Maxwell, S. E., Arvey, R., & Salas, E. (1993). Multivariate group comparisons of variable systems: MANOVA and structural equation modeling. *Psychological Bulletin, 114,* 174–184.

Crockenberg, S., & Litman, C. (1990). Autonomy as competence in 2-year-olds: Maternal correlates of child defiance, compliance, and self-assertion. *Developmental Psychology, 26,* 961–971.

Darling, N., & Steinberg, L. (1993). Parenting style as context: An integrative model. *Psychological Bulletin, 113,* 487–496.

Dodge, K. A., Pettit, G. S., & Bates, J. E. (1990). Mechanisms in the cycle of violence. *Science, 250,* 1678–1683.

Dodge, K. A., Pettit, G. S., Bates, J. E., & Valente, E. (1995). Social information-processing patterns partially mediate the effect of early physical abuse on later conduct problems. *Journal of Abnormal Psychology, 104,* 632–643.

Eccles, J. S., Early, D., Frasier, K., Belansky, E., & McCarthy, K. (1997). The relation of connection, regulation, and support for autonomy to adolescents' functioning. *Journal of Adolescent Research, 12,* 245–262.

Eisenberg, N., & Murphy, B. (1995). Parenting and children's moral development. In M. H Bornstein (Ed.), *Handbook of parenting: Vol. 4. Applied and practical parenting* (pp. 227–258). Mahwah, NJ: Erlbaum.

Fung, H. (1999). *Becoming a moral child: The socialization of shame among young Chinese children*. Manuscript submitted for publication.

Garcia Coll, C. T., Meyer, E. C., & Brillon, L. (1995). Ethnic and minority parenting. In M. H. Bornstein (Ed.), *Handbook of parenting: Vol. 2. Biology and ecology of parenting* (pp. 189–209). Mahwah, NJ: Erlbaum.

Gorman, J. C. (1998). Parenting attitudes and practices of immigrant Chinese mothers of adolescents. *Family Relations, 47*, 73–80.

Gottman, J. M., Katz, L. F., & Hooven, C. (1997). *Meta-emotion: How families communicate emotionally*. Mahwah, NJ: Erlbaum.

Gray, M. R., & Steinberg, L. (1999). Unpacking authoritative parenting: Reassessing a multidimensional construct. *Journal of Marriage and the Family, 61*, 574–587.

Gresham, F. M., & Elliott, S. N. (1990). *Social skills rating system manual*. Circle Pines, MN: American Guidance Service.

Grotpeter, J. K. (1997). *Relational aggression, overt aggression, and family relationships*. Unpublished doctoral dissertation, University of Illinois at Urbana-Champaign.

Hart, C. H., Ladd, G. W., & Burleson, B. R. (1990). Children's expectations of the outcomes of social strategies: Relations with sociometric status and maternal disciplinary styles. *Child Development, 61*, 127–137.

Hart, C. H., Nelson, D., Robinson, C. C., Olsen, S. F., & McNeilly-Choque, M. K. (1998). Overt and relational aggression in Russian nursery-school-age children: Parenting style and marital linkages. *Developmental Psychology, 34*, 687–697.

Hart, C. H., Nelson, D. A., Robinson, C. C., Olsen, S. F., McNeilly-Choque, M. K., Porter, C. L., & McKee, T. R. (2000). Russian parenting styles and family processes: Linkages with subtypes of victimization and aggression. In K. A. Kerns, J. M. Contreras, & A. M. Neal-Barnett (Eds.), *Family and peers: Linking two social worlds* (pp. 47–84). Westport, CT: Praeger.

Hart, C. H., Newell, L. D., & Olsen, S. F. (in press). Parenting skills and social/communicative competence in childhood. In J. O. Greene & B. R. Burleson (Eds.), *Handbook of communication and social interaction skill*. Mahwah, NJ: Erlbaum.

Hart, C. H., Olsen, S. F., Robinson, C. C., & Mandleco, B. L. (1997). The development of social and communicative competence in childhood: Review and a model of personal, familial, and extra familial processes. In B. R. Burleson (Ed.), *Communication yearbook* (Vol. 20, pp. 305–373). Thousand Oaks, CA: Sage.

Hart, C. H., Yang, C., Nelson, L. J., Robinson, C. C., Olsen, J. A., Nelson, D. A., Porter, C. L., Jin, S., Olsen, S. F., & Wu, P. (2000). Peer acceptance in early childhood and subtypes of socially withdrawn behavior in China, Russia, and the United States. *International Journal of Behavioral Development, 24*, 73–81.

Ho, D. Y. F. (1986). Chinese patterns of socialization: A critical review. In M. H. Bond (Ed.), *The psychology of the Chinese people* (pp. 1–37). Hong Kong: Oxford University Press.

Ho, D. Y. F. (1996). Filial piety and its psychological consequences. In M. H. Bond (Ed.), *The handbook of Chinese psychology* (pp. 155–165). Hong Kong: Oxford University Press.

Hoffman, M. L. (1983). Affective and cognitive processes in moral internalization. In E. T. Higgins, D. N. Ruble, & W. W. Hartup (Eds.), *Social cognition and social development* (pp. 236–274). Cambridge: Cambridge University Press.

Holden, G. W. (1997). *Parents and the dynamics of child rearing.* Boulder, CO: Westview Press.

Little, T. D. (1997). Mean and covariance structures (MACS) analyses of cross-cultural data: Practical and theoretical issues. *Multivariate Behavioral Research, 32,* 53–76.

Maccoby, E. E., & Martin, J. A. (1983). Socialization in the context of the family: Parent-child interaction. In P. H. Mussen (Series Ed.) & E. M. Hetherington (Vol. Ed.), *Handbook of child psychology: Vol. 4. Socialization, personality, and social development* (pp. 1–102). New York: Wiley.

Marenko (1937). *The collective family: A handbook for Russian parents* (R. Daglish, Trans.). New York: Anchor Books.

Mason, C. A., Cauce, A. M., Gonzales, N., & Hiraga, Y. (1996). Neither too sweet nor too sour: Problem peers, maternal control, and problem behavior in African American adolescents. *Child Development, 67,* 2115–2130.

McNeilly-Choque, M. K., Hart, C. H., Robinson, C. C., Nelson, L. J., & Olsen, S. F. (1996). Overt and relational aggression on the playground: Correspondence among different informants. *Journal of Research in Childhood Education, 11,* 47–67.

Miller, P. J., Wiley, A. R., Fung, H., & Liang, C. (1997). Personal storytelling as a medium of socialization in Chinese and American families. *Child Development, 68,* 557–568.

Mills, R. S. L., & Rubin, K. H. (1998). Are behavioural and psychological control both differentially associated with childhood aggression and social withdrawal? *Canadian Journal of Behavioural Sciences, 30,* 132–136.

Nelson, D. A. (1997, April). *Family relationships of relationally and overtly victimized children.* Paper presented at the biennial conference of the Society for Research in Child Development, Washington, DC.

Nelson, L. J., Hart, C. H., Robinson, C., & Olsen, S. F. (1997, April). *Relations between three subtypes of withdrawn behavior and peer acceptance in preschool children: A multi-method perspective.* Paper presented at the biennial conference of the Society for Research in Child Development, Washington, DC.

Olsen, S. F., Wells, M. E. W., Hart, C. H., & Robinson, C. C. (2000). *Parental psychological control and preschool children's internalizing and externalizing behavior.* Manuscript in preparation.

Olson, D. H., & Matskovsky, M. S. (1994). Soviet and American families: A comparative overview. In J. W. Maddock, M. J. Hogan, A. I. Antonov, & M. S. Matskovsky (Eds.), *Families before and after Perestroika: Russian and U.S. perspectives* (pp. 9–35). New York: Guilford Press.

Pallock, L., & Lamborn, S. (1997, April). *Russian teens perceptions of parents and self.* Paper presented at the biennial conference of the Society for Research in Child Development, Washington, DC.

Putallaz, M., & Heflin, A. H. (1990). Parent-child interaction. In S. R. Asher & J. D. Coie (Eds.), *Peer rejection in childhood: Origins, consequences, and intervention* (pp. 274–305). Cambridge: Cambridge University Press.

Rollins, B. C., & Thomas, D. L. (1979). Parental support, power, and control techniques in the socialization of children. In W. R. Burr, R. Hill, F. I. Nye, & I. L. Reiss (Eds.), *Contemporary theories about the family: Vol. 1. Research-based theories* (pp. 317–364). New York: Free Press.

Rubin, K. H., Bukowski, W., & Parker, J. G. (1998). Peer interactions, relationships, and groups. In *Handbook of child psychology: Vol. 3. Social, emotional, personality development* (pp. 619–700). Hillsdale, NJ: Erlbaum.

Rubin, K. H., & Coplan, R. J., Nelson, L. J., Cheah, C., & Lagace-Seguin, D. G. (1999). Peer relationships in childhood. In M. A. Bornstein & M. E. Lamb (Eds.), *Developmental psychology: An advanced textbook* (pp. 451–502). Hillsdale, NJ: Erlbaum.

Rubin, K. H., Nelson, L. J., Hastings, P., & Asendorpf, J. (1999). The transaction between parents' perceptions of their children's shyness and their parenting styles. *International Journal of Behavioral Development, 23,* 937–957.

Rubin, K. H., Stewart, S. L., & Chen, X. (1995). Parent of aggressive and withdrawn children. In M. Bornstein (Ed.), *Handbook of parenting: Vol. 1. Children and parenting* (pp. 255–284). Mahwah, NJ: Erlbaum.

Russell, A., Aloa, V., Feder, T., Glover, A., Miller, H., & Palmer, G. (1998). Sex-based differences in parenting styles in a sample with preschool children. *Australian Journal of Psychology, 50,* 89–99.

Russell, A., & Russell, G. (1992). The socialization of Australian boys and girls in middle childhood for independence and achievement. In J. L. Roopnarine & D. B. Carter (Eds.), *Parent-child socialization in diverse cultures: Annual advances in applied development psychology* (Vol. 5, pp. 53–74). Norwood, NJ: Ablex.

Segal, M. H., Lonner, W. J., & Berry, J. W. (1998). Cross-cultural psychology as a scholarly discipline. *American Psychologist, 53,* 1101–1110.

Shulman, S., Collins, W. A., & Dital, M. (1993). Parent-child relationships and peer-perceived competence during middle childhood and preadolescence in Israel. *Journal of Early Adolescence, 13,* 204–218.

Siqueland, L., Kendall, P. C., & Steinberg, L. (1996). Anxiety in children: Family environments and family interaction. *Journal of Clinical Child Psychology, 25,* 225–237.

Stark, K. D., Humphrey, L. L., Crook, K., & Lewis, K. (1990). Perceived family environments of depressed and anxious children: Child's and maternal figure's perspectives. *Journal of Abnormal Child Psychology, 18*, 527–547.

Steinberg, L. (1990). Autonomy, conflict, and harmony in the family relationship. In S. S. Feldman & G. R. Elliott (Eds.), *At the threshold: The developing adolescent* (pp. 255–276). Cambridge, MA: Harvard University Press.

Steinberg, L., Dornbusch, S. M., & Brown, B. B. (1992). Ethnic differences in adolescent achievement: An ecological perspective. *American Psychologist, 47*, 723–729.

Steinberg, L., Elmen, J. D., & Mounts, N. S. (1989). Authoritative parenting, psychosocial maturity, and academic success among adolescents. *Child Development, 60*, 1424–1436.

Steinberg, L., Mounts, N. S., Lamborn, S. D., & Dornbusch, S. M. (1991). Authoritative parenting and adolescent adjustment across varied ecological niches. *Journal of Research on Adolescence, 1*, 19–36.

Stevenson, H. W., Chen, C., & Lee, S. (1992). Chinese families. In J. L Roopnarine & D. B. Carter (Vol. Eds.), I. E. Sigel (Series Ed.), *Parent-child socialization in diverse cultures: Annual advances in applied developmental psychology* (Vol. 5, pp. 17–33). Norwood, NJ: Ablex.

Stevenson-Hinde, J. (1998). Parenting in different cultures: Time to focus. *Developmental Psychology, 34*, 698–700.

Subbotskii, E. V. (1992). Moral socialization of the child in the Soviet Union from birth to age seven. In J. L. Roopnarine & D. B. Carter (Eds.), *Parent-child socialization in diverse cultures* (pp. 89–105). Norwood, NJ: Ablex.

Triandis, H. C. (1994). *Culture and social behavior.* New York: McGraw-Hill.

Wells, M. E. W. (1998). *Psychological control and internalizing and externalizing behavior in early childhood.* Unpublished master's thesis, Brigham Young University.

Widaman, K. F., & Reise, S. P. (1997). Exploring the measurement invariance of psychological instruments: Applications in the substance use domain. In K. J. Bryant, M. Windle, & S. G. West (Eds.), *The science of prevention: Methodological advances from alcohol and substance abuse research* (pp. 281–324). Washington, DC: American Psychological Association.

Wilson, R. W. (1970). *Learning to be Chinese.* Cambridge: MIT Press.

Wilson, R. W. (1981). Moral behavior in Chinese society: A theoretical perspective. In R. W. Wilson, S. L. Greenblatt, & A. A. Wilson (Eds.), *Moral behavior in Chinese society* (pp. 117–136). New York: Praeger.

Wu, D. Y. H. (1985). Child training in Chinese culture. In W. Tseng & D. Y. H. Wu (Eds.), *Chinese culture and mental health* (pp. 113–134). New York: Academic Press.

Wu, D. Y. H. (1996). Chinese childhood socialization. In M. H. Bond (Ed.), *The handbook of Chinese psychology* (pp. 143–154). New York: Oxford University Press.

Wu, D. Y. H. (1997). Parental control: Psychocultural interpretations of Chinese patterns of socialization. In S. Lau (Ed.), *Growing up the Chinese way: Chinese child and adolescent development* (pp. 1–28). Hong Kong: Chinese University Press.

Wu, P., Robinson, C. C., Hart, C. H., Yang, C., Hart, C. H., Olsen, S. F., & Jin, S., Wo, J., & Wu, X. (2000). *Understanding Chinese parenting of preschool children through cultural notions.* Manuscript submitted for publication.

Yau, J., & Smetana, J. G. (1996). Adolescent-parent conflict among Chinese adolescents in Hong Kong. *Child Development, 67,* 1262–1275.

9

EXPANDING THE STUDY AND UNDERSTANDING OF PSYCHOLOGICAL CONTROL

BRIAN K. BARBER, ROY L. BEAN, AND LANCE D. ERICKSON

The two central purposes of this volume are to review the historical, conceptual, and empirical literatures on parental psychological control and to advance the rapidly growing scientific literature on this aspect of the parent–child relationship. Chapter 2 addressed the first task with a review of published material that has specifically investigated psychological control or variables that are conceptually similar to it. From this review of the historical conceptualizations of parental psychological control, we concluded that psychological control is a psychologically oriented, intrusive, constraining, and manipulating form of parental control in which parents appear to maintain their own psychological status at the expense and violation of the child's self. From the review of the empirical literatures, we further concluded that parental psychological control has been consistently linked to difficulties in child functioning, such as self-processes, internalized and externalized problems, and school performance, with emerging evidence that these associations occur in a variety of national, cultural, and ethnic samples.

In chapter 2, we noted that two of the limitations of the growing literature on parental psychological control are (a) that most of the work has investigated adolescents, and not younger children; and (b) that most of the research has been conducted using self-reports of parental psychological control. These two limitations were targeted in chapters 3 to 8 of this volume. Two of these chapters were devoted to expanding the work on adolescents beyond merely documenting the now common finding of a significant association between parental psychological control and difficulties in adolescents. In chapter 3, Stone et al. did this by setting psychological control in the broader family context, finding that it was significantly predicted by measures of interparental conflict and that it was one path through which the negative effects of interparental conflict were transmitted to adolescent difficulty. In chapter 4, Pettit and Laird pioneered work on antecedents of parental psychological control of adolescents, making a number of interesting findings relative to the earlier parenting and child characteristics that differentially predict psychological and behavioral control in adolescence. Both chapters 3 and 4 also illustrated advances in the methodologies used to study psychological control (e.g., multisite replications, multiple informants, and longitudinal design).

Chapters 5 to 8 also illustrated a variety of alternative methodologies for studying parental psychological control (e.g., child, parent, observer, and puppet interview ratings, multi-informant and longitudinal designs, and cross-cultural comparisons) in their investigations of psychological control of children younger than adolescents. Collectively, the findings of these chapters added important validity and specificity to understanding the developmental salience of parental psychological control in demonstrating that, in addition to adolescents, psychological control is similarly predictive of difficulties in younger children. In some cases, the findings of these chapters also added preliminary evidence that suggests qualifications for the relevance of psychological control to child functioning. Specifically, in chapter 5, Morris and colleagues found the negative effects of parental psychological control to be contingent on child temperament (e.g., negative reactivity). In chapter 6, Nelson and Crick found parental psychological control to be related to relational aggression in young girls. In chapter 7, Holmbeck et al. found parental psychological control to be consistently linked with a variety of maladaptive behaviors in young children both with and without physical challenges. Finally, in chapter 8, Olsen et al. demonstrated that maternal psychological control was associated with young children's problem behaviors in U.S., Russian, and Chinese samples, with some variations by type of problem and by sex of child.

In short, the volume establishes that, because of the historical presence of the construct in the work of many scholars of socialization and the consistent empirical findings that are now emerging about the negative role of this form of parental behavior in child and adolescent development, parental psychological control is a phenomenon deserving of consistent and growing attention. This chapter suggests several ways in which this work can proceed. The first part of the chapter highlights the numerous areas that are open for future research regarding psychological control that will provide more detail and clarification as to the use and effects of psychological control. The second part progresses beyond the conceptual and empirical focus on parenting and attempts to set the construct more broadly in a larger context. After linking the literature on psychological control to the literature on child maltreatment, that section lifts the construct out of the exclusive domain of the parent–child relationship in discussing its relevance to other interpersonal and social contexts.

AREAS OF NEEDED SPECIALIZATION

As consistent as are the findings reviewed and presented in this volume relative to parental psychological control, the research effort is still relatively young and in need of much expansion and validation. In particular, there are four tasks that deserve current attention: (a) identifying how levels of parental control vary by important demographic factors, (b) clarifying the effects of psychological control, (c) studying antecedents of psychological control, and (d) implementing new methodologies for measuring psychological control.

Levels of Psychological Control

Although some of the studies reviewed and presented in this volume compared mean levels of parental psychological control across the central demographic groups in the studied samples, many have not. One important way, therefore, that the research literature can be enhanced is to pay more consistent attention to differences in levels of psychological control that are engaged in or experienced by varying groups, such as mothers and fathers, male and female children, children of varying ages, minority and majority groups, and groups varying in socioeconomic well-being. Some trends are apparent in the extant literature, but these and others will need to be validated and extended before we may have a clear understanding of in which demographic circumstances parental psychological control is most prevalent. Here we review the studies covered in chapter 2 of this volume that tested explicitly for differences across groups.

Child Sex Differences

Table 9-1 summarizes the 15 studies that tested for child sex differences. The trend in these studies slightly favors male children experiencing more psychological control (8 of 14 studies). Six studies that used preadolescent or adolescent-reported psychological control, and one study that used parent-reported control, indicated higher levels reported by males than females. Two studies that used observational ratings found the same pattern. In contrast to these findings, two studies found higher levels for females: one study using observational ratings of preadolescent and adolescent Mexican research participants and one using self-reported psychological control from Hispanic adolescents. Finally, five found no child sex differences: four for

TABLE 9-1
Summary of Child Sex Differences in Psychological Control

Article	Measure	Age	Source	Males	Females
Schaefer, 1965	PC	12 to 14	CR	X	
Armentrout & Burger, 1972	PC	9 to 14	CR	X	
Dusek & Litovsky, 1988	PC	12 to 18	CR	X	
Shulman et al., 1993	PC	9 to 11	CR	X	
Bronstein, 1994 (Mexican)	PC	7 to 12	Obs		X
Comstock, 1994	PC	13	CR	Nonsignificant	
Kuczynski & Kochanska, 1995	PC	2 years	Obs	Nonsignificant	
Barber, 1996 (Study 3)	PC	10 to 14	CR	X	
Barber, 1996 (Study 3; Hispanic)	PC	10 to 14	CR		X
Dornbusch et al., 1987	Authoritarian	14 to 18	CR	X	
Crockenberg & Litman, 1990	Negative control	2 years	Obs	X	
Smetana, 1995	PAC	11 to 15	CR, PR	Nonsignificant	
Mason et al., 1996	Restrictiveness	13 to 14	PR	Nonsignificant	
Best et al., 1997	Constraining	14	Obs	X	
Mantzicopoulos and Oh-Hwang, 1998 (Korean)	PPS	14 to 16	CR	Nonsignificant	

Note: "X" signifies higher control; PC = Psychological control; PAC = Parental Authority Questionnaire (Buri, 1989); PPS = Parenting Practices Scale (Steinberg et al., 1989); CR = Child report; Obs = Observation; PR = Parent report.

adolescent or parent reports and one for observational rating of two year old children. In chapter 8 (this volume), Olsen et al. also found no child sex differences in any of their three samples.

As they are, the findings show some consistency in the trend favoring higher psychological control for males across methodologies, but more systematic testing is necessary before any conclusions can be drawn. The possibility that females in Latin cultures receive more psychological control than males also should be pursued systematically, as well as among other ethnic, cultural, and national groups.

Parent Sex Differences

Table 9-2 summarizes the 11 studies that tested for parental sex differences in psychological control. They illustrate a trend favoring higher levels of control for mothers compared to fathers (9 of 12 studies). Seven child-report studies, one parent-report study, and one observational study found mothers rated higher than fathers. In contrast, fathers of preschool children in Russia and China rated themselves higher than mothers, and one study using both child reported data and observational ratings found no parental

TABLE 9-2
Summary of Parent Sex Differences in Psychological Control

Article	Measure	Age	Source	Mother	Father
Schaefer, 1965	PC	12 to 14	CR	X	
Armentrout & Burger, 1972	PC	9 to 14	CR	X	
Rowe, 1980	PC	17	CR	X	
Litovsky & Dusek, 1985	PC	13 to 15	CR	X	
Dusek & Litovsky, 1988	PC	12 to 18	CR	X	
Knowlton, 1988	PC	11 to 18	CR	X	
Boyes & Allen, 1993	PC	15 to 20	CR	X	
Forehand & Nousianinen, 1993	PC	11 to 17	PR	X	
Robinson et al., 1996 (Russia)	PC	Preschool	CR		X
Robinson et al., 1996 (China)	PC	Preschool	CR		X
Dobkin et al., 1997	PC	13	Obs	X	

Note: "X" signifies higher control; PC = Psychological control; CR = Child report; Obs = Observation.

sex differences. Nelson and Crick (chapter 6, this volume) also found fathers to be rated higher than mothers on psychological control.

In addition to those studies summarized in Table 9-2, scattered studies have shown that single mothers and fathers and step-parents scored higher compared to dual-parented families (Dornbusch, Ritter, Leiderman, Roberts, & Fraleigh, 1987); married fathers scored higher than divorced fathers (Teleki, Powell, & Claypool, 1984); and alcoholic mothers more than nonalcoholic mothers (Marcus & Tisne, 1987).

As is the case for child sex differences, this trend favoring higher levels of psychological control by mothers compared to fathers needs additional investigation and verification, as do the scattered findings relative to family structure and other specific family forms.

Developmental Differences

In the few studies that have tested for child age differences in psychological control, the trend is that younger children experience more than older children. Four preadolescent- or adolescent-reported studies have made this finding (Boyes & Allen, 1993; Dornbusch et al., 1987; Fristad & Karpowitz, 1988; Shulman, Collins, & Dital, 1993). In addition, both Stierlin (1974) and Darling and Steinberg (1993) have asserted that younger children experience higher levels of control than older children.

These few studies do not provide adequate information about the developmental differences in psychological control of children. The need to do so is particularly important because of how tightly the construct of psychological control has been linked theoretically with developmental issues in adolescence. Studies need to be conducted that follow children across adolescence to understand if and how parents alter their use of psychological control as a response to developmental changes in themselves or their children or as a strategy to influence those changes.

It is clear, however, that the effects of parental psychological control apply to younger children as well as adolescents (on whom, historically, most of the work has been done). This is evident in the small number of studies that focused on younger children reviewed in chapter 2 of this volume (e.g., Crockenberg & Litman, 1990; Gottman, Katz, & Hoover, 1997; Hart, Nelson, Robinson, Olsen, & McNeilly-Choque, 1998; Robinson et al., 1996), but also in the new findings presented in chapters 5 to 8 of this volume, all of which investigated children younger than adolescents. These findings suggest the possibility that psychological autonomy is an aspect of human experience that is sensitive to intrusion and violation even at very young ages.

Cultural, Minority, and Social Class Differences

The few studies that have looked at cultural, minority, and social class differences together suggest a trend toward higher psychological control among non-Whites, non-Americans, minorities, and families of low socioeconomic status. Specifically, studies have found higher levels of psychological control (or authoritarian parenting) among U.S. Hispanics (Barber, 1996; Dornbusch et al., 1987); U.S. Blacks (Barber, 1996; Dornbusch et al., 1987); U.S. Asians (Chao, 1994; Dornbusch et al., 1987); Black, Asian, and Aboriginal Canadians (Hein & Lewko, 1994); and lower income U.S. families (Barber, 1996; Mason, Couce, Gonzalez, & Hiraga, 1996). Higher levels have also been found for less educated parents (Crockenberg & Litman, 1990; Dornbusch et al., 1987; Mason et al., 1996). In chapter 8 (this volume), Olsen et al. found maternal psychological control to be rated higher in Russian families than in U.S. families.

Caution in generalizing a conclusion from these studies is warranted not only by the relatively small number of studies, but also because many of the findings come from one source (Dornbusch et al., 1987). Moreover, the Avenevoli, Sessa, and Steinberg (1999) study that broke that same sample into multiple ecological niches found that of the 16 niches, authoritarian parenting differed only between intact and single-parented, Asian, working-class families. In addition, most of the studies have measured authoritarian parenting, and thus the extent to which psychological control is implicated in these findings is not clear.

Miscellaneous

Miscellaneous findings relative to level differences in psychological control or similar constructs include higher levels for child reports compared to parent reports (Schwartz, Barton-Henry, & Pruzinsky, 1985); children from divorced homes (Kurdek, Fine, & Sinclair, 1995; Teleki et al., 1984); adolescents who do not work versus those who do (Steinberg, Fogley, & Dornbusch, 1993); non-Mormon adolescents compared to Mormon adolescents (Barber, 1996); and children diagnosed with an anxiety disorder (Siqueland, Kendall, & Steinberg, 1996; this finding was made using independent observers of psychological control, but it did not hold for child reports of parenting). In chapter 7 of this volume, Holmbeck et al. showed that parents of children with spina bifida were rated higher on psychological control that parents of children without physical challenges.

In summary, although there is some evidence for trends in findings, the extant data are not sufficient to make generalizable conclusions about which demographic subsets of parents or children engage in or experience more psychological control. Future studies should attend specifically to group differences to enhance our understanding of the parameters of the use of parental psychological control.

Clarifying Effects and Measurement of Psychological Control

This volume has shown that the negative association between parental psychological control and child and adolescent functioning is quite robust. Now that this basic relationship has been clearly established, there are numerous ways in which this effect can and should be clarified.

Psychological Control and Authoritarian Parenting

In chapter 2 of this volume, Barber and Harmon separated studies that measured psychological control and studies that measured authoritarian parenting. We noted that these two indexes of parenting are linked in that the same concepts of the violation of the child's development of self are explicitly implicated in theoretical and conceptual formulations of both measures. We noted in addition that the link between the two strategies for measuring parenting is further strengthened by the reality that authoritarian parenting in most recent studies has been empirically derived with a specific measure of psychological control or psychological autonomy as one of its key constituents (e.g., the work in the 1990s by Steinberg and colleagues). Despite these conceptual and empirical links between the two ways of measuring psychological control, the separation was made between them in chapter 2 on the basic limitation that when using an aggregated set of parenting dimensions (i.e., a typology), insight into the relative contribution to the effect on child development of the typology's constituent parts is not available (Barber, 1997; Darling & Steinberg, 1993; Gray & Steinberg, 1999; Steinberg, Elmen, & Mounts, 1989; Weiss & Schwarz, 1996). In short, we cannot tell the extent to which psychological control has been a factor in the consistent findings linking authoritarian parenting to child functioning.

Researchers differ with good reason about how they measure parenting. Steinberg (Darling & Steinberg, 1993; Steinberg, Darling, Fletcher, Brown, & Dornbusch, 1995) has argued sensibly that the decision about whether to use the typological versus dimensional approach to measuring parenting should be made on theoretical grounds (i.e., how broad or specific the measure of parenting needs to be to meet a given study's overall purpose). Our aim here is not to discuss the overall benefits of either approach, but to suggest simply that when it comes to achieving a better understanding of the specific nature and role of parental psychological control, it will be important to disassemble the typologies that have psychological control as one of their elements, as in authoritarian parenting. Thus, when significant findings linking authoritarian parenting are made, it would be useful for researchers to attempt to define the relative degree to which psychological control was the operative component of the typology underlying its effect. From the review, findings from studies that used authoritarian parenting (see Table 2-3, this volume) essentially parallel findings from the studies that either measured the dimension of psychological control (Table 2-1, this volume) or a dimension similar to it (Table 2-2, this volume). This would suggest that psychological control is a determining component of the authoritarian typology, but empirical confirmation of this is needed before a conclusion can be drawn.

Psychological Control Versus Psychological Autonomy

A common practice in work on parental psychological control is to imply or to assert that the absence of psychological control equates to the presence of psychological autonomy. This thinking has precedence in the original labeling of the construct, when Schaefer (1965) used *psychological autonomy* versus *psychological control*. In the earlier versions of his Children's Report of Parental Behavior Inventory (CRPBI) there were items that measured both psychological autonomy and psychological control. At least one study (Shulman et al., 1993) used separate scales for these two dimensions, but most work has either combined the two or used psychological control items and referred to them either as a measure of psychological control or autonomy. Others have created or adapted different scales and have referred to them as psychological autonomy when the items actually index psychological control (e.g., Eccles, Early, Fraiser, Belansky, & McCarthy, 1997; Gray & Steinberg, 1999; Herman, Dornbusch, Herran, & Herting, 1997). Other studies have attempted to measure psychological autonomy through other scales (e.g., autonomy/relatedness [Allen, Hauser, Eickholt,

Bell, & O'Connor, 1994; Best, Hauser, & Allen, 1997], autonomy granting [Kurdek et al., 1995], and promotes autonomy [Dobkin, Tremblay, & Sacchitelle, 1997]).

Although it would be possible to construct a continuum of psychological autonomy that ranges from low autonomy (presence of psychologically controlling parental behaviors) to high autonomy (presence of autonomy granting parenting behaviors), such a scale has not been used. Instead, what has been measured mostly is the presence versus absence of psychological control. This is best illustrated by examining the three most commonly used measures currently. All 10 of the psychological control scale items from the 30-item revision of the CRPBI (Schludermann & Schludermann, 1988, personal communication) refer explicitly to forms of parental control to which respondents are asked to rate how well the statements describe their parents (from "not like her/him" to "a lot like her/him"). All eight items of the PCS (Barber, 1996) are psychological control items that have the same response format as for the CRPBI. Eight of nine items from the psychological autonomy scale from the PPS (Steinberg, et al., 1989; responses ranging from "strongly agree" to "strongly disagree") are psychological control items that are reversed-coded to index psychological autonomy. Thus, all three of these measures actually index the presence versus absence of psychological control, not the presence of psychological autonomy.

We see the equating of psychological control and psychological autonomy as a problem that should be clarified in future work. Practically, the fact that a parent does not apply psychological control to a child does not automatically mean that this parent is encouraging or fostering autonomy. It is possible that this parent engages in no explicit encouragement of autonomy. Conversely, a parent who does not encourage autonomy does not necessarily intrude on the child's autonomy through controlling behaviors. It is also possible that a parent could vacillate between both psychological control and psychological autonomy. These ecological realities are not accurately represented by the common tendency in much of the current work to reverse-code psychological control items and label them *psychological autonomy*.

In the latest rounds of our data collection we have begun to deal with this issue by creating an explicit psychological autonomy measure. Initial findings suggest the need to carefully sort out differences between psychological control and psychological autonomy and their varying associations with other parenting variables. For example, the bivariate correlations between psychological control (PCS-YSR) and psychological autonomy (eight items that basically describe the opposite of the PCS-YSR items) are -.61 for adolescent reports of mothers and -.57 for adolescent reports of fathers. Thus, approximately one third of the variance between the scales is shared. However, the bivariate correlations between psychological autonomy and acceptance (10-item CRPBI) are .80 for mothers and .82 for fathers, roughly two thirds shared variance, whereas the bivariate correlations between psychological control and acceptance are -.50 for mothers and -.49 for fathers, or roughly one half shared variance. (Correlations between autonomy and behavioral control [monitoring], though lower overall, are also substantially higher than between psychological control and behavioral control.)

These preliminary findings suggest that, in our data set, psychological autonomy is not correlated highly enough with psychological control to imply that they are at opposite ends of a continuum of autonomy. Also, the difference in strength of the correlations between these two variables and parental acceptance suggests that they are different phenomena, and that psychological autonomy-granting is more closely tied to parental supportive behavior than it is to psychological control. It would be valuable if other data sets were analyzed for differences between psychological control and psychological autonomy, including how they may differentially predict child outcomes in combination with other parenting variables. Until these differences are clarified, it seems advisable not to assume that an absence of psychological control equates with the presence of psychological autonomy.

Specialized Effects and Mediating Effects

Because Steinberg's (Steinberg et al., 1989) disaggregation of authoritative parenting (acceptance, behavioral control, and psychological control), many studies have followed suit in an attempt to understand more precisely the role of these parenting dimensions in child development (see, for example, Barber, 1996; Barber, Olsen, & Shagle, 1994; *Journal of Adolescent Research, 12,*[1], 1997). A particular advantage of isolating individual dimensions of parenting such as this is that one can test for specialized effects; that is, the possibility that specific elements of parenting are predictive of discrete types of functioning in children (Barber, Thomas, Maughan, & Olsen, 2001; Gray & Steinberg, 1999). Both Steinberg (1990) and Barber (1997) have discussed hypothetically the potential specialized associations between the central elements of common parenting typologies and distinct aspects of child development. However, both more theoretical and empirical work is needed to develop this area.

With specific regard to psychological control, Steinberg's (1990) assessment was that the absence of psychological autonomy should be related to deficits in child self-reliance and competence, as opposed, for example, to behavioral control, the absence of which should be related to deficits in impulse control and social responsibility. Similarly, Barber (1992) postulated that psychological control would be uniquely predictive of internalized forms of adolescent problem behavior, in contrast to behavioral control, the absence of which would be uniquely related to externalized problems. Empirical findings to date support the propositions relative to behavioral control clearly, but they also indicate that psychological control is related more broadly to a variety of variables, including disruptions in self-processes, internalized and externalized forms of child and adolescent problem behaviors, and poorer academic achievement (see chapter 2 of this volume for a review).

Part of the reason for the diffuse effects of psychological control, despite the relatively clear theoretical expectations of a more specialized role, may be a lack of adequate model specification in some of the empirical work. Rather than view the list of correlates of psychological control as an accumulated assembly of different aspects of child functioning, it would be more consistent with theory about psychological control to model the interrelationships of these correlates. Specifically, because the child's self-processes are the prime target of psychological control, it would be appropriate to model the direct effects of psychological control on the self, with links extending beyond the self to other aspects of child functioning. Precedent for this was set early by Steinberg et al. (1989), who found that the across-time correlation between psychological autonomy (reverse-coded psychological control) and adolescent grade point average was fully mediated by a measure of adolescent psychosocial maturity. In that study, psychosocial maturity was a composite measure of self-reliance, identity, and work orientation. When this measure was decomposed, it was work orientation (e.g., capacity to experience pleasure in work, aspirations for competent work performance, work skills) that took the burden of the mediation. Given the task-oriented nature of school performance, it is not surprising that this element of self was the operative mediator.

Similarly, Best et al. (1997) found that adolescent ego development partially mediated the association between parental encouragement of relatedness and autonomy during adolescence and young adult educational attainment. In studying depression, Garber, Robinson, and Valentiner (1997) found 12-year-olds' self-worth to significantly mediate the association between mother's psychological control (and acceptance) and child depression. Likewise, Barber and Shagle (1994) found adolescent self-derogation to fully mediate the association between psychological control and depression.

In sum, researchers will gain a more precise understanding of psychological control and how it affects child development if future research more consistently models the fundamental role of the child's self-processes.

Linear Properties and Moderating Effects

Another way to clarify the effects of psychological control is to more thoroughly investigate whether the effects are predominantly linear, and the degree to which or the conditions under which its effects might be moderated by other variables. With regard to the former, most researchers have not tested for possible nonlinear associations, inferring that the more psychological control children experience, the more risk to their development.

Unlike findings for behavioral control that demonstrate consistent curvilinear associations with adolescent functioning (e.g., Kurdek et al., 1995; Mason et al., 1996; Miller, McCoy, Olsen, & Wallace, 1986; Olweus, 1980), results from studies that have tested for nonlinear effects of psychological control are mixed and suggest no pattern of nonlinear effects. No nonlinear effects were discerned between psychological control and psychosocial maturity or academic competence (Steinberg et al., 1989); between authoritarian parenting and multiple indexes of adolescent adjustment across ecological niches (Avenevoli et al., 1999); or between psychological control (reverse-scored as psychological autonomy) and behavior problems, internal distress, or academic competence (Gray & Steinberg, 1999).

Evidence for nonlinear effects include a curvilinear association between psychological control and psychosocial development, suggesting greater effect at low to moderate levels of psychological control (moderate to high levels of psychological autonomy; Gray & Steinberg, 1999), and between parental restrictiveness (labeled as psychological control) and adolescent problem behavior, with moderate restrictiveness posing the least risk (Mason et al., 1996). In sum, the evidence pertaining to the linearity of parental psychological control is minimal and inconsistent. This should be pursued carefully in further investigations.

With regard to moderating effects of psychological control, future research should investigate more thoroughly the extent to which the effects of psychological control are contingent on other dimensions of parenting as well as other processes within and outside the household. Regarding interactions with other forms of parenting, again the findings are limited and mixed. No patterns of interactions among psychological control, acceptance, and behavioral control in predicting several indexes of adolescent functioning (e.g., depression, antisocial behavior, social initiative, substance use, etc.) were found by Barber et al. (2001), Garber et al. (1997), or Herman et al. (1997). Gray and Steinberg (1999), on the other hand, found psychological control to interact with parental acceptance in predicting psychosocial development, internal distress, and academic competence. In this volume, Pettit and Laird (chapter 4) found that psychological control predicted delinquency when parental involvement was low.

Regarding interactions with variables other than parenting, there is initial evidence of some significant interactions between psychological control and variables such as deviant peer association (Mason et al., 1996) and peer norms supporting academic excellence (Kurdek et al., 1995), children's irritable stress and fearful distress (chapter 5 this volume), and adolescents' childhood history of delinquency (chapter 4, this volume). One important additional area for investigation is the degree to which the effects of psychological control might vary depending on the level of risk in the environments families live in. Some recent research suggests that parental undermining of autonomy appears to be interpreted or processed differently by adolescents in high- versus low-risk environments (e.g., McElhaney & Allen, 2001).

As was the case with the issue of linearity, there is currently insufficient evidence to understand the degree to which effects of parental psychological control are conditional on other factors in children and in their various social contexts. Systematic efforts to pin down this specificity would greatly enhance our understanding of the meaning and effects of this form of parental behavior.

Antecedents of Psychological Control

We know very little about the antecedents of parental psychological control. This is an area that is wide open for future research, and one that has a number of different avenues to pursue. Belsky's (1984) three general domains of antecedents of parental functioning—contextual sources of stress and support, child characteristics, and parental psychological resources— would be a good starting point for investigation. Another avenue is to pursue the parenting antecedents of psychological control. For example, Pettit and Laird (chapter 4, this volume) found that mothers' psychological control of their adolescents was predicted by mothers' proactive or hostile parenting style when the adolescents were children. This contrasted with behavioral control that was only predicted by earlier proactive parenting.

Some work on the antecedents of psychological control is being done in the domain of contextual sources of stress and support. For example, Stone et al. (chapter 3, this volume) found psychological control to be predicted by interparental hostility. Additional work needs to extend this focus on stress and support, and also needs to begin examining the extent to which characteristics of children (Bogenschneider, Small, & Tsay, 1997) encourage the use of psychological control. For example, Barber (1996) found year 2 parental psychological control to be predicted by year 1 adolescent depression and delinquency.

In preparing to study the antecedents of psychological control, it seems important to make a fundamental distinction between this form of parenting and most other forms of parenting, particularly forms of parental control. Many discussions of parental control imply that the behaviors parents engage in with their children are strategic attempts to shape children's behavior toward conformity to social regulations, within or outside the family, or to encourage the internalization of motivations to comply (e.g., Grusec & Goodnow, 1994; Rollins & Thomas, 1979). However, as we discussed (chapter 2, this volume), the driving force behind the use of parental psychological control does not appear to be the enhancement of social responsibility in children. Instead, it appears that the impetus for psychological control, at least as far as it is currently being measured, is an attempt on the parent's part to dominate and manipulate the psychological and emotional boundaries between parent and child to the advantage of the parent.

Parental psychological control seems more appropriately conceived of as a negative indicator of the quality of the *relationship* between parent and child. Accordingly, we interpret parental psychological control not as an ineffective socialization strategy but as a violation of healthy and facilitative interpersonal relationships. This distinction is particularly important when it comes to understanding the antecedents of parental psychological control. For example, rather than focus predominantly on the contextual parameters surrounding parenting, such as sources of stress and support, and so forth, we suggest that the most powerful sources of psychological control will be the parent's own psychological status. This is consonant with Belsky's (1984) assertion that parental psychological characteristics (e.g., depression), themselves a product of parent's own developmental history, ought to be prime determinants of parenting.

Because the use of psychological control implies an unhealthy orientation on the part of parents to the psychological and emotional boundaries between parents and children (i.e., it attempts to inhibit the self-development of children or protect the psychological power of parents), it should be particularly informative to investigate the quality of parents' interpersonal relationships with other significant people in their lives to understand why parents engage in psychological control. A study by Wakschlag, Chase-Lansdale, and Brooks-Gunn (1996) illustrated this point by showing that competent parenting (including fostering autonomy) on the part of Black mothers of preschool children was associated positively with the mothers' level of individuation from their own mothers. Similarly, Buehler's measure of covert interparental hostility (see chapter 3, this volume), which she found to be predictive of parental psychological control, may be an indirect measure of the unhealthy psychoemotional boundaries between spouses. Both of these sets of findings echo Stierlin's (1974) clinical notions that parents who bind and constrain their children psychologically may do so to satisfy their own ego deficits.

Another avenue to pursue along this same line is parents' orientation toward emotional expression. Gottman et al. (1997), for example, have demonstrated that parents of young children who coach their children's awareness and expression of emotion are less likely to engage in derogation, a form of parenting very similar conceptually to psychological control.

Emotional coaching, in turn, was highly predicted by parents' awareness of their own emotions, which was also related to marital functioning.

In sum, the field is wide open for studies that enhance our understanding of which parents use psychological control and why. Investigations should focus on contexts and on child and parent characteristics, specifically aspects of parental psychological and relational functioning.

Using New Methodologies to Measure Psychological Control

Several possible explanations for the predominant use of child–adolescent reported indexes of parental psychological control were presented in chapter 2 of this volume. Chapters 3 to 8 of this volume illustrated that parental psychological control also can be reliably assessed on different ages of children via multiple forms of self-report, parent report, and observer report. This methodological variety has provided important confirmation of the validity of the construct of parental psychological control. Here we wish only to make the point that the expansion to various methodologies is valuable not only for validation purposes but also to provide insights that can only be gained by distinct methods of inquiry. Self-reports on surveys from children and adolescents provide their assessment of their parents behaviors toward them. They do not, however, allow for analyses of the extent to which parental behaviors are triggered by aspects of the immediate interaction, including things that children may do or say. Videotaping of actual interactional sequences in which psychological control is observed would, on the other hand, allow for the detection of these important interactional dynamics. Several scholars are currently pursuing video observation of parental psychological control, including Cheryl Buehler (University of Tennessee), Thomas Dishion (University of Oregon), Grayson Holmbeck (Loyola University of Chicago), and Gregory Pettit (Auburn University). Other scholars who have been analyzing videotape family data for constructs similar to psychological control include John Gottman (University of Washington), Stuart Hauser and colleagues (Harvard University), and Joseph Allen and colleagues (University of Virginia).

We also recommend detailed inquiry into the symbolic representations and attributions both parents and children make about psychologically controlling behavior. The understanding that parents and children have of psychologically controlling behavior and the meaning they attach to it that could be assessed through intensive interview methodologies would be very useful data that could increase knowledge of why and how this form of intrusion does and does not effect individual children. This strategy should be particularly useful in clarifying why some children appear to respond to psychological control with internalizing problems and others with externalizing problems.

EXPANDING THE UNDERSTANDING
OF PSYCHOLOGICAL CONTROL

We now shift to elevating the construct of parental psychological control out of its current exclusive domain in the research literatures on normative parent–child relations and link it to a variety of other literatures. We do this both as a corrective to the rather narrow way this construct has been studied (given the existence of other relevant theoretical and empirical literatures) and also as a way of expressing our opinion that the construct has broader relevance than simply a measure of parenting behavior or parent–child relationship quality. Instead, we view parental use of psychologically controlling behaviors as but one manifestation of a kind of interpersonal relationship functioning that occurs broadly throughout human experience that is fundamentally and consistently inhibitive of healthy psychological and social development among people in general. Below, we first link parental psychological control to the well-established, nonnormative parenting literature of child maltreatment, and then proceed with illustrations of how the same processes of intrusiveness are evident in family relationships other than the parent–child dyad, as well as in social settings beyond the family.

Psychological Maltreatment

In many ways, the research literature on psychological maltreatment of children and adolescents—typically a subset of the literatures on child abuse—is a virtual parallel to the literatures reviewed in chapter 2 of this volume on psychological control. We did not integrate this work in that review because, despite the similarities in the content of the two bodies of work, the two literatures have very separate identities (e.g., distinct researchers, publication outlets, and audiences), and also because there are some fundamental controversies in the maltreatment literature that would complicate further the review of psychological control if an integration were attempted. These controversies include debate about the approach to studying maltreatment (e.g., from developmental psychopathological or sociological approaches), conceptual uncertainties about what constitutes maltreatment given historical and cultural parameters and, similarly, at what point psychological aggressiveness becomes maltreatment (e.g., Barnett, Manley, & Cicchetti, 1991; McGee & Wolfe, 1991).

Notwithstanding these issues, on all essential aspects of the research the two literatures are very similar. Characterizations of psychological maltreatment parallel the conceptualization of psychological control as a communication pattern that undermines children's important developmental tasks and inhibits competent emotional, social, cognitive, and social–cognitive functioning of children (Cicchetti, 1989; McGee & Wolfe, 1991).

Specific conceptualizations of psychological maltreatment are similar to that of psychological control. The maltreatment literature contains many parental behavior scales and items that parallel general categories of psychological control (e.g., constraining, invalidating, personally attacking, erratic emotional behavior, and love withdrawal), such as not allowing social and emotional growth (Burnett, 1993), rejecting (Engels & Moisan, 1994; Garbarino, Guttman, & Seeley, 1986), spurning and degrading (Brassard, Hart & Hardy, 1993), ostracism (Claussen & Crittenden, 1991), emotional neglect (Engels & Moisan, 1994), inconsistent responsiveness to social–emotional needs (Claussen & Crittenden, 1991), love withdrawal (Baily & Baily, 1996), blaming and scapegoating (Gross & Keller, 1992; Sanders & Becker-Lausen, 1995), and so forth.

The found correlates of psychological maltreatment also parallel those for psychological control, including dissociation (Sanders & Becker-Lausen, 1995), depression (Claussen & Crittenden, 1991; Gross & Keller, 1992; Swift & Gayton, 1996); interpersonal problems (Vissing, Straus, Gelles, & Harrop, 1991); self-esteem (Gross & Keller, 1992); cognitive and emotional functioning (Burnett, 1993); and aggressiveness, withdrawal, emotional maladjustment, antisocial behavior, and anxious attachment (Claussen & Crittenden, 1991). The assertion in the maltreatment literature that maltreatment is a function of the parent's experiences of psychological abuse as children (Garbarino et al., 1986) mirrors our assertion that a primary source for psychological control is parental dysfunction. Another commonality between the two literatures is the theoretical notion in the maltreatment literature that psychological maltreatment has detrimental effects for preadolescents as well as adolescents (Brassard et al., 1993; Claussen & Crittenden, 1991; Engels & Moisan, 1994; Gross & Keller, 1992). This is consistent with the findings presented throughout this volume of the negative effects of parental psychological control for children of all ages.

Beyond the support for theory and findings related to psychological control, the psychological maltreatment literature offers useful clarifications and additions to understanding psychological control. First, the fact that psychological maltreatment is considered to be abusive and that it has legal implications (e.g., regarding custody of children) underscores the detrimental potential of such psychologically controlling processes. Second, the maltreatment literature includes several specific measures of psychological maltreatment–control heretofore not measured in the research on psychological control that might be considered in future work. These measures include neglect, shaming, threatening, denigrating, name calling, cursing, and ridiculing. Third, the maltreatment literature raises the difficult and interesting question of how different forms of psychological control–maltreatment are related to each other. For example, are the less aggressive forms of psychological control reviewed in this volume precursors to the more aggressive forms sometimes measured in the maltreatment literature? To what extent are these forms of psychological intrusiveness and manipulation related to physical violence or abuse expressed by parents toward children? Can a hierarchy of psychological control–maltreatment–abuse be identified, or are there distinct varieties of psychological intrusiveness that have different antecedents and effects? These and other issues could be addressed in future work that attempted to integrate the psychological control and psychological maltreatment–abuse perspectives.

Beyond the Parent–Child Dyad

Relationship styles that involve the intrusion of one partner into the psychological world of another partner exist in other relationship systems within and outside the family. For example, Conger, Conger, and Scaramella (1997) have demonstrated the salience of psychological control in sibling relationships. They showed that not only do siblings engage in psychologically controlling behaviors of younger siblings (e.g., criticizing, invalidating, threatening, guilt induction), but that these behaviors have the same negative associations with adolescent functioning as does parental psychological control. Their findings included bivariate associations between sibling psychological control and lower self-confidence and higher internalized and externalized problems in male and female adolescents; across-time, multivariate prediction of sibling psychological control to decreases in male and female adolescent self-confidence (both concurrent self-confidence and change over time in self-confidence); and that sibling psychological control explained unique variance to self-confidence, internalized, and externalized problems after controlling for parental psychological control.

Beyond this initial work on sibling interactions, the family process literature is rich with insights regarding the potential of family relationships—including but not exclusive to the parent–child relationship—to violate the psychological autonomy of family members. Basic to this extensive clinical research literature are constructs like enmeshment and overprotectiveness (Colapinto, 1991; Minuchin, Montalvo, Guerney, Rosman, & Schumer, 1967), fusion and undifferentiated family ego mass (Bowen, 1966, 1971; Friedman, 1991), distance or separation (Alexander & Parsons, 1982; Boszormenyi-Nagy, Grunebaum, & Ulrich, 1991), and differentiation (Friedman, 1991). All of these constructs speak to issues directly relevant to psychological control, such as the blurring of interpersonal boundaries, low individual autonomy, exaggerated concern and protectiveness, shared demands for loyalty, and narrow perceptions of self (Colapinto, 1991). As with psychological control, these aspects of interpersonal relationships are seen to compromise self-development:

Individual symptoms, both physical and psychological, take on new meaning when viewed in the context of the loss of self in a relationship. The notion that proximity can induce auto-destruction in one partner ... opens the door to viewing all chronic conditions that manifest themselves in one relative as byproducts of the fusion that characterizes their relationship with each other. (Friedman, 1991, p. 157).

The family process literature does not clearly articulate specific behaviors that create these interpersonal conditions, but some effort has been made to link the specificity of the psychological control literature with family process concepts, suggesting that enmeshment in family relationships—shown to predict adolescent functioning in the same way that psychological control does—reflects aspects of psychological control (Barber & Buehler, 1996).

Two other literatures invoke very similar theoretical constructs and at the same time include specific measures of interrelationships consonant with the work on psychological control. In the psychological abuse literature, O'Leary and Jouriles (1994) discussed name calling, constant criticism, verbal attacks, silent treatment, withdrawing affection or attention, and isolating the person from his or her family and friends. Several different scales are used to measure psychological abuse in married or cohabiting couples (Marshall, 1996), battered women and nonbattered women (Levendosky & Graham-Bermann, 1998), and dating relationships (Jezl, Molidor, & Wright, 1996). The two most comprehensive measures—the Psychological Maltreatment of Women Inventory (Tolman, 1989) and the Severity of Violence Against Women Scales (Marshall, 1992)—measure the frequency of numerous psychologically controlling behaviors referred to as *psychological abuse*. These measures have been related to a variety of indicators of physical and emotional health in women. Marshall (1996, p. 380) contended that they have "the potential to undermine a woman's sense of self in all domains of her life." Women have reported considering psychological abuse to be more damaging than the physical violence they experienced (Follingstad, Rutledge, Berg, Hause, & Polek, 1990; O'Learly & Jouriles, 1994).

Similarly, the literature on expressed emotions invokes behaviors akin to behaviors found in the psychological control literature. In reviewing the expressed emotion literature, Kavanagh (1992, p. 601) identified "unambiguous statements of disapproval or resentment, rejecting remarks, or statements that are delivered in a critical tone" and emotional overinvolvement, overprotection, or overidentification. In that work, the number of critical statements between relatives are counted, and findings show that clinical families with high scores on expressed emotion have substantially higher relapse rates than those with lower scores on expressed emotion.

Extending Outside the Family

Evidence beyond the family realm also shows that psychologically controlling processes exist both in interpersonal and institutional domains. In one study, psychological control from peers was significantly related to adolescent depression and antisocial behavior at the bivariate level but not in multivariate analyses controlling for connection, regulation, and psychological autonomy in other social contexts (Barber & Olsen, 1997). Institutionally, both Barber and Olsen (1997) and Eccles et al. (1997) measured psychological autonomy in the school setting by assessing how involved adolescent students were in decision making in the classroom and how willing teachers were to listen to student suggestions. Both studies found positive bivariate associations between psychological autonomy at school and school performance (either grade point average or academic alienation) and negative bivariate associations (with some gender differences) between school psychological autonomy and adolescent depression and problem behaviors. After controlling for connection and regulation in the school environment and connection, regulation, and psychological autonomy in other social contexts (e.g., family, peer relationship) both studies also found significant, positive, multivariate associations between school psychological autonomy and school performance.

These findings about psychological autonomy in the school context are similar to earlier work in social psychology that has demonstrated that individuals function better in institutional settings that facilitate self-direction. Melvin Kohn's work, for example, has found that conditions that facilitate or restrict the use of initiative, thought, and independent judgment in work in the school and occupational spheres is related to individuals' self-efficacy, ability to accomplish, and positive reactions to job, self, and society (Kohn & Schooler, 1969, 1973; Miller, Kohn, & Schooler, 1986).

In sum, it is evident that the intrusion into or violation of an individual's psychological world is a phenomenon that is not restricted to the parent–child relationship, but that appears to be a feature of a variety of different interpersonal relationships, as well as an individual's experience in institutional settings. Whether the relationship be between parent and child, child and sibling, child and peer, adult and adult, or individual and institution, the findings appear to be consistent that intrusion into a person's psychological autonomy has negative personal consequences for that individual.

CONCLUSION

There are numerous ways in which the current research on parental psychological control of children and adolescents can be enhanced to provide greater detail and specificity related to prevalence, meaning, and effects. Several ways were discussed in this chapter. Work in these areas and others should be useful for theory refinement, advancement in research, and in clinical and applied areas of family functioning. Looking beyond the burgeoning work that is so focused on the parent–child dyad, however, reveals that the processes and behaviors of psychological control characteristic of that dyad are evident in other social interactional situations as reflected both in theory and empirical research presented in the second part of this final chapter. This evidence should lead us to consider and study the extent to which the material reviewed in this volume on parent–child/adolescent interaction is but one indication of human response to psychologically related intrusion and violation wherever it might occur.

REFERENCES

Alexander, J., & Parsons, B. V. (1982). *Functional family therapy*. Monterrey, CA: Brooks/Cole.

Allen, J. P., Hauser, S. T., Eickholt, C., Bell, K. L., & O'Connor, T. G. (1994). Autonomy and relatedness in family interactions as predictors of expressions of negative adolescent affect. *Journal of Research on Adolescence, 4*, 535–552.

Armentrout, J. A., & Burger, G. K. (1972). Children's reports of parental child-rearing behavior at five grade levels. *Developmental Psychology, 7*, 44–48.

Avenevoli, S., Sessa, F. M., & Steinberg, L. (1999). Family structure, parenting practices, and adolescent adjustment: An ecological examination. In E. M. Hetherington (Ed.), *Coping with divorce, single parenting, and remarriage: A risk and resiliency perspective* (pp. 65–90). Mahwah, NJ: Erlbaum.

Baily, T. F., & Baily, W. H. (1986). *Operational definitions of child emotional maltreatment: Final report*. National Center on Child Abuse and Neglect (DHHS 90-CA-0956). Washington, DC: U.S. Government Printing Office.

Barber, B. K. (1992). Family, personality, and adolescent problem behaviors. *Journal of Marriage and the Family, 54*, 69–79.

Barber, B. K. (1996). Parental psychological control: Revisiting a neglected construct. *Child Development, 67*, 3296–3319.

Barber, B. K. (1997). Adolescent socialization in context—Connection, regulation, and autonomy in multiple contexts. *Journal of Adolescent Research, 12*, 173–177.

Barber, B. K., & Buehler, C. (1996). Family cohesion and enmeshment: Different constructs, different effects. *Journal of Marriage and the Family, 58*, 433–441.

Barber, B. K., & Olsen, J. A. (1997). Socialization in context: Connection, regulation, and autonomy in the family, school, and neighborhood, and with peers. *Journal of Adolescent Research, 12*, 287–315.

Barber, B. K., Olsen, J. A., & Shagle, S. (1994). Associations between parental psychological control and behavioral control and youth internalized and externalized behaviors. *Child Development, 65,* 1120–1136.

Barber, B. K., & Shagle, S. C. (1994, Feb.). *Parental control and youth problem behaviors: An analysis of mediators.* Paper presented at the annual Society for Research on Adolescence Conference, San Diego.

Barber, B. K., Thomas, D. L., Maughan, S. L., & Olsen, J. A. (2001). *Central dimensions of parent–child relations: Assessing independent and interactive effects.* Manuscript under review for publication.

Barnett, D., Manley, J. T., & Cicchetti, D. (1991). Continuing toward an operational definition of psychological maltreatment. *Development and Psychopathology, 3,* 19–29.

Belsky, J. (1984). The determinants of parenting: A process model. *Child Development, 55,* 83–95.

Best, K. M., Hauser, S. T., & Allen, J. P. (1997). Predicting young adult competencies: Adolescent era parent and individual influences. *Journal of Adolescent Research, 12,* 90–112.

Bogenschneider, K., Small, S. A., & Tsay, J. C. (1997). Child, parent, and contextual influences on perceived parenting competence among parents of adolescents. *Journal of Marriage and the Family, 59,* 345–362.

Boszormenyi-Nagy, I., Grunebaum, J., & Ulrich, D. (1991). Contextual therapy. In A. S. Gurman & D. P. Kniskern (Eds.), *Handbook of family therapy* (Vol. II, pp. 200–238). New York: Brunner/Mazel.

Bowen, M. (1966). The use of theory in clinical practice. *Comprehensive Psychiatry, 7,* 345–374.

Bowen, M. (1971). Family therapy and family group therapy. In H. Kaplan & B. Saddock (Eds.), *Comprehensive group psychotherapy* (pp. 384–421). Baltimore: Williams & Wilkins.

Boyes, M. C., & Allen, S. G. (1993). Styles of parent–child interaction and moral reasoning in adolescence. *Merrill-Palmer Quarterly, 39,* 551–570.

Brassard, M. R., Hart, S. N., & Hardy, D. B. (1993). The psychological maltreatment rating scales. *Child Abuse & Neglect, 17,* 715–729.

Bronstein, P. (1994). Patterns of parent-child interaction in Mexican families: A cross-cultural perspective. *International Journal of Behavioral Development, 17,* 423–446.

Burnett, B. B. (1993). The psychological abuse of latency age children: A survey. *Child Abuse & Neglect, 17,* 441–454.

Chao, R. K. (1994). Beyond parental control and authoritarian parenting style: Understanding Chinese parenting through the cultural notion of training. *Child Development, 65,* 1111–1119.

Cicchetti, D. (1989). How research on child maltreatment has informed the study of child development: Perspectives from developmental psychopathology. In D. Cicchetti & V. Carlson (Eds.), *Child maltreatment: Theory and research on* the causes and consequences of child abuse and neglect (pp. 37–43). New York: Cambridge University Press.

Claussen, A. H., & Crittenden, P. M. (1991). Physical and psychological maltreatment: Relations among types of maltreatment. *Child Abuse & Neglect, 15,* 5–18.

Colapinto, J. (1991). Structural family therapy. In A. S. Gurman & D. P. Kniskern (Eds.), *Handbook of family therapy* Vol. II, (pp. 417–443). New York: Brunner/Mazel.

Comstock, D. C. (1994). *Parental control and gender-specific etiology of internalized and externalized adolescent deviance.* Master's thesis, Department of Sociology, Brigham Young University, Provo, Utah.

Conger, K. J., Conger, R. D., & Scaramella, L. V. (1997). Parents, siblings, psychological control, and adolescent adjustment. *Journal of Adolescent Research, 12,* 113–138.

Crockenberg, S., & Litman, C. (1990). Autonomy as competence in 2-year-olds: Maternal correlates of child defiance, compliance, and self-assertion. *Developmental Psychology, 26,* 961–971.

Darling, N., & Steinberg, L. (1993). Parenting style as context: An integrative model. *Psychological Bulletin, 113,* 487–496.

Dobkin, P. L., Tremblay, R. E., & Sacchitelle, C. (1997). Predicting boys' early-onset substance abuse from father's alcoholism, son's disruptiveness, and mother's parenting behavior. *Journal of Consulting and Clinical Psychology, 65,* 86–92.

Dornbusch, S. M., Ritter, P. L., Leiderman, P. H., Roberts, D. F., & Fraleigh, M. J. (1987). The relation of parenting style to adolescent school performance. *Child Development, 58,* 1244–1257.

Dusek, J. B., & Litovsky, V. G. (1988). *Maternal employment and adolescent adjustment and perceptions of child rearing.* Paper presented at the Biennial Meeting of the Society for Research on Adolescence, Alexandria, VA, March 26.

Eccles, J. S., Early, D., Frasier, K., Belansky, E., & McCarthy, K. (1997). The relation of connection, regulation, and support for autonomy to adolescents' functioning. *Journal of Adolescent Research, 12,* 263–286.

Engels, M. L., & Moisan, D. (1994). The psychological maltreatment inventory: Development of a measure of psychological maltreatment in childhood abuse in adult clinical settings. *Psychological Reports, 74,* 595–604.

Follingstad, D. R., Rutledge, L. L., Berg, B. J., Hause, E. S., & Polek, D. S. (1990). The role of emotional abuse in physically abusive relationships. *Journal of Family Violence, 5,* 107–120.

Forehand, R., & Nousiainen, S. (1993). Maternal and paternal parenting: Critical dimensions in adolescent functioning. *Journal of Family Psychology, 7,* 213–221.

Friedman, E. H. (1991). Bowen theory and therapy. In A. S. Gurman & D. P. Kniskern (Eds.), *Handbook of family therapy* Vol. II, (pp. 134–170). New York: Brunner/Mazel.

Fristad, M. A., & Karpowitz, D. H. (1988). Norms for the Children's Report of Parental Behavior Inventory—Modified Form. *Psychological Reports, 62,* 665–666.

Garbarino, J., Guttman, E., & Seeley, J. W. (1986). *The psychologically battered child.* San Francisco: Jossey-Bass.

Garber, J., Robinson, N. S., & Valentiner, D. (1997). The relation between parenting and adolescent depression: Self-worth as a mediator. *Journal of Adolescent Research, 12,* 12–33.

Gottman, J. M., Katz, L. F., & Hooven, C. (1997). *Meta-emotion: How families communicate emotionally.* Mahwah, NJ: Erlbaum.

Gray, M. R., & Steinberg, L. (1999). Unpacking authoritative parenting: Reassessing a multidimensional construct. *Journal of Marriage and the Family, 61,* 574–587.

Gross, A. B., & Keller, H. R. (1992). Long-term consequences of childhood physical and psychological maltreatment. *Aggressive Behavior, 18,* 171–185.

Grusec, J. E., & Goodnow, J. J. (1994). Impact of parental discipline methods on the child's internalization of values: A reconceptualization of current points of view. *Developmental Psychology, 30,* 4–19.

Hart, C. H., Nelson, D. A., Robinson, C. C., Olsen, S. F., & McNeilly-Choque, M. K. (1998). Overt and relational aggression in Russian nursery-school-age children: Parenting style and marital linkages. *Developmental Psychology, 34,* 687–697.

Hein, C., & Lewko, J. H. (1994). Gender differences in factors related to parenting style: A study of high performing science students. *Journal of Adolescent Research, 9,* 262–281.

Herman, M. R., Dornbusch, S. M., Herron, M. C., & Herting, J. R. (1997). The influence of family regulation, connection, and psychological autonomy on six measures of adolescent functioning. *Journal of Adolescent Research, 12,* 34–67.

Jezl, D. R., Molidor, C. E., & Wright, T. L. (1996). Physical, sexual and psychological abuse in high school dating relationships: Prevalence rates and self-esteem issues. *Child and Adolescent Social Work Journal, 13,* 69–87.

Kavanagh, D. J. (1992). Recent developments in expressed emotion and schizophrenia. *British Journal of Psychiatry, 160,* 601–620.

Knowlton, S. S. (1998). *Connection, regulation, and autonomy: A comparison of nonclinical adolescents and adolescents in residential treatment.* Master's thesis, Department of Family Sciences, Brigham Young University, Provo, Utah.

Kohn, M. L., & Schooler, C. (1969). Class, occupation, and orientation. *American Sociological Review, 34,* 659–678.

Kohn, M. L., & Schooler, C. (1973). Occupational experience and psychological functioning: An assessment of reciprocal effects. *American Sociological Review, 38,* 97–118.

Kuczynski, L., & Kochanska, G. (1995). Function and content of maternal demands: Developmental significance of early demands. *Child Development, 66*, 616–628.

Kurdek, L. A., Fine, M. A., & Sinclair, R. J. (1995). School adjustment in sixth graders: Parenting transitions, family climate, and peer norm effects. *Child Development, 66*, 430–445.

Levendosky, A. A., & Graham-Bermann, S. A. (1998). The moderating effects of parenting stress on children's adjustment in woman-abusing families. *Journal of Interpersonal Violence, 13*, 383–397.

Litovsky, V. G., & Dusek, J. B. (1985). Perceptions of child rearing and self-concept development during the early adolescent years. *Journal of Youth and Adolescence, 14*, 373–387.

Mantzicopoulos, P. Y., & Oh-Hwang, Y. (1998). The relationship of psychosocial maturity to parenting quality and intellectual ability for American and Korean adolescents. *Contemporary Educational Psychology, 23*, 195–206.

Marcus, A. M., & Tisne, S. (1987). Perception of maternal behavior by elementary school children of alcoholic mothers. *The International Journal of the Addictions, 22*, 543–555.

Marshall, L. L. (1992). Development of the Severity of Violence Against Women Scale. *Journal of Family Violence, 7*, 103–121.

Marshall, L. L. (1996). Psychological abuse of women: Six distinct clusters. *Journal of Family Violence, 11*, 379–409.

Mason, C. A., Cauce, A. M., Gonzales, N., & Hiraga, Y. (1996). Neither too sweet nor too sour: Problem peers, maternal control, and problem behavior in African American adolescents. *Child Development, 67*, 2115–2130.

McElhaney, K. B., & Allen, J. P. (2001). Autonomy and adolescent social functioning: The moderating effect of risk. *Child Development, 72*, 220–235.

McGee, R. A., & Wolfe, D. A. (1991). Psychological maltreatment: Toward an operational definition. *Developmental Psychopathology, 3*, 3–18.

Miller, B. C., McCoy, J. K., Olson, T. D., & Wallace, C. M. (1986). Parental control attempts and adolescent sexual behavior. *Journal of Marriage and the Family, 48*, 503–512.

Miller, K. A., Kohn, M. L., & Schooler, C. (1986). Educational self-direction and personality. *American Sociological Review, 51*, 372–390.

Minuchin, S., Montalvo, B., Guerney, B. G., Rosman, B. L., & Schumer, F. (1967). *Families of the slums.* New York: Basic Books.

O'Leary, K. D., & Jouriles, E. N. (1994). Psychological abuse between adult partners: Prevalence and impact on partners and children. In L. L'Abate (Ed.), *Handbook of developmental family psychology and psychopathology* (pp. 330–349). New York: John Wiley & Sons.

Olweus, D. (1980). Familial and temperamental determinants of aggression behavior in adolescents—A causal analysis. *Developmental Psychology, 16*, 644–660.

Robinson, C. C., Hart, C. H., Mandleco, B. L., Olsen, S. F., Russell, A., Aloa, V., Jin, S., Nelson, D. A., & Bazarskaya, N. (1996, Aug.). *Psychometric support for a new measure of authoritative, authoritarian, and permissive parenting practices: Cross-cultural connections*. Paper presented at the Biennial Conference of the International Society for the Study of Behavioral Development.

Rollins, B. C., & Thomas, D. L. (1979). Parental support, power, and control techniques in the socialization of children. In W. R. Burr, R. Hill, F. I. Nye, & I. L. Reiss (Eds.), *Contemporary theories about the family: Vol. 1. Research-based theories* (pp. 317–364). New York: Free Press.

Rowe, D. C. (1980, April). *Environmental & genetic influence on dimensions of perceived parenting: A twin study*. Paper presented at the 6th biennial southeastern Conference on Human Development. Alexandria, VA.

Sanders, B., & Becker-Lausen, E. (1995). The measurement of psychological maltreatment: Early data on the child abuse and trauma scale. *Child Abuse and Neglect, 19*, 315–323.

Schaefer, E. S. (1965). A configurational analysis of children's reports of parent behavior. *Journal of Consulting Psychology, 29*, 552–557.

Schwarz, J. C., Barton-Henry, M. L., & Pruzinsky, T. (1985). Assessing child-rearing behaviors: A comparison of ratings made by mother, father, child, and sibling on the CRPBI. *Child Development, 56*, 462–479.

Shulman, S., Collins, W. A., & Dital, M. (1993). Parent–child relationships and peer-perceived competence during middle childhood and preadolescence in Israel. *Journal of Early Adolescence, 13*, 204–218.

Siqueland, L., Kendall, P. C., & Steinberg, L. (1996). Anxiety in children: Perceived family environments and observed family interaction. *Journal of Clinical Child Psychology, 25*, 225–237.

Smetana, J. G. (1995). Parenting styles and conceptions of parental authority during adolescence. *Child Development, 66*, 299–316.

Steinberg, L. (1990). Autonomy, conflict, and harmony in the family relationship. In S. S. Feldman & G. R. Elliott (Eds.), *At the threshold: The developing adolescent* (pp. 255–276). Cambridge: Harvard University Press.

Steinberg, L., Darling, N. E., Fletcher, A. C., Brown, B. B., & Dornbusch, S. M. (1995). Authoritative parenting and adolescent adjustment: An ecological journey. In P. Moen, G. H. Elder Jr., & K. Luscher (Eds.), *Examining lives in context: Perspectives on the ecology of human development*. Washington, DC: American Psychological Association.

Steinberg, L., Elmen, J. D., & Mounts, N. S. (1989). Authoritative parenting, psychosocial maturity, and academic success among adolescents. *Child Development, 60*, 1424–1436.

Steinberg, L., Fegley, S., & Dornbusch, S. (1993). Negative impact of part-time work on adolescent adjustment: Evidence from a longitudinal study. *Development Psychology, 29*, 171–180.

Stierlin, H. (1974). *Separating parents and adolescents*. New York: Quadrangle.

Swift, E. E., & Gayton, W. F. (1996). Further validation for the psychological maltreatment inventory. *Journal of Clinical Psychology, 52,* 325–327.

Teleki, J. K., Powell, J. A., & Claypool, P. L. (1984). Parental child-rearing behavior perceived by parents and school-age children in divorced and married families. *Home Economics Research Journal, 13,* 41–51.

Tolman, R. M. (1989). The development of a measure of psychological mistreatment of women by their male partners. *Violence and Victims, 4,* 159–177.

Vissing, Y. M., Straus, M. A., Gelles, R. J., & Harrop, J. W. (1991). Verbal aggression by parents and psychosocial problems of children. *Child Abuse and Neglect, 15,* 223–234.

Wakschlag, L. S., Chase-Lansdale, P. L., & Brooks-Gunn, J. (1996). Not just "Ghosts in the Nursery": Contemporaneous intergenerational relationships and parenting in young African-American families. *Child Development, 67,* 2131–2147.

Weiss, L. H., & Schwarz, J. C. (1996). The relationship between parenting types and older adolescents' personality, academic achievement, adjustment, and substance use. *Child Development, 67,* 2101–2114.

AUTHOR INDEX

Numbers in italics refer to listings in the reference sections; *n* following a page number indicates listings in a note.

McNichol, K., 129, 146, *157*
Measelle, J., 134, *155*
Meece, D. W., 103, 105, 107, 115, 121, *123*
Menaghan, E. G., 66, *94*
Mendleco, B., 189n
Messer, S. C., 127, *155*
Metha, A., 35, *51*
Meyer, E. C., 241, *258*
Midgley, C., 194, *227*
Miller, B. C., 274, *287*
Miller, H., 255, *260*
Miller, K. A., 50, 282, *287*
Miller, P. H., 131, *156*
Miller, P. J., 240, *259*
Mills, R. S. L., 31, 33, 50, 125, 128, 129, 130, 146, *152, 156*, 236, 238, *259*
Millstein, R., 191n
Minchom, P. E., 195, *226*
Minuchin, S., *51*, 53, 56, 59, 86, 87, *94*, 125, *156*, 280, *287*
Mize, J., 101, 120, *122, 123*
Moisan, D., 38, 48, 279, *285*
Molidor, C. E., 281, *286*
Montalvo, B., *51*, 280, *287*
Morgan, S. B., 196, 222, *230*
Morris, A. G., 125n
Morris, A. S., 8–9, 31, 125, 131, 135, 136, 137, *156, 157*, 191, 239, 264
Morris, M. D. S., 125n
Morse, B. J., 163, *184*
Moskowitz, D. S., 63, *94*
Mounts, N. S. 4, *13*, 15, 19, 24, 25, 28, 29, 33, 42, 43, *52*, 99, 101, 107, *121, 122, 123*, 126, *158*, 162, 164, 166, *188*, 193, 193n, 194, 197, 221, 224, 228, 230, 236, *261*, 269, 271, 272, 273, 274, *288*
Mullan, J. T., 66, *94*
Mun, E., 130, 144, *156*
Murch, R. L., 196, 223, *229*
Murphy, B., 245, *258*
Murphy, B. C., 130, *153*
Murphy, C. M., 54, *93*

Neighbors, B., 54, *92*
Nelson, C. A., 132, 144, *152*
Nelson, D. A., 9, 20, 21, 31, 33, 40, 41, 42, 44, 49, *51*, 125, 127, *154*, 161, 163, 164, 167, 168, 169,

170, 180, 181, 182, *184, 185*, *188*, 235, 236, 242, 243, 244, 245, 247, 255, 258, 259, 264, 267, 268, 286, 287
Nelson, L. J., 235, 236, 237, 238, 239, 244, 245, 247, 258, 259, 260
Nelson, R., 197, 226
Newell, L. D., 235, 258
Nielsen, D. M., 35, *51*
Niemela, P., 163, *183*
Nikolopoulos, T., 191n, 214, *228*
Nimick, E., 163, *187*
Noam, G., 5, *12*, 20, 21, 24, 34, 35, *49*
Nolan, D., 194, *229*
Noll, R. B. 196, 222, *227*
Nousiainen, S., 21, 29, 33, *49*, 267, *285*
Nukulkij, P., 164, *185*

O'Brien, K. M., 163, 164, 167, 168, 180, *184*
O'Brien, M., 54, 90, *94*
O'Connor, T. G., 5, *11*, 270–271, 277, *283*
Offord, D. R., 138, *152, 156*
Oh-Hwang, Y., 41, 42, 43, 44, 50, 266, *286*
O'Leary, K. D., 54, 93, 281, *287*
Olsen, J. A., 5, *11*, 18, 19, 30, 33, 47, 57, 58, 61, 90, 99, 101, 107, *121*, 125, 126, 133, *152*, 164, *182*, 193, 202, 221, 226, 235n, 236, 237, 244, 245, 247, 257, 258, 272, 274, 282, 283, 284
Olsen, S. F., 10, 20, 21, 31, 33, 40, 41, 42, 44, 49, *51*, 125, 127, *154*, 161, 164, 167, 169, 170, 172, 180, 181, 182, *185, 187, 188*, 189n, 235, 236, 237, 238, 240, 241, 242, 243, 244, 245, 247, 255, 256, 258, 259, 262, 264, 267, 268, 286, 287
Olson, D. H., 256, *260*
Olson, T. D., 274, *287*
Olweus, D., 274, *287*
Orleans, J., 196, *227*
Osborne, L. N., 54, 92, *94*
Overton, W. F., 41, 43, *48*

Paikoff, R. L., 192, *228*
Pallock, L., 242, *260*

Palmer, G., 255, 260
Panak, W., 133, 146, *154*
Papini, D. R., 221, *229*
Park, S. Y., 129, *156*
Parke, R. D., 131, *156*, 162, 163, 181, 186
Parker, G., 20, *51*
Parker, J. G., 161, 162, *186*, 238, 260
Parsons, B. V., 280, *283*
Paskiewicz, L., 191n
Patterson, C. J., 161, *184*
Patterson, G. R., 59, 87, *94*, 103, 104, 106, 107, *122*, 163, 165, *186*
Paulauskas, S. L., 55, *93*
Pearlin, L. I., 66, *94*
Peevers, B. H., 131, *156*, 157
Pelletier, D., 150, *152*
Pemberton, S., 55, 56, 63, 64, 66, *91*
Perlmutter, M., 132, *153*
Peterson, C., 5, *12*
Peterson, D. R., 61, *94*
Peterson, G. W., 3, *12*, 164, *186*, 187
Pettit, G. S., 7, 8, 31, 32, *51*, 97, 97n, 101, 102, 103, 104, 105, 107–108, 109, 111, 115, 117, 119, 120, *121*, 122, *123*, 128, 129, *152*, 161, 162, *187*, 192, 255–256, *257*, 264, 274, 275, 277
Phares, V., 181, *187*
Piaget, J., 136, 143, *156*
Pianta, R. C., 196, *229*
Pierce, E. W., 35, *48*, 127, *153*
Pine, D. S., 55, *94*
Pleck, J. H., 181, *187*
Plomin, R., 129, *154*
Polek, D. S., 281, *285*
Pollock, M., 55, *93*
Poon, E., 130, 144, *156*
Porter, C. L., 167, 170, 180, 181, *182*, *185*, 240, 243, 244, 245, 247, 255, 258
Powell, J. A., 19, 29, *52*, 267, 269, 288
Powers, S. I., 5, *12*, 20, 21, 24, 34, 35, 49
Press, A. N., 131, *157*
Price, J. M., 161, *186*
Pruzinsky, T., 21, 23, *51*, 201, *230*, 269, 287
Putallaz, M., 162, *187*, 238, 260
Putnam, S., 129, *156*
Puttler, L. I., 130, 144, *156*

Quay, H. B., 61, *94*
Quiggle, N. L., 133, 146, *154*
Quinlin, D. M., 181, *186*

Rabiner, D., 167, *186*
Racine, Y. A., 138, *152*, 156
Rae-Grant, N. I., 138, *152*
Raffaelli, M., 101, 102, *121*
Rajapark, D., 196, *227*
Reber, M., 197, *228*
Reise, S. P., 245, *261*
Reiser, M., 130, 144, *153*
Renson, G. J., 17, 21, *51*
Resnick, G., 55, *91*
Resnick, M. D., 197, *226*
Restrepo, A., 201, 202, *230*
Reynolds, W. M., 54, *94*
Reznick, S., 145, *154*
Rholes, W. S., 131, *152*
Richters, J. E., 54, *93*
Ridge, B., 102, *121*, 128, 129, 144, *152*
Ridgeway, D., 131, *156*
Ritter, P. L., 39, 42, 43, 48, 266, 267, 268, *285*
Roberts, D. F., 39, 42, 43, 48, 266, 267, 268, *285*
Robin, A. L., 201, *229*
Robins, L., 163, *187*
Robins, L. N., 55, *94*
Robinson, C., 20, 21, 31, 33, 40, 41, 42, 44, 49, *51*, 125, 127, *154*, 161, 164, 167, 169, 170, 172, 180, 181, 182, *185*, 187, *188*, 189n, 235, 236, 237, 238, 240, 241, 242, 243, 244, 245, 247, 255, 256, 258, 259, 262, 267, 268, 286, 287
Robinson, N. S., 19, 28, 30, 33, 49, 54, 92, 273, 274, *285*
Rodgers, K. B., 31, *51*
Roggman, L. A., 221, *229*
Rohner, R. P., 223, *229*
Rollins, B. C., 3, *12*, 164, *187*, 192, 193n, *229*, 242, 260, 276, 287
Romney, D. M., 148, *151*
Roosa, M., 224, *228*
Rosenthal, D. A., 224, *226*
Rosete, A., 191n
Rosman, B. L., *51*, 280, *287*
Rotenberg, K. J., 131, *156*

Rothbart, M. K., 102, *123*, 129, 129n, 130, 137, 139, 144–145, 146, 147, 148, *153*, *154*, *156*, *157*
Rowe, 267, *287*
Ruba, J., 191n
Rubin, K. H., 31, 33, 50, 125, 128, 129, 130, 146, *156*, *157*, 161, *186*, 236, 238, 239, 242, 257, 259, 260
Ruble, D. N., 131, *152*
Rueter, M. A., 221, *230*
Russell, A., 40, 41, 42, 44, *51*, 169, 173, 174, 180, *187*, 255, 260, 267, 268, *287*
Russell, G., 169, *183*, 255, 260
Rutledge, L. L., 281, *285*

Sacchitelle, C., 34–38, 48, 267, 271, *285*
Sadock, B., 85, *93*
Saebel, J., 169, 173, 174, 180, *187*
St. Germaine, A., 197, *226*
Salas, E., 249, *257*
Sanders, B., 279, *287*
Sandler, I. N., 144, 148, *155*
Sanford, M., 138, *152*
Scaramella, L. V., 20, 21, 28, 30, 33, 48, 54, *91*, 280, *285*
Scarlett, H. H., 131, *157*
Schaefer, E., 3, 4, 5, *12*, 17–18, 19, 20, 21, 22, 23, 24, 25, 26, 27, 32n, 48, *51*, 67, *94*, 100, *123*, 132, *157*, 166, *187*, 192, 192n, 193, 201, *230*, 246n, 266, 267, 270, *287*
Schludermann, E., 18, 19, 20, 21, 22, 23, 27, *51*, 271
Schludermann, F., 58, 60, 64, *94*
Schludermann, S., 18, 19, 20, 21, 22, 23, 27, *51*, 58, 60, 64, *94*, 201, *230*, 271
Schmidt, G., 60, *94*
Schneider, J., 194, 195, 198, 202, *228*
Schoff, K., 129, *151*
Schooler, C., 50, 282, 286, *287*
Schumer, F., *51*, 280, *287*
Schwarz, J. C., 19, 21, 23, 41, 42, *51*, *52*, 63, *94*, 194, 201, *230*, *231*, 269, *287*, *288*
Secord, P. F., 131, *156*, *157*
Seefeldt, T., 198, *228*
Seeley, J. W., 279, *285*

Segal, M. H., 236, *260*
Segal-Andrews, A., 196, 197, *228*
Seid, M., 64, 92, 132, *154*
Seligman, M. E., 5, *12*
Sesma, A., 197, *227*
Sessa, F. M., 41, 42, 43, 46, 125, 131, 135, 136, 137, *156*, *157*, 268, 274, *283*
Shagle, S., 5, *11*, 18, 19, 24, 25, 28, 33, 47, 57, 58, 61, 90, 99, 101, 107, *121*, 125, 126, 133, *152*, 164, 182, 193, 202, 221, 226, 236, 257, 272, 273, *283*, 284
Shantz, C. U., 131, *157*
Shapera, W., 191, 198, *228*, 229
Shaw, D., 133, 143, *155*
Shelton, K. K., 103, *123*
Shoben, E. J., Jr., 23, *51*
Shulman, S., 24, 28, 29, 33, 44, *51*, 237, 260, 267, 270, *287*
Sickmund, D., 163, *187*
Siegelman, M., 5, *12*, 19, 20, 21, 22, 23, *51*
Siegler, R. S., 136, 143, *152*
Silk, J. S., 125, 136, 137, *156*
Silverberg, S. B., 25, 37, 41, 49, *52*, 54, *93*
Silverthorn, P., 103, *123*
Simon, F., 60, *94*
Simpson, K. S., 54, *91*
Sinclair, R. J., 36, 50, 269, 271, 274, *286*
Siqueland, L., 128, 133, 146, *157*, 192, *230*, 238, 260, 269, *288*
Skinner, M. L., 106, 107, *122*
Skubic, T., 191n
Slaby, R. G., 163, *186*
Slater, C. M., 63, 66, *94*
Small, S. A., 30, 36, 38, 47, 100, *121*, 275, 284
Smetana, J. G., 25, 36, 38, 45, *51*, *52*, 120, *123*, 201, 202, *230*, 256, 262, 266, *288*
Smider, N. A., 137, *151*
Smith, C. A., 98, 119, *122*
Smith, D. A., 54, *93*
Smith, M. A., 55, 89, *93*
Smollar, J., 5, *13*
Snitzer, L., 197, *228*
Snyder, H., 163, *187*
Sobel, M. E., 79, *94*
Spaulding, B. R., 196, 222, *230*

SUBJECT INDEX

Emotional coaching, 277
Emotional expression, 25
Emotional neglect, 279
Enabling interactive style, 169
Enmeshment
    child aggression and, 38, 168
    depression and, 127, 238
    measurement, 24, 280, 279
    parental conflict and, 59
European Americans, 43
Excessive criticism, 126, 281
Excessive expectations, 22
Externalization
    cross-cultural studies, 239–240,
        251–253
    prediction, 138–142
    research, 28–33, 34–35
Externalizing measurement model, 251

Family environment, 127–128, 146
Family ethnocentrism, 24
Family processes, 7, 53
Family structure, 62, 269
Fathers, 170–171, 177–179, 233
Fearful distress, 130, 133, 137, 140–142,
    239
Fearfulness, 103
Firm control, 193n
Frustration, 130

Gender differences
    aggression, 163–164, 167, 170–171,
        175–176
    child's perceptions, 142–143
    cross-cultural, 249–251, 255,
        265–266
    interparental conflict, 61
    parental involvement, 109
    peer interaction, 169
    studies summarized, 265–267
Goodness of Fit Index (GFI), 251
Guilt induction
    as control strategy, 21, 126, 166, 237
    cross-cultural, 242
    interparental conflict and, 85
    measurement, 20

Hispanic Americans
    authoritative parenting, 43, 268

depression, 44, 237
    psychological control effects, 239
    self-esteem, 44
    sex differences, 265–266
Home Visit Report Form, 204, 214
Hostile aggression, 127
Hostile detachment, 22
Hostile interparental conflict styles,
    55–56

Identity, 25
Ignoring, 22
Impulsivity, 165
Income-to-needs ratio, 134n
Independence, 25, 194–195
Independent–additive effects, 68, 84–86
Indifferent–uninvolved parenting style,
    193
Indirect control, 19
Indirect effects, 59–60, 86–87
Individualistic cultures, 45
Individuality, 25
Individuation, 25
Indulgent–permissive parenting style, 193
Infantilization, 23
Interactive-effects model, 102
Internalization
    cross-cultural studies, 237–239,
        251–253
    prediction, 138–142, 146–147
    research, 28–33, 34
Internalizing measurement model, 251
Interparental conflict, 53–90
    covert style, 56
    defined, 55–57
    overt style, 55–56
    youth problem behavior, 53–90
Intrusiveness, 19, 195
Invalidating, 22, 126
Irritable distress, 130, 133, 137, 138–140,
    239
Isolation from parent, 21, 25

Knox County study, 63–87

Love withdrawal
    across cultures, 241–242
    aggression and, 168

ABOUT THE EDITOR

Brian K. Barber, PhD, recently rejoined the faculty of the Department of Child and Family Studies at the University of Tennessee, where he began his faculty career in 1987. Since that time he has held faculty positions in sociology at Brigham Young University (BYU) and in psychology at the University of Utah. His research focuses on the role of family, peer, school, community, and religious influences in adolescent development. In 1993, he received a National Institute of Mental Health FIRST Award to conduct this work in the United States in the form of a five-year longitudinal study of families with adolescents. In addition, he has extended this investigation to numerous cultures in South America, Africa, Europe, the Balkans, the Middle East, Asia, and Australia, and among ethnic minorities in the United States. Since 1994, he has also been studying adolescent development in contexts of political violence, comparing youth from the Gaza Strip, Palestine, and Sarajevo, Bosnia. For this work he was awarded an Advanced Research Fellowship from the Social Science Research Council in 1998 as well as Scholar in Residence positions at the BYU Jerusalem Center for Near Eastern Studies in 1999, the BYU Kennedy Center for International Studies in 2000, and a fellowship at the Rockefeller Foundation's Bellagio Center for 2002. He publishes regularly in the leading family sociology and developmental psychology journals. He is currently associate editor of the *International Journal of Behavioral Development*.